POLITICAL
ECONOMY
for the 21ST
CENTURY

POLITICAL ECONOMY for the 21ST CENTURY

CONTEMPORARY VIEWS ON THE TREND OF ECONOMICS

CHARLES J. WHALEN
editor

M.E. Sharpe

Armonk, New York
London, England

Library of Congress Cataloging-in-Publication Data

Political economy for the 21st century: contemporary views on the
trend of economics / edited by Charles J. Whalen; foreword by
Hyman P. Minsky: contributors, Randy Albelda . . . [et al.].
p. cm. ˙
Includes index.
ISBN 1-56324-648-1 (hardcover: alk. paper).
—ISBN 1-56324-649-X (pbk.:alk. paper)
1. Economic forecasting. 2. Economic policy—Forecasting.
3. Monetary policy—Forecasting. 4. Employment forecasting.
5. International economic relations—Forecasting.
6. Twenty-first century—Forecasts. I. Whalen, Charles J., 1960–
II. Albelda, Randy Pearl.
HB3730.P597   1995
330.1—dc20
95-22497
CIP

Printed in the United States of America

The paper used in this publication meets the minimum requirements of
American National Standard for Information Sciences—
Permanence of Paper for Printed Library Materials,
ANSI Z 39.48-1984.

BM (c) 10   9   8   7   6   5   4   3   2   1
BM (p) 10   9   8   7   6   5   4   3   2   1

Whether economics is a subject of thrilling interests or a dismal pseudo-science depends upon ourselves.

Wesley Clair Mitchell in *The Trend of Economics*

Contents

Contributors

Randy Albelda is Associate Professor of Economics, University of Massachusetts at Boston.

Alice H. Amsden is Ellen Swallow Richards Professor of Political Economy, Massachusetts Institute of Technology.

Barry Bluestone is Frank L. Boyden Professor of Political Economy, University of Massachusetts at Boston.

William M. Dugger is Professor of Economics, University of Tulsa.

Robert Heilbroner is Norman Thomas Professor, Emeritus, New School for Social Research.

Frederic S. Lee is Reader in Economics, DeMontfort University (U.K.).

Ray Marshall holds the Audre and Bernard Rapoport Centennial Chair of Economics and Public Affairs, University of Texas at Austin.

Ann Mari May is Associate Professor of Economics, University of Nebraska at Lincoln.

Brent McClintock is Assistant Professor of Economics, Carthage College.

Hyman P. Minsky is Distinguished Scholar, The Jerome Levy Economics Institute of Bard College.

Wallace C. Peterson is George Holmes Professor of Economics, Emeritus, University of Nebraska at Lincoln.

Chris Tilly is Associate Professor of Policy and Planning, University of Massachusetts at Lowell.

Lester C. Thurow is Professor of Economics and Management, Massachusetts Institute of Technology.

Charles J. Whalen is Resident Scholar, The Jerome Levy Economics Institute of Bard College.

Charles K. Wilber is Professor of Economics, University of Notre Dame.

L. Randall Wray is Associate Professor of Economics, University of Denver.

Foreword

The United States has come to a watershed in public life and economic policy. Changes in the relations among our various levels of government, and between government and the citizenry, are on a very rigid and active political agenda. This agenda, represented most concretely by the Republican "Contract with America," rests on a particular variant of neoclassical economic theory—a variant grounded in two propositions that cannot be proven: (1) that the very complex and ever-evolving set of interrelated markets that constitute modern economies is *stable*; and (2) that the result of unconstrained market processes is *optimal* (that is, no agent can be made better off without another agent being made worse off).

One can only marvel at the heroic jumps in logic that are permitted in our current policy discourse. One can only stand in awe at the consummate economic and historical ignorance displayed by both the architects of the current agenda and their chief political adversaries. It is trite but nevertheless apt to cite Santayana, "Those who cannot remember the past are condemned to repeat it," as we commit our "lives, fortunes and sacred honor" to engage in a discourse where the prize is the development of the policy agenda that will come to the fore after today's agenda leads to an even greater economic and social malfunctioning than that which has troubled us during the past few decades.

Unfortunately, economists are generally ill-equipped to provide much practical guidance. One peculiarity of the preparation of economists at the end of the twentieth century is that the modern graduate curriculum does not require students to study either the history of economics or economic history. In fact the curriculum is extraordinarily anti-intellectual: graduate programs in economics aim to train rather than educate.

Most articles in the academic economics literature are bereft of citations that go back more than a few years. As a result, economists often engage—unknowingly—in the repackaging of old wine in new bottles. What is particularly appalling is that even journal editors and referees are seldom aware that today's "contributions" often merely "reinvent the wheel."

Contemporary neoclassical economics purports to derive propositions about real-world activity that are independent of the actual institutional structure. Thus, it is not surprising that today's dominant policy agenda ignores both the history and the character of our economic institutions. Underlying this agenda is the same combination of arrogance and ignorance that led American academics to prescribe the now clearly failed "shock therapy" for economies in Eastern Europe and the former Soviet Union.

Given the language and temper of the current political and economic discourse, it may seem that neoclassical theory is both a universally accepted way to analyze the American economy and the sole economic-policy guide appropriate for the rapidly approaching third millennium. Although neoclassicalism, in all its variant forms, does indeed dominate American economics today, it is *not* the only economic theory on hand. The essays that Charles Whalen has collected in this volume provide an outline of one very promising alternative.

A capsule history of the economy and economic policy during the twentieth century may help us understand why this collection of essays is important. The United States' economic experience over the past century breaks down into three parts. The first, from 1896 to 1932, was an unstable period in which economic policy leaned strongly toward laissez-faire. It ended with the great contraction of the economy between 1929 and 1933—a contraction that culminated in the collapse of the economic and financial system in the winter of 1933. At the end of the first third of the twentieth century, capitalism was—especially in the United States—a *failed* economic order.

The second third of the twentieth century began with the inauguration of Franklin Delano Roosevelt on March 4, 1933—when the clarion call that "all we have to fear is fear itself" was sounded. It lasted until January 1969 when Lyndon Johnson, defeated by the war in Vietnam, left Washington. The period was characterized by successful government efforts to control cyclical instability; support resource creation; and correct flaws in labor, product and financial markets.

Over the thirty-six years between 1933 and 1969, the United States experienced not only a great growth in economic output but also a society in which income became more evenly distributed than had ever before been achieved. The phrase associated with John F. Kennedy, "A rising tide lifts all boats," seemed validated by events. Perhaps the first twenty or so years after World War II were not a "Golden Age," but they certainly stand as a historical and practical best. At the end of the second third of the twentieth century, American capitalism—though not perfect—was a *successful* economic system.

The final third of the twentieth century began with the 1969 inauguration of Richard Nixon—and is still ongoing. In terms of performance, it is somewhat like the first third of the twentieth century prior to 1929. In this era we observe both that the amplitude of the business cycle is increasing and that incomes are becoming more unequally distributed even as the economy grows. Furthermore, financial "crises," which were well nigh absent during the second third of the century, have returned with a vengeance. In response to the wholesale failure of banks and other financial institutions between 1929 and 1933, federal insurance of bank and thrift deposits was instituted in the New Deal era. This structure was not tested until the past decade—when a huge infusion of public funds was needed to prevent a cascade of bank failures.

Although American economic performance began to exhibit signs of difficulty as early as the late 1960s, economists and political leaders were lulled into thinking that our economic system could be treated as unchanging. But as capitalism evolves, so too should economic theory and policy. The task before today's economists and public officials is to meet the challenges of the present without forgetting the valuable lessons of the past. Since the neoclassical economists and the developers of our current political agenda have chosen to ignore the realities of the present and turn their backs on the past, neither group is capable of leading the country into a new period of sustained prosperity.

As the economy was running toward the 1929–33 debacle, Rexford Guy Tugwell took the initiative and brought together a batch of essays by institutionally oriented economists in a volume published as *The Trend of Economics*. The essays in that volume broke the ground and helped set the agenda for the era of reform and reconstruction that began in 1933. If capitalism is to be successful in the twenty-first century, economists must now apply the orientation of Tugwell's *Trend* to a new era. The thought-provoking essays in the present volume are directed toward precisely this end. After the failure of today's political agenda becomes apparent, our *next* reconstruction will need to draw heavily upon insights contained in the pages that follow.

Hyman P. Minsky

Preface

In the Spring of 1994, I attended a lecture by one of the economics profession's newest Nobel recipients, Douglass North. North's message was that economics must account for the passage of time—an element that not only draws our attention to the interaction of individuals and social institutions but also demands that we recognize that institutions, knowledge, and values are subject to change. North added that ignoring this element can lead to poor—even disastrous—policy guidance. Unfortunately, while over two centuries have passed since Adam Smith penned *The Wealth of Nations*, conventional economic theory still does not account for this all-important factor. The present volume unites non-neoclassical traditions in an effort to offer a coherent alternative to standard theory—a *political economy* that incorporates time into analyses that are not only relevant to today but also useful as a starting point for work in the twenty-first century.

The contributors to this book were brought together to rethink economic theory and policy in terms of the central issues of the 1990s. Challenges addressed include a number of often interrelated matters including economic stabilization, rising inequality, wage stagnation, labor-market dislocation, international competitiveness, and economic development. Each author was also asked to keep in mind the needs of economics as it prepares to enter the next century. Chapter 1 underscores the important methodological, theoretical, and policy connections that are brought to the surface as a result of attention to these needs.

Chapters 2 through 4 place special emphasis on conceptual aspects of "redefining economics." Each presents elements of a political economy that not only sheds new light on familiar terrain but also extends research boundaries beyond those imposed by neoclassical thought. The authors of these chapters are William M. Dugger, Charles K. Wilber, and Ann Mari May, respectively.

Chapters 5 through 13 are grouped into sections that reexamine microeconomics, macroeconomics, and international issues, respectively. The contributors to these sections are: Frederic S. Lee, Ray Marshall, and L. Randall Wray; Wallace C. Peterson, Barry Bluestone, and Chris Tilly and Randy Albelda; and Lester C. Thurow, Brent McClintock, and Alice H. Amsden. Their chapters produce a social-market framework that demonstrates the compatibility and complementarity of insights generated by institutionalism, post-Keynesianism, and other non-neoclassical traditions.

According to political economists, practical problem solving requires analyses that are institutionally grounded. Political economists also maintain that today's economic challenges require us to give attention not only to the *level* but also to the *composition* of public outlays. In the international arena, meanwhile, they emphasize that the traditional comparative-advantage model must be augmented by one that allows advantage *creation*.

The volume closes with a chapter by Robert Heilbroner. That chapter exposes the myopic vision beneath conventional economic analyses by probing the relationship between economics and capitalism. The chapter also suggests that economics may be *fatally* flawed by its treatment of time. In its present condition, economics is a discipline that has nothing to say on matters as fundamental as where capitalism is heading and how—indeed, even if—it can survive.

As indicated in the chapter by William Dugger, neoclassical theory is rooted in the economics of contentment while political economy is the economics of discontent. Neoclassicals see economic problems as exceptions to the general thrust of a market system. Moreover, they tend to identify government action (a price-system "interference") as the source of the trouble when problems do appear.

In contrast, political economists are problem oriented. Their goal is to understand and resolve practical economic problems—and they observe no shortage of such problems in today's world. Public action may not always be the answer—and even when some action seems unavoidable, the appropriate form of action is seldom self-evident—but for political economists there is also no a priori reason to place faith in market-generated solutions. Besides, as a number of contributors to the present work observe, markets and the state are inextricably linked in capitalist society. (The same point was stressed by a key founder of the very market-oriented Chicago School of economics, Henry Simons, who long ago noted that free-enterprise capitalism must place "heavy responsibilities" upon the public sector.) Alas, individuals can view government policy as merely redistributive and/or disruptive only by abstracting from the passage of time.

The idea for the present book came a few years ago as I was reading about a collaborative volume published in the early decades of this century as *The Trend of Economics* (*The Trend*). That volume brought together over a dozen of its era's most creative and influential economists—including Wesley Mitchell, Paul Douglas, Sumner Slichter, Frank Knight, Morris Copeland, John M. Clark, and Rexford G. Tugwell—for the purpose of exploring standard theory's strengths, weaknesses, and alternatives in light of the major issues of the day. It struck me that a similar work was again needed, for all around were signs that economics had advanced little since the early 1970s when Wassily Leontief, Robert Gordon, Joan Robinson, and others criticized the profession severely for losing touch with reality.

The suggestion that I edit a new volume in the tradition of *The Trend* received an overwhelmingly favorable response. In fact, my toughest task stemmed from the fact that there was simply no way to include all the very talented political economists expressing an interest in the effort. My thanks—and hopes for an opportunity to collaborate in the future—go to each of them.

My thanks go also to the following: Dick Bartel, Karen Byrnes, and Christine Florie of M.E. Sharpe, John Adams, Richard Brinkman, Gladys Foster, Margarita Garza, Robert Kuttner, Judith McKinney, Robert Prasch, Anthony Scaperlanda, Beth Yarbrough, and Linda Whalen. Each provided assistance that contributed to the present book. Finally, I would like to thank my contributors for their enthusiasm, encouragement, and high-quality work. Bob Heilbroner has been especially helpful. The suggestions he offered during the project's early stages were invaluable.

Charles J. Whalen

Part I
Introduction

1

Beyond Neoclassical Thought: Political Economy for the Twenty-first Century

Charles J. Whalen

This volume brings together economists from a range of non-neoclassical traditions. All agree that mainstream economic theory is incapable of adequately addressing the real-world challenges of the late 1990s and early twenty-first century. The alternative they provide unites institutionalism, post-Keynesianism, social economics, and other perspectives. This forward-looking collaboration points toward construction of a coherent and broadly defined *political economy*.[1]

Concerns similar to the one that has produced this book are certainly not new. John Kenneth Galbraith, for example, noted more than two decades ago that neoclassical economics has "a decisive flaw" in that it "offers no useful handle for grasping the economic problems that now beset the modern society."[2] In fact, this volume follows in the tradition of a collection of essays published early in the century as *The Trend of Economics* (*The Trend*).[3] What is new today, however, is the pace and extent of structural economic change—change that is transforming not only firms and industries but also individual nations and the entire global economy.

During this century, members of the economics profession produced many developments in the realm of theory. But the neoclassical theories now dominant in English-speaking nations have retained key methodological elements from the distant past. Those elements place severe constraints on both theory and policy—and continue to restrict the ability of economics to offer practical insights. In the course of seeking to provide a more secure foundation for policy, the alternative outlined in this volume breaks free from these constraints.

Economics in the Twentieth Century

From Confusion to Contentment

Advanced capitalist nations experienced severe macroeconomic fluctuations in the early decades of the twentieth century. Moreover, the boom-and-bust cycles were complicated and exacerbated by persistent distributional problems and occasional structural adjustments. As real-world problems mounted, economics in the 1930s found itself in what Joan Robinson described as a "pitiful state of confusion."[4] The most pressing problems of the era were resolved only after the adoption of numerous recommendations not grounded in traditional economic analysis.[5]

Despite policy achievements, individuals with a non-neoclassical outlook were unable to dislodge conventional economic theorists from their position of dominance in academia. This is explained in part by the fact that many non-neoclassicals failed to develop theoretical foundations for their work. Academic economists influenced by the University of Wisconsin's John R. Commons, for example, were often content to seek resolution of practical problems without any regard for theory. Many other innovative thinkers left academia entirely and devoted their careers to government service. But the resilience of economic orthodoxy is also explained by the ability of mainstream economists to reconcile countercyclical policies with standard theory through construction of the "neoclassical synthesis."[6]

The development of economics in the twentieth century has also been influenced by the increased use of quantitative methods. While contributors to *The Trend* stressed the need for a more empirical economics, they also warned readers to avoid becoming blind to economic reality through the relentless pursuit of rigor.[7] Unfortunately, conventional economics—which has long sought to model itself after the "hard" sciences—found the attraction to mathematical techniques and modes of expression irresistible. In a discipline where formalism is not a secondary feature but often "a central programmatic aim," we should not be surprised to find neoclassicalism in a dominant position—for there is no question that this approach permits a high degree of mathematization.[8]

The fact that economics has sacrificed relevance for rigor received much attention during the 1970s as conventional policies proved ineffective in the face of rising inflation and unemployment.[9] But after citizens became accustomed to higher levels of unemployment (a development accompanied by upward revisions of the notion of the "natural" rate of unemployment), and conservative public policies and international developments kept inflation in check, English-speaking economists were able to return again to their world of "splendid isolation" and "scholarly contentment."[10] In fact, one of the most prestigious mainstream developments of the past few decades has been the rise of the "new classical economics"—a body of analyses (by Robert Lucas, for example) that offer an equilibrium account of business cycles and an elegant rationalization of monetarism.[11]

Disenchantment Returns

The contributors to this volume believe the present era demands more than conventional economics provides—indeed, more than economic orthodoxy is capable of providing. In the 1992 U.S. presidential election, for example, citizens expressed their frustration with an economy weakened by cyclical, structural, and distributional ills. In the agenda-setting Little Rock conference that followed, however, economists devoted most of their attention to rehashing debates regarding the appropriateness of deficit reduction and stimulative fiscal action.

Even those touted as being among the most progressive and innovative within the neoclassical camp seem out of touch. Consider the work of Paul Krugman as an example. The United States has faced serious competitiveness problems and a "silent" depression (involving slow productivity growth and stagnant earnings) during the past two decades.[12] Krugman, meanwhile, considers competitiveness "a largely meaningless concept" and "a dangerous obsession."[13] His latest book devotes some critical attention to Lucas and other conservatives, but the volume and a related article unleash a much more vicious attack on problem-oriented supporters of "strategic" trade.[14] In contrast, Krugman explains that his own "new international economics" leads to "a sadder but wiser argument for free trade."[15]

Perhaps the most disturbing of all recent evidence regarding the detached nature of economics comes from a 1991 report by the American Economic Association's Commission on Graduate Education in Economics (COGEE). The commission noted that many top students from the nation's best liberal-arts colleges either decide against graduate economics programs or drop out during their first year because "the abstract, technical nature" of the curriculum "is not *economics* as they know it."[16] COGEE also expressed the fear "that graduate programs may be turning out a generation with too many *idiot savants*, skilled in technique but innocent of real economic issues."[17] On the matter of technique versus substance, the commission concluded, "We feel that the balance is not quite right at present."[18]

Will the neoclassical wing of the U.S. economics profession change in response to these recent findings? Probably not in any meaningful way. COGEE recommends that professors devote more course attention to applying economic theory to real-world matters. But that practice will not be enough—for the narrow vision of our prevailing paradigm is itself part of the problem. Moreover, economics has long operated under a scoring system that rewards technical wizardry and discourages investigations of real economic issues.[19] COGEE offers no recommendations that would alter this arrangement.

Conventional economics is likely to persist, but so too will citizen disenchantment with both economists and real-world economic performance—unless economists outside the thrall of neoclassicalism join forces and both offer and build support for an alternative. Kevin Phillips argued in 1993 that how officials address the public's widespread uneasiness regarding economic security is the key to the politics of the 1990s.[20] Contributors to this volume understand that addressing the sources of such uneasiness is one important task of any economic alternative that seeks to provide a more secure policy foundation for the years ahead.

An Overview of the Present Volume

Redefining Economics

The perspective presented in this volume does *not* involve a complete rejection of neoclassical insights. Conventional concepts such as "marginal utility" and "opportunity cost" are indeed valuable. In addition, orthodox theories provide important insights into the impact of scarcity on market allocation—the interaction of supply and demand as described in standard theory does indeed contribute to understanding real-world economic activity. Nevertheless, neoclassicalism offers a weak methodological foundation, an incomplete picture of reality, and equilibrium requirements that are satisfied only in unreal, idealized cases.

In light of the narrowness of economic orthodoxy, we begin this effort to improve the discipline by redefining it. A shift from the perspective of neoclassical orthodoxy to that of our "political economy" involves defining economics not as the study of market allocation under the constraint of scarcity but instead as the study of the much broader terrain of "social provisioning." This permits economists to shape theory to reality rather than the reverse. It also permits them to infuse their work with greater attention to both the moral dimension of human behavior and the economic significance of gender and marginality. Chapters by William M. Dugger, Charles K. Wilber, and Ann Mari May (in a section entitled "Provisioning, Ethics, and Gender") underscore the elements of such a redefinition.

The wider scope of this political economy authorizes explorations of more questions than are permissible within neoclassicalism. For example, the perspective allows researchers to investigate the impact of culture on individual desires. It *also* permits questions of allocation and distribution—matters central to orthodoxy—to be considered from a more expansive viewpoint. Markets are important contemporary provisioning mechanisms, but market activity is neither independent of other social spheres nor the only realm in which provisioning occurs. Thus, our alternative encourages a study of the entire social landscape (including, for example, institutions and practices involving the workplace, state, and family) rather than analyses of just markets alone.

This more expansive outlook enables economists to consider provisioning influences other than scarcity, and to explore motives or objectives beyond short-run self-interest. In particular, political economists recognize the economic significance of not only additional influences such as custom and power but also altruism and morally grounded behavior. Indeed, Wilber's chapter suggests that the latter is a prerequisite to achieving allocative efficiency even in the conventional sense.

The shift from neoclassical orthodoxy to political economy offers even more than a *broader* focus—it also provides a foundation that is fundamentally *different* from the one supporting traditional economics. In particular, this political economy offers a foundation that:

- rejects the idea of "value-neutral" economics and instead acknowledges both the influence that an economist's "world view" has on professional research and the fact that economics seeks ultimately to guide public policy;
- focuses on actual events, not hypothetical ones—and wants to *explain* as well as *predict*;
- emphasizes historical processes and institutional adjustment;[21]
- does not ignore harmony and contentment, but—unlike orthodoxy—puts issues of conflict and disorder at the center of its attention; and
- acknowledges the inseparability of the market and the state.

This foundation is firmly rooted, as Dugger's chapter indicates, in the tradition of institutional economics. But Dugger also explains that the approach shares important elements with the work of Karl Marx and contemporary Marxists—and Wilber's chapter identifies an important link to the viewpoint of Adam Smith. Further, as Wilber and May suggest, social economists and feminists can also employ—and contribute to—the pretheoretic groundwork that supports this political economy. Moreover, chapters found in later sections of this volume suggest that the adoption of such an approach enables members of the aforementioned traditions to develop stronger ties to other non-neoclassicals—including post-Keynesians and structuralists.[22]

May makes the important point that what economists see depends not only on where they look but also on the lens through which they gaze. The foundation outlined above (and developed more fully by Dugger, Wilber, and May) describes the contours of the political economist's lens. As May notes, this lens reveals the fact that production and exchange are not merely individualistic and competitive but also collective and cooperative. May's chapter also explains that the political economist's lens helps not only to expose the ideological and gendered nature of traditional economics (features that obscure sexism, androcentrism and the issues and concerns of marginalized people) but also to point political economists in the direction of a more "objective" and useful economics.

Wilber agrees that adopting a lens or "world view" is a prerequisite to economic analysis. He also stresses that neoclassical notions of "equilibrium" and "efficiency" are troublesome standards for reality, not merely because of economic dynamics and "social traps" but also because these concepts come from a world view that excludes important aspects of human welfare (such as the value of work and community life). Wilber encourages political economists to propose and develop alternatives to the neoclassical definition of economic welfare, and his chapter mentions one approach to this matter. As he explains, evaluation of public policies can be very different once we adopt an alternative to the conventional economic perspective of human well-being.

Dugger's chapter also underscores the importance of developing alternatives to economic orthodoxy. In addition, it notes that political economists have produced a number of theories that explore neglected aspects of social provisioning.[23] As Dugger states in his chapter's final paragraph: "Institutionalism has developed theories of the resource process, the want process, the production process, and the meaning process. Neoclassicalism has not. Whether most economists realize it or not, institutionalism has matured into a paradigm with a fully developed body of theory."[24]

Fundamental Ingredients

The section on "Firms, Human Resources, and Money" (chapters 5 through 7) takes us from a discussion of political economy's foundations to a consideration of some of its fundamental ingredients. If political economists are to influence not only ongoing policy discussions but also the trend of economics as it enters the next century, then they must offer a new look at both the role of human resources and the nature of important market institutions such as the business enterprise and money. Frederic S. Lee, Ray Marshall, and L. Randall Wray each contribute to this end.

Relying on empirical evidence from the United States and United Kingdom, Lee develops a model of business pricing—a framework identifying the general factors determining prices in these two nations. His review of numerous studies indicates that business prices in these countries are not subject to constant renegotiation or revision in response to supply and demand forces. Rather, prices are administered to the market and often do not change for a period of three months to a year or more. Moreover, Lee suggests that nearly all firms rely on some "cost markup" procedure that enables them to cover expenses and obtain a desired rate of return.

Lee's framework indicates that firms consider supply and demand factors in pricing decisions—factors including not only competitive pressures but also sales estimates and input costs. But the framework recognizes that pricing is also a *social* process. For example, the corporate goals that help determine prices are not universal—they often vary with time and place. In addition, pricing activities are often constrained by tax laws and other public policies. Further, evidence indicates that pricing administrators base their decisions heavily on "custom, convention, and reasonableness."[25] In short, prices are determined in a "social market" by custom, command (the state), and competition (and its inverse, market power).

A major implication of this work on pricing is that a useful twenty-first–century political economy must offer empirically grounded and historically specific analyses and theories of firm behavior. (Note that this point is thoroughly compatible with May's call for an emphasis on the "cultural, temporal, and specific," rather than on "what is universal, timeless, and static."[26]) While economists have largely abandoned such efforts in favor of applications of standard theory, researchers in business schools and other applied academic units continue to produce some work of this type. Political economists should seek not only to revitalize this work within economics departments but also to develop stronger ties to the units in which such work is now being undertaken.[27]

Another significant implication of Lee's pricing analysis—one that he identifies as "the most important contribution of the model to future work"—is that his chapter "highlights the obvious fact that competition in the [global] market stems largely from the clash of different goals that can be traced back to different social values. Thus, the evolution of capitalism in the twenty-first century will reflect the outcome of these clashes." Lee cites the specific example of competition between Japanese and U.S. firms. In particular, he indicates that different social values cause these nations' companies not only to set prices differently but also to respond differently to the resulting competition.[28]

While Lee's view of *product markets* as "social markets" may strike some as novel, economists had precisely this view toward *labor markets* until the past few decades.[29] Although neoclassical views have recently become dominant even in this realm, institutionalists have not only developed a labor-market framework that is similar to Lee's pricing model but they have also established academic units of "industrial relations" where such research and teaching can occur. They have also established professional associations, such as the Industrial Relations Research Association, to foster such efforts. One past president of this association is Ray Marshall. To set the stage for Marshall's chapter, I offer a brief summary of the institutionalist view of labor markets.

In *The Transformation of American Industrial Relations*, Thomas Kochan, Harry Katz, and Robert McKersie—three of the most prominent industrial-relations scholars in the United States—develop a broad framework for understanding the outcomes and dynamics of employment relationships.[30] This "strategic-choice" framework explains wages, employment levels, and other labor-market outcomes in terms of the interaction of a specific *context* for industrial-relations activity and the *actors* (that is, employers, employees, citizens, and the representatives of each) who operate within that given context. The context for such activity includes the scarcity-driven labor- and product-market factors that conventional economists would consider in their analyses. But this institutionalist framework brings additional elements of the external environment in for consideration as well—including technological, demographic, social, historical, institutional, and political factors. The framework also draws attention to the many organizational and societal levels (from the workplace to the level of national policy determination) at which the plans, practices, and values of different industrial-relations actors must interact.

Marshall's chapter rests implicitly on the strategic-choice framework. In particular, Marshall uses international comparisons of the Commission on the Skills of the American Workforce and other empirical evidence to argue that there is ultimately only one path that will permit us to enhance national prosperity while competing in global markets—a path that requires that we compete on the basis of productivity, (product and process) innovation, and product quality. Moreover, he explains that while human resources have always been a major determinant of economic performance, this factor is currently of fundamental importance.[31] Marshall's chapter also indicates that a wide range of institutional structures, strategies, and practices must be modified if the United States is to develop and utilize its human resources more effectively in the years ahead.[32]

The analysis and conclusions offered by Marshall are reinforced by a new volume by Eileen Appelbaum and Rosemary Batt. Their book, *The New American Workplace*, argues that the future success of both American companies and the nation as a whole will depend on our ability to transform work systems that have become obsolete in recent decades.[33]

Unfortunately, despite identifying the emergence of "a broad and diverse constituency" in support of workplace change, and evidence that some companies have committed themselves to becoming "high-performance organizations," Appelbaum and Batt explain that "only a few organizations have achieved major transformations and the accompanying performance improvements, and these have done so under unique circumstances." Moreover, the authors emphasize that "the U.S. institutional environment provides virtually no support for transforming work systems. If anything, it is hostile to such attempts."[34] This finding is especially troubling in light of the fact that they cite approvingly the following point (one consistent with views expressed by both Lee and Marshall in this volume) from a recent article in the *Harvard Business Review*: "In the global economy, competition isn't just between companies; it is between entire socioeconomic systems. These systems set the all-important context that shapes the actions and the fortunes of individual companies."[35]

In an essay written during the 1970s for a volume on post-Keynesian economics, Appelbaum noted that "the labor market is not a 'market' as that term is usually understood, for the labor market does not possess a market-clearing price mechanism."[36] This perspective is not only the same as the present volume's view of the labor market but, as we have seen, it is also compatible with our view of product markets. The fact that Appelbaum's statement represents a "post-Keynesian" viewpoint, meanwhile, demonstrates that there is at least some connection between post-Keynesian and institutionalist works at the level of analysis. In "Monetary Theory and Policy for the Twenty-first Century" (chapter 6 in the present volume), Wray's post-Keynesian approach to money contributes further to the linking of these non-neoclassical traditions by suggesting that the *money market* is no more a conventional "market" than labor and product markets.

The market for money is different from that for labor or goods and services because while markets of the latter sort are social institutions, *money itself is a social institution.*[37] As Wray describes in this volume, money is "a unit of account," and as he has written elsewhere, "a unit of account is by its very nature *social.*"[38] Not only is money "social" because it cannot have meaning outside a particular social context (outside our social context, for example, a dollar bill is just a piece of green paper), but money is created not for inventory but as part of a social relationship between a borrower and lender. Moreover, this relationship bestows social rights and obligations on both parties—and enforcement of the relationship is also social. In fact, Wray has noted that even debt repayment is social, "for the ability to do so will depend to a great extent on economic performance of society."[39]

A money market is also not a conventional market in that there can be no "efficient" allocation of credit. As Wilber's chapter indicates, *scarcity* is required for economic orthodoxy to identify a set of prices that allocate resources efficiently. But since credit is a social institution, *credit* scarcity is fundamentally different from *resource* scarcity. Central banks can, as Wray notes in this volume, control a particular type of money-denominated liability. But money demand and supply are not independent—and "an increase of money demand normally induces an increase of money supply."[40] Further, the "price" of credit is not determined by scarcity alone—it is also shaped by the purely psychological, expectational and volatile concept of *liquidity preference.*[41]

Wray's chapter also dovetails with those of Lee and Marshall in that he ties his analysis to both a historical—not hypothetical—account of money and banking, and a view of monetary production as a process occurring in calendar time. Thus, we can conclude that chapters 5 through 7 analyze their respective political-economy ingredients in precisely the institutionally oriented, empirically grounded, and historically specific manner mandated by the redefinition of economics outlined in chapters 2, 3, and 4.

Finally, a word must be said about Wray's views on monetary policy. Like Marshall, Wray rejects laissez-faire in favor of a more active set of domestic and international policies. More active institutional and policy guidance by the public sector does indeed raise questions such as whether these additional government actions can be taken without manipulation by special interests; whether public officials can be expected to have the skills and information needed to perform their new tasks in an effective manner; and whether any public body can successfully counter efforts by profit-seeking firms to circumvent state policies through innovation. But while there are dangers to moving away from conventional monetary policies, there is also *no reason to believe that neoclassical policies always yield the best possible outcomes.*

If financial markets allocated money efficiently, then perhaps political economists could argue for monetarism to deal with the quantity of money, for laissez-faire with respect to the qualitative aspects of credit, and for flexible exchange rates in the international realm. In reality, though, we do not merely have the obstacles to static efficiency noted earlier, for—as the post-Keynesian work of Hyman Minsky makes clear—the view of money described above leads also to a recognition of endogenously generated business cycles.[42] Moreover, these cycles are *exacerbated* (as both Minsky and Wray have explained) by mainstream policies of both the monetarist and "Keynesian" varieties.[43]

Output, Growth, and Inequality

Chapters 8 through 10 focus attention on macroeconomics and distribution. Wallace C. Peterson opens the section ("Macroeconomics, Structural Change, and Distribution") with a discussion of cyclical macroeconomic dynamics. Barry Bluestone then presents an analysis of structural trends that have affected the U.S. economy in recent years. Chris Tilly and Randy Albelda complete this part of the volume with a chapter that enriches the discussion of income distribution. The discussions of output, growth, and inequality found in these chapters draw attention not only to some of our most pressing national economic issues but also to important analytical matters relevant to the construction of a political economy for the next century.

Peterson's chapter draws on insights from Marx, Veblen, Keynes, and others in the institutionalist and post-Keynesian camps to develop a monetary theory of production relevant to the present era. As Peterson explains this theory and links it to an analysis of macroeconomic cycles, we find a non-neoclassical synthesis that is indeed a coherent alternative to economic orthodoxy. Moreover, we find many ways in which the cyclical analysis builds on insights presented in earlier chapters.

Peterson shows the very close connection between the methodological foundation outlined in chapters 2 through 4, the social-market perspective presented in chapters 5 through 7, and his own views on macroeconomic theory and policy. Like both Marshall and Wray, Peterson suggests that public officials interested in resolving real economic problems cannot rely on either self-regulating markets or control of the aggregate level of a few economic variables (such as the size of public expenditures and the money supply) to produce a stable, prosperous, and growing national economy. For example, policy makers must consider not only the appropriateness of fiscal stimulus (or restraint) but also the matter of "how" demand is to be stimulated—that is, consideration must be given to both the *level* and *composition* of taxes and expenditures.[44]

One point stressed by Peterson's chapter is that the need to give attention to the composition of fiscal policy has recently been underscored by economic developments of a structural nature. Bluestone's chapter develops this point further by explaining the structural roots of recent problems with U.S. economic growth and distribution. In fact, Bluestone provides evidence suggesting that structural factors have recently begun to overwhelm cyclical ones.

Conventional economists have been understandably slow to acknowledge structural economic change. The ahistorical nature of standard theory does not easily allow a consideration of this matter. But even when such developments are acknowledged, orthodoxy's faith in market self-regulation leads generally to a laissez-faire policy stance. In contrast, Bluestone argues that *structural problems* demand *structural policies*—especially in the realms of labor markets, manufacturing, and trade. While there are certainly dangers associated with such policies, Bluestone's chapter contains the same message found in Wray's discussion of a more active set of monetary policies—namely, that even greater harm may be done by policies based on neoclassicalism.

Bluestone's contribution warrants two final comments. First, his chapter provides evidence of the fact that the political-economy perspective outlined in this volume does not involve a complete rejection of neoclassical insights. In fact, Bluestone argues that insights contained in the neoclassical notion of "factor-price equalization" may now be more valuable than ever to those seeking to understand real-world trends. Nevertheless, he explains that other forces are also involved in determining wage patterns—forces with elements that undermine both the descriptive and normative power of economic orthodoxy.

Finally, while mainstream economists have been slow to recognize the trends discussed by Bluestone, research by non-neoclassicals of many different camps has been converging not only in the methodological realm (as indicated above) but also in the realm of macroeconomics—and the convergence in the latter area has centered on the contemporary importance of structural change. Of course, both convergences are related in that the methodological foundation developed by political economists helps one to analyze the impact of a changing institutional setting upon economic performance. But even those outside orthodoxy who avoid methodological discussions have devoted increasing attention to the structural trends of the past few decades.[45]

The rising economic inequality mentioned by Bluestone sets the stage for the examination of income distribution offered by Tilly and Albelda. But as Tilly and Albelda note at the outset of their chapter, although our current situation lends urgency to the task of developing a richer theory of distribution, political economists are interested in distribution for *many* reasons. Indeed, distribution has been a central issue of concern to economists throughout the history of economic thought.

Despite the attention distribution has received from scholars for over two centuries, Tilly and Albelda argue that orthodox economists have an "underdeveloped and distorted" view of this issue. Their critique challenges conventional economics on methodological, theoretical, empirical, and ethical grounds. Their alternative, meanwhile, contains both a macro and a micro dimension. The macro discussion focuses on the fact that the relationship of growth to distribution depends on the institutional environment. This leads them to conclude that "we must analyze inequality directly, in a way that is historically specific and institutionally grounded." The conclusion is not only fully consistent with views outlined in chapters 2 through 4 of this volume but it also calls for precisely the type of analysis offered in Bluestone's chapter.

The micro discussion of distribution also contains links to earlier chapters. For example, this discussion is consistent with chapters 5 through 7 in that Tilly and Albelda offer a social market view of labor markets—markets, they note, that exist in the context of a historically unique (not natural or inevitable) capitalist mode of production. The discussion also identifies other determinants of income distribution, including the class structure, the family, and the state. As suggested in the chapters on provisioning, ethics, and gender, studies of social provisioning will require political economists to cross traditional boundaries and explore terrain beyond market exchange. Indeed, an important message of the work of Tilly and Albelda is not merely that the state and market are inseparable but that the institutions of market, state, *and family* are all interrelated.[46]

The Global Economy

The last four chapters of the book are by Lester C. Thurow, Brent McClintock, Alice H. Amsden, and Robert Heilbroner. All but Heilbroner's conclusion appear in a section devoted to international economics and development. Each chapter in that section ("Competitiveness, Trade, and Development") offers a number of insights relevant to the global economy. As chapters 5 through 10 suggest, few areas of practical economics are likely to be unaffected by recent trends toward an internationalized economy. Thus, political economists of the twenty-first century must have a firm grasp of international issues.

Thurow's chapter begins our exploration of the world economy with a discussion relating to national economic competitiveness. His approach to this topic involves a critical assessment of a fundamental concept of conventional economics—comparative advantage. In particular, Thurow explains that today's neoclassical theory of comparative advantage is outdated because it was designed for an era where such advantage was predetermined by a nation's physical (natural-resource and capital) endowments. The present, he argues (in a manner compatible with Marshall's chapter), is an era of "brain power" industries—an era in which comparative advantage is "man-made" in that such industries "will be located wherever someone organizes the brain power to capture them."[47]

Like Bluestone, Thurow also argues that globalization trends have caused factor–price equalization to exert a more powerful influence than ever before—

and that this influence has had a negative impact on U.S. workers. Thurow's conclusion, which is similar to both Bluestone and Marshall, is that the rise of both human-resource–determined comparative advantage and factor–price equalization creates a need for industrial strategies and trade tactics that foster national economic development.

Thurow makes it clear that this new comparative-advantage era raises new questions and dangers. But he says that government and industry have no choice but to work together to develop the strategies and tactics required for economic success: "Governments cannot successfully give orders to industrial firms; markets cannot successfully make the necessary long-run investments." Moreover, it is clear that the sort of economic research needed to answer today's new questions—and to help us avoid the political and administrative dangers associated with policy development and implementation—is not the type that can be undertaken with neoclassical tools. Instead, we need work that is holistic, historical, and comparative in nature.[48]

McClintock explores both the national and supranational dimensions of international trade. His chapter begins by providing evidence of the trend toward international trade and production, and by explaining that this trend has generated significant economic and social dislocation. He then argues that adapting to such developments will require both national adjustment policies (for workers and industries) and greater supranational governance.[49]

McClintock's discussion of public action includes a critical assessment of neoclassical trade theories—theories that argue for free trade and a laissez-faire approach to economic adjustment. One important point made in this assessment is that individuals (in both the public and private sectors) can be—and often are—*creators* of productive capacities, not just agents who maximize objective functions under conditions of *fixed* endowments. This point is compatible with what Marshall calls the rise of human-resource–driven "competitive" advantage, and what Thurow calls the rise of "man-made" (versus physically predetermined) comparative advantage.[50] It is also a point that conventional economists might understand as the shift from a static to a *dynamic* conception of efficiency.

Another valuable point made by McClintock is that the public-choice view of the state would be inaccurate even if we could ignore the variable nature of productive capacities. Political economists understand that the state is more than a collection of vote-maximizing representatives. In fact, they recognize that it is also more than just an umpire. This leads McClintock to present an alternate view of the state—one grounded in institutional economics.

McClintock's perspective on the state is not only compatible with that of Tilly and Albelda but it is also consistent with what I have elsewhere outlined as the "creative" state.[51] This approach is different from the conventional—"corrective"—view because it acknowledges that the state plays a role in *creating social order.* In fact, according to this alternative, the state helps shape the social preferences that permit a society both to define "order" and to determine which methods are most appropriate for establishing it. Moreover, unlike the "protective" state found in traditional Marxism, the creative state is considered capable of being an oppressor and an emancipator—and it is likely often to be a bit of both.[52]

Yet another important point offered by McClintock is that there is no a priori reason why a society should choose efficiency considerations (even in a dynamic sense) over other values, such as those relating to security, democracy, and equity. In other words, political economists believe in a world where society drives the market rather than the reverse.[53]

Amsden's chapter argues for approaching issues of economic development from a perspective that is broader in scope and more sensitive to institutional and historical factors than neoclassicalism. Not only is this position consistent with the perspective described by contributors to this volume who are working in other branches of political economy, but it also leads her to join Tilly and Albelda in stating that economists have much to learn from sociologists and historians. She believes that the highly abstract models and market-failure policy focus of economic orthodoxy offer little guidance to nations seeking to develop today and in the next century.

Amsden observes that successful future development will depend heavily on a country's ability to learn from other nations and to modify aspects of its own economy accordingly. Yet conventional economics is a weak guide to this process of "country model transfer" because it fails to produce even an effective analysis of what made a country succeed. Thus, Amsden's chapter identifies a number of methodological principles to be followed—and potential pitfalls to be avoided—by economists seeking to contribute more effectively to questions of economic development.

A particularly difficult issue for standard economics is the evaluation of government's role in the development process. This has been especially challenging since some of the most successful development experiences since World War II have been in East Asian economies where the state has exerted a pervasive influence on economic activity. Amsden argues that mainstream economists respond to this issue by allowing their belief in laissez-faire to control their work. For example, she shows how such economists formulate tests for industrial policies in which these policies cannot win regardless of observed performance. Amsden's suggestions for development research allow political economists to look beyond the mere existence or absence of government activism and to explore the actual *nature* of public-sector efforts.

Themes and Conclusions

The preceding overview indicates that four themes receive special attention from contributors to this volume: redefining economics; reexamining fundamental ingredients of microeconomic analysis; reconsidering macroeconomic questions of output, growth, and inequality; and reconceiving the nature and needs of our global economy. An important conclusion of this work as a whole is that it demonstrates the compatibility and complementarity of the methodological, analytical, and policy research of institutionalism, post-Keynesianism and other heterodox traditions. Another conclusion is that while conventional economics often impedes resolution of our most pressing real-world problems, analyses rooted in a political-economy perspective offer the starting point for a more useful twenty-first-century economics.

In addition to these overall findings, other conclusions are generated by explorations into each of the volume's central themes. For example, the attempt to redefine economics as the study of social provisioning engenders the conclusion that it is indeed possible to synthesize neoclassical and non-neoclassical insights into a broad yet coherent alternative to the methodology of economic orthodoxy— an alternative that is holistic, processual, empirical, historically grounded, and institutionally oriented. The reexamination of product, labor, and financial markets, meanwhile, produces the conclusion that each is a *social* market—indeed, a social *institution*—governed by custom, command, and competition. It also leads to the conclusion that output, growth, and inequality are determined not by price-system imperatives but by a complex social process with historical, political, and cultural dimensions.

Additional conclusions that are produced by work at the macro level are as follows: (1) current and future discussions of fiscal and monetary policy should give attention to both the quantitative and qualitative dimensions of such policies (that is, we should be concerned with both the level and the composition of variables such as public spending and the supply of money); (2) business cycles can and should be understood as endogenously generated phenomena; and (3) economists must be prepared to shed light on structural dynamics, for these factors have played a major role in shaping recent economic activity and are likely to remain significant in the coming decades. Finally, one finds the following conclusions when the realm of international economics is reconceived from a political-economy perspective: (1) structural problems require structural solutions—solutions to be implemented at both the national and the international level; (2) the static, comparative-advantage model of orthodoxy must be supplemented, if not supplanted, by a more dynamic view that allows for *creation* of a competitive advantage through concerted action by public and private economic actors; (3) both descriptive and normative economic research must recognize that a given society may choose to forego some economic efficiency (even in the most dynamic sense of this term) in an effort to achieve other social goals; and—in a conclusion that brings us full circle by emphasizing the need to redefine economics—(4) future research in the field of economic development must be broader in scope and more institutional and historical in nature than neoclassicalism allows.

A Look Ahead

This volume suggests that the interdisciplinary and eclectic traditions of political economy and institutionalism must be revived if economics is to be a vital field of inquiry in the next century. Today, however, "political economy" is used by some to refer to public-choice economics or to Marxist scholarship. "Institutionalism," meanwhile, has become a pejorative—a label to be avoided by those who seek respectability and professional acclaim.

But as Raymond Bye wrote in *The Trend*, Adam Smith saw political economy as "a broad study of all forces contributing to national wealth."[54] And it was not Veblen but Richard T. Ely, founder of the American Economic Association, who once proclaimed: "I am an institutional economist or I am nothing."[55] As the chapters of this volume indicate, both of these valuable traditions—and the important non-neoclassical insights of Keynes and others—have been ignored at great expense.[56]

Unfortunately, neoclassicals are not likely to rediscover the neglected insights of either political economy or institutional economics on their own. As Peterson wrote recently, if this "discovery" work is to be done at all, "it will be done by those outside the mainstream."[57] Non-neoclassical economists have taken the lead in creative thinking and practical problem solving in the past. This volume demonstrates that they are poised to do the same in the years ahead.

Of course, obstacles to a revival of political economy and institutionalism are indeed formidable. Before concluding this introduction, let us give attention to a few of these impediments.

Rigor versus Relevance

One obstacle to the revival of political economy is the fact that many economists prefer mathematical rigor and technique over practical relevance and problem solving. This issue is often discussed as the matter of "rigor versus relevance." But the key to this dispute hinges ultimately on the *purpose* of economic inquiry. As Marshall writes, "The main assessment of a theory depends on the use one wishes to make of it."[58]

As long as most economists see development of mathematical models and use of the most advanced quantitative methods as chief objectives of their work, neoclassicalism will remain dominant within university economics departments. Political economists, however, have a *different* primary objective—they seek to understand and contribute to the resolution of real-world concerns. These economists are not hostile to theory and models. But as Gunnar Myrdal put it, "We just want our theory and models, indeed even the concepts we use, to be more adequate to the reality we are studying."[59] Similarly, while political economists do not reject quantitative methods, they believe "it is better to have imprecise or approximate answers to the right questions than to have precise answers to the wrong questions."[60]

Mechanism versus Volition

Another obstacle to the revival of political economy and institutionalism is that these traditions require viewing the economy not as a mechanism but as a product of human volition. A mechanistic conception of the economy engenders the notion of an automatic equilibrium. It also offers a clear standard—efficiency—for use in evaluating economic activity. In contrast, by insisting that society drives the market, our volitional perspective offers only a managed (and temporary) equilibrium—and reveals that efficiency is only one possible measure of social well-being. A general-equilibrium theory of value—price theory—provides a set of ready-made answers to economic questions; a volitional theory of value does not. In fact, by drawing attention to a broader set of possibilities than we find in orthodoxy, political economy often raises as many questions as it answers.[61]

Economists are understandably reluctant to shift from a paradigm of self-regulating markets and efficiency to one that emphasizes institutional adjustment, demands analyses of nonmarket institutions, and questions one-dimensional conceptions of human welfare. But political economists respond that these adjustments, analyses, and alternate conceptions can be ignored only by adopting a definition of economics that produces an incomplete and distorted view of reality. Political economy may indeed raise as many questions as it answers. But these new questions are essential—how we answer them will fundamentally determine the future shape of our local, national, and international economies.

Political economists also underscore the fact that their questions are not merely matters ignored by standard theory; these are questions that cannot be answered by conventional economic tools. For example, neoclassicalism offers no details on the best way to secure competitive advantage or promote positive economic adjustment. These issues require analyses that reflect a deep understanding of institutional reality and the passage of historical time. Mainstream research, with its attention to market clearing and its suggestion that realistic assumptions are unimportant, pulls us in precisely the wrong direction.

Research Methods

Yet another obstacle to the development of a revived political economy is the fear that research methods required for institutionalist analyses are either unavailable or too demanding. While economics programs devote much attention to training students in econometrics, they generally ignore techniques such as participant observation, (single and comparative) case studies, interviews, and surveys. But the fact that economists ignore such approaches makes the methods neither unavailable nor "unscientific." Institutionalists have long been eclectic in the realm of research methods, and they have long advocated use of a variety of techniques in comparative analyses that seek to identify and help diffuse "best existing practices." This tradition continues to this day—in fact, it may now be more important than ever in light of global competition and the need for structural adjustment at many levels of economic activity.[62]

In response to the question of whether the work of political economy is too demanding, institutionalists acknowledge that their broader, empirically grounded approach is more demanding than neoclassical economics. Nevertheless, political economists do *not* need to be superhuman—the contributors to the present volume, and the many insightful non-neoclassical publications they cite in their chapters, demonstrate that valuable, holistic analyses are indeed possible. Moreover, political economists do not have to work alone. They not only can but should build bridges to scholarship in other disciplines. They also can and should undertake research through collaborative projects and commissions.[63]

Twenty-first Century Economics

Will there be a revival of institutionalism and political economy during the next century? While the obstacles mentioned above are formidable, none is insurmountable. Perhaps the most significant challenge ahead, however, is securing what Galbraith calls "the emancipation of belief."[64] If non-neoclassicals fail to halt the economics profession's current tendency to define economic inquiry as a realm inhabited by only one paradigm, political economy will remain marginalized.

The present volume takes a step toward the emancipation of belief by presenting an alternative to neoclassicalism. This may not be enough—for as Keynes wrote in the preface to *The General Theory*, "the difficulty lies, not in the new ideas, but in escaping from the old ones, which ramify, for those brought up as most of us have been, into every corner of our minds."[65] In fact, escaping the "old ideas" is made especially difficult today by a rewards system that discourages unconventional explorations. Nevertheless, one fact is now clear: mainstream economics is *not* the only game in town.

Political economists understand that there is no "once-and-for-all" cure for economic ills. But if these economists do not succeed in the emancipation of belief, then their future policy successes—*our* future policy successes—will be even that much more precarious and fleeting. The work to be done is substantial; but so is what is at stake.

A Remade World

In his introduction to *The Trend*, Rexford Tugwell expressed the following reaction to the collaborative effort in which he had just participated: "It stirs the imagination profoundly; in it, and the like cooperations of the other sciences, together with the possibility of their successful interchange of thought, there lies the possibility of a remade world—no less."[66] The present volume suggests a similar possibility. In particular, our call for a political economy grounded in a volitional view of economic activity is one that unlocks the door not just to the resolution of contemporary problems but also to an entire new era of *economic democracy*.

Although citizens in English-speaking nations have long rejected the idea of autocratic government in favor of political democracy, we continue to believe that the market must function as a Leviathan in the realm of economic life. But the volitional political economy outlined in this volume suggests that democracy may be as superior to authoritarianism in the economic realm as it is in politics. Indeed, a message throughout this book is that if we cannot find some way to add a greater element of cooperation and vision to all aspects of our domestic and international economic relations (while retaining the important benefits of individualism and competition), we are *all* likely to be affected adversely in the years ahead.

Of course, economic democracy has its own formidable obstacles. In fact, it is clearly much more a goal or direction than a "state." But the thought of more democratic decision making from the workplace to the global realm is an ideal that certainly stirs the imagination and contains the possibility of a remade world. Making the shift from neoclassical economics to political economy does not guarantee any progress on this front, but it *does* allow us to begin asking the right questions.

Notes

1. The author would like to thank Linda Whalen, Dick Bartel, and Bill Waller for comments on an early version of this chapter.

2. John Kenneth Galbraith, "Power and the Useful Economist," *American Economic Review*, *63*, 1 (March 1973), 1–11.

3. According to Galbraith, *The Trend* was a pioneer document in institutional economics. The book, edited by Rexford Tugwell, included chapters by a number of influential economists including Wesley Mitchell, Paul Douglas, Morris Copeland, and Sumner Slichter. Historians of economic thought indicate not only that the collection received much attention in the 1920s but also that it remains among the most notable survey volumes of its era.

The bulk of *The Trend* was written by institutionalists who were concerned that conventional economics did not provide sufficient insight into practical problems. All chapters—including one by Frank Knight—offer important criticisms of standard economic theory; but constructive discussions of methodology, theory, and policy are also provided. In an *American Economic Review* article commemorating the centennial of the American Economic Association, Martin Bronfenbrenner argues that institutionalism seemed likely to assume a commanding post in American economics only once—in the decade following publication of *The Trend*. See Rexford G. Tugwell (ed.), *The Trend of Economics* (New York: Alfred A. Knopf, 1924); John Kenneth Galbraith, *Economics in Perspective: A Critical History* (Boston: Houghton Mifflin, 1987), p. 197; Joseph Dorfman, *The Economic Mind in American Civilization* (New York: Viking Press, 1959); and Martin Bronfenbrenner, "Early American Leaders—Institutional and Critical Traditions," *American Economic Review*, *75*, 6 (December 1975), 20.

4. Joan Robinson, "The Second Crisis of Economic Theory," *American Economic Review, 62*, 2 (May 1972), 2.

5. In the United States, for example, Tugwell and others with non-neoclassical views served in President Franklin D. Roosevelt's "Brains Trust," a position that allowed them to contribute significantly to development of the New Deal.

6. Still another factor explaining the resilience of orthodox economics is the fact that standard theory cannot be refuted by *any* real-world developments. A mainstream economist can always find a way to reconcile reality with theory—if only by arguing that market adjustment requires just a bit more time.

7. See, for example, pp. 69 and 79 of *The Trend*.

8. Bruna Ingrao and Giorgio Israel, *The Invisible Hand: Economic Equilibrium in the History of Science* (Cambridge, MA: MIT Press, 1990), p. 1.

9. See, for example, Wassily Leontief, "Theoretical Assumptions and Nonobserved Facts," *American Economic Review, 61*, 1 (March 1971), 1–7; Edward H. Phelps Brown, "The Underdevelopment of Economics," *Economic Journal, 82*, 1 (March 1972), 1–10; G.D.N. Worswick, "Is Progress in Economic Science Possible?," *Economic Journal 82*, 1 (March 1972), 73–86; Robert A. Gordon, "Rigor and Relevance in a Changing Institutional Setting," *American Economic Review, 66*, 1 (March 1976), 1–14; and John T. Dunlop, "Policy Decisions and Research in Economics and Industrial Relations," *Industrial and Labor Relations Review, 30*, 3 (April 1977), 275–82.

10. Wassily Leontief, "Foreword," in Alfred S. Eichner (ed.), *Why Economics Is Not Yet a Science* (Armonk, NY: M.E. Sharpe, 1983), p. xi; John Kenneth Galbraith, "Economists and the Economics of Professional Contentment," in his *Annals of an Abiding Liberal* (New York: Meridian, 1979), p. 22.

11. See Robert E. Lucas, Jr., *Studies in Business-Cycle Theory* (Cambridge, MA: MIT Press, 1981), especially p. 234.

12. See, for example, the following: Competitiveness Policy Council, *Promoting Long-Term Prosperity* (Washington, DC: Competitiveness Policy Council, 1994); Wallace C. Peterson, *Silent Depression: The Fate of the American Dream* (New York: W.W. Norton, 1994); Thomas Karier, "Competitiveness and American Enterprise," *Challenge, 37*, 1 (January–February 1994), 40–44; Laura D'Andrea Tyson, *Who's Bashing Whom? Trade Conflict in High-Technology Industries* (Washington, DC: Institute for International Economics, 1992); Competitiveness Policy Council, *Building a Competitive America: First Annual Report to the President and Congress* (Washington, DC: Competitiveness Policy Council, 1992); Michael L. Dertouzos, et al. (The MIT Commission on Industrial Productivity), *Made in America: Regaining the Productive Edge* (Cambridge, MA: MIT Press, 1989); and President's Commission on Industrial Competitiveness, *Global Competition: The New Reality* (Washington, DC: U.S. Government Printing Office, 1985), volume 1.

13. Paul Krugman, "Competitiveness: A Dangerous Obsession," *Foreign Affairs, 73*, 2 (March–April 1994), 41.

14. Ibid., pp. 28–44; Paul Krugman, *Peddling Prosperity: Economic Sense and Nonsense in the Age of Diminished Expectations* (New York: W.W. Norton, 1994).

15. Paul Krugman, "Is Free Trade Passé?," *Economic Perspectives, 1*, 2 (Fall 1987), 143.

16. Anne O. Krueger, et al., "Report of the Commission on Graduate Education in Economics," *Journal of Economic Literature, 29*, 3 (September 1991), 1040–41. While evidence regarding the career choices of *university* graduates was not available, Commission members noted both that the colleges studied "have traditionally been a major source of future Ph.D.'s in economics" and that "it is not obvious that—at least in this respect—undergraduates at Amherst and Oberlin are so different from students at Harvard and Princeton" (p. 1041).

17. Ibid., pp. 1044–45.

18. Ibid., p. 1045.

19. Wassily Leontief, "Theoretical Assumptions and Nonobserved Facts," p. 3.

20. Kevin Phillips, "Down and Out: Can the Middle Class Rise Again?," *New York Times Magazine* (January 10, 1993), 34. It is interesting to note that during a late 1994 speech, Labor Secretary Robert Reich acknowledged that the middle class has become "an anxious class, most of whom are justifiably uneasy about their own standing and fearful for their children's futures" (quoted in Bob Herbert, "Workers Unite!," *New York Times* [September 14, 1994], A19). At about the same time, *Time* magazine reflected citizen concerns with a cover story that asked: "Boom for Whom?" The abstract to that ten-page story noted that "for many ordinary Americans, beating overseas competitors has carried a bitterly high price" (October 24, 1994).

21. As Yngve Ramstad wrote in 1985, one fundamental insight of institutional economics is that *institutional adjustment*, not the price system, provides the "balancing wheel" of an economy. See Ramstad, "Comments on Adams and Brock Paper," *Journal of Economic Issues*, *19*, 2 (June 1985), 509. For a similar perspective, see Michael J. Piore, "American Labor and the Industrial Crisis," *Challenge*, *25*, 1 (March–April 1982), 6. In contrast, orthodoxy emphasizes price-system equilibrium and market self-regulation.

22. In this volume, see the chapters by Wray and Peterson for links to post-Keynesian economics. For related post-Keynesian discussions outside this volume, see Sheila Dow, "The Post-Keynesian School," in Douglas Mair and Anne G. Miller (eds.), *A Modern Guide to Economic Thought: An Introduction to Comparative Schools of Thought in Economics* (Aldershot, UK: Edward Elgar, 1991), pp. 176–206; Philip Arestis, "Post-Keynesianism: A New Approach to Economics," *Review of Social Economy*, *48*, 3 (Fall 1990), 222–46; Marc Lavoie, *Foundations of Post-Keynesian Economic Analysis* (Aldershot, UK: Edward Elgar, 1992); and Charles K. Wilber and Kenneth P. Jameson, *An Inquiry into the Poverty of Economics* (Notre Dame, IN: University of Notre Dame Press, 1983).

For structuralist perspectives, see Bluestone's chapter (chap. 9) in the present volume. See also Stephen A. Marglin and Juliet B. Schor, *The Golden Age of Capitalism: Reinterpreting the Postwar Experience* (Oxford: Clarendon Press, 1990). A similar neo-Marxian account of structural change is contained in Samuel Bowles, David M. Gordon, and Thomas E. Weisskopf, *After the Waste Land: A Democratic Economics for the Year 2000* (Armonk, NY: M.E. Sharpe, 1990).

For more on the institutionalist, feminist, and social-economic dimensions of our foundation for political economy, see the following: William M. Dugger and William T. Waller, Jr. (eds.), *The Stratified State: Radical Institutionalist Theories of Participation and Duality* (Armonk, NY: M.E. Sharpe, 1992); Janice Peterson and Doug Brown (eds.), *The Economic Status of Women Under Capitalism: Institutional Economics and Feminist Theory* (Aldershot, UK: Edward Elgar, 1994); Marianne A. Ferber and Julie A. Nelson (eds.), *Beyond Economic Man: Feminist Theory and Economics* (Chicago: University of Chicago Press, 1993); and Mark A. Lutz (ed.), *Social Economics: Retrospect and Prospect* (Boston: Kluwer Academic Press, 1990).

For related discussions of the traditions of the French "regulation" school and both socio- and humanistic economics, see Robert Boyer, *The Regulation School: A Critical Introduction* (New York: Columbia University Press); Amitai Etzioni, "Founding a New Socioeconomics," *Challenge*, *29*, 5 (November–December 1986), 13–17; and Mark A. Lutz and Kenneth Lux, *Humanistic Economics: The New Challenge* (New York: The Bootstrap Press, 1988).

23. For an opposing (and widely held) viewpoint, see David Colander, *Why Aren't Economists as Important as Garbagemen?* (Armonk, NY: M.E. Sharpe, 1991), p. 163.

24. See chapter 2 for Dugger's contribution.

25. It should also be stressed that Lee's chapter makes it clear that business leaders do not relish competition. In fact, Lee explains and describes a "custom-creating" process whereby such leaders establish their own institutions to eliminate destructive price competition.

26. The chapters of Dugger and Wilber both make a similar suggestion.

27. Some important publications on U.S. business practices in this tradition are the following: Adolf A. Berle, Jr., and Gardiner C. Means, *The Modern Corporation and Private Property* (New York: Macmillan, 1933); Fred Korfman, Nelson Repenning, and John Sterman, "Unanticipated Side Effects of Successful Quality Programs," MIT Sloan School Working Paper (March 1994); Robert T. Averitt, *The Dual Economy: The Dynamics of American Industry Structure* (New York: W.W. Norton, 1968); Alfred D. Chandler, Jr., *The Visible Hand: The Managerial Revolution in American Business* (Cambridge, MA: Belknap Press, 1977); Robert H. Hayes and William J. Abernathy, "Managing Our Way to Economic Decline," *Harvard Business Review*, 58 (July–August 1980), 67–77; Robert B. Reich, *The Next American Frontier* (New York: Times Books, 1983); John R. Munkirs, *The Transformation of American Capitalism: From Competitive Market Structures to Centralized Private Sector Planning* (Armonk, NY: M.E. Sharpe, 1985); Bennett Harrison, *Lean and Mean* (New York: Basic Books, 1994); and Michael L. Dertouzos, et al., *Made in America: Regaining the Productive Edge*. For an international perspective, see Michael E. Porter (ed.), *Competition in Global Industries* (Boston: Harvard Business School Press, 1986); Alfred D. Chandler, Jr., *Scale and Scope: The Dynamics of Industrial Capitalism* (Cambridge, MA: Belknap Press, 1990); Martin Kenney and Richard Florida, *Beyond Mass Production* (New York: Oxford University Press, 1993); and Michael E. Porter, *The Competitive Advantage of Nations* (New York: Free Press, 1990).

28. An article by another contributor to this volume, Lester C. Thurow, has explored this international business conflict and its likely outcome. His view does not favor the United States. Thurow's conclusion underscores the need for a shift from neoclassical orthodoxy to political economy—his article suggests that one important obstacle to improved U.S. performance is our traditional approach to economics. See Lester C. Thurow, "Competing Games: Profit Maximization versus Strategic Conquest," in Richard M. Coughlin (ed.), *Morality, Rationality, and Efficiency: New Perspectives on Socio-Economics* (Armonk, NY: M.E. Sharpe, 1991), pp. 119–31. For related discussions of the cultural, structural, and strategic dimensions of competition in a global economy, see Lester C. Thurow, *Head to Head: The Coming Battle among Japan, Europe, and America* (New York: Morrow, 1992); and Jeffrey E. Garten, *A Cold Peace: America, Japan, Germany, and the Struggle for Supremacy* (New York: Times Books, 1993).

29. For evidence and discussions of this view toward labor markets, see Paul J. McNulty, *The Origins and Development of Labor Economics* (Cambridge, MA: MIT Press, 1980); John T. Dunlop, "Industrial Relations and Economics: The Common Frontier of Wage Determination," in *Proceedings* of the Thirty-Seventh Annual Meeting of the Industrial Relations Research Association (Madison, WI: Industrial Relations Research Association, 1985), pp. 9–23; and John T. Dunlop, "Labor Markets and Wage Determination: Then and Now," in Bruce E. Kaufman (ed.), *How Labor Markets Work* (Lexington, MA: Lexington Books, 1988), pp. 47–87. Two valuable institutionalist discussions of the labor market are the following: Bennett Harrison and Andrew Sum, "The Theory of 'Dual' or Segmented Labor Markets," *Journal of Economic Issues*, 13, 3 (September 1979), 687–706; and William M. Dugger, "The Administered Labor Market: An Institutional Analysis," *Journal of Economic Issues*, 15, 2 (June 1981), 297–407.

30. Thomas A. Kochan, Harry C. Katz, and Robert B. McKersie, *The Transformation of American Industrial Relations* (New York: Basic Books, 1986).

31. The development and use of human resources has been seen as an important determinant of the "wealth of nations" at least since the days of Adam Smith. Marshall's chapter explains how such resources "have become even more important in a highly competitive, knowledge-intensive, global economy." For Smith's view of the significance of human resources, see *An Inquiry into the Nature and Causes of the Wealth of Nations* (New York: The Modern Library, 1937 [1776]), especially p. 1vii.

32. For another excellent discussion of human resources from an institutionalist perspective, see Vernon M. Briggs, Jr., "Human Resource Development and the Formulation of National Economic Policy," *Journal of Economic Issues, 21,* 4 (December 1987), 1207–40.

33. Eileen Appelbaum and Rosemary Batt, *The New American Workplace: Transforming Work Systems in the United States* (Ithaca, NY: ILR Press, 1994).

34. Ibid., pp. 6 and 8.

35. Ibid., pp. 52–53. For a similar view of competition between firms in a global economy, see Laura D'Andrea Tyson, *Who's Bashing Whom?*, p. 31.

36. Eileen Appelbaum, "The Labor Market," in Alfred S. Eichner (ed.), *A Guide to Post-Keynesian Economics* (Armonk, NY: M.E. Sharpe, 1979), p. 115.

37. Paul Davidson, one of America's most prominent post-Keynesians, has written: "Money is first and foremost a human institution." As Thorstein B. Veblen, a founder of institutional economics, might have put it, while labor and products have some direct "serviceability," money has only "ceremonial" value. Davidson's post-Keynesian view of money is discussed in his "Post Keynesian Economics," in Daniel Bell and Irving Kristol (eds.), *The Crisis in Economic Theory* (New York: Basic Books, 1981), pp. 151–173; Veblen's distinction between the serviceable and ceremonial aspects of economic life is discussed in various chapters of his *The Place of Science in Modern Civilisation and Other Essays* (New York: Viking Press, 1919).

38. L. Randall Wray, "Can Free Markets Efficiently Allocate Credit?," paper presented at the Association for Institutional Thought Annual Meeting, April 1993, p. 6, emphasis in original.

39. Ibid., pp. 6–8.

40. Ibid., pp. 6–7. The view of money described above is, as Wray notes in his chapter, usually called the "endogenous" approach. As Wray explained in a 1990 volume, this approach leads to the post-Keynesian contention that "the economy cannot be dichotomized into real and monetary sectors, and the IS and LM curves are not independent." See his *Money and Credit in Capitalist Economies: The Endogenous Money Approach* (Aldershot, UK: Edward Elgar, 1990), p. 171.

41. Post-Keynesians, building on John Maynard Keynes's liquidity-preference theory, maintain that the price of credit reflects "the premium required to induce agents to hold illiquid portfolios" (this quote comes from L. Randall Wray, *Money and Credit in Capitalist Economies*, p. 169). For a concise discussion of liquidity preference by Keynes himself—and an attempt to link it to his "general theory of output and employment"—see his "The General Theory of Employment," *Quarterly Journal of Economics, 51,* 1 (February 1937), 209–23.

42. For Minsky's views, see his *John Maynard Keynes* (New York: Columbia University Press, 1975); *Can "It" Happen Again? Essays on Instability and Finance* (Armonk, NY: M.E. Sharpe, 1982); and *Stabilizing an Unstable Economy* (New Haven, CT: Yale University Press, 1986).

43. For Minsky's views on how business cycles are exacerbated by conventional economic policies, see his works cited in the preceding footnote; for Wray's views on this matter, see chapter 7 in the present volume.

44. One aggregate variable receiving much attention in recent years is the size of the U.S. federal budget deficit. In a recent *Eastern Economic Journal* article, Martin Wolfson

contrasted the orthodox deficit analysis to an alternative consistent with Peterson's chapter. Wolfson's work demonstrates that our political-economy alternative can indeed shed valuable light on current issues. His article also provides additional evidence of the need for policies that look at not only the *level* but also the *composition* of public spending. (See Martin H. Wolfson, "Corporate Restructuring and the Budget Deficit Debate," *Eastern Economic Journal, 19*, 4 (Fall 1993), 495–520.)

In her Richard T. Ely lecture before the American Economic Association in 1971, Joan Robinson argued that conventional economic theory was in crisis because it did not address the composition of government expenditures. (See Joan Robinson, "The Second Crisis of Economic Theory," pp. 1–10.) The political-economy perspective mentioned by Wolfson and developed in this volume seeks to help economists find a way out of that still unresolved crisis.

45. For some structural-change analyses presented by other non-neoclassical authors, see Stephen A. Marglin and Juliet B. Schor, *The Golden Age of Capitalism*; Samuel Bowles, David M. Gordon, and Thomas E. Weisskopf, *After the Waste Land*; Robert B. Reich, *The Next American Frontier*; Michael J. Piore and Charles F. Sabel, *The Second Industrial Divide: Possibilities for Prosperity* (New York: Basic Books, 1984); Michael Aglietta, *A Theory of Capitalist Regulation: The U.S. Experience* (London: Verso, 1979); Allan G. Gruchy, *The Reconstruction of Economics*, pp. 89–116; Robert Kuttner, *The End of Laissez-Faire: National Purpose and the Global Economy after the Cold War* (New York: Knopf, 1991); Robert Kuttner, "Keynes, Schumpeter, and High-Growth Economics in the 1990s," paper presented at a conference on Economic Growth and International Competitiveness at The Jerome Levy Economics Institute of Bard College, November 12, 1993; Ray Marshall and Marc Tucker, *Thinking for a Living: Work, Skills, and the Future of the American Economy* (New York: Basic Books, 1992); Barry Bluestone and Bennett Harrison, *The Deindustrialization of America* (New York: Basic Books, 1982); Bennett Harrison and Barry Bluestone, *The Great U-Turn* (New York: Basic Books, 1988); and Charles J. Whalen, "Structural Change and the Compulsive Shift to Institutional Analysis," in Charles M.A. Clark (ed.), *Institutional Economics and the Theory of Social Value* (Boston: Kluwer Academic Press, 1995), 179–94. Structural-change analyses are also offered in the following: President's Commission on Industrial Competitiveness, *Global Competition: The New Reality*; Competitiveness Policy Council, *Building a Competitive America*; and Cuomo Commission on Competitiveness, *America's Agenda: Rebuilding Economic Strength* (Armonk, NY: M.E. Sharpe, 1992).

For labor-market perspectives of structural change, see Thomas A. Kochan, Harry C. Katz, and Robert B. McKersie, *The Transformation of American Industrial Relations*; Peter B. Doeringer, et al., *Turbulence in the American Workplace* (New York: Oxford University Press, 1991); and Eileen Appelbaum and Rosemary Batt, *The New American Workplace*. Finally, see Karen Pennar, "The Business Cycle Isn't Dead, Just Resting," *Business Week* (October 4, 1993), 76, for evidence that both the U.S. business press and private-sector economists have become aware of the significance of structural change in recent years.

46. For three discussions of the family—and the connections among work, state, and family—that seem consistent with the political-economy perspective outlined in this volume (in terms of both their implicit methodology and their attention to recent structural change), see Bernadette Lanciaux, "The Role of the State in the Family," in William M. Dugger and William T. Waller, Jr. (eds.), *The Stratified State*, pp. 195–215; and Alice H. Cook, "Work and Family: Juncture and Disjuncture," and Marsha Love, Ellen Galinsky, and Diane Hughes, "Work and Family: Research Findings and Models for Change," both in Cornell University's *ILR Report, 25*, 1 (Fall 1987), 5–9 and 13–20, respectively.

47. The term "man-made" is not intended, of course, to be gender-specific. Rather,

this form of comparative advantage is merely "human-resource–determined" (instead of being produced by inherited physical endowments).

48. For some examples of the type of work called for above (including discussions of what other nations do in the realm of industrial policy), see the following: Ray Marshall, "Industrial Policy and Competitiveness in the United States," in M. Donald Hancock, John Logue, and Bernt Schiller (eds.), *Managing Modern Capitalism* (Westport, CT: Praeger, 1991), pp. 265–81; Lester C. Thurow, *Head to Head*; Jeffrey E. Garten, *A Cold Peace*; and John Zysman and Laura Tyson (eds.), *American Industry in International Competition: Government Policies and Corporate Strategies* (Ithaca, NY: Cornell University Press, 1983).

49. The national adjustment policies suggested by McClintock are compatible with— and are often very similar to—recommendations offered in other chapters, including those by Marshall, Bluestone, and Thurow.

50. To distinguish neoclassical (physically predetermined) comparative advantage from what Thurow calls "man-made" comparative advantage, Marshall uses the label "competitive advantage" for the latter and reserves the notion of "comparative advantage" for the orthodox case. We should also note that Thurow sometimes refers to "man-made" comparative advantage as "strategic advantage."

51. See Charles J. Whalen, "Schools of Thought and Theories of the State: Reflections of an Institutional Economist," in William M. Dugger and William T. Waller, Jr. (eds.), *The Stratified State*, pp. 55–85.

52. As John R. Commons explained decades ago, public policies (and other forms of collective action) can restrain individuals, but policies can also *liberate* and/or *expand* our capacity for action. See Commons, "Institutional Economics," *American Economic Review*, *21*, 4 (December 1931), 651.

53. For a similar perspective, see Amsden's discussion in chap. 13 of the need to move from a "market-failures" discussion of development to a "historical trade-offs" approach.

54. Raymond T. Bye, "Some Recent Developments of Economic Theory," in *The Trend*, p. 272.

55. Richard T. Ely, in "Roundtable Conference on Institutional Economics," *American Economic Review*, *22*, 1 (March 1932), Supplement, 116.

56. We should also note that the founders of the American Economic Association (AEA) proclaimed the following in their first public statement: "We regard the state as an agency whose positive assistance is one of the indispensable conditions of human progress." This quote, along with a discussion of the role played by institutionalists in the founding of the AEA, is contained in "History of the Founding of the American Economic Association," *Journal of Economic Issues*, *20*, 2 (June 1986), i-iii.

57. Wallace C. Peterson, "The Silent Depression," *Challenge*, *34*, 4 (July–August 1991), 34.

58. Ray Marshall, "Commons, Veblen, and Other Economists," *Journal of Economic Issues*, *27*, 2 (June 1993), 303.

59. Gunnar Myrdal, "The Meaning and Validity of Institutional Economics," in Rolf Steppacher, Brigitte Zogg-Walz, and Hermann Hatzfeldt (eds.), *Economics in Perspective* (Lexington, MA: Lexington Books, 1977), p. 5.

60. K. William Kapp, "In Defense of Institutional Economics," *Swedish Journal of Economics*, *70*, 1 (March 1968), 18. The credo suggested by Robert A. Gordon during his 1975 AEA presidential address—namely that economics should pursue "relevance with as much rigor as possible" rather than "rigor regardless of relevance"—seems thoroughly compatible with the perspective of political economists in this volume. See Robert A. Gordon, "Rigor and Relevance in a Changing Institutional Setting," p. 12.

61. Readers familiar with the institutionalist work of Commons will observe that the

distinction between an economics of mechanism and volition is one he sought to draw and develop throughout his career. For example, see Commons, *Institutional Economics: Its Place in Political Economy* (New York: Macmillan, 1934).

62. For Commons's emphasis on identifying and diffusing best practices, see his *Institutional Economics*, pp. 860–75. Today evidence of this approach can be found not only in the present volume but also in works such as Eileen Appelbaum and Rosemary Batt, *The New American Workplace*; Michael L. Dertouzos, et al., *Made in America*; and Thomas A. Kochan and Joel Cutcher-Gershenfeld, *Institutionalizing and Diffusing Innovations in Industrial Relations* (Washington, DC: U.S. Department of Labor, 1988).

63. For a recent example of excellent collaborative research, see Michael L. Dertouzos, et al., *Made in America*.

64. John Kenneth Galbraith, *Economics and the Public Purpose* (Boston: Houghton Mifflin, 1973), pp. 221–32.

65. John Maynard Keynes, *The General Theory of Employment, Interest, and Money* (New York: Harvest/HBJ, 1964 [1936]), p. viii.

66. Rexford G. Tugwell, "Introduction," in *The Trend*, p. x.

Part II

Provisioning, Ethics, and Gender

2

Redefining Economics:
From Market Allocation to
Social Provisioning

William M. Dugger

The Institutional Definition of Economics

The Search for an Alternative Definition

Neoclassical economics is clearly defined, and its definition is the generally accepted one for all of economics.[1] The definition of Lionel Robbins in particular has served to unify most practitioners of the dismal science. According to Robbins, "Economics is the science which studies human behavior as a relationship between ends and scarce means which have alternative uses."[2]

Institutional economists, however, rely on an alternative definition formulated by Allan Gruchy. Gruchy found institutionalism a very difficult discipline to define. Institutionalists have been notoriously quarrelsome and independent cusses, so getting them all within the perimeters of a manageable definition is not easy—it is a bit like herding stray cats. Nevertheless, over several decades, Gruchy patiently tried to define institutional economics. At the end of his long career, he succeeded in herding his beloved cats together by defining institutionalism as "the science of social provisioning." He emphasized that it was a "processual paradigm," a study of the changing economic processes taking place in a specific, dynamic, cultural context.[3]

Gruchy also identified the originator of institutional economics. Surprisingly, it was not Thorstein Veblen. According to Gruchy, "Karl Marx was the originator of institutional economics, for he was the first nineteenth-century economist to direct attention to the processes of institutional change within the economic system."[4]

Progressive Implications of the Institutional Definition

We should drop the neoclassical definition of economics because it is narrowing and conservative. In its place we should adopt Gruchy's definition of institutionalism because it is broadening and progressive. Institutionalism is the antidote needed to cure the narrowness and regressiveness of neoclassicism. Defining economics as a study of social provisioning and insisting that economics adopt a processual paradigm to replace the neoclassical equilibrium paradigm has six major implications: (1) While neoclassical inquiry is directed into mathematical analysis and away from social analysis, institutional inquiry is directed into historic-empirical analysis and away from formal mathematics. (2) While neoclassicists conduct static equilibrium analysis and take equilibrium to mean optimum, institutionalists conduct historical investigations or case studies of ongoing processes and take economic process to mean the continual conflict and adjustment that arise from evolving economic problems. (3) Neoclassical equilibrium implies that economic forces naturally come to a beneficent balance, while institutional process implies that evolving economic forces frequently give rise to conflict, power, and domination. (4) Neoclassicism focuses on individual choice and relies on methodological individualism. Institutionalism, on the other hand, focuses on collective action and relies on methodological collectivism. (5) Neoclassicism omits important questions. Institutionalism questions how resources come into use, how wants arise, and what economic activities mean. (6) In neoclassicism values are obscured by the attempt to be a value-free science. Institutionalism involves the open statement of values in a value-directed inquiry.

Implication 1: Historico-Empirical Analysis

First, if economics is redefined as the study of social provisioning, then economic inquiry must deal with actual social processes rather than with the mathematical logic of individual choice. Mathematical logic is neat and precise and has a beauty, an elegance, and a rigor that appeal to many students of economics. So it is no coincidence that John R. Commons, pioneering institutionalist, kept pushing his students out of his classroom at the University of Wisconsin and into the factories, sawmills, and other workplaces in Wisconsin, urging them to find out what people were actually doing and to find out what problems, conflicts, and working rules those people were facing. Commons devoted his life to the study of actual economic processes, not formal analytical techniques. He was actively involved in progressive reforms at the Wisconsin state level and also at the national level. He saw economics as the study of social provisioning, even though he did not define what he was doing in that way.[5] Wesley C. Mitchell, another leading institutionalist, devoted his life to the study of actual business cycles. He saw the business cycle as a cumulative process, inherent to the system of investing for money profit. His avoidance of mathematical formalism allowed him to see an actual process instead of a theoretical equilibrium.[6]

The historico-empirical bent of institutionalism, with its focus on process instead of equilibrium, makes it much easier for institutionalists to see the problems and conflicts that arise in their economy than it is for the neoclassicals to see them. The neoclassicals, focused on the optimality of equilibrium, find it hard to see, let alone understand, real economic problems. Neoclassicists are idealists. They see temporary deviations from social optimality. But institutionalists are pragmatists. They see social problems every place they look. And so institutionalists become interested in dealing with social problems rather than in solving mathematical problems.

Implication 2: Evolving Conflict

Economic process, the subject of institutionalism, is dynamic. Economic equilibrium, the subject of neoclassicism, is static. But what is far more important, neoclassical equilibrium is optimal. In equilibrium, we live in the best of all possible worlds, barring minor frictions. In equilibrium unemployment is natural, pollution is not a political problem but an individual problem handled through individual negotiation à la the Coase theorem, race and sex discrimination are forms of statistical errors or individual preferences, and in equilibrium the market optimizes consumer and producer surplus.

Institutional economics, on the other hand, takes as its subject dynamic change. Institutional economics could even be called the economics of maladjustment, of cultural lag. Under the constant drive of changing processes, our economy is suboptimal. It suffers from maladjustment, from leads and lags. Dynamic change gives rise to new conflicts between those who benefit from the old status quo and those who stand to gain from change. Dynamic change opens up new struggles between the underdogs and the topdogs. Equilibrium is order. Dynamic change is disorder. Equilibrium resolves conflicts of interest. Dynamic change creates conflicts of interest anew. So while neoclassicism is an antidote to economic discontent, institutionalism is the economics of discontent.[7]

Implication 3: Domination and Unbalanced Growth

The economics of discontent, the processual paradigm of institutionalism, implies that the conflict and discontent that continually arise in a changing economy are due to processes that are not automatically balanced in equilibrium. Processes of change do not necessarily come to rest in optimal balance. Instead, in societies possessed of significant economic, political, and social inequalities, processes of change more often lead to cumulative inequalities and outright domination. Dominant classes and interest groups can influence the direction of change in their favor. Using their economic power, they can invest in new areas and in new technologies that benefit them at the expense of others. Using their political power, they can define new property rights that give them advantageous access to resources or that give them differential bargaining advantages. They can use political power to influence the enforcement of existing property rights and laws in their favor. They can manipulate the nature and the flow of information. Furthermore, they can use their social power to impose new meaning for economic activities and repress old meanings in such a way as to elevate their own standing and lower the standing of others. Such power is cumulative and can give rise to increasing domination of one class or interest group over others. Institutionalism, then, is the economics of domination while neoclassicism is the economics of balance. Unfortunately, while the theory of general equilibrium (balance) is highly developed, the general theory of domination is not.[8]

The theory of cumulative causation of Gunnar Myrdal, however, is a big step in the right direction. Myrdal explained the equilibrium assumption as a belief that "a change will regularly call forth a reaction in the system in the form of changes which on the whole go in the contrary direction to the first change."[9] But actual changes usually occur in a cumulative rather than an offsetting fashion. Myrdal laid out in general terms how circular and cumulative causation worked:

> [T]here is no such tendency toward automatic self-stabilization in the social system. The system is by itself not moving toward any sort of balance between forces but is constantly on the move away from such a situation. In the normal case a change does not call forth countervailing changes but, instead, supporting changes, which move the system in the same direction as the first change but much further. Because of such circular causation a social process tends to become cumulative and often to gather speed at an accelerating rate.[10]

Cumulative change and domination, not quiescence and equilibrium, are the norms. This is particularly true for modern social systems that are already in an unbalanced state, that are already operating with gross economic, political, and social inequalities. Institutionalism is the economics of cumulative change and domination, the economics of racism and sexism and classism. Neoclassicism is the economics of equilibrium and quiescence, the economics of social harmony.

Implication 4: Culture Matters

Individuals choose. That much is indisputable. But while neoclassicism is the economics of individual choice with the culture that molds the individual left out, institutionalism is the economics of individual choice in its cultural context.

A culture is a system of interrelated patterns of behavior, meaning, and belief.[11] Economies and the economic choices individuals make are part of a culture. They are influenced by the cultural context in which they take place and, in turn, influence that cultural context. This, in a general sense, is what Stephen A. Resnick and Richard D. Wolff mean when they say that their new Marxian theory is characterized by "overdetermination." Economic factors are determined by other cultural factors and other cultural factors are, in turn, determined by economic ones.[12] For economic terms to mean anything, they must be related to other terms, to their cultural context.

Applying this contextual definition of meaning to economic ideas makes it essential to connect them to the other ideas and relations of the culture to which they belong. For the individual to mean anything and for individual choice to mean anything, they must be put into a cultural context. Neoclassicism does not do so. Institutionalism does.

Implication 5: Asking the Important Questions

An economics defined to be the logic of individual choice regarding the use of scarce means for alternative uses, which is narrowed down so as to leave out the meaning of the individual and is narrowed down so as to leave out the meaning of choice itself, omits important questions. Economic behavior means something to those performing it and economic behavior has motives behind it. Neither behaviors nor motives just drop out of the sky. Nor do economic resources just drop out of the sky. They all come from somewhere. Behaviors and motives are learned, so, unless we beg the questions, we must investigate how they are learned. J. Ron Stanfield argues that "the treatment of behavior as learned behavior" is the essence of institutionalism.[13] Institutionalists take the "givens" of neoclassicism and incorporate them into their theory of the economy. Or, as Geoffrey Hodgson sees it, we make the exogenous variables endogenous.[14] We do so by asking the important questions regarding the learning of wants and the source of resources.

But institutionalism does more than just make the exogenous variables endogenous. It also inquires into the meaning of wants, choices, and resources. For example, Thorstein Veblen's works still provide some of the most penetrating analyses of the questions begged by neoclassicism. Veblen's *Theory of the Leisure Class* investigated the nature of consumer wants and choices in the cultural context of gross inequality and industrial capitalism. His essay on the nature of capital probed the sociotechnological nature of resources and of productivity.[15] After Veblen, a number of works probed into related questions. Let me cite just three of them: Adolf A. Berle and Gardiner C. Means investigated the nature of private property in the corporate age; Erich W. Zimmerman explained that resources are functional (that is, he explained that they are a function of new technology); and John R. Commons investigated the nature and evolution of property rights.[16]

When the important questions are asked, insight can be gained into how resource availability changes, how wants change, and into the formation and reformation of economic meaning. Such insights are the subject matter of institutionalism.

Implication 6: Economics Cannot Be Value-Free

Economics is a cultural science and since we are all part of a culture and since we all place positive value on some aspects of our culture and negative values on other aspects of our culture, we cannot purge all values from our inquiries. Nevertheless, we can be effective. To be effective we cannot pretend to be value-free, because then values enter our inquiry unconsciously, as it were. They enter unanalyzed and unchallenged. To be effective we must begin by explicitly stating our values so they can be analyzed and challenged. This is the method used and proposed by institutionalist Gunnar Myrdal.[17] Institutionalists are instrumentalists regarding the value question.[18] That is, they favor values produced by a continuing process of democratic policy making, policy correcting, and policy remaking that is based on participatory decision making. In the instrumentalist tradition, values are never definitive, never absolute. But they must be explicit and open to challenge. As Myrdal explained it,

> I am not pretending to have arrived at a final and fully satisfactory solution. . . . But I do insist that if we . . . spell out, in as definite terms as possible, a set of instrumental value premises—however they have been reached and whichever they may be—and if we allow them to determine our approach, the definitions of our concepts, and the formulation of our theories, this represents an advance towards the goals of honesty, clarity, and effectiveness in research. These are steps in the direction of "objectivity" in the only sense this concept can be understood.[19]

Economics should be redefined to be the study of social provisioning. It should be a processual paradigm defined to ask the important questions. Economics should be institutional and not rely on a facile, subjective–objective dualism that draws a distinction between the subject (the value-free scientist) and the object (the allocation of scarce resources to alternative uses).

Process: The Central Feature of Economics

All economies involve processes that expand or retard social provisioning. Socialist economies, capitalist economies, anarchist economies, industrial economies, and pastoral economies all involve intricate webs of social provisioning processes. These processes are all interrelated, "overdetermined." These processes produce goods and services, but they also produce people. These processes are the result of individual choices but they also give substance to individual choice and set limits on individual choice. These processes continually change. They do not tend toward equilibrium, balance, or optimality. Instead, they tend to change, and generally in a cumulative fashion. I find the following fourfold grouping to be helpful in approaching social provisioning problems: (1) the resource process, (2) the want process, (3) the production/re-production process, and (4) the meaning process.

The Resource Process

The resource process involves the creation and discovery of new resources on one hand, and the allocation and destruction of existing resources on the other hand. Clarence Ayres and Erich Zimmermann emphasize the significance of technology in the resource process.[20] In their technological view, resources do not just exist; they become. The neutral stuff of nature becomes useful resources because new technologies make it possible to find, or to extract, or to process them, or because new technologies transform previously useless materials into useful ones. From the technological point of view, resources are not scarce. They are not given, not exogenous. Instead, they are a function of technological advance itself. This is not to say that scientists and engineers are magicians who can pull rabbits out of their hats whenever they need them, however. Nor is it to say that society should grant huge rewards to inventors and entrepreneurs who implement the accumulated knowledge of their culture and push it a tiny bit further. But it is to say that social policy regarding public education, research, and science can have strongly positive effects on the rate at which new resources can be discovered and created.

The allocation and destruction of existing resources are largely legal and political processes, the significance of which is heavily emphasized by the followers of John R. Commons. The allocation of existing resources has to do with the determination and enforcement of property rights. Property rights are not god-given and immutable. They change through the actions of adjudication, legislation, and revolution. Property rights are complex bundles of *liberty, capacity, compulsion*, and *exposure*, all of which are made effective through collective action—through the coercion of the state, if necessary. *Liberty* establishes what may be done without interference from others. *Capacity* establishes what can be done with the support of collective action. *Compulsion* establishes what must or must not be done, under threat of collective action. *Exposure* establishes what collective action will not do on behalf of one party to protect it from the compulsion of others.[21] Property rights have not and do not evolve through simple individual bargaining à la the Coase Theorem. Instead, Commons explained how the property rights system of feudalism evolved into the property rights system of capitalism. It evolved as the underdogs pressed to expand their capacities and liberties against the topdogs. It evolved as the underdogs pressed to contract their exposures and compulsions at the hands of the topdogs. And property rights continue to evolve in the same way today—as a collective push from below against privilege and as a collective defense from above against usurpation, with the "establishment" resisting those from below.

The resource process also involves cultural norms. In patriarchical societies, the creation and use of resources within the family are usually invisible. The resource process within the family is invisible because the family is largely a sphere of traditional female activity. According to the cultural norms of patriarchy, housewives and mothers do not really "work." They receive no pay. They do not make anything. So, they do not create or allocate resources. They are dependents of men, not producers and allocators of resources. They just keep house and watch the children. Furthermore, according to the cultural norms of patriarchy, women should stay home. They should not "work." Hence, women are not considered resources; they are not part of the work force or labor supply. Such cultural norms have enormous crippling and limiting impacts on the creation and allocation of resources. So changing cultural norms can significantly affect both the quantity and the quality of resources.[22]

The theory of the resource process, as built up by institutionalists, makes resources endogenous. Resources are not scarce, not given as in neoclassical economics. Instead, resources are functions of technological change, evolving property rights, and changing cultural norms. Institutionalism has a theory of resources. Neoclassicism takes them as given.

The Want Process

Rather than beginning with given individual preferences, institutionalism makes wants endogenous. It explains them as the products of individual learning and collective action in the context of a specific ongoing culture. The want process involves the creation and expansion of new wants along with the destruction of old wants. Commodity fetishism, conspicuous consumption, and the theory of the revised sequence explain wants in affluent societies. Neoclassicism has no corresponding theories of wants, just the logic of individual choice with wants taken as given.

Commodity fetishism refers to a cumulative process of buying more and more consumer commodities without ever receiving any intrinsic, consummating satisfaction from them but only being driven to buy more of them. Conspicuous consumption refers to trying to keep up with the "Joneses" while the "Joneses" are themselves trying to keep up in a vain attempt to acquire status in the eyes of others by consuming more than they do. The theory of the revised sequence is John Kenneth Galbraith's explanation that we no longer produce in order for others to consume badly needed goods. Instead, we consume in order for others to have jobs and profits as they produce.

Marx refers to "the fetishism of commodities" in section 4 of the first chapter of *Capital*.[23] Although this passage may be the most widely read of his passages on commodity fetishism, it is not the clearest statement of his views; nor is it the most powerfully moving. Marx's best writings on commodity fetishism are contained in his *Economic and Philosophical Manuscripts*.[24] Under capitalism, Marx explains,

No eunuch flatters his tyrant more shamefully or seeks by more infamous means to stimulate his jaded appetite, in order to gain some favor, than does the eunuch of industry, the entrepreneur, in order to acquire a few silver coins or to charm the gold from the purse of his dearly beloved neighbor. (Every product is a bait by means of which the individual tries to entice the essence of the other person, his money. Every real or potential need is a weakness which will draw the bird into the lime. . . .)[25]

Veblen did not base his theory of conspicuous consumption on capitalism itself, but on the struggle for invidious distinction that arises in pecuniary culture. As Veblen put it:

The decent requirements of waste absorb the surplus energy of the population in an invidious struggle and leave no margin for the non-invidious expression of life. . . . The canons of decent life are an elaboration of the principle of invidious comparison, and they accordingly act consistently to inhibit all non-invidious effort and to inculcate the self-regarding attitude.[26]

More recent works on commodity fetishism and conspicuous consumption analyze consumerism as a continual round of working harder and feeling worse.[27] The harder we work, the more we have to spend on commodities to try to overcome the effects of our alienated work, and the more we spend on conspicuous consumption, the more other consumers spend on it, depriving us of the invidious distinctions we seek from it. Spending on commodities that satisfy artificial wants does not overcome the effects of alienation. Nor does conspicuous consumption make us feel better about ourselves. They both just leave us deeper in debt and more dependent on our paychecks. With commodity fetishism and conspicuous consumption, more is not better. It is worse.[28]

The theories of commodity fetishism and conspicuous consumption lay down an epistemological foundation for a critique of the want process in affluent societies. They show that individual utility is not the causal factor in want creation and want satisfaction. The causal factors are external to the subjective preferences of the individual consumer because those preferences are learned, not inherent. Only such basics as hunger and thirst are inherent. A desire for potato chips and beer is learned. The Galbraithian theory of the revised sequence fills in the actual details of how advertising and salesmanship teach us what we want: "The revised sequence sends to the museum of irrelevant ideas the notion of an equilibrium in consumer outlays which reflects the maximum of consumer satisfaction."[29]

The Production/Reproduction Process

The production/reproduction process involves a whole series of social relations: the ownership of the means of production, the organization of the workplace, relations within the family and between the sexes, policies of the state, and continuous struggle over the control of all these relations. Neoclassical economics reduces the production/reproduction process down to the theory of the firm. The theory of the firm then reduces the firm down to little more than a production function and an individual chooser who maximizes his profits within a set of given constraints. With the substance squeezed out of the production/reproduction process, neoclassicism then proceeds to develop an elaborate analysis of the logic of individual choice as applied to production/reproduction. The social relations of ownership, management, patriarchy, politics, and conflict are replaced by isoquants, budget lines, and equilibrium conditions which become the mathematical abstractions analyzed. Neoclassicism substitutes the logic of individual choice as applied to production/reproduction for explanations of production/reproduction itself.

Marxists who inquire into institutional issues have made significant contributions to the theory of production. Such Marxists have constructed a number of powerful theories of ownership of the means of production, theories of control of the workplace, and theories of class conflict in the workplace. For example, Harry Braverman's *Labor and Monopoly Capital* is a theory of private property in the means of production that explains how private ownership has affected the production process at every turn. To Braverman's theory of ownership, Richard Edwards's *Contested Terrain* adds a theory of workplace conflict. Edwards shows how continued struggle over control of the workplace has shaped the production process in the United States. Then, Stephen A. Marglin's "What Do Bosses Do" rounds out the Marxist-institutionalist theory of the production process by explaining how managerial hierarchy has shaped the evolution of the production process.[30]

To these Marxist-influenced theories of the workplace and class conflict, institutionalists add theories of the state and theories of gender, to round out the explanations of the production/reproduction process. The state and the political process are shown to have profound effects, both positive and negative, on the production/reproduction of the material means of life. Furthermore, gender inequality is shown to distort both the way we understand the economy and the way the economy itself actually works.[31]

The Meaning Process

The meaning process involves assigning meaning to the three other processes. To understand what the economic activities mean to the people involved in them does not involve reading their minds or prying open their heads to get at their individual subjectivity. Understanding meaning does not require that we project our own introspections onto other people. Those other people can talk. They can write. They can tell their own stories. What economists need to do is learn how to ask questions and learn how to listen to people's stories. The collection and interpretation of oral histories already provide us with considerable insight into the meanings of economic activities.[32] The meaning of the life process lies out there in the hearts and minds of millions of folks, just waiting for us to ask the right questions and to listen to the answers.

To inquire into meaning, however, is to go to the very heart of the economic system. And that, neoclassicism fails to do. Instead, it retreats from a theory of meaning by posing as a value-free science. For at the heart of any class system is the conflict between class interest and general interest, the contradiction between the general will and the particular will. In the old Soviet system it was the contradiction between the class interest of the state bureaucracy and the underlying populations. In the U.S. system it is the contradiction between the class interest of monopoly capital and the broad public. Marx emphasized,

> For each new class which puts itself in the place of one ruling before it, is compelled, merely in order to carry through its aim, to represent its interest as the common interest of all the members of society put in an ideal form; it will give its ideas the form of universality, and represent them as the only rational, universally valid ones.[33]

If we do not inquire into the meanings of economic processes, we run the danger of having an economic theory that, at best, does not mean anything and, at worst, serves merely to obscure and preserve the position of those who derive wealth and power from the status quo. It is in the understanding of the meaning process that institutionalism becomes particularly significant. Most important is the contribution made by Thorstein Veblen. He lifted the myths that had shrouded the meaning of the predatory processes of our economy.[34] Important recent contributions to the Veblen branch of institutionalism can be found in work produced by "radical institutionalists."[35]

Institutionalism has developed theories of the resource process, the want process, the production process, and the meaning process. Neoclassicism has not. Whether most economists realize it or not, institutionalism has matured into a paradigm with a fully developed body of theory.

Conclusion

Due to its broad definition of economics as the study of social provisioning, institutionalism has become a synthesis. The synthesis includes the commonly recognized institutionalism of Veblen, Commons, Mitchell, and Ayres—traditional institutionalism. But the synthesis also includes the originator of institutionalism, Karl Marx, and it includes some contemporary Marxists like Stephen Resnick, Richard Wolff, Samuel Bowles, Herbert Gintiss, Thomas Weisskopf, and Howard Sherman. Furthermore, institutionalism has been enriched by the works of many others who have inquired into the social provisioning process, whether or not they call themselves institutionalists (Douglass North and Oliver Williamson, for example). Considerable disagreement exists within the synthesis, but then considerable disagreement always exists within any paradigm.[36] What is significant about this synthesis is its very real theoretical depth and breadth. Its broad definition encompasses a theoretical body of knowledge far surpassing what can be fit within the narrow confines of the neoclassical definition. Furthermore, the institutionalist definition focuses inquiry on social processes rather than on mathematical forms, on dynamic change rather than on optimal equilibrium. Economics should be redefined to be the study of social provisioning.

Notes

1. The views expressed in this chapter benefited from the contributions of Warren J. Samuels, J. Ron Stanfield, Marc Tool, William Waller, and Charles Whalen.

2. Lionel Robbins, *An Essay on the Nature and Significance of Economic Science*, 2d ed. (London: Macmillan, 1935), p. 16.

3. Allan G. Gruchy, *The Reconstruction of Economics* (New York: Greenwood Press, 1987), pp. 4–7 and 21.

4. Allan G. Gruchy, *Modern Economic Thought* (New York: Augustus M. Kelley, 1967), p. 275.

5. John R. Commons, *Myself* (Madison: University of Wisconsin Press, 1964).

6. Wesley C. Mitchell, *Business Cycles, The Problem and Its Setting* (New York: National Bureau of Economic Research, 1927).

7. A similar view of orthodox and institutional economics is suggested by John M. Clark; see his "The Socializing of Economics," in Rexford Tugwell's *The Trend of Economics* (New York: Knopf, 1924), p. 85.

8. But see François Perroux, "The Domination Effect and Modern Economic Theory," *Social Research*, *17* (1950), 188–206.

9. Gunnar Myrdal, *Economic Theory and Underdeveloped Regions* (New York: Harper and Row, 1957), p. 13.

10. Ibid., p. 13.

11. For further discussion, see William T. Waller, "Methodological Aspects of Radical Institutionalism," in William M. Dugger (ed.), *Radical Institutionalism: Basic Concepts* (New York: Greenwood Press, 1989), pp. 39–49; J. Ron Stanfield, "Phenomena and Epiphenomena in Economics," *Journal of Economic Issues*, *13* (1979), 885–98; J. Ron Stanfield, "Learning from Primitive Economies," *Journal of Economic Issues*, *16* (1982), 471–79; and Anne Mayhew, "Culture: Core Concept Under Attack," *Journal of Economic Issues*, *21* (1987), 587–603.

12. Stephen A. Resnick and Richard D. Wolff, *Knowledge and Class* (Chicago: University of Chicago Press, 1987).

13. J. Ron Stanfield, "Learning from Primitive Economies," p. 471.

14. Geoffrey M. Hodgson, *Economics and Institutions* (Philadelphia: University of Pennsylvania Press, 1988), pp. 13–17.

15. Thorstein Veblen, *The Theory of the Leisure Class* (New York: Augustus M. Kelley, 1975); and Thorstein Veblen, *The Place of Science in Modern Civilization and Other Essays.* (New York: B. W. Huebsch, 1919), pp. 325–86.

16. Adolf A. Berle and Gardiner C. Means, *The Modern Corporation and Private Property*, rev. ed. (New York: Harcourt, Brace and World, 1968); Erich W. Zimmermann,

World Resources and Industries, rev. ed. (New York: Harper and Brothers, 1951); and John R. Commons, *Legal Foundations of Capitalism* (Madison: University of Wisconsin Press, 1968).

17. Gunnar Myrdal, *Objectivity in Social Research* (New York: Pantheon, 1969).

18. See Marc Tool, *Essays in Social Value Theory* (Armonk, NY: M.E. Sharpe, 1986).

19. Gunnar Myrdal, *Objectivity in Social Research,* p. 72.

20. Clarence E. Ayres, *The Theory of Economic Progress*, 2d ed. (New York: Schocken Books, 1962); Erich W. Zimmermann, *World Resources and Industries*; and Thomas R. DeGregori, *A Theory of Technology* (Ames: Iowa State University, 1985).

21. John R. Commons, *Legal Foundations of Capitalism*, p. 6.

22. Further discussion is in Barbara Bergmann, *The Economic Emergence of Women* (New York: Basic Books, 1986).

23. Karl Marx (ed. by Frederick Engels), *Capital* (New York: International Publishers, 1967), pp. 71–83.

24. I have relied on T.B. Bottomore's translation in Erich Fromm, *Marx's Concept of Man* (New York: Frederick Ungar, 1966), pp. 90–257.

25. Ibid., p. 141, parentheses in original.

26. Thorstein Veblen, *The Theory of the Leisure Class*, p. 362.

27. Juliet B. Schor, *The Overworked American* (New York: Basic Books, 1991).

28. J. Ron Stanfield and Jacqueline B. Stanfield, "Consumption in Contemporary Capitalism: The Backward Art of Living," *Journal of Economic Issues, 14* (1980), 437–51. For an analytical framework, see William M. Dugger, "The Analytics of Consumer Externalities," *Review of Social Economy, 43* (1985), 212–33.

29. John Kenneth Galbraith, *The New Industrial State* (Boston: Houghton Mifflin, 1967), p. 213.

30. Harry Braverman, *Labor and Monopoly Capital* (New York: Monthly Review Press, 1974); Richard Edwards, *Contested Terrain* (New York: Basic Books, 1979); Stephen A. Marglin, "What Do Bosses Do? The Origins and Functions of Hierarchy in Capitalist Production," *Review of Radical Political Economics, 6* (1974), 33–60.

31. Recent works in this line include William M. Dugger and William T. Waller (eds.), *The Stratified State* (Armonk, NY: M.E. Sharpe, 1992); and Janice Peterson and Doug Brown (eds.), *The Economic Status of Women Under Capitalism* (Aldershot, UK: Edward Elgar, 1994).

32. See the following books by Studs Terkel: *Hard Times* (New York: Pantheon Books, 1970); *Working* (New York: Pantheon Books, 1974); and *The Great Divide* (New York: Pantheon Books, 1988).

33. Marx in Erich Fromm, *Marx's Concept of Man*, p. 214.

34. Thorstein Veblen, *Absentee Ownership and Business Enterprise in Recent Times* (New York: Augustus M. Kelley, 1964).

35. See William M. Dugger, *Radical Institutionalism: Basic Concepts*, for an introduction to radical institutionalism and its recent contributions to economics.

36. See William M. Dugger and Howard J. Sherman, "Comparison of Marxism and Institutionalism," *Journal of Economic Issues, 28* (1994), 101–27.

3

Ethics and Economics

Charles K. Wilber

Economics and ethics are interrelated because both economists (theorists and policy advisers) and economic actors (sellers, consumers, workers) hold ethical values that help shape their behavior. In the first case economists must try to understand how their own values affect both economic theory and policy. In the second case this means economic analysis must broaden its conception of human behavior.

In this chapter I will focus on the importance of these two issues. First, economists construct theory upon a particular world view, resulting in basic concepts, such as efficiency, being value-laden. Second, economic theory, with its myopic focus on self-interest, obscures the fact that preferences are formed not only by material self-interest but also by ethical values, and that market economies require that ethical behavior for efficient functioning.

Values, World Views, and the Economist

In recent years there has been a flurry of literature on methodological issues in economics, much of it calling into question its supposed scientific character. Part of that literature deals explicitly with the impact of ethical value judgments on economics as a science. Of this literature a greater amount argues the value-permeation thesis than defends the idea of value neutrality. However, value neutrality of economics as a science is the dominant position in the day-to-day work of contemporary economists. It seems expedient to begin by laying out its arguments.

Value Neutrality

There are two pervasive tenets to the value-neutrality argument. The first is a reliance on the Humean guillotine which categorically separates fact ("what is") from value ("what ought to be"); this is also known as the positive/normative dichotomy. The second basic tenet strongly supports the first by claiming that since we have objective access to the empirical world through our sense experience, scientists need not concern themselves with "what ought to be." This second tenet is the really crucial point and the one that postpositivist philosophy of science has sought to undermine.

The value-neutral position argues that scientific economics comprises three separate components: prescientific decisions, scientific analysis, and postscientific application. However, there is a difference between the value judgments of pre-science and of post-science. Hume's guillotine is protected by drawing a distinction in social science between two types of value judgments. A *characterizing value judgment* expresses an estimate of the degree to which some commonly recognized (and more or less clearly defined) type of action, object, or institution is embodied in a given instance. An *appraising value judgment* expresses approval or disapproval either of some moral (or social) ideal, or of some action (or institution) because of commitment to such an ideal. Some value judgments are thus not really value judgments of any ethical significance, but judgments that merely allow one to carry on the scientific enterprise.[1]

Other attempts to reconcile value judgments and objective science often use the notion of "brute fact." This is the claim that facts are in some sense "out there" for all to see, independent of scientific theory.[2] Unfortunately for the value neutral position, the idea of brute fact has fallen on hard times in the philosophy of science literature. Today it is generally recognized even by sophisticated logical empiricists that facts are theory-laden and that theories are tested by the facts designated as of interest by the theory.[3] The more important question then becomes whether theory itself is, in part, value determined, for if it is, then theory-laden facts would also appear to be value-laden.

The defense of value neutrality still stands, but the pillars seem to be weakening. Blaug concedes that both "factual" and "moral" arguments rest ultimately "on certain definite techniques of persuasion, which in turn depend for their effectiveness, on shared values of one kind or another."[4] Even more damaging is his comment that "no doubt Hume's Guillotine tells us that we cannot logically deduce ought from is or is from ought. We can however, influence ought by is and vice versa: moral judgments may be altered by presentation of the facts, and facts are theory-laden so that a change of values may alter our perception of the facts."[5]

Let us now consider recent criticisms of the value-neutrality thesis.

Value Permeation

The value permeation position argues that while science is driven by a search for truth, it is not interested in just any truth. The relevant truth must be both "interesting" and "valuable," and thus all science is goal-directed activity. Further, the criteria for a "good" or "acceptable" scientific theory cannot be ranked in terms of their intrinsic importance, but only in relation to the degree to which they serve particular goals of the scientific community.[6]

Theory choice is not, therefore, based objectively on noncontroversial criteria (e.g., degree of verification or corroboration), but on criteria that are inevitably value-laden (i.e., the extent to which each theory serves specific ends). The scientists' search for "valuable truth" is directed by what they think society (and science) ought to do. No amount of evidence ever completely confirms or disconfirms any empirical hypothesis but only renders it more or less probable.

Another line of reasoning, Kuhnian in character, is more convincing to many. Kuhn, referring to the natural sciences, speaks of paradigms, characterized by the shared values of a given scientific community.[7] It is Kuhn's rejection of the second tenet—that we have objective access to the empirical world through our sense experience—that is important for those opposed to the value-neutrality position. He argues that the empirical world can be known only through the filter of a theory; thus, facts are theory-laden.

One major argument of those who build on Kuhn's approach runs as follows: A world view greatly influences the scientific paradigm out of which one works; value judgments are closely associated with the world view; theories must remain coherent with the world view; facts themselves are theory-laden; therefore, the whole scientific venture is permeated by value judgments from the start. This world view, or *Weltanschauung*, shapes the interests of the scientist and determines the questions asked, the problems considered important, the answers deemed acceptable, the axioms of the theory, the choice of "relevant facts," the hypotheses proposed to account for such facts, the criteria used to assess the fruitfulness of competing theories, the language in which results are to be formulated, and so on.

The Neoclassical World View: A Case in Point

At this point let me illustrate the world view argument with neoclassical economics.[8] The world view of mainstream neoclassical economics is closely associated with the notion of the good embedded in its particular scientific paradigm.

Neoclassical economics is founded on a world view made up of the following propositions:

1.   Human nature is such that humans are:
      a. self-interested;
      b. rational—that is, they know their own interest and choose from among a variety of means in order to maximize that interest.
2.   The purpose of human life is for individuals to pursue happiness as they themselves define it. Therefore, it is essential that they be left free to do so.
3.   The ideal social world is a gathering of free individuals who compete with

each other under conditions of scarcity to achieve self-interested ends. As in the natural world with physical entities, in the social world, too, there are forces at work that move economic agents toward equilibrium positions.

Neoclassical economists either accept the preceding empirically unverifiable and unfalsifiable statements or, barring overt acceptance, conduct scientific inquiry with methods based thereon.

To state it simply, neoclassical economists believe that humans are rational maximizers of their own self-interest and that humans act in a rational world characterized by forces that move things toward equilibrium.[9] The first two propositions contain the motivating force in economic life (satisfaction of self-interest) and the third proposition spells out the context in which that force works itself out.

It seems fairly clear that judgments of value, of a particular notion of the good, are directly implied by the first two propositions of this world view. If the purpose of life is that individuals pursue happiness, and if they do so self-interestedly, then it certainly would be good for individuals to receive what they want. Here is the basic notion of the good permeating all neoclassical economics: individuals should be free to get as much as possible of what they want. Other value judgments of the neoclassical paradigm either qualify what types of individual wants will be considered or are derivative from this basic value judgment. That this basic position is, in fact, a judgment of value, or of the good, is a point willingly granted by many economists.[10] There are two basic judgments in any use of economic theory, such as cost–benefit analysis. The first of these is that individual preferences should count. Also, the use of economic theory requires a value judgment on distributional equity. But this value judgment is rather superficial, for it is external to the neoclassical paradigm. Because it is external, it often obstructs our view of the more fundamental value judgments, those deeply embedded in the paradigm itself.

These other value judgments, along with the basic value judgment, can be summarized in this way:

1. Individuals should be free to get what they want.
2. Competitive market equilibrium is the ideal economic situation.
    a. Competitive market institutions should be established whenever and wherever possible;
    b. Market prices should be used to determine value.
3. Means and ends should be bifurcated into two mutually exclusive categories.
4. Means and ends should be measured quantitatively.

The second value judgment derives from elements one and three of the neoclassical world view and from the basic value judgment that individual preferences should count. If one takes the core ideas of individualism, rationality, and the social context of harmony among diverse and conflicting interests, along with a number of limiting assumptions, it can be shown that competitive equilibrium maximizes the value of consumption and is therefore the best of all possible economic situations. The second value judgment is thus a different sort than the first, because it is conditional on the first. It does not stand alone. Competitive market equilibrium is good, in part, because it allows the greatest number of individual wants to be satisfied. Moreover, this value judgment is also determined by the world view. Without the third proposition such a judgment could not be made, for then some other economic condition could be found to satisfy individual wants. Competitive market equilibrium is good because the world view insists that only this condition can be ideal.

The notion of competitive equilibrium carries out two basic functions: it serves as an ideal and as a standard by which to measure the real value of current economic conditions. Because it serves as an ideal for which we strive, it leads directly to the value judgment that wherever competitive markets do not exist or are weak, they should be instituted or promoted. Wherever markets do not exist, the natural competitiveness of human beings will be channeled into nonproductive directions. It would be better to establish markets where this competitiveness and self-interest-seeking behavior could be channeled into mutually satisfying activities. Wherever markets are weak and distorted due to monopoly power or government interference, there is sure to be a reduction in actual consumption. Therefore, perfectly competitive markets should be promoted so that the ideal competitive equilibrium can be achieved.

The third and fourth value judgments do not spring directly from the world view. Instead, they make the paradigm based thereon operational. The separation of means and ends is not strictly required by the world view itself, but is an operational requirement, without which the paradigm could generate no meaningful research or study. If means and ends were not mutually exclusive, then neoclassical economics would be nothing more than a simple statement that humans do what they do because they wish to do it. There could be, for example, no inquiry into how satisfaction is maximized by choosing among various alternatives. If some activity (e.g., production or consumption) could be both means and end, then one could not determine which part is which. As Jerome Rothenberg concedes, the intermixing of means and ends "does violence to our paradigm."[11] This results in the value judgment that consumption is the end or "good" to be achieved. In so doing, any good inherent in the process or means for obtaining higher consumption is ignored. For example, if the production activity of human labor were more than just a means—if work were good in and of itself regardless of the final product—then it would be impossible for the neoclassical economist to discover how much individual wants are satisfied by the activity. The ends and the means would be all mixed together and it would be impossible to speak independently of the value of the product and the cost of the resources.

The splitting of economic activities into means and ends by its very nature promotes a particular notion of the good. It may be an operational necessity, but it is also a judgment of value. With means and ends separated, it becomes convenient to measure the satisfaction given by particular ends and the dissatisfaction (costs) resulting from employing various means. It becomes possible to measure how much better one situation is than another, by comparing numbers instead of concepts or ideas. Things that are apparently incommensurable thus become commensurable. This is evident in many branches of neoclassical analysis; when money values are unavailable or inappropriate, quantified units are used in their place.

The emphasis on quantification in neoclassical economics adds another element to its particular notion of the good. While the third value judgment separates means and ends, the fourth value judgment tells us to focus on means and ends that can be quantified. One practical outcome of this is a heavy emphasis on "things" over interpersonal relationships, education, cultural affairs, family, workplace organization, and so on. Things are countable, while the quality of these other spheres of human life is not. In the area of economic policy especially, such concerns are treated often as obstacles to be removed or overcome.[12] To the extent that this occurs, the notion of the good that focuses on quantifiable inputs and outputs is embedded in the paradigm.

Within neoclassical economics there are thus judgments of value that are rooted in a fundamental world view. There are also judgments of value that operate in concert with the world view and that allow the neoclassical approach to be operational. Together these judgments make up the neoclassical position on the character of the good, and when an economic policy is planned, implemented, and evaluated, it is done on the basis of these clearly defined standards.

To conclude this discussion, the paradigm or research program of *any* scientific community is circumscribed by boundaries laid out in a world view that, while not perhaps individually subjective, is nevertheless empirically untestable, or metaphysical as Boland would say.[13] How, then, do value judgments about the good, the just, and the right enter into scientific analysis? Such value judgments are themselves entailed by the same world view that gives rise to theoretical and factual analysis. "What is" and "what ought to be" are thus inextricably commingled in the data, the facts, the theories, the descriptions, the explanations, the prescriptions, and so on. All are permeated by the a priori world view.

As economics enters the next century, it must recognize that there is no alternative to working from a world view. Making explicit the values embodied in that world view will help keep economics more honest and useful. For example, many institutional economists see the social world as characterized by interdependence of economic actors with the result that "externalities" are ubiquitous. The assignment of rights by the political and legal systems, therefore, determines "who gets what." The distribution of income, wealth, and rights that results from economic transactions and public policies becomes as important as efficiency.

Therefore, economists with this world view believe every policy should be evaluated for its impact on distribution as well as on efficiency.[14]

Furthermore, it is not sufficient to simply reject the neoclassical position that
satisfying individual preferences, as expressed in the market, is the only measure
of economic welfare. Alternatives must be proposed and developed. Let me
sketch out one possible alternative.[15]

We must broaden our view of human welfare from that of a simple consumer
of goods and services with consumer sovereignty as the goal. Rather, once
biological needs are met, people derive welfare primarily from social activities
such as working, dancing, theorizing, playing golf, painting, partying, and so
forth. In order to engage in such activities, people need instruments, capacities,
and a social context or environment.

People need instruments (goods and services) to engage in activities—fishing
poles to fish with, tools to work with, shoes to dance in. Traditional economics
focuses solely on this need. However, the instruments are worthless unless people have the capacity to use them—training is needed to learn how to fly-fish, to
use tools to repair a car, to dance the Tango. Finally, people need a social context
or environment to carry out these activities—a clean river is needed to fish in,
good working conditions are needed to enjoy working, clean air and safe streets
are needed to enjoy jogging.

The result of such a world view is that the measure of human welfare expands
from consumer sovereignty to include worker sovereignty (do people have the
jobs they want; are the jobs fulfilling; does the work enhance people's capacities?) and citizen sovereignty (do people have the communities and environments they want; do they have the power to construct the social contexts within
which they can develop their capacities?). With this expanded conception of
human welfare, the evaluation of economic policies can be quite different.

Now it is time to turn from the economist's world view to analyze the impact
of ethical values on the behavior of economic actors.

Values of Economic Actors

If economic theory is to make progress in understanding how the economy
operates, then a better conception of human behavior is needed. Social economists and institutionalists have always understood this. Belatedly, even neoclassical economists are becoming aware of the problem. Basically, the argument is
that (1) people act on the basis of embodied moral values as well as from
self-interest, and (2) the economy needs that ethical behavior to be efficient.

The assumption that self-interest in a competitive environment is sufficient to
yield the common good is an illusion. Pushed to its logical extreme, individual
self-interest suggests that it would usually be in the interest of an individual to
evade the rules by which other players are guided. Therefore, what constrains
individuals from doing so? The answer is that our selfishness or tendency to

maximize our material welfare at the expense of others is inhibited by a deeply ingrained moral sense, one often based on religious convictions.

I argue that subordination of short-run interests to long-run interests and moral behavior which constrains free riding, in addition to being good in themselves, are essential for the efficient operation of the economy. The claim that individual self-interest is sufficient to achieve efficient market outcomes is wrong. The next section outlines the theory underlying this claim. The remainder of the chapter applies the theory to the supply of blood and then examines the relationship between self-interest and internalized moral behavior.

Imperfect Information, Interdependence, and Social Traps

Under conditions of interdependence and imperfect information, rational self-interest frequently would lead to socially irrational results unless that self-interest was constrained by an internalized moral code.[16] Traditional economic theory assumes independence of economic actors and perfect information. However, the more realistic assumptions that one person's behavior affects another's and that each has less than perfect knowledge of the other's likely behavior can give rise to strategic behavior, or what game theorists call "moral hazards."

A classic example is the situation where both the employer and worker suspect that the other one cannot be trusted to honor their explicit or implicit contract. For example, the employer thinks the worker will take too many coffee breaks, spend too much time talking with other workers, and generally work less than the employer thinks is owed. The worker, on the other hand, thinks the employer will try to speed up the pace of work, fire her or him unjustly if given the chance, and generally behave arbitrarily. When this is the case, the worker will tend to shirk and the employer will increase supervision to stop the expected shirking. If the worker would self-supervise, production costs would be lower. Thus, this distrust between employer and worker reduces efficiency.

In this case the pursuit of individual self-interest results in the worker and the employer as individuals and as a group becoming worse off than if they had been able to cooperate, that is, not shirk and not supervise. The problem is simple and common. The employer and worker are interdependent and do not have perfect knowledge of what the other will do, and the resulting lack of trust leads to behavior that is self-defeating. This outcome is made worse if distrust is accompanied with feelings of injustice. For example, if the worker feels that the contract is unfair (low wages, poor grievance machinery, etc.), the tendency to shirk will be increased.

There are numerous other cases—for example, inflation. A labor union fights for a wage increase only to find that others also have done so and thus the wage increase is offset by rising consumer prices. No one union alone can restrain its wage demands and maintain the support of its members. Business firms are caught in the same dilemma. They raise prices to compensate for increased labor

ETHICS AND ECONOMICS 53

and other costs only to discover that costs have increased again. Distrust among unions, among firms, and between unions and firms makes impossible a cooperative agreement on price and wage increases.

The case of recession is similar. As aggregate demand in the economy declines, each company attempts to cope with its resulting cash flow difficulties through employee layoffs. However, if all companies pursue this strategy, aggregate demand will decline further, making more layoffs necessary. Most companies agree that the result is undesirable for each company and for the whole economy, but no one company on its own can maintain its work force. In effect, each company says it will not lay off its employees if all the others do not also lay off their employees. Again, no agreement is concluded.

These cases have two things in common. They all have a group (in these cases, workers and their employers) with a common interest in the outcome of a particular situation. And, second, while each attempts to choose the best available course of action, the result is not what any member of the group desires. For example, employers must pay for additional supervision costs and workers receive lower wages because of lowered productivity. In these cases the individual motives lead to undesired social and individual results.

Why is it so difficult for the individuals involved to cooperate and make an agreement? One reason is that exit is cheap, but voice is expensive.[17] Exit means to withdraw from a situation, person, or organization and depends on the availability of choice, competition, and well-functioning markets. It is usually inexpensive and easy to buy or not, sell or not, hire or fire, and quit or shirk on your own. Voice means to communicate explicitly your concern to another individual or organization. The cost to an individual in time and effort to persuade, argue, and negotiate will often exceed any prospective individual benefit.[18]

In addition, the potential success of voice depends on the possibility of all members joining for collective action. But then there arises the "free rider" problem. If self-interested persons cannot be excluded from the benefits of collective action, they have no incentive to join the group agreement. Self-interest will tempt them to take the benefits without paying the costs—such as watching educational television without becoming a subscriber. This free riding explains why union organizing is next to impossible in states that prohibit union shops (where a majority of the workers voting for a union means all workers must join and pay dues).

The problem is further complicated by the possibility that what started simply as a self-interested or even benevolent relationship will become malevolent. Face-to-face strategic bargaining may irritate the parties involved if the other side is perceived as violating the spirit of fair play. This can result in a response of hatred rather than mere selfishness. Collective bargaining between Eastern Airlines and its unions is a good example. The distrust and hatred generated by the negotiations led to the shutting down of the airline with the result that everyone suffered.

Allan Schmid refers to these problems as "social traps." These are situations where there is some act under the individual's unilateral control that promises to produce a short-run welfare improvement for that individual but at the same time is not consistent with what individuals who share a common preference want to obtain as a long-run result. An alternative line of action that would be consistent with the more preferred long-run result is marked by the fact that no matter how hard the individual tries, *alone* he or she can produce no net benefits or fewer than in the unilateral activity.[19] So the social trap exists because the alternative line of action requires some level of trust that can lead all to engage in the process necessary to reach group agreement. In social traps, cooperative behavior by an individual will achieve nothing unless it changes the actions of others.

Thus, for an individual or organization to break out of a social trap requires a common consciousness of one's interdependence with others: the realization that, in fact, the group is more than a collection of individuals. This consciousness does not have to be benevolent or altruistic, though it undoubtedly would make collective action easier to attain. It certainly requires a degree of mutual trust. If malevolence arises, the trap will be strengthened. In addition, morally constrained behavior is necessary to control free riding. And it is here that self-interested individualism fails—for social traps are ubiquitous in the economy, constraining the beneficent invisible hand that supposedly brings social good from individualistic behavior.

How can we spring the social traps generated by interdependence and imperfect information? The resolution of the problem is not easy, for they are persistent and intractable. There are at least three possibilities: government intervention, group self-regulation, and institutional reinforcement of those moral values that constrain self-interested behavior.

Market failures such as pollution or monopoly have generally been seen as warrants for government intervention. However, there are ubiquitous market failures of the moral hazards variety in everyday economic life. In these cases private economic actors can also benefit from government measures for their protection, because interdependence and imperfect information generate distrust and lead the parties to self-defeating behavior. Certain kinds of government regulation—from truth-in-advertising to food-and-drug laws—can reduce distrust and thus economic inefficiency, providing gains for all concerned. However, government regulation has its limits. Where the regulated have concentrated power (e.g., electric companies), the regulators may end up serving the industry more than the public. In addition, there are clearly situations in which government operates to serve the self-interest of the members of its bureaucratic apparatus. Free market economists would have us believe that such is always the case. This is an exaggeration. Government can serve the common good, but it has clear limits. One major limitation on the ability of government to regulate is the willingness of people to be regulated.

The Kennedy administration's wage-price guidelines were a partially successful attempt to control inflation through public encouragement of labor and management cooperation to limit wage increases to productivity increases. The cooperation broke down because of the growing struggle among social classes and occupational groups for larger shares of GNP. More formal cooperation between labor and management, monitored by government, might reduce the distrust that cripples their relationship. In order to do so, government would have to be accepted by all sides as above the fray and willing to encourage agreements that would benefit society. The experience of the 1970s in which government activity delivered less than it promised, and of the 1980s when it was used to serve the agenda of bureaucrats and to facilitate the goals of the powerful both imply a diminished capacity of government to play this role.

The second way to spring these social traps is self-regulation. Sellers could voluntarily discipline themselves not to exploit their superior information. This is the basis of professional ethics. Surgeons, for example, take on the obligation, as a condition for the exercise of their profession, to avoid performing unnecessary operations, placing the interest of the patient first. The danger is that their professional association will end up protecting its members at the expense of others.

This leads us to the final possibility—developing institutions to heighten group consciousness and reinforce moral values that constrain self-interested behavior so that the pursuit of short-run rewards and free riding can be controlled. Is it possible to rebuild institutional mechanisms so that long-run interests and moral values become more important in directing economic behavior? Yes, but we must rethink our view of people as simply self-interested maximizers.

Arrow, for example, states that he does not "wish to use up recklessly the scarce resources of altruistic motivation."[20] While it is possible that altruism may become ineffective if overused, there is no evidence that this motivation can be likened to a scarce resource. Economists have made a major mistake in treating love, benevolence, and particularly public spirit as scarce resources that must be economized lest they be depleted. This is a faulty analogy because, unlike material factors of production, the supply of love, benevolence, and public spirit is not fixed or limited. These are resources whose supply may increase rather than decrease through use. Also, they do not remain intact if they stay unused.[21] These moral resources respond positively to practice, in a learning-by-doing manner, and negatively to nonpractice.

People learn their values from their families, their religious faith, and from their society. In fact, a principal objective of publicly proclaimed laws and regulations is to stigmatize certain types of behavior and to reward others, thereby influencing individual values and behavior codes. Aristotle (in *Nicomachean Ethics*) understood this: "Lawgivers make the citizens good by inculcating habits in them, and this is the aim of every lawgiver; if he does not succeed in doing that, his legislation is a failure. It is in this that a good constitution differs from a bad one."

Habits of benevolence and civic spirit, in addition to heightened group consciousness, can be furthered by bringing people together to solve common problems. Growth of worker participation in management, consultation between local communities and business firms to negotiate plant closings and relocations, establishment of advisory boards on employment policy that represent labor, business, and the public all are steps toward a recognition that individual self-interest alone is insufficient, that mutual responsibilities are necessary in a world where interdependence and imperfect information generate distrust and tempt individuals into strategic behavior that, in turn, results in suboptimal outcomes.

Ethical Values in Practice: The Supply of Blood

An example of the problem of relying solely on self-interest is given by a comparison of the system of blood collection for medical purposes in the United States and in England. In his book, *The Gift Relationship*, Richard Titmuss questions the efficiency of market relationships based on purely monetary self-interest principles.[22] Instead he hypothesizes that in some instances, such as blood giving, relying on internalized moral values (in this case, altruistic behavior) results in a more efficient supply and a better quality of blood. Kenneth Arrow's response to Titmuss questions the extent to which altruism or other internalized moral values may be counted upon as an organizing principle, yet he acknowledges that there may, indeed, be a role for altruistic giving.

Arrow summarizes Titmuss's book as a "close study intended as something of a searchlight to illuminate a much broader landscape: the limits of economic analysis, the rival uses of exchange and gift as modes of allocation, the collective or communitarian possibilities in society as against the tendencies toward individualism."[23] The following covers some of the more salient points in the debate and reflects on these issues in an attempt to clarify the role that virtues or moral values may play in the economy.

Titmuss focuses on the blood supply system in Great Britain and the United States. The United States system has moved toward a commercialized market system in which suppliers of blood are paid for the service while in Great Britain the supply of blood depends on voluntary and unpaid individual blood donors. Titmuss argues that the commercialization of blood giving produces a system with many shortcomings. A few of these shortcomings are the repression of expressions of altruism, increases in the danger of unethical behavior in certain areas of medicine, worsened relationships between doctor and patient, and shifts in the supply of blood from the rich to the poor. Furthermore, the commercialized blood market is bad even in terms of nonethical criteria:

> In terms of economic efficiency it is highly wasteful of blood; shortages, chronic and acute, characterize the demand-and-supply position and make illusory the concept of equilibrium. It is administratively inefficient and results

in more bureaucratization and much greater administrative, accounting, and computer overheads. In terms of price per unit of blood to the patient (or consumer), it is a system which is five to fifteen times more costly than voluntary systems in Britain. And, finally, in terms of quality, commercial markets are much more likely to distribute contaminated blood; the risks for the patient of disease and death are substantially greater. Freedom from disability is inseparable from altruism.[24]

It is noteworthy that since the AIDS crisis started in the United States, physicians have regularly recommend that patients scheduled for nonemergency surgery donate their own blood in advance.

Arrow attempts to restate Titmuss's arguments in terms of utility theory. Thus, the motivation for blood giving is reduced and reformulated in the form of a utility function. One such form is "(1) the welfare of each individual will depend both on his own satisfaction and on the satisfactions obtained by others. We here have in mind a positive relation, one of altruism rather than envy." Another form is "(2) The welfare of each individual depends not only on the utilities of himself and others but also on his contributions to the utilities of others."[25]

By representing altruism in this way, the incommensurability of self-interest and altruism that is crucial to Titmuss's analysis is ignored. The commercialization of certain activities that historically were perceived to be within the realm of altruism results in a conceptual transformation that inhibits the expression of this altruistic behavior. Contrary to the commonly held opinion that the creation of a market increases the area of individual choice, Titmuss argues that the creation of a market may inhibit the freedom to give or not to give.

Robert Goodin develops this theme in an article entitled "Making Moral Incentives Pay." Taking moral principles "seriously" implies that they must not be "*contaminated* by association with more mundane (and especially egoistic) concerns."[26] If this is true, then Arrow's model, which treats apparent morally based behavior as a simple addition to an ordinary utility function, seriously misrepresents these issues.[27] What is only mentioned in passing and downplayed by Arrow is that market relations may often drive out nonmarket relations. As Goodin states, "Material incentives destroy rather than supplement moral incentives."[28]

The supply of blood provides a clear illustration of the problem. A person is not born with a set of ready-made values; rather, the individual's values are socially constructed through his or her being a part of a family, a church, a school, and a particular society. If these groups expect and urge people to give their blood as an obligation of being members of the group, that obligation becomes internalized as a moral value. Blood drives held in schools, churches, and Red Cross facilities reinforce that sense of obligation. As commercial blood increases, the need for blood drives declines. Thus, the traditional reinforcement of that sense of obligation declines with the result that the embodied moral value atrophies. In addition, the fact that you can sell your blood creates an opportunity cost of donating it free. Finally, there is an information problem. As blood drives decline, it is rational for an individual to assume that there is no need for donated blood. The final outcome is that a typical person must overcome imperfect information, opportunity costs, and a lack of social approbation to be able to choose to donate blood.

This suggests that the type of policy enacted by public officials will have implications for the type of society that will develop. Inherent in the type of policy suggested is a preference as to the motivational attitudes that are appropriate and should be encouraged.

As already discussed, economists often claim value neutrality in their analysis. But value neutrality cannot be achieved merely by focusing on the efficiency results of a policy recommendation derived from a theoretical model. The motivations on which the results are based are also important—that is, *how* we achieve these results needs to be addressed.

This problem arises because economists take preferences as given—they neither change over time nor are affected by the preferences of other individuals or society. Consequently, the process of preference formation and the nature of the preferences that people have are ignored. That the distribution of beliefs and behaviors at time t influences individual beliefs and behaviors at time $t+1$ is, however, the single most basic finding of the voluminous research within sociology on the behavior of groups.[29]

Beliefs and preference structures are important because they are the basis for individual motivation. An understanding of these also gives us a notion as to what are and what will encourage the continuation of certain valued feelings. When economists look to self-interest to solve social problems, they are placing a higher value on and promoting their own beliefs about what is proper motivation. Similarly, "through a decision that endorses self-interest in achieving environmental policy goals, society makes a statement, both to polluters and to citizens in general, that people's motivations in behaving how they do are a matter of indifference."[30]

Even though neoclassical economists are seldom interested in why people behave the way they do, society usually places a high value on motivations. This is readily evident if one looks at the legal system. Consider a situation in which a person shoots and kills someone else. The end result is the same but depending on the motivation the act may be judged to be murder, justifiable homicide, or even just an accident.

In short, three conclusions can be derived from our discussion of issues raised by the Titmuss–Arrow debate. First, economic policies have a direct effect on both market outcomes and individual values. Second, economists should drop their narrow approach to human behavior and join the rest of society in giving attention to the effect that policies have upon values. How we achieve results *is* important. Finally, economists must recognize that the policy impact upon values exerts its own influence on future market activity. Thus, over time the type of values promoted by public action has significance even within the "efficiency" realm of traditional economic analysis.

Economists are often reluctant to depend on ethics. Ethics are perceived to be a less stable attribute of human behavior than self-interest. As Arrow states: "I think it best on the whole that the requirements of ethical behavior be confined to those circumstances where the price system breaks down. . . . Wholesale usage of ethical standards is apt to have undesirable consequences."[31]

Certainly individuals, with particular needs and abilities, motivated by self-interest do create consequences that often are benevolent. But there is also a role for ethically based behavior. In response to Adam Smith's "it is not from the benevolence of the butcher, the brewer, and the baker that we expect our dinner, but from their regard to their own interest," Edmund Phelps noted, "More than half of the American population depend for their security and material satisfaction not upon the sale of their services, but rather on their relationships with others."[32] There are many occasions on which reliance on the goodwill of others is not merely rational but necessary.

Internalized Moral Behavior versus Self-Interest

The way that ethically based behavior and self-interest are often juxtaposed gives the impression that they are mutually exclusive. But proximity to self-interest alone does not defile morality. Moral values are often necessary counterparts in a system based on self-interest. Not only is there a "vast amount of irregular and informal help given in times of need,"[33] there is also a consistent dependence on moral values upon which market mechanisms rely. Without a basic trust and socialized morality, the system would be much more inefficient.

Traditional economics has forgotten one of Adam Smith's key insights. It is true he claimed that self-interest leads to the common good if there is sufficient competition; but also, and more important, he claimed that this is true only if most people in society have internalized a general moral law as a guide for their behavior.[34]

Peter Berger reminds us that "No society, modern or otherwise, can survive without what Durkheim called a 'collective conscience,' that is without moral values that have general authority."[35] Fred Hirsch reintroduces the idea of moral law into economic analysis:

> [T]ruth, trust, acceptance, restraint, obligation— these are among the social virtues grounded in religious belief which . . . play a central role in the functioning of an individualistic, contractual economy. . . . The point is that conventional, mutual standards of honesty and trust are public goods that are necessary inputs for much of economic output.[36]

Some argue that there has been an erosion of this internalized moral code as religious belief has declined. This has "freed" economic actors of the old religious and moral constraints; but the self-interest–led growth process has not provided any ready substitute social morality. Thus, the previously effective inhibitions on lying, cheating, and stealing have lost their effectiveness and the functioning of both the public and private economy has suffered.[37] The legacy is an upperclass bent upon immediate gains and conspicuous consumption and an underclass frequently hungry, homeless, and incapacitated by drug dependency. The growth of the illegal components of the irregular sector are logical outcomes of the process, as is the dramatic increase in the number of security guards in the work force. Another outcome is the dramatic increase in the prison population of the country, from 200,000 in 1970 to 300,000 in 1980 and to 500,000 in 1987— the highest rate of incarceration in the world.[38]

The expectation that public servants will not promote their private interests at the expense of the public interest reinforces the argument that the economy rests as importantly on moral behavior as self-interested behavior. As Hirsch wrote:

> The more a market economy is subjected to state intervention and correction, the more dependent its functioning becomes on restriction of the individualistic calculus in certain spheres, as well as on certain elemental moral standards among both the controllers and the controlled. The most important of these are standards of truth, honesty, physical restraint, and respect for law.[39]

Attempts to rely solely on material incentives in the private sector, and more particularly in the public sector, suffer from two defects. In the first place, stationing a policeman on every corner to prevent cheating simply does not work. Regulators have a disadvantage in relevant information compared with those whose behavior they are trying to regulate. In addition, who regulates the regulators? Thus, there is no substitute for an internalized moral law that directs persons to seek their self-interest only in "fair" ways.[40] The second shortcoming of relying on external sanctions alone is that such reliance can further undermine the remaining aspects of an internalized moral law. As discussed above, by promoting solely self-interest, society encourages that type of behavior rather than ethical behavior. The argument is not that there is no role for self-interest, but rather that there is a large sphere for morally constrained behavior. To distinguish in which sphere self-interest should be used and in which sphere altruism should be promoted is very important and sends signals to society as to what we value.

In summary, the erosion of society's religious-based moral code has important practical results. As Hirsch says:

> Religious obligation performed a secular function that, with the development of modern society, became more rather than less important. It helped to reconcile the conflict between private and social needs at the individual level and did it by internalizing norms of behavior. It thereby provided the necessary social binding for an individualistic, *non*altruistic market economy. This was

the non-Marxist social function of religion. Without it, the claims on altruistic feelings, or on explicit social cooperation, would greatly increase, as was foreseen, and to some extent welcomed, by a long line of humanists and secular moralists. Less love of God necessitates more love of Man.[41]

Conclusion

This chapter has identified a number of weaknesses in the neoclassical treatment of economics and ethics. But despite its dominant contemporary position, the neoclassical perspective is only one approach to economics. Social economists, for example, have always insisted that economies are embedded in social systems and that it is economistic and reductionistic to abstract out the economy and claim that objective knowledge can be obtained without reference to values or the context of decision making.

Three claims of social economists have been demonstrated in this chapter: (1) efficiency is not a value-neutral concept; (2) self-interest does not adequately explain actual economic behavior because economic actors are also motivated by internalized moral values, such as trust and honesty, though they may be eroding; and (3) self-interest does not lead to efficient outcomes in the absence of these moral values. The irony of mainstream economic theory is this: on the one hand it is permeated, despite repeated denials, with ethical values imported from its governing world view; on the other hand it fails to fully understand that economic actors are driven by more than material self-interest *and need to be* if a market economy is to function efficiently.

In demonstrating these claims, I have attempted to chart out the direction we should be moving in constructing a more realistic and useful economic theory. To move in this direction, we must: (1) accept the fundamental role of a world view in economics, and make explicit the values embodied in our own world view; (2) propose and develop alternatives to the neoclassical definition of economic welfare; (3) broaden our conception of economic behavior beyond the motive of self-interest; (4) examine the actual nature of human preferences, including the processes by which they are formed and change over time; (5) recognize the reality of economic interdependence and imperfect information, including the fundamental uncertainty of the future; (6) shed light on the nature, existence, and resolution of social traps; (7) counter the notion of altruism or other moral values as scarce resources with an alternative perspective emphasizing that they respond positively to practice; (8) counter the notion that creation of a market necessarily increases the area of individual choice; (9) study not only the efficiency effects of public policies but also their effects on values and income and wealth distribution; and we must (10) be able to distinguish between cases where self-interested behavior and internalized moral behavior are substitutes and where they are complements. Clearly, there is much work to be done as economics enters the next century.

Notes

1. See Mark Blaug, *The Methodology of Economics: Or How Economists Explain* (Cambridge: Cambridge University Press, 1980). Also see Ernest Nagel, *The Structure of Science: Problems in the Logic of Scientific Explanation* (New York: Harcourt, Brace and World, 1961).

2. See Timothy J. Brennan, "Explanation and Value in Economics," *Journal of Economic Issues, 13*, 4 (December, 1979), 911–32.

3. See David Thomas, *Naturalism and Social Science: A Post-Empiricist Philosophy of Social Science* (Cambridge: Cambridge University Press, 1979). Also see Bruce J. Caldwell, *Beyond Positivism: Economic Methodology in the Twentieth Century* (London: Allen and Unwin, 1982).

4. Mark Blaug, *The Methodology of Economics*, p. 132.

5. Mark Blaug, "Kuhn vs. Lakatos, or Paradigms vs. Research Programs in the History of Economics," *History of Political Economy, 74* (Winter, 1975), 406.

6. See Larry Dwyer, "The Alleged Value-Neutrality of Economics: An Alternative View," *Journal of Economic Issues, 16,* 1 (March 1982); Jon D. Wisman, "The Naturalistic Turn of Orthodox Economics: A Study of Methodological Misunderstanding," *Review of Social Economics, 36*, 3 (December 1978).

7. Thomas S. Kuhn, *The Structure of Scientific Revolutions*, 2d ed. (Chicago: University of Chicago Press, 1970); "Reflections on My Critics," in Imre Lakatos and Alan Musgrave (eds.), *Criticism and the Growth of Knowledge* (Cambridge: Cambridge University Press, 1970); "Notes on Lakatos," in R.C. Buck and R.S. Cohen (eds.), *Boston Studies in the Philosophy of Science*, vol. 8 (Dordrecht, Netherlands: Reidel, 1971).

8. This section is drawn from Charles K. Wilber and Roland Hoksbergen, "Ethical Values and Economic Theory: A Survey," *Religious Studies Review, 12*, 3–4 (July–October 1986), 211–12.

9. It is interesting that experimental studies by psychologists indicate that people are concerned about cooperating with others and with being fair, not just preoccupied with their own self-interest. Ironically, these same studies indicate that those people attracted into economics are more self-interested and taking economics makes people even more self-interested. Thus, economic theory creates a self-fulfilling prophecy. See Robert H. Frank, Thomas Gilovich, and Dennis T. Regan, "Does Studying Economics Inhibit Cooperation?" *Journal of Economic Perspectives, 7*, 2 (Spring 1993), 159–71.

10. D.W. Pearce and C.A. Nash, *The Social Appraisal of Projects* (New York: John Wiley and Sons, 1981).

11. Jerome Rothenberg, "Cost-Benefit Analysis: A Methodological Exposition," in M. Guttentag and S. Strueninge (eds.), *Handbook of Evaluation Research*, vol. 2 (Beverly Hills, CA: Sage Publications, 1975), p. 57.

12. A classic example is the construction of public housing for the poor. Square footage per household is the key variable, not such intangibles as neighborhood, community, or access to services. Another example is welfare policy that concentrates on levels of support and ignores the psychological impact of means testing or the prohibition of able-bodied males in the household.

13. See Lawrence Boland, "On the Futility of Criticizing the Neoclassical Maximization Hypothesis," *American Economic Review, 71*, 5 (December 1981), 1031–36, and *The Foundations of Economic Method* (London: Allen and Unwin, 1982). The recent literature on "rhetoric" takes the argument another step—economic theory is a conversation, and different groups of economists (neoclassicals, Marxists, institutionalists, et al.) have their own conversations which are different. See Donald N. McCloskey, *The Rhetoric of Economics* (Madison: University of Wisconsin Press, 1985) and the voluminous literature

generated by it.

14. See A. Allan Schmid, *Property, Power, and Public Choice: An Inquiry into Law and Economics* (New York: Praeger, 1978), and *Benefit–Cost Analysis: A Political Economy Approach* (Boulder, CO: Westview Press, 1989). Also see the exchange of correspondence between Warren Samuels and James Buchanan, "On Some Fundamental Issues in Political Economy: An Exchange of Correspondence," *Journal of Economic Issues, 9* (March 1975), 15–38.

15. See Herbert Gintis and James H. Weaver, *The Political Economy of Growth and Welfare*, Module 54 (MSS Modular Publications, 1974); Denis Goulet, *The Cruel Choice: A New Concept in the Theory of Development* (New York: Atheneum, 1971); Charles K. Wilber and Kenneth P. Jameson, *Beyond Reaganomics: A Further Inquiry into the Poverty of Economics* (Notre Dame, IN: University of Notre Dame Press, 1990).

16. See A. Allan Schmid, *Property, Power, and Public Choice*; Robert H. Frank, *Passions within Reason: The Strategic Role of the Emotions* (New York: W.W. Norton, 1988); Jane J. Mansbridge (ed.), *Beyond Self-interest* (Chicago: University of Chicago Press, 1990); Amitai Etzioni, *The Moral Dimension: Toward a New Economics* (New York: Free Press, 1988); George A. Akerlof, *An Economist's Book of Tales* (Cambridge: Cambridge University Press, 1984); Kenneth E. Boulding, *The Economy of Love and Fear* (Belmont, CA: Wadsworth, 1973); Fred Hirsch, *Social Limits to Growth* (Cambridge, MA: Harvard University Press, 1978); Albert O. Hirschman, *Exit, Voice, and Loyalty: Responses to Decline in Firms, Organizations, and States* (Cambridge, MA: Harvard University Press, 1970); Andrew Schotter, *Free Market Economics: A Critical Appraisal* (New York: St. Martin's Press, 1985), pp. 47–88; Mark A. Lutz and Kenneth Lux, *Humanistic Economics: The New Challenge* (New York: The Bootstrap Press, 1988).

17. See Albert O. Hirschman, *Exit, Voice, and Loyalty*, and Albert O. Hirschman, *Rival Views of Market Society* (New York: Viking, 1986), pp. 77–101.

18. Exit is more difficult in Japan where social tradition is more binding than it is in other industrial countries. As a result, with much greater emphasis on harmony and consensus at all levels, voice is more appreciated and cultivated.

19. A. Allan Schmid, *Property, Power, and Public Choice*, pp. 162–69.

20. Kenneth Arrow, "Gifts and Exchange," *Philosophy and Public Affairs, 1,* 4 (Summer 1972), 343–62.

21. See Albert O. Hirschman, *Rival Views of Market Society*, p. 155.

22. Richard M. Titmuss, *The Gift Relationship: From Human Blood to Social Policy* (London: Allen and Unwin, 1970). I want to thank my research assistant, Steven Brinks, who prepared a preliminary draft of this section.

23. Kenneth Arrow, "Gifts and Exchange," p. 343.

24. Richard Titmuss, *The Gift Relationship*, p. 205.

25. Kenneth Arrow, "Gifts and Exchange," p. 342.

26. Robert Goodin, "Making Moral Incentives Pay," *Policy Sciences, 12* (1980), 137.

27. For some other attempts to model ethical behavior while remaining within a general utility framework, see Amartya Sen, *On Ethics and Economics* (Oxford: Basil Blackwell, 1987).

28. Robert Goodin, "Making Moral Incentives Pay," p. 141.

29. Steven Kelman, *What Price Incentives? Economists and the Environment* (Boston: Auburn House, 1981), p. 31. Also see note 9 above.

30. Ibid., p. 32.

31. Kenneth Arrow, "Gifts and Exchange," p. 355.

32. Quoted in Steven Kelman, *What Price Incentives?*, p. 40.

33. Kenneth Arrow, "Gifts and Exchange," p. 345.

34. See Adam Smith, *Theory of Moral Sentiments* (London: Henry Bohn, 1861), and A.W. Coats (ed.), *The Classical Economists and Economic Policy* (London: Methuen, 1971). It is interesting that Milton Friedman, in his *Essays in Positive Economics* (Chicago: University of Chicago Press, 1966), has a similar starting point when he says, "Differences about policy among disinterested citizens derive predominantly from different predictions about the economic consequences of taking action . . . rather than from fundamental differences in basic values" (p. 5).

35. Peter Berger, "In Praise of Particularity: The Concept of Mediating Structures," *Review of Politics* (July 1976), 134.

36. Fred Hirsch, *Social Limits to Growth*, p. 141.

37. Ibid.; Charles K. Wilber and Kenneth P. Jameson, *Beyond Reaganomics*, pp. 230–34. This also appears to be a growing problem in the new capitalist Russia. One of the new "whiz kids" who are taking leading positions in the new banks, finance, and trading companies gave his explanation for why young people are in such high demand: "Older people have an ethics problem. By that, I mean they *have* ethics. To survive, I can break a law if I need to and if the risks aren't too large. Older people wouldn't even think in such a way" (quoted in *The Wall Street Journal* [August 2, 1993], A1).

38. *Sourcebook of Criminal Justice Statistics* (Washington, DC: 1987). Editor's Note: According to the U.S. Department of Justice, the nation's prison population reached nearly 1.5 million in 1994.

39. Fred Hirsch, *Social Limits to Growth*, pp. 128–29.

40. This casts new light on the recent attempts to construct theories of justice that are acceptable to all. See John Rawls, *A Theory of Justice* (Cambridge, MA: Harvard University Press, 1971) and the literature spawned by that work. The whole endeavor can be seen as an attempt to create a substitute moral law based on rationality rather than religion.

41. Fred Hirsch, *Social Limits to Growth*, pp. 141–42.

4

The Challenge of Feminist Economics

Ann Mari May

When asked to speak on the subject of women and fiction, Virginia Woolf mused that the suggestion may have meant for her to discuss "women and what they are like; or it might mean women and the fiction that they write; or it might mean women and the fiction that is written about them." Pondering these alternatives, she responded by simply saying "a woman must have money and a room of her own."[1]

Substituting economics for fiction, which may not be altogether difficult or inappropriate, we might begin by examining women and what they are like. That is, do the assumptions of self-interested economic behavior attributed to "economic man" also apply to women? (Even more interesting, why is the theoretical core of our discipline grounded on the assumption of self-interested behavior to begin with?) Or, we might examine women and the economics that they write. Does the experience of being a woman lead women economists to examine economic phenomena differently? More generally, how has the discipline of economics been influenced by the inclusion or exclusion of women? Or, we might examine women and the economics that is written about them—which may bring us closer to the title of Woolf's speech than we would like.

However we choose to look at women and economics, it is noteworthy that Woolf, like other feminists from Mary Wollstonecraft to Charlotte Perkins Gilman, believed that feminism must be grounded, at least, in economic independence. That feminism has historically been intimately concerned with economic independence for women makes it all the more curious that economics, as a discipline, has been one of the last social sciences to develop a feminist voice.[2] In practice, the discipline of economics has been, as Paul Samuelson so aptly put it, "the study of how men [sic] and society *choose*, with or without the use of money, to employ scarce productive resources to produce various commodities over time and distribute them for consumption."[3] One might add that the discipline of economics has been, in reality, the study of how *men study* how men in society choose to employ scarce resources to produce commodities and distribute them for consumption.

A casual examination of the institutions that generate and reproduce knowledge in the discipline of economics reflects both the continuance of male dominance as well as the potential for great change. Women are still rarely seen, much less heard, in those institutions vested with the responsibility for conferring the authority to speak about economic matters in the United States. In 1989, only 9 percent of all faculty in Ph.D.-granting institutions in economics were women. Moreover, fewer than 3 percent of full professors at these institutions were women. Of the over one hundred departments with Ph.D. programs in economics in the United States, less than a handful of departments have women as chairs.

While there is nothing inevitable about the movement of women into or out of the academy, it is also true that by the late 1980s around 20 percent of Ph.Ds awarded in economics went to women. Moreover, by 1989 around 20 percent of assistant professors at Ph.D.-granting institutions were women, up from 8 percent in 1974. In 1993, for the first time, a woman was appointed to serve as chair of the Council of Economic Advisors. While the overall figures continue to be disappointing, they do reflect a gradual increase in participation by women.[4] As higher education in general becomes more diverse in the twenty-first century, economics will undergo change as well. Just as the inclusion of women in the study of literature has forever altered perceptions of what we consider great literature to be, and the inclusion of women in the study of history has forever altered our knowledge of the past, so too the inclusion of women in the discipline of economics will alter our knowledge of material reproduction.[5]

Feminist economics, that growing body of thought that has largely been developed by women and is still in its initial stages, represents a fundamental challenge to economics in the twentieth century and offers the potential for substantially altering our perceptions about material reproduction in the twenty-first century.[6] It is a challenge that is radical by virtue of the fact that it is based upon the fundamentally radical notion of equality. It is radical in the sense that it challenges the very categories of discourse that mainstream neoclassicism takes for granted. And it is radical in the sense that it is, like previous feminist discussions, intimately concerned with economic independence for women—a notion that would, if implemented, radically alter the structure of society.

The Gendered Nature of Economic Discourse

Quite clearly, the absence of women from the discipline of economics has affected the content and scope of economics. More often than not, what women do, what return they receive for doing what they do, and the particular problems that women experience by virtue of their location in society have been outside the boundaries of most economic discourse. In fact, the very categories of discourse are laden with metaphors that reflect dualisms and dualistic thinking that are heavily influenced by gender.[7]

Even the most hardened apologists will concede that economics, which comes from the Greek word meaning "management of the household," does not examine the management of the household, except when such management involves market exchange.[8] That work, a fundamental ingredient in the management of the household, is not truly work unless done in a marketplace is as much testimony to the pervasive influence of gender bias as it is testimony to the influence of the market mentality.

The absence of any serious examination of the economics of housework, for example, reflects a strong element of androcentrism present in most economic inquiry. As Nancy Folbre demonstrates, there was nothing natural about conceptualizing work such that the work of women did not really count. In her study of the evolution of the "unproductive housewife," Folbre shows how notions of what constitutes productive activity were heavily influenced by neoclassical economists' acceptance of the "cult of domesticity," which not only assigned women's sphere to the home but devalued that sphere relative to the market.[9] Although most economists continue to utilize national income accounting statistics without a hint of shame about their shortcomings, there is some acknowledgment (even by hardened apologists) that these commonly used measures of productive activity reflect a significant gender bias in failing to recognize women's work in the home.[10]

Acknowledgement is one thing—a footnote as it were, that is appreciated on one level—and perhaps, depending upon the contribution, an outright insult on another level. The national income and product accounts have not been adjusted to include household labor. As a result, and perhaps more importantly, governmental programs such as Social Security and Unemployment Compensation do not acknowledge the contributions of women's unpaid labor in the home.

Even when women work in the market economy, their contributions have largely been overlooked by economists. In their study of women and minorities in economics textbooks, for example, Susan F. Feiner and Barbara A. Morgan show that women and minorities are seldom discussed. When they are discussed, Feiner and Morgan find that women's roles are narrowly defined and they are often subject to pejorative labeling. Even more disturbing is the finding that while there was a general increase in topics relating to women and minorities in the 1970s, the trend sharply reversed itself in the 1980s when, Feiner and Morgan suggest, introduction of Reaganomics and the new classical macroeconomics demonstrated their own form of "crowding out" in the marketplace of ideas.[11]

Despite the wage disparity between men and women that has existed since the origins of a paid labor force, economic theory since the late nineteenth century has largely failed to acknowledge this differential. Interestingly, as the word "discrimination" entered the lexicon of social discourse surrounding women's wages, economic theory began to expand in ways that would explain away, at least in part, some of the disparity.[12] Human capital theory, which gained authority in the early 1960s, explained differentials in wages as a function of individual choices in education, occupation, and family priorities that might interrupt the accumulation of job skills.[13] Yet, despite attempts to account for wage disparities between men and women through differences in human capital investments, these studies themselves fail to account for a significant amount of the wage disparity.[14]

The concept of labor market segmentation, which has been put forward by non-mainstream economists, is an attempt to address this oversight in economic theory. According to the theory, women are more likely to be employed in "secondary" labor markets characterized by low wages, instability, and poor working conditions.[15] Yet, the theory does not adequately explain differentials in earnings that exist within occupations, nor does it explain why race, sex, or ethnicity are determinants of labor market categorizations.[16] Explanations that might examine, for example, patriarchal cultural norms and the ways in which they influence material reproduction remain, of course, outside the boundaries of economics.

Upon examination, many of the problems that women have encountered, such as occupational segregation and wage differentials, have historically been all but ignored by economic theory. Moreover, many concepts such as unemployment, inflation, income distribution, and poverty have not been examined by economists in terms of their differential impact on various groups. That women represent a particularly vulnerable group in society who quite often and increasingly have been included, for example, in the legions of "the poor" may explain, in part, the invisible aspect of these problems.

One could, of course, argue that economists are simply hardened and impervious to social problems in general in their steadfast pursuit of knowledge. However, economists, particularly since World War II, have increasingly been active participants in the political process, helping to define what it is that we consider society's problems to be. For example, what person, on his or her own, would consider the national debt, the budget deficit (most informed journalists on the economics beat don't even know the difference between the two), the level of capital formation, or the balance of trade to be major social problems worthy of considerable attention? So effective have economists been at heightening our (heretofore latent?) interest in such things as the balance of trade and the budget deficit, that presidential candidates have actually begun to run campaigns in which the central feature of the message is a graph with the national debt invidiously displayed.[17]

What we see depends not only upon where we look, but also upon the lens through which we view the expanse of social interactions. The lenses of economists are molded by the metaphors that give intellectual form to the "facts" we choose to identify. Most importantly, these metaphors that shape and constrain our thinking are heavily influenced by gender. Nowhere is this more obvious than with the metaphor so central to economics, that of "economic man."

Economic man, that "Western romantic hero"[18] of academic economic culture, is unapologetically self-interested, unidimensional, and autonomous—self-directed as it were. We care not how *he* got that way or even if *he* is that way at all. Nor do we allow *him* to be any other way. Economic man is the norm—the center, from which all else is a mere digression. When we examine "the other," *it* (not *he*) is trivialized or subsumed such that all behavior must be ultimately self-interested.

As Diana Strassmann has observed, economic man is also empowered and, therefore, a distinctly androcentric metaphor. Empowered, economic man is free to choose in a variety of realms and free to act in such a way that *his* utility is maximized. As Strassmann writes, "economic theory presents the ability to choose as the normal state of being."[19] The only constraint on choice admitted into the equation is that of a budget constraint. Yet, conceptions of self, such as the one presented to us by economists in the metaphor of economic man, are intimately related to notions of gender which are themselves shaped and molded by institutional arrangements.[20] (Not to worry, however: these institutional arrangements are conveniently outside the boundaries of economic theory.) That women might not envision the general state of affairs to be that of freedom to choose is obvious. As feminists have often pointed out, women have historically been constrained by a variety of institutional arrangements that have functioned in very effective and pervasive ways to limit even the most fundamental of choices.

Not only is economic man free to choose, but those preferences that guide choice are assumed to be "given" according to economic theory. What appears to the "untrained observer" to be a virtual reality piped into almost every home, feeding freeze-framed erotic images (guess whose?) selling everything from Land Rovers to margarine is, according to economic theory, merely a goods market in which individuals are voluntarily entering into contracts to purchase goods for which they have some latent or realized desire. What appears to the "untrained observer" to be a society in which certain privileges are awarded on the basis of sex and race is, according to economic theory, merely a labor market in which certain individuals are expressing their own (given) preferences for less responsibility, low wages, and part-time work. Preferences that might be thought to have been generated and shaped through a complex set of cultural cues that serve to rationalize societal biases and neutralize dissension are reinterpreted as voluntary associations as American as apple pie. As Nancy Hartsock points out, the emphasis on voluntary exchange reflected in neoclassical theory allows economists to "reinterpret coercion as choice."[21]

The unit of analysis reflected in the notion of economic man is, after all, the individual—autonomous, with given preferences, not preferences shaped by virtue of experience and location. Neither television, nor peers, nor even spouse can penetrate the psyche of economic man. Whereas anthropologists begin with the notion of kinship, economists have historically chosen to ignore the complex and problematic institution of the family. Perhaps because of the obvious contradiction between the alleged behavior of economic man and the complex ways in which individuals actually interact and behave within the family, the formation and expression of preferences through choice remain primarily in the realm of the individual, not the family.[22]

Of course, not all economists have ignored the family as a unit of analysis.[23] Gary Becker, after all, has gained considerable recognition and notoriety for his inclusion of the family as a legitimate focus of analysis.[24] However, as Donald McCloskey points out, "the family in Becker's world has one purpose, one utility function—guess whose?—unproblematically unified in the way that the neoclassical firm is supposed to be."[25] Since comparisons of interpersonal utility functions are impossible (just as it would be impossible to compare the horns of unicorns) and tastes are exogenous (could they be anything else?), Becker's monumental contribution to our understanding of choice within the family reflects little more than the imposition of patriarchal assumptions on a distinctly patriarchal institution in society. In reality, the family is an institution that, despite the economistic assumptions that are imposed upon it, is wrought with complex interactions, behaviors, and quite often conflict.[26]

Although not elevated to the status of "economic man," economists have implicitly sculpted a prototypical version of "economic woman." "*Femina economica*," as McCloskey has labeled her,[27] is altruistic, naturally affectionate, nurturing, and, most likely, always home when the kids get out of school. She is never prone to avarice but displays considerable consensus-building skills and deference (which is most conducive to consensus building). And best of all, she doesn't even need to learn these traits but comes to them quite naturally.[28]

While it is nice to have clean clothes, food on the table, and children who grow to adulthood, economists are inherently ambivalent about *"femina economica."* "We" are simultaneously appreciative and suspicious of *"femina economica,"* precisely because she is "the other." "The other," in economic theory, displays behavior that is, after all, irrational—aberrant, impulsive, and unpredictable (and more difficult to control?).[29] It is interesting to note that *"femina economica"* displays behaviors that have culturally been associated with childhood, reflecting perhaps the cultural tendency toward denigration through resistance to accept the other as adult and hence equal. (It is no small coincidence that "boy" was the term used by white southerners for black men and that the legions of women working for male managers in offices are, whatever their age, alas, only "girls.")

When we examine some of the essential underlying assumptions behind much of economic theory, it is not difficult to identify the ways in which the narrow framework of most economic inquiry has hampered economists' efforts to examine the often messy world of material reproduction. The dichotomy presented between rationality and altruism, and the assignment of one to the realm of the market and one to the realm of the family, masks the collective and cooperative nature of production and exchange as much as the self-interestedness that may exist in nonmarket realms. In both realms, Nancy Folbre and Heidi Hartmann contend, "complex overlays of self-interest and reciprocity are at work."[30]

Largely unexplored is the influence of gender upon the content, scope, and methodology of economic inquiry. The feminization of economic discourse clearly cannot take place merely by accepting women and women's issues as legitimate categories of study. However professionally rewarding, understanding the process of material reproduction will not be enhanced by attempts to apply simplistic and unrealistic assumptions and axioms to new groups of individuals. Nor will it be accomplished through rejection of the entirety of economistic reasoning. Instead, what feminist economics proposes is a framework for critical, systematic reevaluation that is pluralistic and heterogeneous rather than monistic and homogeneous, mindful of the ideologically charged nature of all economic discourse, and value driven rather than value neutral.

The Feminization of Economic Discourse

To provide a framework for a feminist economics, ontological and epistemological assumptions previously applied to economic discourse must be reexamined. Ontological assumptions in economics define the boundaries of the discipline, inform our views about the nature of reality, and shape the outcomes of theorizing.[31] As we have seen, the ontological framework of neoclassicism to a very large extent shapes the reality that economists choose to accept as worthy of study. This reality focuses on individual behavior over group behavior and accepts only the most limited notion of self-interest as ontologically important. The assertion that tastes and preferences are given is far more than an incidental assumption inserted to allow the development of a model. Instead, it is an ontological assumption of the largest kind that frames, to a very large extent, the boundaries of the discipline and precludes examination of potentially significant activity.

Another monumental ontological assumption that has, to a very large extent, shaped the boundaries of the discipline of economics, as well as all other social sciences, is the public/private split. This public/private split, which reflects a Cartesian dualistic mode of thought, contrasts the public sphere (which includes production, exchange, and activities of the state) with the private sphere (which includes reciprocity, nurturing, and the family). According to Judith Howard, while there are many disagreements as to the origins of the public/private split, there is no disagreement about the gender-orientation of the split or its importance for feminist theory.[32] While men are associated with the public realm, women are relegated to the private realm.

The significance of the public/private split for feminist economics is also discussed by Ann Jennings, who argues that the ontological assumptions embedded in the public/private split serve to "distinguish and prioritize 'the economy' or 'the market' over other spheres in conventional understandings, and to rank social groups according to their presumed relationships to the privileges and spheres defined."[33] Indeed, much of what has not been examined in the development of the history of economic thought involves just those constructions that involve the female side of the dualism Jennings mentions—family, woman, reciprocity and, more generally, institutions centered around something other than market exchange and based upon something other than self-interestedness and acquisitiveness.

While ontological assumptions determine the boundaries of the discipline, epistemological considerations guide us in the process of knowledge creation. In the twentieth century, the epistemological framework that gained ascendancy within the philosophy of science is that of positivism.[34] Positivism has largely defined itself around ideals of "objectivity" and "value neutrality" and is reflected in the obligatory references to the normative/positive distinction found in most economics textbooks.[35] According to this view, knowers are "detached, neutral spectators, and the objects of knowledge are separate from them; they are inert items in the observational knowledge-gathering process."[36]

That the ideal in scientific inquiry would posit the existence of a disinterested, detached, neutral observer is, itself, reflective of the androcentric nature of knowledge creation. Disengagement is, after all, a stereotypically male perspective and, perhaps, not surprisingly therefore, the model behavior for proper scientific inquiry. As Lorraine Code has argued, "In view of the fact that disengagement throughout a changing history and across a range of class and racial boundaries has been possible primarily for *men* in western societies, this aspect of the adrocentricity of objectivist epistemologies is not surprising."[37]

The positivist view of knowledge creation has gained ascendancy, in part, because of the claims (by positivists) that positivism is synonymous with "science." The power of staking out the only path to knowledge is, like religions that claim to know the only path to god, quite powerful—in McCloskey's words, "a verbal weapon within the intelligentsia."[38] As a weapon, positivism has been very effective at limiting debate even within those disciplines, such as economics, that cannot adhere to its strict imperatives. However, philosophy of science, which economists invoke with great enthusiasm when it advocates an intolerance of methodological pluralism, has increasingly moved beyond positivism through the growth of knowledge tradition.[39] More recently, postpositivist feminist epistemologies have developed within this growth of knowledge tradition that offer profound critiques of positivism along with guidelines for feminist theorizing in a variety of disciplines.

Feminist epistemologists most often begin with the belief that the context of inquiry (context of discovery) is inseparable from the context of justification. More specifically, feminist epistemological accounts start with the hypothesis that knowledge is socially constructed *and* that this is ontologically significant.

The implications of this particular ontological assumption are many. The insistence on examination of the context of inquiry has led many feminist epistemologists, according to Linda Alcoff and Elizabeth Potter, to "skepticism about the possibility of a general or universal account of the nature and limits of knowledge, an account that ignores the social context and status of the knowers."[40] In contrast to the positivist perspective that presumes there is one unique truth about the world awaiting discovery, feminist epistemologists, along with other postpositivist epistemologists, often argue that theories are inherently "underdetermined."[41] Hence, feminist epistemologists often view knowledge claims as inherently partial and tentative.

In addition, Lynn Nelson, for example, argues that knowledge claims, as a social construction, are developed in communities—both scholarly and otherwise—that are multiple and shifting, historically contingent, and dynamic. As such, the selection of facts to be considered is determined by the subjective awareness, informed by communities and experience, of a problem situation worthy of notice. In feminist epistemological accounts, gender enters into the "objective" selection of these facts. Facts, as such, are not "self-announcing." Observation of the facts involves subjective perceptions shaped by the communities and experiences of the knower. Facts do not exist independently of scientific theories. According to Nelson, "the sensory experiences currently recognized as relevant to such knowledge are themselves shaped and mediated by a larger system of historically and culturally specific theory and practice . . . a system which not only constitutes part of the evidence for current knowledge . . . but also shapes the experiences of individuals into coherent and relevant accounts."[42]

In the positivist tradition, which posits the existence of value neutrality, normative or subjective influences have generally been looked upon with disdain as producing "bad science." However, according to many feminist epistemological accounts, additional data, even those relating to the knower, have the benefit of producing more objective knowledge claims. Indeed, as Code argues, "Objectivity *requires* taking subjectivity into account."[43]

According to Sandra Harding, whose book *The Science Question in Feminism* provides the starting point for what has come to be known as "standpoint theory," knowledge about the experiences and perspectives of the knower is important for better science. Harding identifies the origins of standpoint theory in Hegel's observations about the master/slave relationship.[44] The Hegelian view, adopted by Marxists and other liberatory movements, recognizes that insights can be gained from examining situations from the standpoint of the oppressed or marginalized. Moreover, Harding contends that only by entertaining these perspectives can a more objective discussion take place. According to Harding, "Knowledge claims are always socially situated, and the failure by dominant groups critically and systematically to interrogate their advantaged social situation and the effect of such advantages on their beliefs leaves their social situation a scientifically and epistemologically disadvantaged one for generating knowledge."[45]

In addition to providing a framework for the examination of the gendered nature of knowledge claims, standpoint theory also provides a framework for the examination of additional markings and locations that affect experience, perspective, and standards of evaluation. Gender hierarchy is not, after all, the only hierarchy reflected in stratified societies. As Alcoff and Potter explain, "Cognitive authority is usually associated with a cluster of markings that involve not only gender but also race, class, sexuality, culture, and age."[46] Feminist standpoint theory allows for a stronger objectivity through inclusion of these perspectives. However, the recognition of the interconnectedness of these categories of stratification is also necessary for understanding. As Alcoff and Potter point out, "gender can never be observed as a 'pure' or solitary influence. Gender identity cannot be adequately understood—or even *perceived*—except as a component of complex interrelationships with other systems of identification and hierarchy."[47] This assumption, common to standpoint theory and many feminist epistemologies, reflects a rejection of reductionism in favor of more holistic approaches. While there continues to be considerable debate among feminist scholars as to the usefulness of gender as *the* primary ontological reality, feminist epistemologies often provide a framework for alternative ontological assumptions that allows for examination of the influence of many categories of stratification.

That economics has been one of the last of the social sciences to acquire a feminist perspective bears some reflection. The firm acceptance of positivism, which allows economics to claim for itself the unlikely title of "queen of the social sciences," no doubt marginalizes feminist epistemologies present in other social science disciplines. In addition, the strict adherence to the public/private split and other ontological assumptions prevalent within economics severely limits the possibilities for feminist theorizing. However, recognition of these barriers does not explain why the discipline has so effectively imposed these barriers and why the "recalcitrant discipline" continues to embrace epistemeological and ontological perspectives that limit the acceptance of feminist theorizing (not to mention practical problem solving).

To understand why economics has been so inhospitable to feminist inquiry requires recognition of the fact that economic inquiry is, at its base, highly political and intimately associated with rationalizing a particular distribution of power—which, in a pecuniary society, translates into a particular distribution of wealth and income. Perhaps because of the adamant claims that economics is scientific and, hence, apolitical, economic theory is all the more effective in mystifying the political nature of its inquiry.

In contrast, feminist economics is explicitly political. Feminist theorizing requires that we ask the sometimes troublesome questions about the effects of disparate power relations in the identification and generation of knowledge claims, and ultimately that we ask the question, "Who *is* empowered by the theory?" As Harding points out, feminist theorizing is intended to produce more objective knowledge claims *and* "produce knowledge that can be *for* marginalized people (and those who would know what the marginalized can know) rather than *for* the use only of dominant groups in their projects of administering and managing the lives of marginalized people."[48]

Despite what we have often been told, recognition of the political nature of economic inquiry will not diminish, taint, or lessen our understanding of economic matters. Such recognition offers, instead, the hope of having an honest, intelligent conversation about material reproduction. More generally, feminist economics offers the possibility of expanding the boundaries of economic theorizing to embrace new views, new problems, and new solutions through critical, systematic self-reflective conversation— something the profession has not demonstrated much interest in or tolerance for in the past.

The Future of Feminist Inquiry in Economics

Feminist research, in economics and elsewhere, is currently in the process of sketching out the contours of feminist inquiry. The process requires communities of scholars to reexamine previous ways of knowing, previous "facts" used to formulate our perceptions, and prior assumptions about what is worthy of intellectual inquiry. Because the framework in which intellectual inquiry occurs is indeed influenced by the larger culture as well as the academic culture, epistemological *and* ontological assumptions must be systematically exposed and evaluated. Much of feminist economics suggests that these contours are beginning to shape a discipline in which knowledge claims are informed by inquiry that is sociological in nature, historical, political, and explicitly normative.

As we have seen, feminist economics asserts that individual behavior cannot be a starting point in economic inquiry. Methodological individualism must be replaced by a sociological perspective that examines the context in which decisions are made and that allows for a complex set of constraints, goals, and motivations to enter into the decision-making process. Moreover, feminist inquiry further asserts that the process through which these knowledge claims are created must be viewed in sociological terms as well. It is, for feminist scholarship, important to remember that knowledge creation itself is a social process undertaken in communities and through institutions rather than by dispassionate, untainted, disinterested, and hence objective individuals.

Feminist inquiry reflects what might be called a historical rather than a theoretical tradition. According to Paul Feyerabend, "members of theoretical traditions identify knowledge with universality. . . . Theories, according to them, identify what is permanent in the flux of history and thereby make it unhistorical."[49] In contrast, feminist inquiry rejects the notion of universality of knowledge claims and instead views these knowledge claims as temporal and contextual. Knowledge claims are therefore provisional in nature.

Finally, feminist inquiry is unapologetically and self-consciously political and value-driven. Feminist inquiry is explicit about its desire to produce knowledge claims that can promote democratic and liberatory movements. Although all knowledge claims are value-driven in a variety of ways, feminist inquiry attempts to identify explicitly the value orientation informing the process of inquiry.

The contours of a feminist economics then, vary considerably from those of mainstream economics. Moreover, acceptance of these contours as legitimate for economic inquiry would require a fundamental reconceptualization of the discipline. The impediments to such a reconceptualization are enormous.

As already discussed, the epistemological foundations of much feminist inquiry is, according to the positivist tradition, "unscientific." The positivist claim of authorship to *the* scientific approach is made all the more powerful by the progressive view of science embodied in the theoretical tradition of positivism. The progressive view of science assumes that scientific progress is "cumulative" and "self-erasing," leaving only those elements of theory that can withstand the scrutiny of scientific inquiry. Moreover, the progressive view of science is powerful in the sense that it encourages the view that knowledge about the history of the development of scientific thought is not important for understanding phenomena. From this perspective, one need not study the history of plate tectonics to evaluate the theory of continental drift. In economics, it reflects the view that one need not study classical economics of the eighteenth century to understand the economy of the twentieth century. As anyone who has studied Reaganomics will attest, this is a very dangerous assumption.

While acceptance of the progressive view of science in economics no doubt leads to shallow understandings of current phenomena, it has also had a very powerful impact on the culture of the discipline that affects future possibilities for feminist inquiry. The progressive view of science, along with the wholesale acceptance of positivism, has led economics to devalue those traditions and fields that value the past—fields that might encourage us to view economic theory as a product of a discrete society with oftentimes not so discrete objectives, activities, and outcomes. The history of economic thought, for example, has been virtually eliminated in graduate programs in economics throughout the United States.[50] As Kenneth Boulding notes, the "antihistorical school" prevails in the United States such that "the history of thought is regarded as a slightly depraved entertainment."[51]

While the progressive view of science makes feminist inquiry more difficult through devaluing whatever is cultural, temporal, and specific relative to what is universal, timeless, and static, the compartmentalized, reductionist nature of academic disciplines such as economics tears at the interdisciplinary aspect of feminist inquiry. The discipline of economics displays a curious mix of ontological compartmentalization and methodological universality. Mainstream economics, as we have seen, has defined away many questions and problematics by asserting that they are outside the boundaries of economics. Yet, mainstream economics at the same time has developed what is by now a rather elaborate framework in which to view these narrow sets of questions. Indeed, it is only by narrowing the domain of the subject that economics has been able to develop such an elaborate scheme with universal knowledge claims. The problem, however, is worse than knowing more and more about less and less. The problem may be that we know less and less about less and less. Strict compartmentalization may lead to distortion rather than refinement, which, along with the universality of knowledge claims, fosters a lack of critical analysis.

Of course, the ontological assumptions and the gender composition of the discipline continue to serve as impediments to feminist economics. As Howard points out, "feminist theory and research is much less likely to develop in disciplines that focus primarily on the public (male) arena than in disciplines that focus on the private (female) arena (or in disciplines that rigidly separate the two)."[52] In economics, the acceptance of the public/private split serves to frame not only the discipline but also the discourse within the discipline. However, the potential influence of the discipline on current social relations that might be reflected in such things as the distribution of income and wealth—not to mention who does the laundry—may well be one of the most significant factors affecting the development of a feminist perspective. As Howard points out in her examination of feminist theorizing in the social sciences, the pattern of scholarship suggests that "theoretical perspectives that may be threatening to the status quo will be more successful in fields that study something other than modern societies. . . . The resistance of economics to feminist analyses is equally consistent; in a capitalist society, economics is deeply wedded to the prevailing power structure."[53] Recognition that the power structure is patriarchal as well helps to explain much of the resistance.

While impediments for the development of feminist economics are daunting, especially those within the academic culture where academic freedom and the free marketplace of ideas are so highly valued; in the rough and tumble world of the larger culture, development of a grassroots feminist economics may stand a better chance, largely because of demographics. While on its face the Reagan decade of the 1980s might not appear to have been a period of progressive change for women, it may indeed go down in history as just that; for it was in the 1980s that women moved from being the silent majority to being the majority that voted, for the first time in U.S. history, at the same rates as men. This fact did not go unnoticed, and the "gender gap," which reflects differences in voting behavior between men and women, gained considerable attention.[54] In the past decade, more women have been elected and appointed to positions of power within government than at any time in U.S. history.

At the same time that women have become more prominent electorally, there has been an increased recognition of the political nature of women's economic status.[55] Growing numbers of women, particularly since the late 1960s, have become employed in government jobs associated with the social safety net. The feminization of poverty has resulted in an increased attachment to the state.

Working women in all socioeconomic groups have become increasingly aware of the political nature of their economic status because of the protection offered to women through legislation such as Title VII of the Civil Rights Act and other legislation pertaining to sexual harassment.[56]

The implications of these changes are many. Most obviously, as women and women's issues become more salient, information about women and women's issues will have more "currency," so to speak. Moreover, information about women and women's issues had better be useful to women in their liberatory movements. This information had better take into account the realization of women's work experiences and not reflect some outdated ontological assumption about women's proper sphere, and it had better be careful to craft its policy recommendations on empirical grounds rather than theoretical models that are designed merely to entrench and protect the status quo. In short, economics in the twenty-first century may have to get real.

Of course, feminist research programs are expanding in think tanks, such as the *Institute for Women's Policy Research*, which have often become productive havens for some of the best feminist research economists.[57] These research institutions may continue to provide access to the kinds of information that women and policy makers need about economic matters and academic institutions may continue to lag behind the larger community in addressing the needs of society. The struggle for information about material reproduction that is currently going on inside academic culture will most likely continue as more women enter the realms of higher education. This struggle may, however, become increasingly public. Academic institutions may be called upon to provide information *for* new constituencies that also attend alumni functions, sit on boards of directors, and schmooze with legislators.

Conclusion

Economics as a discipline has, in the late nineteenth and twentieth centuries, developed as a hypothetical-deductive tradition rather than an empirically based social study. The pretense of science, which economists have carefully cultivated, reinforces the authenticity of its conclusions and generally insulates economics from any untoward criticism. However, the hegemony of mainstream economics is more a result of the utility of economics in rationalizing a particular distribution of wealth and income. In this sense, mainstream economics functions as an "animating myth" that preserves the status quo and entrenches a particular distribution of power.[58]

Heterodox economists have long been aware of the usefulness of the mainstream theoretical core in rationalizing a particular distribution of wealth and income and in promoting a particular social configuration of status and power. They have often exposed the gulf between the theoretical and the empirical, the hypothetical and the actual, the individual as autonomous agent and society as socializing agent. Yet, heterodox economists are only now beginning to explore the ways in which the concepts and theoretical constructs of economics are themselves gendered. They are only now beginning to examine the ways in which these gendered concepts and theories help to distribute power, confer status, and limit the boundaries and outcomes of theorizing.

Feminist economics offers a substantive challenge to the content, scope, and methodology of economics. Feminist economics has already produced revealing insights about the ontological assumptions that impose limits on discourse and obfuscate the gendered nature of that discourse. Feminist epistemologists have begun to provide frameworks for a more critical, systematic analysis of the gendered nature of economic inquiry—frameworks that will serve as guides to a more objective and inclusive economic inquiry in the future. Feminist economists have begun the process of demystifying economic inquiry by further exposing the ideology underlying the neoclassical mainstream economic core.

More profoundly, however, feminist economics challenges the legitimacy of societal arrangements surrounding provisioning. Through the questioning of categorical assumptions, theoretical constraints, and the policies that flow from them, feminist economics represents a challenge to the existing social order that mainstream economics has so subtly and carefully helped to construct and to legitimate. Perhaps, like any good deed, it will not go unnoticed or unpunished. As such, the challenge presented *to* feminist economics is, itself, defined by the challenge that it presents—a formidable one to be sure.

Notes

1. Virginia Woolf, "A Room of One's Own," in Miriam Schneir (ed.), *Feminism: The Essential Historical Writings* (New York: Vintage Books, 1972), p. 345.

2. See Judith A. Howard, "Dilemmas in Feminist Theorizing: Politics and the Academy," *Current Perspectives in Social Theory, 8* (1987), 279–312.

3. Paul A. Samuelson, *Economics: An Introductory Analysis* (New York: McGraw-Hill, 1964), p. 5.

4. Summary statistics on women in the economics profession can be found in the *CSWEP* (Committee on the Status of Women in the Economics Profession) *Newsletters* of February 1990, March 1991, and February 1992. For a good summary of broader indicators of the relative lack of women in the economics profession, see Marianne A. Ferber and Michelle L. Teiman, "The Oldest, the Most Established, the Most Quantitative of the Social Sciences—and the Most Dominated by Men: The Impact of Feminism on Economics," in Dale Spender (ed.), *Men's Studies Modified: The Impact of Feminism on the Academic Disciplines* (New York: Pergamon Press, 1981), pp. 125–39.

5. For a discussion of the impact of feminism on research in the academy, see Christie Farnham (ed.), *The Impact of Feminist Research in the Academy* (Bloomington: Indiana University Press, 1987).

6. For an excellent introduction to feminist economics, see Marianne A. Ferber and Julie A. Nelson (eds.), *Beyond Economic Man: Feminist Theory and Economics* (Chicago: University of Chicago Press, 1993).

7. For a discussion of Cartesian dualism, see Susan Bordo, *The Flight to Objectivity:*

Essays on Cartesianism and Culture (Albany, NY: SUNY Press, 1987). Interesting discussions on gender and metaphor in economics can be found in Donald N. McCloskey, "Some Consequences of a Conjective Economics," in Ferber and Nelson (eds.), *Beyond Economic Man*, pp. 69–93, and Julie A. Nelson, "Gender, Metaphor, and the Definition of Economics," *Economics and Philosophy*, 8 (1992), 103–25.

8. As Marjorie Cohen points out, "That women were at the centre of this activity is obvious and is clearly reflected in the first English use of the term which refers to woman who 'doth employ her Oeconomick Art . . . her Household to preserve.' " See Marjorie Cohen, "The Razor's Edge Invisible: Feminism's Effect on Economics," *International Journal of Women's Studies*, 8, 3 (May–June 1985), 290.

9. According to Folbre, while early nineteenth-century censuses focused on families rather than individuals, census categories in England and Wales dealt with the problematic of women's work inside the home by identifying them, over time, as members of a "Domestic Class," "Unoccupied Class," and finally as "Dependents." By 1900, the U.S. Census, as well, adopted the practice of designating women without a paid job as "Dependents." See Nancy Folbre, "The Unproductive Housewife: Her Evolution in Nineteenth-Century Economic Thought," *Signs*, 16, 3 (Spring 1991), 463–84.

10. There are a few studies that attempt to estimate productive activity in nonmarket sectors. See, for example, R. Gronau, "The Measurement of Output of the Nonmarket Sector: The Evaluation of Housewives' Time," in Milton Moss, (ed.), *The Measurement of Economic and Social Performance* (New York: National Bureau of Economic Research, 1973), pp. 163–90, and Robert Eisner, "Extended Accounts for National Income and Product," *Journal of Economic Literature*, 26, 4 (December 1988), 1611–74.

11. Feiner and Morgan found that in one textbook the example of opportunity cost includes men as "gambler, playwright, TV news watcher, bachelor, doctor, general, and political contributor. . . . [T]he two women in this example include a widow who hides her life savings in the mattress and 'Minnie the Moocher.' " See Susan F. Feiner and Barbara A. Morgan, "Women and Minorities in Introductory Economics Textbooks: 1974 to 1984," *Women's Studies Quarterly*, 14, 4 (1990), 46–67 (quote on p. 54).

12. According to Claudia Goldin, "there was no clear movement prior to the 1960s to define differences in incomes and occupations between men and women as resulting from discrimination, and history is virtually silent on the impressions of female workers." See Claudia Goldin, *Understanding the Gender Gap: An Economic History of American Women* (New York: Oxford University Press, 1990), p. 205.

13. Examples of the human capital literature include Gary S. Becker, "Investment in Human Capital: A Theoretical Analysis," *Journal of Political Economy*, 70, 5 (October 1962), Special Supplement, Part 2, 9–49; Theodore W. Schultz, "Investment in Human Capital," *American Economic Review*, 51, 1 (March 1961), 1–17; and Jacob Mincer and Solomon Polachek, "Family Investments in Human Capital: Earnings of Women," *Journal of Political Economy*, 82, 2 (March–April, 1974), Part 2, s76–s108.

14. For example, Jacob Mincer and Solomon Polachek entertain the possibility that numerous unmeasured factors might explain the "unexplained" portion (59 percent) of the wage gap; however, they fail to mention discrimination by employers as a possible explanation. See Mincer and Polachek, "Family Investments in Human Capital."

15. See, for example, Peter B. Doeringer and Michael J. Piore, *Internal Labor Markets and Manpower Analysis* (Lexington, MA: D.C. Heath, 1971), and Michael Reich, David M. Gordon, and Richard C. Edwards, "A Theory of Labor Market Segmentation," *American Economic Review*, 63, 2 (May 1973), 359–65.

16. See, for example, Francine D. Blau and Carol L. Jusenius, "Economists' Approaches to Sex Segregation in the Labor Market: An Appraisal," *Signs*, 1, 3 (Spring 1976), Part 2, 181–99.

17. All presidents in the postwar era have, to varying degrees, sought to use economics as a weapon in the symbolic uses of politics—some more successfully than others. The rehabilitation of economics, following the embarrassment of the Great Depression, was hastened by the visibility of Kennedy's "Harvard Brain Trust," which romanticized economics using the metaphor of a "new frontier." Who can forget (who can remember?) Gerald Ford and his campaign to raise awareness of economic issues by asking the all important question "How is your EQ (economics quotient)?" The underlying message was, of course, if you think there is really something wrong with 9 percent unemployment, you might want to take a course in economic theory. Perhaps the height of absurdity came when H. Ross Perot played upon our anxieties about negative derivatives with his ostentatious displays of graphs in the 1992 presidential election.

18. Diana Strassmann, "Not a Free Market: The Rhetoric of Disciplinary Authority in Economics," in Ferber and Nelson (eds.), *Beyond Economic Man*, p. 61.

19. Ibid., p. 62.

20. See Dorinne K. Kondo, *Crafting Selves: Power, Gender, and Discourses of Identity in a Japanese Workplace* (Chicago: University of Chicago Press, 1990), and Nancy C.M. Hartsock, *Money, Sex, and Power: Toward a Feminist Historical Materialism* (Boston: Northeastern University Press, 1983), pp. 41–42.

21. See Nancy C.M. Hartsock, ibid., p. 42.

22. A few notable exceptions are beginning to emerge. See, for example, the use of game theory in joint decision making within the household in Marjorie B. McElroy and Mary Jean Horney, "Nash-Bargained Household Decisions: Toward a Generalization of the Theory of Demand," *International Economic Review*, 22, 2 (June 1981), 333–49.

23. Clearly, when neoclassical economists have chosen to view a phenomenon in sociological terms, it has often merely reflected the cultural biases that recognize difference primarily when the differences are assumed to reinforce the presumption that women's sphere is in the home and men's sphere is in the public arena. The categories that have been allowed into the discourse reflect the willingness to accept group behavior as ontologically important only when those groups consist primarily of white males (government, firms, etc.), while there has been a lack of attention to groups in which women are more prevalent, such as the family, nonprofit organizations, and volunteerism.

24. See, for example, Gary S. Becker, *A Treatise on the Family* (Cambridge, MA: Harvard University Press, 1981).

25. Donald McCloskey, "Some Consequences of a Conjective Economics," p. 77.

26. Heidi Hartmann, "The Family as the Locus of Gender, Class, and Political Struggle: The Example of Housework," *Signs*, 6, 3 (Spring 1981), 366–94.

27. Donald McCloskey "Some Consequences of a Conjective Economics," p. 79.

28. Diana Strassmann points out that "the story that women do not work is slowly giving way to other stories, many of them told by the women who have become economists in recent decades." Strassmann cites the following research which demonstrates how the "discovery" of women's work outside the home coincides with the entry of these economist's wives into the workplace: Lisa Jo Brown, "Gender and Economic Analysis: A Feminist Perspective," presented at the American Economic Association annual meetings, December 1989. See Diana Strassmann, "Not a Free Market," p. 60.

29. See Gary S. Becker, *The Economic Approach to Human Behavior* (Chicago: University of Chicago Press, 1976).

30. Nancy Folbre and Heidi Hartmann, "The Rhetoric of Self-interest: Ideology and Gender in Economic Theory," in Arjo Klamer, Donald N. McCloskey, and Robert M. Solow (eds.), *The Consequences of Economic Rhetoric* (New York: Cambridge University Press, 1988), p. 197.

31. Judith A. Howard, "Dilemmas in Feminist Theorizing," p. 283.

32. For an extended discussion of the influence of the public/private split on a variety of social-science disciplines, see Judith A. Howard, "Dilemmas in Feminist Theorizing," p. 283.

33. See Ann L. Jennings, "Public or Private? Institutional Economics and Feminism," in Ferber and Nelson (eds.), *Beyond Economic Man*, p. 119.

34. See, for example, Karl R. Popper, *Objective Knowledge: An Evolutionary Approach* (Oxford: Clarendon Press, 1972). For a discussion of positivism and its impact on economics, see Bruce Caldwell, *Beyond Positivism: Economic Methodology in the Twentieth Century* (London: Allen and Unwin, 1982).

35. As my former colleague writes in his best-selling textbook "*Positive economics* deals with facts (once removed at the level of theory) and is devoid of value judgments. . . . *Normative economics*, in contrast, embodies someone's value judgements about what the economy should be like or what particular policy action should be recommended on the basis of some given economic generalization or relationship." See Campbell R. McConnell and Stanley L. Brue, *Economics* (New York: McGraw-Hill, 1990), p. 6.

36. Lorraine Code, "Taking Subjectivity into Account," in Linda Alcoff and Elizabeth Potter (eds.), *Feminist Epistemologies* (New York: Routledge, 1993), p. 17.

37. Ibid., p. 33.

38. Donald McCloskey, "Some Consequences of a Conjective Economics," p. 73.

39. See, for example, Thomas S. Kuhn, *The Structure of Scientific Revolutions* (Chicago: University of Chicago Press, 1970), and Paul K. Feyerabend, *Against Method* (London: NLB, 1975).

40. Linda Alcoff and Elizabeth Potter, "Introduction: When Feminisms Intersect Epistemology," in Alcoff and Potter (eds.), *Feminist Epistemologies*, pp. 1–14 (quote on p. 1).

41. According to Nelson, "However much evidence we have for that account and however much we could have, we are not in a position (and never will be) to know that future experience will not cause us to abandon it or to organize things in ways that no longer include it." See Lynn Hankinson Nelson, "Epistemological Communities," in Alcoff and Potter (eds.), *Feminist Epistemologies*, p. 133.

42. Ibid., pp. 122, 125, and 138.

43. Lorraine Code, "Taking Subjectivity into Account," p. 32.

44. Sandra Harding, "Rethinking Standpoint Epistemology," in Alcoff and Potter (eds.), *Feminist Epistemologies*, p. 53.

45. Ibid., p. 54.

46. Linda Alcoff and Elizabeth Potter, "Introduction: When Feminisms Intersect Epistemology," p. 3.

47. Ibid., p. 3.

48. Sandra Harding, "Rethinking Standpoint Epistemology," p. 56.

49. Paul K. Feyerabend, "Knowledge and the Role of Theories," *Philosophy of the Social Sciences*, *18*, 3 (September 1988), 169.

50. As Geoffrey Harcourt points out, most noted economists trained after the 1920s belong to the "do it yourself" generation where their understanding and perspectives on the discipline were acquired as the result of outside reading. See Geoffrey C. Harcourt, "Reflections on the Development of Economics as a Discipline," *History of Political Economy*, *16*, 4 (Winter 1984), 492–93.

51. Kenneth E. Boulding, "After Samuelson Who Needs Adam Smith?," *History of Political Economy*, *3* (1971), 232.

52. Judith A. Howard, "Dilemmas in Feminist Theorizing," pp. 283–84.

53. Ibid., p. 303.

54. See, for example, Robert Y. Shapiro and Harpreet Mahajan, "Gender Differences in Policy Preferences: A Summary of Trends from the 1960s to the 1980s," *Public*

Opinion Quarterly, *50* (1986), 42–61. Also, for a discussion of the response to the gender gap by the Reagan administration see Ann Mari May, "Women, Economics, and the Concept of the Market: A Second Look at Reaganomics," *Journal of Economic Issues*, *27*, 2 (June 1993), 471–80.

55. Barbara J. Nelson, "Women's Poverty and Women's Citizenship: Some Political Consequences of Economic Marginality," *Signs*, *10*, 2 (1984), 209–31.

56. Ann Mari May and Kurt Stephenson, "Women and the Great Retrenchment: The Political Economy of Gender in the 1980s," *Journal of Economic Issues*, *28*, 2 (June 1994), 533–42.

57. Despite her many valuable and recognized contributions to economics, which now include a prestigious MacArthur Foundation grant, Heidi Hartmann has never been given tenure in a department of economics. As Director of the Women's Studies Program at Rutgers University, she was granted tenure in the department of sociology.

58. Gareth Stedman Jones, *Languages of Class: Studies in English Working Class History* (New York: Cambridge University Press, 1983).

Part III

Firms, Human Resources, and Money

5

Pricing and the Business Enterprise

Frederic S. Lee

This chapter provides an empirically grounded pricing model centered on the business enterprise. The model, while not a theory of prices, provides a framework from which it is possible to concretely examine the business enterprise basis of the historical and social development of capitalism in the twenty-first century as well as in the past.

To set out the model, the chapter is divided into four sections. The first lays the foundations of the model by delineating both the business enterprise's approach to pricing and the features of the prices set and administered to the market, while the second section outlines the relationship between the goals of the individual business enterprise and its markups for profit that are part of the pricing equation. Integral to the discussion is the role that power plays in the determination of the profit markups. The third section deals with the establishment of the market price and the determination of the "market" markups for profit. The discussion is based on the competitive-social interaction of a community of enterprises that inhabit a specific market and on the role of social power and social decision making. The final section delineates the properties of an empirically grounded pricing model, and its implications for future work on the business enterprise are noted.

Before proceeding, it should be noted that the ensuing discussion is conducted without reference to neoclassical price theory; thus, the empirically grounded pricing model that eventually emerges is conceptually independent of it. The model is broadly consistent with many of the empirical tenets found in post-Keynesian and institutional economics while at the same time it is inconsistent with many of their theoretical tenets (such as the emphasis on a single pricing procedure). Consequently, the model represents an advance beyond both post-Keynesian and institutional economics in the quest to develop an alternative to orthodox price theory.

Pricing and Administered Prices

The activity of pricing is carried out within the business enterprise by an individual, such as its owner, or by a committee made up of business administrators or managers drawn from different departments and levels of management.[1] In either case, pricing is an administrative activity in that the kind of pricing procedures used, especially with regard to the determination of costing procedures, depreciation, and normal output, are administratively determined, and the prices determined are administered to the market. Moreover, these activities are constrained by the prevailing social–legal environment in which the pricing administrators find themselves. For example, the tax codes in the United States prescribe to the administrators the procedures for valuing the plant and equipment for depreciation/pricing purposes.

The administratively determined pricing procedures that are the focal point of this chapter are markup, normal cost, and target rate of return pricing. Markup pricing procedures consist of marking up average direct costs based on normal or estimated output to set the price, with the markup being sufficient to cover shop and firm expenses and produce a profit. Normal cost-pricing procedures consist of marking up average direct costs based on normal output to cover shop expenses which gives normal average factory costs, then marking up normal average factory costs to cover firm expenses which gives normal average total costs, and then marking up normal average total costs to set the price, with the markup producing a desired margin for profit. Finally, target rate of return pricing procedures consist of marking up normal average total costs (including shop and firm expenses) by a certain percentage that will generate a volume of profits at normal output that will produce a specific rate of return with respect to the value of the enterprise's capital assets.[2]

Markup, normal cost, and target rate of return pricing procedures have been used by large and small business enterprises under various *competitive market conditions* since before the 1930s. It is also clear from many pricing studies that normal cost and target rate of return pricing are the pricing procedures most used by business enterprises. For example, Black and Eversole found, in their study of cost accounting in American industry, that of the 20,282 enterprises that used a recognizable system to calculate their costs, nearly 90 percent could calculate their average factory costs and nearly 80 percent could calculate their average total costs.[3] It can then be argued that the enterprises would use the developed cost base when pricing.[4] Various cost accounting studies, including Govindarajan and Anthony, do in fact support this argument, while over fifty pricing studies report the usage of the above pricing procedures by business enterprises, with normal cost pricing mentioned the most often.[5]

Various pricing studies reveal that pricing administrators who used markup, normal cost, and target rate of return pricing procedures adopted policies designed to maintain prices for the selling season and in the face of fluctuations in sales. Moreover, Blinder noted that the business leaders of the enterprises thought that use of cost-based or normal cost-pricing procedures was an important factor in explaining infrequent price changes.[6] Finally, research by Means, Riley, Carlton, and Blinder has established that in the United States prices of most industrial and retail goods remain unchanged for extended periods of time and for many sequential transactions.[7]

This result is further reinforced by various case studies of business enterprises and industries where we find, for example, Lever maintaining the same retail price of his Sunlight soap for the period 1896 to 1906; and for the years 1896 to 1915 and 1920 to 1939, the price of Sunlight soap changed only fourteen times, or on average only once every thirty-two months.[8] Another example is Cassady's 1954 study of the U.S. petroleum industry where he noted that crude petroleum prices were stable for periods of twelve to thirty months, whereas dealers' prices of gasoline changed every two or three months.[9] Other supporting evidence can be found in journalist publications where they report, for example, "a pledge from Marks & Spencer yesterday that most prices in its shops this autumn will be the same as, or lower than, last year laid down a high street marker for rivals."[10] Finally, supporting evidence can also be garnered from one's daily activities, such as buying a national newspaper whose price has not changed for months and many millions of transactions or using a local launderette whose price for a wash has changed only once over an eighty-month period.

Thus, one can conclude that an essential facet of markup, normal cost, and target rate of return pricing procedures is that pricing administrators use them to set prices that they intended to maintain for periods of time and many sequential transactions. Conversely, one can also conclude that prices of products that change infrequently have been set by administrators using the above pricing procedures. Consequently, one can generally conclude that a significant proportion of industrial and consumer products in a capitalist economy, as indicated in Table 5.1, have prices that are based on markup, normal cost, and target rate of return pricing procedures.

One feature of stable, cost-based prices is that they are determined before transactions take place, and are administered to the market—hence their name of administered prices. A second feature is the absence of any determinate inverse price–sales relationship facing the individual business enterprise or for the market as a whole. Where documented in pricing studies, pricing administrators stated that variations in their prices within practical limits, given the prices of their competitors, produced virtually no change in their sales and that variations in the market price, especially downward, produced little if any changes in market sales in the short term. Moreover, when the price change was significant enough to result in a significant change in sales, the impact on profits has been negative enough to persuade enterprises not to try the experiment again.[11] The absence of any significant market price–sales relationship in the short term has been noted as well in various industry studies.[12] Consequently, pricing administrators do not utilize an inverse price–sales relationship when making pricing

Table 5.1

Product Groups and Infrequent Price Changes

Product Groups	Means*		Carlton**	
	No. of products	No. of products whose average length of price stability was 3 months or longer	No. of products	Average length of price stability (months)
Farm Products	64	3		
Foods	126	30		
Hides and leather products	39	27		
Textile products	105	60		
Fuel and lighting	16	3	4	5.9
Metal and metal products	111	75	21	4.3–13
Building materials	96	65	5	4.7–13.2
Chemicals and drugs	83	64	23	12.8
Housefurnishing goods	35	31		
Miscellaneous	70	58	13	8.1–8.7

Sources: *G.C. Means, *The Structure of the American Economy, Part 1: Basic Character-istics* (Washington, DC: U. S. Government Printing Office), 1939; **D.W. Carlton, "The Rigidity of Prices," *American Economic Review,* 76 (September 1986), 637–58.

decisions, nor do they set their prices to achieve a specific volume of sales; instead, the prices they set are maintained for a variety of sales volumes over time, since they believe that sales are almost entirely a function of buyer income, level of aggregate economic activity, government demand for armaments, population growth, product design, and perhaps advertising.[13]

The final feature of administered prices is that they change over time. As the evidence indicates, pricing administrators work with pricing periods of three months to a year in which their administered prices remained unchanged; and then at the end of the period, they decide whether to alter them. The factors most important when alterations in prices are considered are changes in labor and material costs, changes in normal output or capacity utilization based on expected future sales, and changes in the markup for profit. Regarding the latter, factors prompting the administrators to *alter* their profit markups include short-term and long-term competitive pressures, the stage the product has reached in its life-cycle, and the need for profit. Consequently, administered prices can change from one pricing period to the next in any direction, irrespective of the state of the business cycle. However, evidence does suggest that within short periods of time (such as two-year intervals), changes in costs will dominate the price changes, whereas over longer periods of time changes in the profit markup will play a more important role.

Business Goals and Profit Markups

One feature of administered prices not discussed above is their role in helping to achieve the goals pursued by leaders of the business enterprise. The business leaders of an enterprise hold a hierarchical set of goals and objectives they wish to attain, the most basic of which is the continuation of the enterprise for at least some undefined period of time into the future. In addition, they will pursue a variety of higher-order goals and objectives that will vary over time and may be different from country to country. Some of the higher-order goals include sales growth and diversification, maintenance of a fully employed work force, high-quality craftsmanship, and a healthy flow of dividends. They may also include social and political goals, such as trying to stem the tide of inflation or funding political pressure groups. A closer look at the higher-order goals also reveals that they are multifaceted in that, for example, growth may be achieved by simultaneously expanding sales in established lines, diversifying into new but established lines, and by eliminating dying lines and replacing them with totally novel products.

Any goals the business leaders adopt can be attained only if the enterprise produces profits. In this sense, profits are a means to an end, not a goal in themselves. Consequently, business leaders are not simply interested in "maximizing" profits (whatever that means); rather, they are interested in generating profits in order to attain their goals, and the more goals they have, the more profits they want.

In deciding the goals pursued, the business leaders of the enterprise exercise the power of direction vis-à-vis other groups in or associated with the enterprise. This power to direct, hence power to control, the economic activities of the enterprise may rest on legal rights or it may simply be the result of leading the enterprise. In either case, this power can only be sustained if the business leader can increase, or at least maintain, the flow of profits. Consequently, since some of the business leaders in the enterprise will be part of the committee assigned to set prices, their power to direct will be reflected in the markups for profits utilized by the price administrators when setting prices. Thus, the business leaders as pricing administrators can translate their goals into profit markups and prices.

To meet the basic goal of reproduction, the pricing administrators can use cost-based pricing procedures to set prices that enable their enterprise to engage in sequential acts of production over time and thereby reproduce itself. If additional goals are pursued, the administrators must determine profit markups. Establishing profit markups in the modern business enterprise is a complex task involving the setting of prices on a wide range of products situated in a variety of market conditions.

The relationship among business goals, profit markups, and pricing can be explored further with the aid of the following simplified model of the business enterprise. At a point in historical time, the business enterprise has, by implication, its complement of fixed capital; thus, for production to take place, the business leaders must have cash on hand to procure the necessary direct and indirect labor and material inputs. Once the necessary productive inputs are obtained, production is undertaken, the output sold, and the revenue collected. The period of time from the initial buying of the inputs through production to the collection of revenue is called the turnover period. Assuming normal output is produced, if the amount of total revenue received at the end of the turnover period equals the initial expenditure of working capital for the inputs (implying that the price administrator sets the price equal to average total costs at normal output), the enterprise has met its basic reproduction goal and can repeat the process for the next production period. If total revenue is greater than total costs at normal output (implying that the pricing administrators applied a profit markup to normal average total costs when setting the price), the enterprise could not only repeat the process again, but could also engage in discretionary activities directed at fulfilling the other goals of the business leaders.

To enable such discretionary activities, the leaders of the business enterprise utilize a variety of multitemporal, multiobjective pricing strategies. In particular, the pricing administrators need to establish a range of markups for profit for the enterprise's various products. Each markup will be intended to achieve a particular pricing objective, while the overall markup structure is intended to achieve the goals of the business leaders. Thus, the administered prices of a business enterprise are strategic prices designed to achieve the goals of business leaders—goals that are often reproduction and growth, but there could be others as well.[14]

Since pricing administrators must set specific markups for profit on a wide range of products, the power to direct a business enterprise is supported by the power to establish acceptable prices in the market. The source of such power is usually attributed to barriers to entry, the potency of potential competition, and the unresponsiveness of market sales to price changes.[15] However, there are also other sources.

One such source of power comes from the institutional makeup of the market. That is, markets in this chapter are not organized like auction markets where enterprises cannot set their own prices and determine their own profit markups, or like the early retail markets and oriental bazaars where the retailer engaged in individual price, hence profit margin, negotiation for each transaction. Rather, enterprises that desire to enter these markets must first announce a price for their product and then enter into direct buyer–seller interaction to obtain sales. Thus, the necessity of setting prices clearly means that the institutional nature of the market is a source of market power for the enterprise.

A second source of power comes from the product itself. If the flow of the product can be regulated either by regulating the pace of production or through the use of inventories, then the enterprise will not be forced to simply dump the product on the market and accept whatever price it will obtain. Moreover, if the product is in continuous demand, because of the consumption patterns of the population, then a market price must always exist for it. This need for a continuously posted market price implies yet another source of power—the enterprise must have the power to set this market price if its product is to be sold at all.

Although the above represent sources of market power, the empirical studies on pricing do not lend support to the position that the pricing administrators consciously base their determination of the markup for profit or the price on them. This is due to the fact that these sources of power have no quantitative dimension that can be directly associated with the magnitude of the profit markups and prices. It is also because the sources of power are so pervasive in the market that the pricing administrators are unable to identify them clearly so as to use them consciously in their pricing decisions.

Consequently, the pricing administrators prefer to base their pricing decisions regarding the markups and prices on custom, convention, and reasonableness, and on short-term and long-term competitive pressures within the context of the sources of market power. Each of these variables clearly implies that the magnitudes of the markups for profits and the price are determined in a social/market context that varies not only historically but also geographically. Moreover, the use of these variables in pricing means that the pricing administrators cannot unilaterally determine the markups for profit and prices simply by reference to desire to increase market share, to fund investment, or anything else—because each action affects both the market as a whole and various enterprises within and outside the market. Thus, the determinants of the magnitudes for the markup for profit can only be found within the context of the determination of the market price.

The Market Price and "Market" Markups

A decline in the business enterprise's price below normal average total costs will prevent it from engaging in sequential reproduction at normal output. Moreover, if its pricing administrators are forced to set a price below their desired price, the flow of profits needed for the attainment of the higher-order goals will be disrupted. For the isolated enterprise and its administrators, the price problem described above would not occur; but it does occur when the enterprise inhabits a market that includes other enterprises. That is, in a market that has more than one enterprise, there exists the potential problem of destructive price competition as the pricing administrators of each enterprise search independently of the others for "the" market price. If the individual prices are highly dispersed, then the low-price enterprises would have increased sales while the high-price enterprises would have a decline in sales. Consequently, the high price enterprises would respond with lower prices in an effort to increase their sales themselves. But such a response and the ensuing counterresponses would drive the market price so low without a corresponding increase in market sales that the reproductive ability of all the enterprises in the market would be endangered. Therefore, in order to enhance their chances of survival, the business leaders and pricing administrators of the enterprises within the market are driven to establish market institutions that would eliminate the problem of destructive price competition and establish a stable market price.

The leaders of the business enterprise must continually invest in plant, equipment, and product innovation in order to maintain the enterprise's existence and to grow. In making their investment decisions, they must look to the market for the necessary information, such as sales trends, stock movements, the state of orders, and market shares. Because each of the indicators is singularly dependent on the prices charged at each act of exchange, the existence of prices based on market conditions specific to the exchange cannot generate the information needed by the business leaders for making investment decisions. On the one hand, buyers cannot make long-term buying plans based on the goods' relative prices since these prices could change in a haphazard, unpredictable manner; on the other hand, if the total sales of the enterprise are associated with many different prices, then they cannot make long-term sales predictions based on sales trends, stock movements, state of orders, or market share. Consequently, the information needed by the leaders to make investment decisions would simply not exist. Therefore, to eliminate fluctuating exchange-specific prices, business leaders establish market institutions that would generate a single market price that can remain unchanged for many exchanges, with the result that sales trends, stock movements, state of orders, and market shares can then provide the information they needed to make long-term investment decisions.

The types of market institutions organized by business leaders vary considerably, depending on laws, customs, and personal trust. However, three generic institutions can be identified: private institutions, quasi-public/private institutions, and purely public institutions. Private institutions include cooperative price setting through trade associations (which includes cartels and open price associations) and individual leadership price setting where the leaders and price administrators of the "following" enterprises voluntary accept the leadership price. Quasi-public/private institutions, such as U.S. regulatory commissions and the trade associations established under the National Industrial Recovery Act, also engage in cooperative price setting, the process of which is sanctioned by law and supported by government bureaucracy, but initiated and carried out by the leaders and price administrators of the business enterprises. Finally, in the case of purely public institutions, their administrators engage in leadership pricing and establish prices that must by law be accepted by the price administrators of the enterprises operating in the market.

In spite of the variations in market institutions used to determine profit markups and set the market price, the actual administering of the pricing process can be summarized under two headings: cooperative price setting and leadership price setting. In the case of cooperative price setting, pricing administrators may take an average of the average total costs of the member enterprises with the lowest costs adjusted for share of market sales, or they may take an average of costs of all their member enterprises. In either case, a "market" markup for profit is applied to the costing equation to set the market price. On the other hand, they may adopt the pricing equation and price of the lowest-cost enterprise as the market pricing equation and market price. Finally, administrators may simply specify the costing and pricing procedures and suggest normal "market" markups for profit, but not specify a particular market price with the consequence that in some markets, such as printing and book selling, there will not be a single market price.

As for leadership price setting, the price leader uses its own pricing procedures and determines its own "market" markup for profit when setting its price, while the pricing administrators of the price following enterprises accept the price and adjust their markups for profit accordingly. Similarly, government price administrators, using the same costing and pricing procedures as private enterprise, themselves determine the "market" profit markup when setting a market price.[16]

It is obvious from the above discussion that the markups for profit are socially determined. That is, in the case of cooperative price setting, the pricing administrators from the various enterprises have to decide upon a mutually acceptable figure for the markup. To reach such a figure involves a social process where the different beliefs as to what is an appropriate markup have to be reconciled if stable relationships among the competing business leaders are to be established and maintained. This process of reconciliation is a process of custom-creation and the extent to which a business leader is able to influence it indicates his or her competitive strength (i.e., market power) relative to the other leaders. Similarly, in the case of leadership pricing, the pricing administrators have to take into account the probable competitive responses of the opposing business leaders if a set of stable market relationships is to emerge. Hence, it can be concluded that this process of determining the "market" profit markup is also a process of custom-creating.[17] Thus, the determinants of the "market" markup for profit are competition and custom, or, more generically, market power. That is, market power as a competitive edge contributes to determining the markup for profit, and once the markup has been determined, it contributes to maintaining the stable market relationships, which makes the markup "customary" in the minds of the business leaders and price administrators. Over time, competitive edge and custom become so intermingled and mutually reinforcing that the determinants of the profit markup—namely, market power—become indistinguishable from the social and historical fabric that constitutes the market and thus completely unamenable to quantification.

The Empirically Grounded Pricing Model

The market-price equation that emerges from the above discussion has a number of significant features, the most notable of which is that it has no one universal specification. That is, given the various ways in which the market-price equation is and historically has been specified, it is not empirically valid to claim, for example as Eichner does, that all market pricing equations in industrial and wholesale markets are simply those of the reigning price leader.[18] Moreover, it is also not legitimate to argue for fictional "representative firm" market pricing equations. Since all equations are based on real-life enterprises, it is impossible to identify one as "representative" of the enterprises in the market.

A second salient feature of the market pricing equation is that it is not an average aggregate of all the individual pricing equations. Consequently, the averaging procedure used by Kalecki to obtain a general market pricing equation has no empirical support.[19]

The third salient feature of the market pricing equation is that it is determined by price administrators within the context of market-based social relationships, social institutions, and legal constraints.

The final salient feature of the market pricing equation is that the resulting market price is an administered price.

A model of interdependent market-pricing equations consistent with the single market pricing equations described in this chapter is presented in the appendix. The remainder of this section discusses the properties and implications of that general pricing model.

Because the coefficients of the pricing model can differ from the coefficients of the corresponding quantity model, the dual price–quantity relationship of the Leontief post-Keynesian input–output models does not exist for the empirically grounded pricing model. This property of the model has three implications: first, that empirical investigations on industrial pricing based on production coefficients are flawed; second, that no substantive meaning can be attached to the term *profit maximization*, which suggests that market prices are not a resource allocation mechanism; and third, that the model does not represent the actual technological and institutional constraints of the economy. A second property of the model is that custom and competition are predominant among the determinants of the "market" markup for profit and the market price. Consequently, since the motivation for profits is historically specific and capitalist societies are beset with varying customs and conventions and cultural lags, it is empirically and theoretically inappropriate to assume that all price administrators have the same motivation regarding the determination of the markup. Thus, the determinants of the markup for profit in the pricing model—hence, the markup itself— must necessarily vary from market to market at a single point in time, and in a particular market over time as is suggested by the empirical evidence.[20] Finally, the persistence of custom and convention in the determination of the markup for profit undermines the often-stated view that a tendency toward a uniform rate of profit is a persistent and structural feature of a competitive capitalist economy. The final property of the model is that its prices are tied to time and hence are historical.

As constituted, the model suggests that future work on the business enterprise and pricing must be historically and socially specific. For example, since business leaders in Japan and in the United States hold different sets of social values, their higher-order goals, markups for profit, and market prices will be qualitatively different. Moreover, as the model suggests, different legal traditions will generate different types of market institutions that will try to prevent price wars in different ways. However, the most important contribution of the model to future work is that it highlights the obvious fact that competition in the market stems largely from the clash of different goals that can be traced back to different social values. Thus the evolution of capitalism in the twenty-first century will reflect the outcome of these clashes. Or, to put it another way, the model makes transparent the argument that capitalist development is simply social conflict and cultural conquest carried out by less violent, although no less ruthless, means.

Conclusion

It was not the purpose of this chapter to demonstrate that manufacturing, wholesale, and retail business enterprises used cost-plus pricing procedures—the facts speak for themselves. Rather, my purpose was to develop an empirically grounded pricing model, starting with the pricing procedures of the individual business enterprise and ending with a general pricing model that covers all industrial, wholesale, and retail enterprises and their respective markets. In achieving this, pricing procedures were found to vary considerably, leading to a variety of pricing equations, of which normal cost and target rate of return pricing equations were the most common; normal capacity utilization and prices themselves were found to be administratively determined, which meant prices changed infrequently; administered prices were found to be strategic prices designed to achieve particular socially agreed-upon goals, none of which was profit maximization; and historical factors, customs, and competition (i.e., market power) were found to contribute to the determination of the profit markups and market prices.

To flesh out and extend the model and its implications, integrated theoretical and historical research is needed in a number of areas, of which the following are the most important. One is the tied historical evolution of cost accounting, pricing procedures, and management control of the labor force, while a second area is research on the relationship between social values and entrepreneurial goals and their evolution over time in the United States. A third area of research is in the determination of profit markups in specific markets, especially with regard to the contribution of customs and laws in their determination. For example, the rise and fall of fair trade laws provides a ready-made case study of the interaction of customs and laws in the determination of profit markups. The final area of research is in the clash of social values, entrepreneurial goals, and profit markups. The social and economic clash between big and small business, local communities and national markets, and the established social and business elite and newcomers are just three of the many projects that could be pursued in this area. Secondary areas of research include surveys of costing and pricing procedures, collection of data on the frequency of price changes and on profit markups, historical and contemporary surveys of entrepreneurial goals, and an examination of auction versus administered price markets. The research suggested will keep non-neoclassical economists busy well into the twenty-first century, with the result that a historically grounded theory of prices will emerge that will be different from and will replace neoclassical price theory.

Appendix

To move from a single market pricing equation to a model of interdependent market pricing equations, it is necessary to delineate the material, labor, and other inputs included in the markup, normal cost, and target rate of return pricing equations:

Markup Pricing Equation

$$[\sum_{i=1}^{n} md_{li}p_i + \sum_{v=1}^{z} ld_{lv}\, w_v][1 + rk_1] = p_1.$$

Normal Cost-Pricing Equation

$$[\sum_{i=1}^{n} md_{li}p_i + \sum_{v=1}^{z} ld_{lv}\, w_v][1 + g_1][1 + h_1][1 + r_1] = p_1.$$

Normal Cost-Pricing Equation

$$[\sum_{i=1}^{n} md_{li}p_i + \sum_{v+1}^{z} ld_{lv}\, w_v + \sum_{i=n+1}^{a} mo_{1i} + \sum_{v=z+1}^{e} lo_{lv}w_w + d_1][1 + r_1] = p_1.$$

Target Rate of Return Pricing Equation

$$[\sum_{i=1}^{n} md_{li}p_i + \sum_{v=1}^{z} ld_{lv}\, w_v + \sum_{l=n+1}^{a} mo_{1i} + \sum_{v=z+1}^{e} lo_{lv}w_w + d_1][1 + t_1] = p_1.$$

Where md_{1i} is the ith normal average direct material pricing coefficient;
ld_{1v} is the vth normal average direct labor pricing coefficient;
mo_{1i} is the ith normal average overhead material pricing coefficient;
lo_{1v} is the vth normal average overhead labor pricing coefficient;
d_1 is the normal average depreciation pricing coefficient;
p_i is the market price of the ith material input;
w_v is the wage rate of the vth labor input; and
p_1 is the market price for good 1.

Assuming the existence of, say, f markets whose prices are based on the above pricing equations, it is possible to rewrite the above equations into a general pricing model:

$$[R][Mp^*_t + Lw + d] = [p^*_{t+1}] = p_{t+1},$$
$$p+1$$

Where M is the matrix of material pricing coefficients of $f \times a$ dimension ($f \neq a$);
L is the matrix of labor pricing coefficient of $f \times e$ dimension ($f \neq e$);
D is a column vector with f depreciation pricing coefficients;
R is a diagonal matrix of $f \times f$ dimension of overhead and profit markups;
w is a column vector with e wage rates;
p^*_t is a column vector with a material input market prices at time t;
p^0_{t+1} is a column vector with f market prices at time $t+1$ which do not include the a material market prices at time $t+1$; and
p_{t+1} is a column vector that includes p^*_{t+1} and p^0_{t+1}.

M is semi-decomposable because all material overhead inputs do not necessarily appear in all the market pricing equations and because some of the material inputs may not originate in markets that use the above pricing equations. However, because the same direct (and some overhead) material inputs appear directly and indirectly in all the pricing equations, the above pricing model is interdependent. The labor matrix may also be semi-decomposable, but given that different products and industrial/competitive environments require different laboring skills, the matrix may well be largely decomposable, punctuated with pockets of quite interrelated groups of markets. Finally, the fth element of R consists of $[1 + k][1 + g][1 + h][1 + r][1 + t]$, where k, g, h, r and/or t may be zero depending on the market pricing equation under consideration.

Aside from the obvious feature that the model is empirically grounded since each of its market pricing equations is based on a "real-world" pricing equation, a number of other features need to be delineated. First, it is a single-product pricing model, even though the underlying structure of production includes much joint production. This is based on the fact that enterprises use single-product pricing equations when setting prices. A second feature of the model, which follows from the first, is its incomplete, imprecise correspondence with the underlying model of production. That is, assuming a surplus-producing economy and that the level of output in each market is normal with respect to pricing, the resulting production coefficients in the material and labor matrices will not necessarily correspond to the pricing coefficients of those same matrices. This is due to the fact that many of the market pricing equations do not explicitly include all the material and labor inputs actually used in production; to the mismeasurement by the market price setting administrators of the pricing coefficients vis-à-vis the actual production coefficients (which accounts for the existence of variance analysis); to the inability of the pricing administrators actually to determine all the pricing coefficients needed for pricing; and to the obvious existence of joint production. The final feature of the model is that depreciation pricing coefficients are in money terms, determined prior to the pricing process, and largely determined by the tax code.

Notes

1. See Edwin G. Nourse, *Price Making in a Democracy* (Washington, DC: The Brookings Institution, 1944); Robert A. Gordon, *Business Leadership in the Large Corporation* (Washington, DC: The Brookings Institution, 1945); Alfred D. Chandler, *Strategy and Structure* (Cambridge, MA: MIT Press, 1962); and Alfred D. Chandler, *The Visible Hand* (Cambridge, MA: MIT Press, 1977).

2. The pricing procedures can be delineated in the following manner:

Markup pricing:	$[NADC][1 + k] = \text{price};$
Normal cost pricing:	$[(NADC)(1 + g)][1 + h][1 + r] = \text{price};$
	$[(NAFC)(1 + h)][1 + r] = \text{price};$
	$[NATC][1 + r] = \text{price};$
Target rate of return pricing:	$[NATC][1 + t] = \text{price}.$

Where $NADC$ is normal average direct costs;
$NAFC$ is normal average factory costs;
$NATC$ is normal average total costs;
k is the markup for overhead costs and profits;
g is the markup for shop expenses;
h is the markup for firm expenses;
r is the markup for profit; and
t is the markup for profit that will produce the target rate of return with respect to the value of the enterprise's capital assets.

3. Martin L. Black and Harold B. Eversole, *A Report on Cost Accounting in Industry* (Washington, DC: U.S. Government Printing Office, 1946).

4. Herbert A. Simon, et al., *Centralization vs. Decentralization in Organizing the Controller's Department* (New York: Controllership Foundation, 1954); and Alfred D. Chandler, *Strategy and Structure.*

5. Vijay Govindarajan and Robert N. Anthony, "How Firms Use Cost Data in Price Decisions," *Management Accounting (USA)* (July 1983), 30–36; and Frederic S. Lee, "From Post Keynesian to Historical Price Theory: Facts, Theory and Empirically Grounded Pricing," *Review of Political Economy* (forthcoming).

6. Alan S. Blinder, "Why are Prices Sticky? Preliminary Results from an Interview Study," *American Economic Review, 81* (May 1991), 89–96.

7. Gardiner C. Means, *The Structure of the American Economy, Part 1: Basic Characteristics* (Washington, DC: U.S. Government Printing Office, 1939); Hersey E. Riley, *Frequency of Change in Wholesale Prices: A Study of Price Flexibility, Report no. 142* (Washington, DC: U.S. Department of Labor, Bureau of Labor Statistics, 1958); Dennis W. Carlton, "The Rigidity of Prices," *American Economic Review, 76* (September 1986), 637–58); and Alan S. Blinder, "Why Are Prices Sticky?"

The adoption of the one-price plan by retailers in the middle 1800s contributed significantly to retail prices remaining unchanged for extended periods of time and for many sequential transactions. Previously, retailers were more likely to engage in individual negotiation of prices with buyers with the result that the same product could be sold to different buyers at different prices on the same day. However, such selling activity was time-consuming and costly and therefore not universally practiced especially with regard to prices of staple goods. See Lewis Eldon Atherton, "The Pioneer Merchant in Mid-America," *University of Missouri Studies, 14* (April 1939), 1–135; and Donald L. Shawver, *The Development of Theories of Retail Price Determination in England and the United States* (Urbana: University of Illinois Press, 1956).

8. Charles Wilson, *The History of Unilever*, vol. 2 (London: Cassell and Company, 1954), app. 9.

9. Ralph Cassady, *Price Making and Price Behavior in the Petroleum Industry* (New Haven, CT: Yale University Press, 1954).

10. *The Guardian* (July 18, 1992), 35.

11. Carolyn Shaw Bell, "On the Elasticity of Demand at Retail," *American Journal of Economics and Sociology, 20* (1960), 63–72.

12. See, for example, Ralph Cassady, *Price Making and Price Behavior in the Petroleum Industry.*

13. See Frederic S. Lee, "From Post Keynesian to Historical Price Theory." This necessarily means that administered prices are not market-clearing prices, nor do they vary with each change in sales (or shift in the virtually nonexistent market or enterprise "demand curve"). For further discussion, see the following by Frederic S. Lee: "Full Cost Pricing: A New Wine in a New Bottle," *Australian Economic Papers, 24* (June 1984), 151–66; " 'Full Cost' Prices, Classical Price Theory, and Long Period Analysis: A Critical Evaluation," *Metroeconomica, 37* (1985), 199–219; and "Marginalist Controversy and Post Keynesian Price Theory," *Journal of Post Keynesian Economics, 13* (Winter 1990–91), 252–63.

14. Frederic S. Lee, " 'Full Cost' Prices, Classical Price Theory, and Long Period Analysis"; and "Marginalist Controversy and Post Keynesian Price Theory."

15. See Philip W.S. Andrews, *Manufacturing Business* (London: Macmillan, 1949); Joseph Steindl, *Maturity and Stagnation in American Capitalism* (Oxford: Basil Blackwell, 1952); Paolo Sylos-Labini, *Oligopoly and Technical Progress*, rev. ed. (Cambridge, MA: Harvard University Press, 1969); and Alfred S. Eichner, *The Megacorp and Oligopoly, Micro Foundations of Macro Dynamics* (New York: Cambridge University Press, 1976).

16. Frederic S. Lee, "From Post Keynesian to Historical Price Theory."

17. While changes in economic conditions can disrupt the competitive/social relation-

ships that determine the markup for profit, it is evident from the empirical evidence that business leaders continually work at restoring them.

18. Alfred S. Eichner, *The Macrodynamics of Advanced Market Economies* (Armonk, NY: M.E. Sharpe, 1991).

19. Michal Kalecki, *Theory of Economic Dynamics* (London: Allen and Unwin, 1954).

20. Frederic S. Lee, "From Post Keynesian to Historical Price Theory."

6

Human Resources, Labor Markets, and Economic Performance

Ray Marshall

The main theme of this chapter is that human resources, which have always been a major determinant of personal, enterprise, and national economic progress, have become even more important in a highly competitive, knowledge-intensive global economy. The most basic cause of economic progress is improvements in productivity, or the way factors are organized and focused to improve output. The most fundamental process used to improve productivity is the organization of human resources to make the most effective use of technology, defined as how goods and services are produced. The most important feature of technology is not machines, but the ideas, skills, and knowledge embodied in machines. Technology is improved primarily through the interactions of human resources and machine technology within organizational forms controlled by various actors in the process. Depending on the context, those who control production processes may or may not be interested in maximizing productivity or efficiency in the use of all resources. It can be demonstrated, moreover, that technological innovation increasingly takes place in the production process, not in separated laboratories and research centers.

Changing technology, markets, and the organization of work cause constant shifts in the kinds of skills workers need for optimal performance. In technology-intensive workplaces, manual skills become increasingly less important and thinking skills, especially abstract learning, become much more important. Indeed, superior economic performance increasingly depends on the quality of individual, group, and organizational learning. As the intellectual content of goods and services increases, superior returns will accrue to those who can improve productivity and quality with fewer physical resources and more ideas, skills and knowledge. This is so because standardized machine technologies become commodities requiring only basic intellectual skills.

Learning Systems and Labor Markets

Learning Systems

Learning, or the acquisition of ideas, skills, and knowledge, takes place in many different places. The family is the most basic learning system, which is one of the reasons why family income often predicts educational achievement better than years of schooling.[1] The condition of families also is an important reason many children start school behind.[2] There is evidence, moreover, that the education of parents, especially mothers, can do much to break the intergenerational cycles of poverty. Unfortunately, the status of families is a major problem for the United States since it has a much larger proportion of its children in poverty than any other major industrial country. Moreover, the number of poor preschool-aged children increased 28 percent during the 1980s, compared with an increase of only 16 percent for all preschool-aged children.[3] The good news is that interventions have demonstrated their ability to help families improve the education of parents as well as children.[4]

Schools are, of course, also important learning systems, although most productivity-enhancing learning (55 percent between 1929 and 1982) takes place at work.[5] Here again, however, the United States has major problems. American schools were organized primarily to meet the needs of the mass-production, natural-resource–oriented economy that predominated in the early part of this century. Elite private schools, tracks within public schools for those expected to do postsecondary education and training, and colleges and universities produced the relatively small managerial, professional, and technical elites needed for the mass-production system while most public schools, organized like factories, turned migrants and immigrants into literate workers able to perform the routine work required on farms or in most mass-production workplaces. The best American graduate and research universities are still world class, but most of the public schools are not. American workers have more years of schooling than those in most other industrialized countries, but consistently place near the bottom in international student assessments, particularly in math and science. Moreover, American schools are becoming even more polarized than they were earlier in the century. The problem is particularly serious in large metropolitan areas, where low income whites, minorities, and immigrants are concentrated in grossly inadequate public schools while higher income minorities and whites attend suburban and private schools.[6]

The problems created by school polarization are compounded by demographic changes. Sometime during the next century, non-Hispanic whites will become a minority of the U.S. population. Much earlier, minorities will become majorities in our public schools, as they already have in most large cities and a number of states, including Texas and California. Since minorities are not well served by our public schools, they will not be well enough educated to perform effectively in a high-wage, high-productivity economy.

Clearly, increasingly segregated schools where elite private institutions serve mainly high-income groups and where public schools are attended mainly by low-income students are a recipe for social, political, and economic disaster. Again, the good news is that we know how to cause schools to provide quality education for even the most disadvantaged children.[7] Indeed, restructuring schools for high performance would do much to improve education for *all* students, including disadvantaged minorities.

Most economically important learning takes place at work, not in schools. Unfortunately, job-related education and training reflect the schools. Well-educated workers receive most of the training and frontline workers receive very little.[8] American companies also spend less on workplace education and training than do their competitors in most other industrialized countries.

Other important learning systems are political processes and community organizations and institutions. Unfortunately, American political and governmental processes are excessively adversarial and provide few opportunities for consensus building. Consensus-building mechanisms in other countries balance adversarial processes and contribute to superior learning about public issues and superior performance on many economic indicators.[9] Increasing racial, ethnic, and class fragmentation are major barriers to the joint learning required to improve U.S. economic and social policy. Income polarization is closely related to the basic economic policies pursued in the United States during the 1980s. A fundamental political problem is that high-income people increasingly see little need to make the investments in human resources required to enable the United States to remain a country with high incomes and equal education and economic opportunity.

Labor Markets

So far we have focused on learning systems. But labor markets also exert a great influence on human resource development and economic performance. Labor markets provide signals to workers and potential workers about job opportunities and provide signals to employers about the cost and qualifications of labor. Well-functioning labor markets therefore influence national and enterprise economic performance. If markets do not perform very well, economies will experience skill shortages and inflation, as well as high levels of frictional and structural unemployment, and will be unable to take full advantage of opportunities to improve productivity and incomes. If labor markets are fragmented so that some workers are denied access to better jobs and learning opportunities, economic performance is stunted, many individuals are discouraged from acquiring knowledge, and incomes reflect race, gender, class, or other factors unrelated to performance. Well-functioning labor markets require the ready availability of information and learning opportunities on the basis of motivation and ability.

American labor markets are more fragmented and less efficient than those in most other industrial countries.[10] Some of the reasons for this state of affairs include the absence of effective linkages between school and work, tracking according to income within schools, and the monopolization of information and opportunities by private labor exchanges, families, enterprises, schools, and other institutions. Some other industrialized countries have developed public institutions to provide better information about jobs and training opportunities and have fewer financial barriers for people who wish to take advantage of education and training opportunities.

The United States probably has the worst school-to-work transition system of any major industrial country, and has no effective national labor market system. We do much more relative to gross domestic product (GDP) for college-bound students but spend much less on elementary and secondary students and pre-employment training for the non-college-bound.[11] Indeed, the United States probably has the most elitist schools and learning systems of any major industrial democracy. We have a public employment service and provide some public work-oriented education and training facilities, many of which are of very high quality, but there is no national labor market system and federal training programs are fragmented, stigmatized, very inefficient, and serve a relatively small percentage of our population. Similarly, the U.S. Employment Service suffers from a lack of identity because it is not clearly either a federal or a state system, it does not have very good information, and it serves mainly low-income, unskilled workers and employers seeking to hire such workers.

Other industrialized countries have learned that public interventions and institutions are needed to make labor markets more efficient. They also have learned that what Swedish labor economists call "active labor market policies" can do much more to improve individual, enterprise, and national economic performance than is possible with "passive" income support systems or "natural" labor markets alone. "Active" means encouraging workers to train, take jobs, or relocate, not merely to depend on "passive" measures like income maintenance, which the Swedes call the "dole." They reason that better use of labor-market resources will result from active measures to make workers more productive or to improve labor-market efficiency. Moreover, active labor-market processes enhance the performance of macroeconomic policies by improving productivity growth and helping combat both unemployment and inflation simultaneously.[12] Some nations, especially those dominated by Keynesian macroeconomic policies, have tried unsuccessfully to reduce inflationary pressures by wage and price controls—which have never worked for very long except in times of severe national emergencies.[13] A major problem for inflationary pressures induced by shortages or excess aggregate demand is that controls do not relieve the pressures by eliminating supply constraints or increasing supplies. The Swedes thought it much more equitable and efficient to work with basic market forces to overcome shortages and remove bottlenecks than to adopt controls that merely suppress problems temporarily.

While the evaluations of selective employment policies in the United States have generally been positive, there are some important limitations that have caused these programs to be less effective in the United States than in other countries.[14] A major problem (discussed at greater length below) is the absence in the United States of an effective labor market infrastructure to ensure that resources are used efficiently to get workers employed or trained. In addition, there has been great resistance to these programs for a variety of reasons. Keynesian macroeconomists, who dominated U.S. economic policy throughout most of the postwar period, accepted neoclassical microeconomics—mistakenly, in my judgment—and therefore generally minimized the significance of structural problems and the need for selective labor market policies—arguing that monetary-fiscal policies and markets would overcome these problems. They consequently joined forces with conservatives who resisted active labor market policies except as a component of welfare policies. Orthodox economists, who often let the perfect be the enemy of the good, could always point to methodological problems in ascertaining whether or not the programs achieved their objectives. Indeed, these economists often evaluated programs in terms of objectives they imposed, not those specified in the legislation. For example, public-service employment was designed mainly to put unemployed workers who could not find private-sector jobs to work doing useful things. Public-service programs were not necessarily to enhance participants' job skills and long-run earnings, a function of training programs. In short, U.S. selective employment programs have had many problems but have nevertheless had modest positive benefits for participants. They have, however, been too stigmatized, fragmented, inefficient, and underfunded to realize their full potential as complements to general economic and social policies. We should learn from the experiences of other countries as well as our own and develop effective labor-market infrastructures as instruments for more effective labor-market policies. The recommendations at the end of this chapter are designed to achieve this objective.

The Case for a High-Productivity, High-Wage Strategy

America's Choice

Under modern conditions, companies in the United States, or in any other country, can compete either by reducing wages or by improving productivity and quality—there are no other options. The United States, unlike most other developed democratic countries, has been pursuing the low-wage option by default—that is, because of its aversion to economic strategies, it has left competitiveness mainly to market forces, which, under conditions in the United States in the 1990s and beyond, will lead inevitably to the low-wage option. Other countries have rejected this course, not only because they understand that it leads to lower and more unequal incomes, but also because it greatly limits their ability to upgrade people and companies.

The most important components of a high-productivity strategy are measures that (a) greatly improve work-force quality; (b) encourage companies to organize for high performance and discourage reliance on low-wage competition; and (c) develop supporting national and international economic policies.

In explaining the reasons for these conclusions, I would like to develop two points. First, "brain power" (knowledge and higher-order thinking skills) is likely to be the chief source of economic success in the 1990s and beyond. This has always been true, but is likely to be more so in the future, as an increasingly knowledge-intensive world makes thinking skills essential to personal and national success. I emphasize the economic role of thinking skills, but these same intellectual skills are now required for good decision making in other aspects of life. Although economists often forget it, I am very mindful that there is much more to life than making a living—though you won't have much of a life if you can't make a living. And most adults identify themselves, organize their lives, gain their sense of self-worth, and contribute to the human community by what they do for a living.

Second, the world has changed so that economic success requires all workers to have the thinking skills formerly required only of the 25 percent of our labor force who were college-educated professional, technical, and managerial workers. In the past, most American workers with a high school education who were willing to work hard have been able to earn middle-class incomes. There is mounting evidence that this has become much more difficult.

Economic research has fairly consistently found that investments in education yield very high personal and social returns. Although real or "inflation-adjusted" earnings for most Americans have fallen over the last twenty years, the returns to education have increased with education. Since 1987, however, real earnings have fallen even for college-educated workers. Only those with advanced degrees continued to experience rising earnings in the late 1980s and early 1990s.[15] This suggests that declining economic competitiveness threatens real wages at every education level, even though those with higher levels of education will be better off than those with less knowledge and fewer thinking and learning skills. Moreover, the evidence shows that the education wage gap is growing mainly because of the declining earnings of less educated workers, not because of increasing demand for college-educated workers.

Why will educated people have higher earnings? In the first place, people with good thinking skills can make better decisions and have more choices.

Second, educated people are more productive and therefore earn higher incomes. Productivity is an efficiency concept—it is a measure of output per unit of input of labor, capital, or natural resources. Higher productivity is related to better decision making because those who make good decisions can identify and select more productive activities. But educated people also improve productivity because they are better able to understand, adapt, and develop and use sophisticated technologies; in other words, they are better able to substitute ideas, skills and knowledge for physical resources.

There are many illustrations of this process: Agricultural economists, following the work of 1981 Nobel laureate Theodore Schultz at the University of Chicago, have demonstrated that American farmers use no more land, labor, or machine capital than they did in the 1920s, yet output has tripled and quadrupled, depending on the crop. How did this happen? Ideas, skills, and knowledge were substituted for physical resources. Schultz and other human-capital researchers have also demonstrated that the returns to human capital are higher than the returns to physical capital, and that almost all of the improvements in productivity since the 1920s are due to technology and human capital; 20 percent or less is attributable to physical capital and zero to natural resources.[16]

The process of substituting ideas, skills, and knowledge for physical resources is not restricted to agriculture, even though it is more obvious there. Peter Drucker tells us that the value of the strategic product of the 1920s, the automobile, contained 60 percent raw materials and energy; by contrast, the computer chip, the strategic product of the 1990s, contains only 2 percent energy and raw material.[17]

Finally, we know from sophisticated research that national and personal incomes are highly correlated with education. This research also has found that such social pathologies as drug abuse, unwanted teen pregnancies, involvement with the criminal justice system, unemployment, and low wages are inversely related to educational achievement.[18]

Before concluding this discussion, we should note some problems related to determining the impact of education on economic performance. Although it is generally recognized that human capital increases earnings, education also has a positive effect on the quality of life of educated persons and produces social benefits or "externalities" that exceed the benefits to individuals. For example, education improves the rate at which educated individuals are absorbed in productive work, their productivity and entrepreneurship, and the extent to which they contribute to technological progress by their ability to appropriate and improve on existing knowledge and technology.

The empirical research of the last thirty years generally supports the human-capital perspective, whatever the method used—whether growth accounting, rate of return, or productivity studies. One widely used measure of the productivity impact of education is a summary of more than thirty studies that concludes that four years of elementary education increases productivity on average by 8.7 percent.[19] A later study estimated that a 1 percent increase in agricultural college graduates raises productivity in that sector by about 10 percent.[20] Several nonagricultural productivity studies reached similar conclusions.[21] A 1993 summary of numerous rate-of-return studies by the World Bank for many countries also concluded that overall "the evidence . . . suggests that the economic payoff to education is high and remains sizable with economic growth, even as educational systems expand the supply of educated workers."[22]

Some critics of the human-capital approach concede the value of education but argue that empirical studies inflate rates of return because of the "screening" effects of schooling.[23] These analysts agree that employers pay higher salaries to educated workers, but, they argue, this is because of their innate aptitudes and behavioral traits, not solely or even mainly because their education makes them more productive.

While the screening hypothesis has some validity when it refers to schooling, it is less of a factor in productivity studies, or in studies that relate various outcomes to educational achievement instead of years of schooling. I am, moreover, very skeptical that educational attainment is due in any significant way to "innate ability." The evidence suggests that educational achievement is due mainly to supportive learning systems and hard work, not inherited intellectual abilities.[24]

Skill Requirements in a Changing Global Economy

The world economy has changed from one where the United States had enormous economic advantages to one in which we have serious disadvantages. Our advantages in the first two-thirds of this century were due to: (a) abundant natural resources; (b) economies of scale, made possible by a large internal market; and (c) supportive policies and institutions. Economies of scale were particularly important because they made it possible to greatly increase productivity and living standards. Thinking skills were required only for managerial, professional, and technical workers; the majority of workers needed only basic literacy to earn middle-class incomes. This system was sustained by policies to maintain economic growth, provide social safety nets, and support mass education and higher learning systems that were the envy of the world. Between 1945 and 1973, this American system produced the longest period of sustained and equitably shared prosperity in history.

Technological change and international competition changed all of this. Technology not only reduced the significance of natural resources, but also made less viable the hierarchical organization of work that characterized the mass-production system. New technology also eliminated the need for large plants and layers of supervision. Information technology, if used most effectively, is inherently democratizing and decentralizing and is best used by frontline workers at the point of production.

Technological change has, in addition, contributed to the internationalization of the American economy, and internationalization has made it much more difficult for countries to maintain full employment and economic growth by domestic policies alone. Countries, companies and people must now yield to the imperatives of global competition. The most basic of these imperatives, as we have noted, is that we can compete in only one of two ways: (a) reduce wages and income, or (b) increase productivity and quality. We can no longer rely on natural resources and economies of scale in domestic markets insulated from international competition.

Most high-income industrial countries have rejected the low-wage option because it creates lower and more unequal wages—which is exactly what the United States has experienced in the last twenty years. Wages in most other major industrialized economies have continued to increase and are now higher in those countries than they are in the United States. According to the most recent U.S. census data, developed by the Economic Policy Institute, the median hourly wage of men was 14 percent less in 1989 than it was in 1979. The only workers whose incomes had increased since 1979 were the college-educated. Young male high school graduates' earnings were 26.5 percent lower in 1991 than in 1979. Among all male college graduates, earnings increased only for those with advanced degrees; young male college graduates actually earned 5.1 percent less in 1991 than they did in 1979, with most of the drop coming after 1987. Men's gains in earning were significantly lower than those of women; between 1979 and 1991 real wages for high school dropouts declined 23.2 percent for men and 11.0 percent for women. For those with four years of college, earnings dropped 2.3 percent for men but rose 13.6 percent for women; for those with college plus two years, the gains were 10.2 percent for men and 13.2 percent for women. These improvements for women are relative, however, because women still earn considerably less than men, regardless of education. In 1991, for example, a woman at the eightieth earnings percentile was paid $13 an hour, only slightly more than the median $12.59 paid to a male in 1979, twelve years earlier.[25]

The U.S. experience illustrates why most other industrialized countries have rejected the low-wage option—they see that lower and more unequal incomes threaten their political, social and economic health. The only way for those following the low-wage option to improve total incomes is to work more, a reality that clearly limits economic progress.

The high-wage, high-productivity option, by contrast, is based on the substitution of ideas, skills, and knowledge for physical resources and therefore holds the promise of rapidly increasing personal, organizational, or national advancement.

High-Performance Organizations, High-Skill Workers

High-Performance Organizations

What must we do if we want to pursue the high-productivity option? Worldwide experience suggests that we must first develop a national consensus to follow that option and then support the policies and strategies to achieve it. The laissez-faire policies followed by the United States during the 1980s will lead inevitably to lower and more unequal real wages for most workers. National policies must create an environment that encourages companies to organize for high performance.

In a 1990 report, the Commission on the Skills of the American Workforce

(CSAW) found that relative to six other countries studied (Japan, Singapore, Germany, Sweden, Denmark, and Ireland), very few American companies have moved to the high-wage option.[26] This report was based on over 2,800 in-depth interviews of people at every level in 550 companies in a broad cross section of industries. Information from these interviews was supplemented with written material and interviews with numerous experts and public officials.

The CSAW found that 95 percent of major American companies cling to the mass-production organization of work. The commission also found that a much larger proportion of companies in the other countries studied are shifting to more competitive systems. The most successful companies in the United States and other countries share the following characteristics:

1. They are quality-driven and therefore establish closer and more cooperative relations with customers and suppliers. Quality, best defined as meeting customers' needs, becomes much more important in market-driven systems. Mass production systems, by contrast, are producer-driven and have more adversarial relations with suppliers, who are played off against each other through price competition.

2. They have lean management structures that promote horizontal cooperation, foster participative management styles, and decentralize decisions to the workplace. This contrasts with the hierarchical, segmented mass production approach to management that is more prevalent in the United States. Participative management systems improve quality, productivity, and flexibility by decentralizing decisions to frontline workers, whose responsibilities are broadened, thereby eliminating the need for supervisors and other indirect workers.

3. They stress internal and external flexibility to adjust quickly to changing technology and markets. The mass-production system seeks stability through rules, regulations, and contractual relationships. High-performance organizations achieve stability through quality, productivity, and flexibility.

4. The most successful enterprises likewise give high priority to positive incentive systems to relate rewards to desired outcomes. Such incentive systems are important because the efficient use of leading edge technology gives workers considerable discretion.[27] Mass-production systems stress negative (punishment and layoffs) or even perverse incentives that make it more difficult to achieve desired outcomes, as when workers believe improving productivity will cost them their jobs or some valued job benefits. Mass production hierarchical arrangements, fragmented work, and adversarial relations discourage the kind of cooperation required for high levels of quality and productivity. Positive incentives used by high-performance organizations include bonus compensation systems, job security, the ability to participate in decision making, and institutional arrangements that promote internal cohesion, fairness, and equity.

5.   High-performance organizations develop and use leading-edge technology through constant improvement on the job and by adapting advanced technologies produced elsewhere. They understand that standardized technologies are highly mobile and therefore imply competing mainly according to wages.

6.   These enterprises give heavy attention to education and training of frontline workers. The mass-production system stresses education and training mainly for managerial and technical workers. The most successful organizations know that higher-order thinking skills are required for high performance and the development and use of leading-edge technologies.

There also seems to be growing international consensus about the kinds of skills workers must have in high-performance workplaces. One of the most important of these is the ability to impose order on the mass of chaotic information made available by modern technology. This skill makes it possible to improve productivity and quality by seeing more effective ways to do things, discovering patterns and relationships, solving problems, and preventing or correcting defects. High-performance workers are more likely to work in groups and therefore must have the interpersonal skills to work in teams, communicate with precision, manage their own work, solve problems, deal with ambiguity, and think systematically. One of the most important skills frontline workers must have is the ability to learn using abstractions as well as through observation. As noted earlier, the mark of a high-performance organization is its focus on learning in order to develop the ideas, skills, and knowledge needed to innovate, improve productivity and quality, and adapt to changing markets, technologies, and work organizations.

7.   One of the most controversial aspects of high-performance production systems is the role of labor organizations. I am persuaded that high-performance systems work best when workers have an independent source of power. It is not a coincidence that businesses in other industrialized countries that are taking market share from American companies usually have stronger worker organizations, through works councils, other shop floor organizations, and trade unions. It is unlikely that workers will "go all out" to improve productivity unless they have the power to protect their interests. This is especially true in the transformation of traditional mass production systems where workers have feared that going all out to improve productivity might cost them their jobs. Workers understand, moreover, that unrestrained decision processes make it possible for managers to appropriate to themselves most of the productivity gains from high-performance systems. It is also difficult to maintain cooperative relationships between parties of unequal power. Sooner or later the stronger party will be inclined to assert unilateral control, ending the cooperative relationship, as happened with the so-called "employee representation plans" in the United States during the 1920s. Finally, labor–management relationships contain elements of both cooperation and conflict. Adversarial

relationships provide ways to resolve inherent differences; they are therefore both inevitable and functional. The trick, of course, is to prevent
conflict from making relationships so adversarial that all sides are worse
off. The greatest danger in the American setting is that a diminished right
of workers to organize and bargain collectively will, in the long run, make
positive incentive systems difficult to sustain.[28]

Will the Jobs of the Future Require Higher Thinking Skills?

There seems to be little question that education is highly correlated with positive
social and economic outcomes or that high-performance organizations require
higher-order thinking skills. There are, however, doubts that most jobs in the
United States will require significantly higher skills,[29] or that there is much that
can be done to cause schools to improve incomes.[30] With respect to the first
point, the critics are right: unless we adopt a high-productivity competitiveness
strategy, most jobs in the United States will not require much more than basic
literacy. As critics point out, most of the jobs being created in the United States
require only modestly higher intellectual skills, even though the highly skilled
jobs are increasing at a rapid rate.

There is, moreover, some confusion on the relationships between schools and
education achievement as defined here. Indeed, some who doubt the importance
of public expenditures to improve education often equate education and schooling. As I use the term, however, education refers to *educational achievement*, not
years of schooling. Because of the absence of national standards in the United
States, it is hard to know what years of schooling mean. Confusion is caused by
studies that declare that expenditures on schooling have not improved education
as measured by standardized test scores.[31]

There are several things wrong with these studies. The first is that standardized tests are a poor measure of thinking skills. Moreover, these studies rarely
control for things other than schooling that could affect test scores—especially
the number and characteristics of people taking the test, student motivation, and
family income. Studies also often have serious timing and identification problems. It
is commonly argued, for example, that expenditures on schooling during the 1980s
did not improve student performance. Some studies that make this claim use data
for, say, 1984, when the first round of 1980s reforms started in 1983—hardly long
enough to make a difference.[32] Actually, there were some impressive improvements
in student performance by 1990, despite seriously flawed assessment tools. Gains
were especially significant for minorities, who are not well served by the present
public school system. We should also note that many studies average poor schools
and good schools and conclude that schools do not make a difference.

What should be done is to assess student achievement by performance measures, much as is done with scout merit badges, and to learn how schools can be
restructured to improve student performance. We have numerous examples of

effective schools that have significantly improved student performance. One of my favorite examples is the work done by James Comer and his colleagues, at first in New Haven, Connecticut, and now in schools all over the United States.[33] By changing attitudes and school management, the Comer schools have achieved remarkable improvements in student achievement. The attitudinal changes involved demonstrating and convincing teachers, parents, and students that all students, however disadvantaged, can learn. This is particularly important for poor minorities, like those in Comer's original New Haven schools, where most students, teachers, and parents had been conditioned to expect that students would fail in school. Indeed, the myth that learning is due mainly to "innate abilities" is more prevalent in the United States than in most other countries where people understand that learning is due mainly to hard work and supportive learning systems. Comer's experience, and that of other behavioral and cognitive scientists have demonstrated the validity of the conclusion that "any student can learn."

The second major change by Comer and his colleagues was to make student achievement the schools' main objective and to organize the school to focus the efforts of parents, teachers, and child-development specialists on achieving that objective. The Comer schools' governing committee is chaired by the principal, who works with representatives of parents, teachers, and child-development specialists. This governing mechanism, which includes a high degree of parental involvement at every level in the school, is designed to overcome the cultural barriers between students and schools that often prevent students from understanding the schools' requirements and make it difficult for teachers to know how to help students learn. Comer's is one very successful model, but there are others.[34]

Unfortunately, most American schools lack uniform achievement standards and are still organized to mass-produce students with only basic literacy skills. Therefore, they do not necessarily produce educated students who can think. We have evidence, however, that schools can be restructured to give graduates higher-order thinking skills. The keys to restructuring are to make student achievement the main driving force, staff schools with highly professional teachers, administrators, and support workers, and reward student achievement. In other words, schools must become high-performance organizations. They must be restructured for much the same reason that traditional mass-production companies must be restructured. Indeed, the "scientific" management system developed in American companies during the early part of this century was applied as rigorously to American schools as it was to any industry.[35]

What Is to Be Done?

Principles

As noted earlier, CSAW found that enterprises in other countries were much more committed to high-performance work organizations than most of their

American competitors. Despite very different cultures and social systems, these other countries have adopted the same goals and strategies, though implementation varies widely. They all agree on the following fundamental principles:

1. National consensus-based policies are needed to actively promote high-performance work organizations that can maintain and improve incomes in a highly competitive global economy.
2. We must set high academic expectations for all young people, whether college-bound or not.
3. Well-developed school-to-work transition systems are necessary to provide young people with solid, recognized occupational skills.
4. Public labor-market organizations are needed to provide training, counseling, information, and placement services for all workers. The United States invests much less in employment and training policies than other countries. In 1987, for example, it invested only 0.9 percent of GDP on these programs compared with 5.9 percent in Denmark, 4.8 percent in Ireland, 3.7 percent in France, 4.2 percent in Sweden, and 3.2 percent in the U.K.[36]
5. These countries all value the skills of frontline workers very highly. Companies and governments are therefore strongly committed to providing lifelong training and employment opportunities to workers. While American companies spend only between 1 and 2 percent of payroll on training, two-thirds of which goes for management, companies in leading foreign countries spend up to 6 percent of payroll and devote a significant share to frontline workers. Less than 10 percent of American non–college-educated workers receive any formal training for work.

The commission did not analyze all of the reasons why so few American companies are pursuing the high-performance option, but the factors include:

1. Inertia has been fostered in the United States because traditional mass production systems and their supporting institutions were both more successful and more deeply entrenched here than elsewhere.
2. The United States has no national strategy to be a high-income country and therefore has not created incentives and disincentives for companies to make the necessary investments to become high-performance organizations. Indeed, our policies and financial institutions have discouraged such investments with high capital costs, limited social support services, uncertain and erratic economic policies, an ideological commitment to market forces, relatively unfettered business decision making, and an aversion to consensus-based public goals and strategies. Leaders in other countries have a greater sense of community and believe that companies that do not pay wages high enough to sustain workers and their families are being subsidized by governments or workers. These countries understand the

obvious importance of markets, but they also understand that markets must operate within the framework of policies and institutions to maintain order and equity as well as efficiency. As a consequence, in these countries collective bargaining and government regulations limit companies' ability to pursue low-wage options.

3.   We are especially handicapped by the absence of a coherent human resource development strategy to give frontline workers the kind of thinking and learning skills required for high-performance work organizations.

4.   American workers have less control over their working conditions than their counterparts in any other major industrial country. In other countries, workers are more likely to be covered by collective-bargaining agreements or to participate, by law or custom, in company decisions.

The United States still has some advantages in terms of work-force quality, but it also has serious disadvantages. It still has some of the world's leading public and private research institutions and the top 20 to 25 percent of its work force is world class. Its best higher-education institutions are world class, due in large part to some outstanding universities and graduate schools and to past successes, which gave the country the resources and intellectual environments to attract many of the world's leading scholars and scientists. American learning systems also provide opportunities for second chances for people who have failed at various stages in the education process, and some of the United States' leading companies have high-performance learning systems.

The United States' main disadvantages relate to the uneven quality of our colleges and universities, many of which have very poor standards for entry or graduation; the absence of effective mechanisms to commercialize scientific knowledge, which becomes a free good to foreign competitors who have adopted high-performance organizations and strategies and therefore have stronger incentives than most of their American competitors to commercialize basic research; and the poor quality of most of the United States' non-college learning systems. Families are the most basic learning systems, but a much larger proportion of American children live in poverty than is the case with most other developed democratic countries. And the United States alone among the major industrial countries has no family policy. Similarly, our elite schools are very good, but, as noted, most of our public schools are oriented toward mass-producing literates, not ensuring that all students have high-order thinking skills. And there are no uniform standards that *all* students are expected to meet. Schools therefore channel students into or out of the elite tracks at very early ages. And the United States probably has the weakest school-to-work transition system of any major country. Finally, as noted, most American companies do not provide education and training opportunities to frontline workers.

Recommendations

If the United States wants to remain a world-class, high-income country, it must build consensus for that outcome and develop the strategies to achieve it. It is naive to assume that these outcomes will result from "natural" forces or passive strategies. Unlike its major competitors, the United States has no process to facilitate consensus. Adversarial relations like ours focus attention on differences, however small; consensus processes focus on, and therefore encourage cooperation to achieve, common objectives.

In addition to developing consensus-building mechanisms, the United States should adopt macroeconomic policies to achieve a better balance between production and consumption by encouraging higher levels of investment in physical and human capital. It must, in addition, develop strategies to translate its world-class science into leading-edge commercial technologies. It needs an industrial extension service patterned after its fairly successful agricultural system to help enterprises, especially smaller businesses, adapt technologies to their needs.

To facilitate the development of a highly skilled work force needed for high-performance work organizations, CSAW advanced five major recommendations:

1. A new educational performance standard should be set for all students, to be met by age sixteen. This standard should be established nationally and benchmarked to the highest in the world. Students passing a series of performance assessments that incorporate this standard would be awarded a Certificate of Initial Mastery (CIM). Such a standard would provide greater incentives to students, better information to employers, and a way to provide success indicators for restructured schools. In other words, schools, like enterprises, must be high-performance organizations where much better educated and professional teachers are given positive incentives to improve student learning.

2. The states should take responsibility for assuring that virtually all students achieve the CIM. About 20 percent of our students drop out of high school. We cannot give up on these students because they will constitute one-third of our work-force growth during this decade. Through new local Employment and Training Boards, states—with federal assistance—should therefore create and fund alternative learning systems for those who cannot attain the CIM in regular schools. There are many examples of creative alternative learning systems at the local level—examples include the Job Corps and the Comprehensive Competencies Program developed by Remediation and Training, Inc. and U.S. Basics. Once these alternative learning systems are in place, children should not be allowed to work before the age of 18 unless they have attained the CIM or are enrolled in a program to attain it.

3. A comprehensive system of technical and professional certificates and

associates' degrees should be created for the majority (70 to 75 percent) of our students and adult workers who do not pursue a baccalaureate degree. The standards for these certificates and degrees should be defined by business, labor, education, and public representatives. These programs should combine general academic education with the development of occupational skills and should include a significant work component. All students should have financing for these programs. It would be a wise public investment to guarantee to everyone who had attained a CIM four years of education and training in accredited institutions. An alternative approach would be to provide postsecondary loans to be repaid as a surtax on earnings or through national service. This system could be patterned after the very successful GI Bill of Rights which provided education and training to millions of veterans after World War II.

4.   All employers should be given incentives and assistance to invest in the further education and training of their workers and to pursue high-productivity forms of work organizations. The commission proposed a system whereby all employers would invest at least 1 percent of payroll for this purpose. The Clinton administration proposed raising this requirement to 1.5 percent of payroll. Those who do not wish to participate would contribute to a general training fund. Public assistance should be provided to help employers move to high-performance work organizations.

5.   A system of Employment and Training Boards should be established by federal and state governments, together with local leadership, to organize and oversee the proposed school-to-work transition programs and training systems. These boards could consolidate many of the fragmented, incoherent, and largely ineffective councils and advisory committees that currently characterize many contemporary human-resource development activities. Two of the most important needs for improving the U.S. employment and training system are a simplified human-resource development infrastructure and a cadre of highly motivated human-resource professionals, particularly at the local level.

It is encouraging to see that the Clinton administration has adopted most of these recommendations. It is hoped that they will receive wide congressional and public support. I would add three additional recommendations:

1.   Labor laws should be reformed to remove the barriers workers face in organizing and bargaining collectively. And joint labor–management committees should have responsibility for occupational safety and health, training, and the administration of pensions and other employee benefits. Serious consideration should be given to mandating works councils in larger firms.

2. The federal government should establish a technical assistance program to

help companies reorganize for high-performance while wage, full employment, income support, tax, trade and other policies discourage low-wage competitiveness policies.
3.   A global strategy must be developed.

These recommendations would help make it possible for the United States to develop a decentralized, world-class, human-resource development and labor-market system. Workers, employers, students, and others interested in jobs would have a ready source of information and counseling from highly automated local labor-market offices staffed by highly qualified professionals. Such entities would greatly improve the effectiveness of other economic and social policies.

No one should assume, however, that even highly effective human-resource and labor-market policies could function, or even be developed, except as part of an overall high-productivity, high-wage economic strategy. Education, training, and labor-market systems alone will not guarantee enough growth to provide good jobs for all who would like to have them. Indeed, without growth, high-productivity strategies displace workers and contribute to rising unemployment.

There is thus a need for macroeconomic policies to promote job growth. Clearly, moreover, macroeconomic policies must be considered in an international context. There is a need to be concerned about much more job growth in an open and expanding global economy. It is particularly important for the United States and other developed countries to help stimulate growth in the developing countries, which offer great potential for increased demand. Indeed, it is fairly clear that transactions between the industrialized countries are unlikely to generate enough growth to prevent global stagnation.[37]

However, just as national and enterprise policies have to change to reflect the realities of a more competitive world economy, there must be a reexamination of international economic policies and institutions, and these must be based on more appropriate economic theories. Present international policies and institutions are rooted in the realities of the 1940s and 1950s and assume mainly national economies where international transactions were "second-order" considerations and where the United States could provide an international "engine of growth." These institutions and policies are not appropriate for a more dynamic, competitive, knowledge-intensive globalized world economy where international transactions are "first-order" considerations, and where no one country can be the engine of growth.

Comparative advantage, the dominant international trade theory, no longer provides an adequate guide for international economic policy. Comparative advantage assumed voluntary transactions mainly in final goods and services, not the mobility of whole companies, industries, and technologies. Under modern conditions, competitive advantage—with its emphasis on high-performance rather than low wages—is a much better concept. And all countries and international institutions should be encouraged to adopt high-productivity, high-wage strategies that could improve the conditions of people everywhere. A low-wage strategy, by contrast, will diminish the incomes of most people in high-wage countries like the United States, and could suppress the conditions of workers in countries like Mexico. It is in our interest for productivity and wages in Mexico and other developing countries to rise. Indeed, low-wage competition could be to the 1990s what a "beggar thy neighbor" tariff policy was to the 1930s. The United States should therefore follow the example of most other major industrialized countries and adopt a high-productivity strategy. We should also take the lead in urging this strategy on the GATT, IMF, the World Bank, regional trade agreements like NAFTA, and other international institutions.

Notes

1. Educational achievement can be measured in many ways. The typical approach in the United States has been to use standardized tests. However, there is growing consensus that performance assessments that measure ability to use knowledge are much better measures of achievement. Such measures are produced by the National Assessment of Educational Progress (NAEP). A more sophisticated system is being produced by the New Standards Project, sponsored by the National Center on Education and the Economy. See Ray Marshall and Marc Tucker, *Thinking for a Living: Education and the Wealth of Nations* (New York: Basic Books, 1992).

2. Ibid.

3. U.S. General Accounting Office, *Poor Preschool-Aged Children: Numbers Increase but Not in Preschool* (Washington, DC: Report no. GAO/HRD–93–111BR, July 1993).

4. Ray Marshall, *Losing Direction: Families, Human Resource Development, and Economic Performance, State of Families* series, vol. 3 (Milwaukee, WI: Family Service America, 1991).

5. Anthony Carnevale and Leila J. Gainer, *The Learning Enterprise* (Washington, DC: U.S. Department of Labor, 1989); Edward Denison, *Trends in American Economic Growth: 1929–1982* (Washington, DC: The Brookings Institution, 1985).

6. Quality Education for Minorities Project, *Education That Works*, report of the Action Council on Minority Education (Cambridge, MA: MIT, 1989).

7. James P. Comer, "Educating Poor and Minority Children," *Scientific American* (November 1988), 44–48; Quality Education for Minorities Project, *Education That Works*; Ray Marshall and Marc Tucker, *Thinking for a Living*.

8. Commission on the Skills of the American Workforce, *America's Choice: High Skills or Low Wages* (Rochester, NY: National Center on Education and the Economy, 1990); Lee A. Lillard and Hong W. Tan, *Private Sector Training: Who Gets It and What Are Its Effects?* (Santa Monica, CA: Rand Corporation, 1986).

9. Ray Marshall, *Unheard Voices: Labor and Economic Policy in a Competitive World* (New York: Basic Books 1987).

10. Commission on the Skills of the American Workforce, *America's Choice*; Ray Marshall and Marc Tucker, *Thinking for a Living*.

11. M. Edith Rasell and Lawrence Mishel, *Shortchanging Education: How U.S. spending on Grades K–12 Lags behind Other Industrial Nations*, Briefing paper for the Economic Policy Institute (Washington, DC: EPI, n.d.).

12. Robert M. Solow, "Employment Policy in Inflationary Times," in Eli Ginzberg (ed.), *Employing the Unemployed* (New York: Basic Books, 1980), pp. 129–42.

13. Robert J. Flanagan, David Soskice, and Lloyd Ulman, *Unionism, Economic Stabilization, and Incomes Policies: The European Experience* (Washington, DC: The Brookings Institution, 1983).

14. Ray Marshall, "Selective Employment Programs and Economic Policy," *Journal of Economic Issues* (March 1984): 117–42.

15. Lawrence Mishel and Jay Bernstein, "Declining Wages for High School and College Graduates," Economic Policy Institute Briefing Paper (Washington, DC: EIP, May 14, 1992).

16. Anthony Carnevale, *Human Capital: A High Yield Corporate Investment* (Washington, DC: American Society for Training and Development, 1983), pp. 8–9; Denison, *Trends in American Economic Growth: 1929–1982.*

17. Peter Drucker, *Managing for the Future: The 1990s and Beyond* (New York: Truman Talley Books, 1992).

18. Gordon Berlin and Andrew Sum, *Toward a More Perfect Union: Basic Skills, Poor Families and Our Economic Future* (New York: Ford Foundation, 1988).

19. Dean T. Jamison and Lawrence J. Lau, *Farmer Education and Farmer Efficiency* (Baltimore: Johns Hopkins Press, 1982).

20. Lawrence Lau and P.A. Yotopoulos, "The Meta-Production Function Approach to Technological Change in World Agriculture," *Journal of Development Economics, 31* (1989): 241–69.

21. William P. Fuller, "More Evidence Supporting the Demise of Pre-employment Vocational Trade Training: A Case Study of a Factory in India," *Comparative Education Review, 20* (1976): 30–41; Wei-Fang Min, "The Impact of Vocational Education on Productivity in the Specific Institutional Context of China," Ph.D. dissertation, Stanford University, 1987.

22. John Middleton, Adrian Ziderman, and Avril Van Adams, *Skills for Productivity* (New York: Oxford University Press, 1993).

23. E.S. Phelps (ed.), *Altruism, Morality and Economic Theory* (New York: Russell Sage Foundation, 1972); Paul Taubman and Terence Wales, "Higher Education, Mental Ability and Screening," *Journal of Political Economy, 81*, 1 (1973): 28–55; Joseph Stiglitz, "The Theory of Screening, Education, and the Distribution of Income," *American Economic Review, 65* (1975): 283–300.

24. Ray Marshall and Marc Tucker, *Thinking for a Living.*

25. Lawrence Mishel and Jay Bernstein, "Declining Wages for High School and College Graduates."

26. Commission on the Skills of the American Workforce, *America's Choice.*

27. Shoshona Zuboff, *In the Age of the Smart Machine* (New York: Basic Books, 1988).

28. Ray Marshall, *Unheard Voices.*

29. Ruy Teixeira and Lawrence Mishel, "Whose Skills Shortage—Workers or Management?," *Issues in Science and Technology* (Summer 1993), and by the same authors, *The Myth of the Coming Labor Shortage: Jobs, Skills and Incomes of America's Workforce 2000* (Washington, DC: Economic Policy Institute, 1991).

30. James S. Coleman, et al., *Equality of Educational Opportunity* (Washington, DC: U.S. Government Printing Office, 1966); James S. Coleman, Thomas Hoffer, and Sally Kilgore, *Public, Catholic, and Private Schools Compared* (New York: Basic Books, 1982); Christopher Jencks, et al., *Inequality: A Reassessment of the Effects of Family and Schooling in America* (New York: Basic Books, 1972).

31. John Chubb and Terry Moe, *Politics, Markets, and America's Schools* (Washington, DC: Brookings Institution, 1990).

32. Ibid.

33. James P. Comer, "Parent Participation in the Schools," *Phi Delta Kappan* (Febru-

ary 1989), 42–47; "Educating Poor and Minority Children," pp. 34–40; *School Power* (New York: The Free Press, 1980).

34. Edward B. Fiske, *Smart Schools, Smart Kids* (New York: Simon and Schuster, 1991); Ray Marshall and Marc Tucker, *Thinking for a Living*.

35. Raymond Callahan, *Education and the Cult of Efficiency: A Study of the Social Forces That Have Shaped the Administration of the Public Schools* (Chicago: University of Chicago Press, 1962).

36. Commission on the Skills of the American Workforce, *America's Choice*, p. 64.

37. John Sewall and Stuart Tucker (eds.), *Growth, Exports and Jobs in a Changing World Economy: Agenda 1988* (Washington, DC: Overseas Development Council, 1988).

7

Monetary Theory and Policy for the Twenty-first Century

L. Randall Wray

The theory that has guided monetary policy in most of the capitalist countries for the past several decades is flawed, and the adopted policies have had disastrous consequences. Orthodox monetary theory misunderstands the nature of money, the role money plays in the process of accumulation, the importance of accumulation for capitalist economies, and the role that monetary authorities should play in capitalist economies. As a consequence, orthodox monetary policy (based on flawed theory) has played a major role in the development of a long list of maladies infecting capitalist countries, including more than two decades of economic stagnation, with high unemployment and falling living standards in most of the developed countries; a series of increasingly worse recessions throughout the capitalist world; "deindustrialization" of some of the developed countries; devastating recessions (or depressions) in most of the developing countries; rising inequality both within and among countries; and high government deficits.

This chapter presents an alternative based on post-Keynesian endogenous money theory. In this approach, money is the social unit of account whose quantity increases as accumulation proceeds. The capitalist system requires accumulation, which takes the form of expansion of the money-denominated aggregate social measure of value. Because accumulation and growth of the "money supply" are inextricably linked, growth of money cannot be constrained without hindering accumulation. Tight money policy cannot slow the growth of money unless it disrupts the accumulation process. Indeed, tight money policy initially increases interest rates, inflation, and the rate of growth of the money supply as financial and nonfinancial institutions attempt to maintain rates of accumulation. However, higher interest rates produce a fragile financial system and tend to direct the pursuit of profit toward speculation. "Industry" suffers at the expense of "finance." Eventually, a crisis occurs that halts accumulation and lowers the rate of growth of the money supply, while inflation is reduced as the economy slows during the following recession. At this point, the central bank must act as a lender of last resort to set a floor to asset prices in order to prevent a debt deflation that could generate a depression.

We will also see that the endogenous money approach, when applied to international monetary policy, leads to the conclusion that the international financial system as presently designed generates stagnation in the world economy. The current policy is comprised of movement toward "free international trade" in conjunction with a movement toward "freely flexible exchange rates." This combination has contributed toward the development of stagnationist pressures for "real" economies throughout the globe even as it has fueled speculative "booms" and "busts" in world financial markets. Keynes's call for a fixed exchange rate system, for policies that would reduce international financial flows, and even for some protectionist policies is consistent with the endogenous money approach.[1]

The Orthodox Approach to National and International Money

Since the orthodox approach is well known, I only briefly outline its method and conclusions. Orthodoxy begins with individual utility maximization over *real* variables, achieved through self-interested barter of scarce resource endowments. Equilibrium is defined as a vector of relative prices that emerges through a tatonnement process operating in logical time (in which it is possible to move forward *and* backward through time) in the presence of perfect foresight. While rigorous orthodox analysis has not been able to identify any reason for the use of money in such a society, if money *is* used, its sole function is as a medium of exchange that lubricates the market mechanism.[2] Unfortunately for orthodox analysis, it does not seem to be possible to demonstrate that such an equilibrium price vector exists (much less that it would be stable or unique) once money is added to the model.[3] In spite of this, *all* orthodox analysis accepts as a matter of faith that money *must be* neutral in equilibrium; this means that introduction of money has no impact on the vector of relative (real) prices and quantities of marketed resources.[4] In other words, the behavior of agents of the neoclassical model is not influenced by *nominal* values, but only by real variables.

However, short-run non-neutrality of money is permitted in some orthodox models through the adoption of *ad hoc* assumptions. These include imperfect foresight, temporary fooling, menu costs, and transactions ("shoe leather") costs. It is important to note, however, that all orthodox economists recognize these "imperfections" as short-run phenomena that have no long-run impact. As such, the neoclassical *dichotomy* is maintained: that is, nominal variables cannot affect the long-run equilibrium price vector, which is determined solely by real variables. Long-run non-neutrality is rejected by all neoclassical economists as *irrational money illusion*. The only difference of opinion among orthodox economists on this score is with respect to the rapidity with which the economy moves to the equilibrium real price vector; the "new classicals" argue that the economy is always in long-run equilibrium, while "neoclassical Keynesians" believe that short-run non-neutrality of money may persist for significant periods.

Orthodox economists adopt an "exogenous money" approach in which money is theoretically exogenous and is exogenous in the control sense. A theoretically exogenous money supply is one that does not respond to the demand for loans. In other words, orthodox economists deny that banks would supply more money simply because borrowers wish to take out more loans in order to increase spending.[5] Orthodox economists emphasize a "money multiplier" approach to the supply of deposits, in which banks passively expand the money supply only when they find themselves with excess bank reserves. Exogeneity in the control sense applies to the case in which the central bank is able to control the money supply (including the private supply of money, such as bank deposits) through use of its three "tools": required reserve ratios, discount interest rates, and open market operations.[6] According to almost all orthodox economists (whether of monetarist or neoclassical Keynesian persuasion), the Federal Reserve (Fed) *could* hit monetary targets if it chose to do so through the manipulation of its tools; there is some difference of opinion, however, over whether this would be *good* policy and over whether the Fed has actually *tried* to do so in the past.

It is the difference of opinion regarding short-run non-neutrality that leads to some divergence among orthodox proposals for domestic monetary policy. The new classicals, emphasizing even short-run neutrality of money, argue that monetary policy has *no effect* on real variables, but only determines nominal prices. The old-style monetarists believe monetary policy may have short-run effects through temporary money illusion by agents that mistake nominal changes in prices for real changes. Both groups would advocate a simple money growth rate rule: let the money supply grow at a rate equal to the rate of growth of real output. This would then eliminate inflation according to both approaches, and would eliminate short-run fooling, according to monetarists. Finally, neoclassical Keynesians used to believe that the monetary authorities could exploit short-run non-neutrality through discretionary policy to "fine-tune" the economy. However, this view has very nearly disappeared due to the apparent inability of the Fed to fine-tune the U.S. economy during the 1970s. The overwhelming consensus among orthodox economists seems to be a monetary rule under which the central bank's monetary policy would target inflation, either directly (e.g., policy would "set" inflation at zero by continually adjusting "tightness" of policy in response to information regarding inflation) or indirectly (policy would set the rate of money growth at a rate believed to be consistent with zero inflation).[7]

The orthodox view of international money is similarly based on the real barter paradigm. If all relative prices were "free" to adjust instantaneously within all countries, an equilibrium *international* vector of relative prices would emerge from barter, with each country specializing according to the law of comparative advantage in order to take advantage of its unique national environment.[8] Again, rigorous analysis can find no reason to use money in the neoclassical model. However, if countries do adopt different national currencies based on a gold standard, we find again that addition of money to the neoclassical model has no impact on the equilibrium vector of real prices.[9] Under this *fixed exchange rate system* (each currency is made convertible into gold at a fixed rate; this means each is convertible into any other currency at a fixed ratio), a country that imported more than it exported would quickly lose gold reserves as its currency was converted into gold by foreign recipients. Such *short-run* trade deficits would be quickly rectified through the "specie-flow mechanism": the outflow of gold would cause its domestic money supply and prices to fall, lowering domestic wealth through the "real cash balance effect"; its imports would then fall and its exports would rise, quickly restoring a balance on its trade account. Orthodox *international* monetary policy would then simply advocate maintenance of fixed exchange rates and convertibility to gold on demand.

Some orthodox economists promote, instead, *freely flexible* exchange rates. The justification for this appears to be the recognition that in the "real world," domestic prices are not perfectly flexible.[10] This is true, according to some orthodox economists, especially in the case of wages. When nominal wages are rigid downward, if the marginal (revenue) productivity of labor measured in nominal terms falls below the nominal wage, then unemployment results *because* workers stubbornly refuse to accept lower nominal wages which are required merely to maintain constant *real* wages. Thus, rigid wages lead to domestic unemployment. However, perfectly flexible exchange rates can solve the problem associated with inflexible domestic nominal prices: if nominal domestic wages and other prices are too high, imports will rise (due to high *real* domestic incomes and prices relative to foreign incomes and prices at the going exchange rate) while exports fall (because domestic prices are too high); this results in a trade deficit. The trade deficit then forces a devaluation of the domestic currency, leading to lower domestic wealth and restoring balanced trade through the real cash balance effect previously described. In this sense, the flexible exchange rate is seen as an alternative to flexible domestic prices that will allow the economy to operate continuously at full employment even when wages are rigid. The appropriate international monetary policy in this case is laissez-faire: the domestic central bank merely ensures convertibility of the domestic currency on demand at the exchange rate determined by free market forces. The "invisible hand" of the international financial system eliminates the need for any international monetary policy coordination among central banks as international "free markets" achieve "efficient allocations" of all "scarce resources" (including credit) in the world economy at real prices established in the equilibrium relative price vector.

The Post-Keynesian View of Money

This necessarily brief introduction to orthodox analysis provides a useful coun-terpoint to the post-Keynesian approach to money. The main features of ortho-doxy include barter as the point of reference, the focus on "real" values, the dismissal of the importance of nominal values as irrational money illusion, and the *ad hoc* introduction of money as a medium of exchange. This then leads directly to domestic policy prescriptions that emphasize control of money and/or inflation, and to international policy prescriptions that emphasize free markets and flexible exchange rates. In contrast, post-Keynesian theory begins with money as a *unit of account*; it insists that production for market is always *mone-tary production*; it emphasizes uncertainty and denies that money can *ever* be neutral in an economy that operates in *historical* time, and it calls for active domestic and international monetary policy.

The neoclassical preoccupation with barter is historically inaccurate and logi-cally flawed.[11] Money was not injected into a well-functioning barter economy as a medium of exchange that lubricates the market mechanism. Rather, the necessary existence of uncertainty in an economy that operates in historical time that proceeds in one direction only (from the irreversible past to the unknowable future) leads to the use of monetary contracts as the development of private property results in individual responsibility for one's welfare. While it is cer-tainly true that uncertainty existed before private property, it would not lead to the use of money or market exchange. This is because the development of private property destroys the collective security of tribal or command society and generates "existential uncertainty" for individual households, who then attempt to accumulate a surplus (mainly in the form of grain reserves) in order to survive adverse periods. In contrast, under tribal or command societies, the accumulated surplus would be divided among members according to well-established rules of reciprocity and redistribution—in other words, members of these societies face only "collective uncertainty" that the collective reserves, distributed according to societal rules, will not be sufficient to see them through bad times.[12] In contrast, members of the private property economy will survive adverse conditions only if their individual reserves are sufficient, or *if they can borrow reserves from other individual households*.

However, any household that lends a portion of its, say, wheat reserves to the borrowing household faces the possibility that it might need these reserves *be-fore* the borrower can "repay" the loaned wheat. This is why all private loans must include interest; thus, any private loan of reserves must take the form of "wheat now for more wheat later." As Keynes correctly observed, any contract of this sort *is a monetary contract*, which necessarily includes interest as part of its "money now for more money later" proposition.[13] The key role played by "money" in this contract is as a unit of account, or, as the terms in which the contract is written. At first, this would be in "wheat terms" (a bushel now for a bushel and a half at the end of the harvest). Indeed, *all* the early units of account *were* wheat units; later, barley units were substituted due to the uniform size of barley grains.[14] In fact, *all* monetary units of account (whether the English pound, the Italian lira, or the French livre) were *weight* units until quite recently, reflecting their origins in the early development of wheat and barley units as the terms in which private contracts were written.[15]

Money thus developed first as a unit of account in which the terms of private debts are standardized once private property is developed and loans become possible. The money of account is developed *before* market exchange—developed, that is, prior to the use of money as a medium of exchange. In the next section, we will return to the development of production for markets, which evolves with the creation of the medium of exchange function of money. However, at this point it is important to note that the forward contract that is created when one promises to deliver "more money later" requires that one discharge one's debt at the later date. This can be done either by actually delivering "more wheat" later or by delivering something with equivalent value in terms of wheat. Once we have the development of a standard money of account, it becomes possible to deliver "more money later" in the form of a *means of payment* rather than in physical wheat terms. This can be much more convenient and can reduce transactions costs.

In other words, suppose you have obtained "wheat now" on the promise of "more wheat later" by writing an IOU that will be held by the lender until you are able to discharge your debt. However, rather than actually delivering "more wheat later," you deliver another *third-party IOU* (that is, an IOU that has been issued by a third party—neither by you nor by your creditor) whose money-denominated value is exactly sufficient to discharge your debt. In this case, if your creditor is willing to accept the third-party IOU, it functions as a *means of payment* that allows you permanently to discharge your debt (so that you may destroy your IOU). This brings us to the second historical "function" of money: means of payment that allow one to meet the terms of a forward contract and discharge one's debt.

Privately issued third-party liabilities could act as means of payment so long as they were accepted by creditors. Generally, this required either that the creditors knew and trusted the issuers of these IOUs, *or* that the IOUs were "endorsed" by wealthy, credit-worthy individuals who promised to place their own nominally valued wealth at risk should the issuer default. This brings us to three essential functions that must be fulfilled in any economy that uses forward contracts: a *witness* is required to verify contract terms, an *endorser* is needed to reduce default risk, and an *enforcer* is needed to ensure that debtors do not voluntarily abrogate contractual commitments. While governmental and quasi-governmental agencies have played all these roles, the first two roles have been more frequently performed by private agents (who even, on occasion, perform the enforcer role).

Obviously, however, uncertainty involved in private forward contracts can never be eliminated completely; even endorsed liabilities involve uncertainty because the *endorser* might also default. In order to increase the ability of privately issued third-party liabilities to circulate as means of payment, they could be made convertible *on demand* into other money-denominated assets. Thus, if a holder of the liability became worried about the economic situation of the issuer, the holder could demand conversion into another money-denominated asset. This would require that the issuer hold *reserves* of the asset into which conversion was required. For example, the issuer (or the endorser standing behind the issuer) would hold money-denominated liabilities issued by the most credit-worthy members of society as reserves that would allow the issuer to "liquidate" position by substituting the reserve asset on demand for the issuer's liabilities.

All money-using private property economies develop a "pyramidal" debt structure in which liabilities lower in the pyramid are made convertible on demand into liabilities higher in the pyramid; as we move higher in the debt pyramid, perceived credit-worthiness rises.[16] For example, in a debt pyramid in a modern capitalist economy the debt of households would be at the bottom of the pyramid; this must normally be endorsed by agents higher in the pyramid before it is accepted. Somewhat higher in the pyramid we would find small and medium sized firms; again, their debt (for example, paper representing accounts receivable) would be endorsed by agents standing above them in the pyramid. Commercial banks are the primary endorsers of the debt of smaller firms. Large firms would be found even higher in the pyramid, with their debt endorsed by commercial and investment banks. Still higher, we would find various types of banks, whose debt is backed by, and made convertible into, central bank and government liabilities. Finally, governmental (e.g., Treasury) and quasi-governmental (e.g., Fed) liabilities are found at the top of the pyramid.

While we don't have space to go into the details, it is interesting to note that historically, government debt *was not* at the apex of the debt pyramid; indeed, government debt normally was not accepted without *private* endorsements until quite recently.[17] Instead, for most of the period since the private invention of the money of account, governments could not issue money-denominated liabilities. Unlike privately issued credit money (which was nothing more than a money-denominated debt), until recently, government money had to take the form of *precious metal coin*, or, commodity money. The value of this commodity money would be determined by its weight equivalent to the wheat money unit of account. For example, the early money of account used in Babylonia was the *mina*, equivalent in weight to 10,800 grains of wheat.[18] A *mina* of gold coins would thus have to weigh the equivalent of a *mina* of wheat—or, 10,800 grains of wheat.

Due to the relative scarcity of gold, governments would try to *debase* coin—that is, to mix common metals with gold so that more coins could be stamped per pound of gold. However, debased coin would then lose value relative to the money of account because private agents became quite adept at detecting debased coin.[19] Since a debased coin is really government debt (for example, if a quantity of gold coins that is purported to be worth a *mina* only contains half a *mina* of gold, half of its purported worth is nothing more than debt), it can circulate at nominal value *only* if private agents will accept government debt. In this case, the debased coin is said to be "fiat money" because its "real" value in terms of gold is less than its stated nominal value. For the most part, however, government debt was not acceptable, thus, (most) governments were not able to issue fiat money until very recently.

This brings us to an interesting point: in some sense, private IOUs have *always* been "fiat"—denominated in the money of account, with their value fixed in nominal terms *so long as their holders believed issuers and/or endorsers were credit-worthy*. On the other hand, governments could not issue fiat money, but instead had to rely on commodity money. The commodity money gradually evolved into the riskless representation of the social unit of account. Thus, the wheat and barley units were eventually replaced by a precious metal weight equivalent—usually a gold weight unit, such as the Roman pound. In fact, the gold pound unit of account was adopted almost universally throughout Europe. It eventually became the ultimate reserve at the very apex of the pyramid of liabilities—that is, the "mono-reserve."

The gold standard was adopted by many countries both domestically and internationally. This would allow each domestic unit of account to have a fixed exchange rate in terms of gold, *and* in terms of foreign units of account. This facilitated international trade by making domestic IOUs convertible at known exchange rates into foreign moneys. Note that this arrangement was *not* necessitated by the use of different *coins* among countries, for the value of coins was easily determined by gold content. It is because most transactions take place in *privately issued* money denominated assets in a variety of national units of account that the gold standard became necessary. The gold standard, in fact, was not the first attempt to establish an international standard of value; there had previously been experiments with "ghost monies" or "giro monies" which were *international* pound units of account into which domestic units of account were converted at fixed exchange rates.[20] These ghost monies (so called because no coins were denominated in them) would be used internationally to clear accounts among agents operating in different countries. For example, if a Florentine merchant had a net claim on a Parisian merchant, this could be cleared using the books of the Bank of Amsterdam which offered clearing house payment services in terms of a ghost money of account.

The first central banks were established to provide government finance; as mentioned above, governments were constrained in their ability to borrow and could not issue fiat money.[21] One of the earliest central banks was the Bank of England, specifically created to buy the debt of the English Crown so that it could conduct a war with France. The Bank of England would issue notes denominated in a sterling pound unit of account (a "fiat" money) to finance its position in Crown debt. This essentially allowed the Crown to *indirectly* issue money-denominated IOUs; it must be emphasized, however, that the Bank of England was doing nothing out of the ordinary when it issued pound-denominated notes—all private banks could "create money" by issuing notes denominated in the social unit of account whenever they made loans (bought the IOUs of "borrowers"). It was only the Crown that could *not* issue pound-denominated IOUs and that was constrained by the amount of gold it could obtain for coinage. This arrangement seems exceedingly strange to the modern reader because the government is seen as the most credit-worthy borrower (thus, can issue money-denominated IOUs)—but the situation was precisely the reverse until the nineteenth century.

The Bank of England, however, was given several advantages over other private banks; the most important was the monopoly right of note issue in London.[22] In England, private banks outside London ("country banks") already pyramided reserves on London—in other words, they made their IOUs convertible on demand into London bank notes. When all London banks save the Bank of England were prohibited from issuing notes, it became quite natural to make country bank notes convertible into Bank of England notes. Eventually, the Bank of England became the preferred *reserve bank*, with its liabilities serving as the ultimate reserve for the liabilities of all other private banks. As such, a *mono-reserve* system was created with the liabilities of the Bank of England serving as the reserve for all private banks.[23] Under the gold standard, the Bank of England liabilities were then made convertible into gold; gold, then, was the ultimate reserve at the apex of the debt pyramid. The Bank of England became the *central bank*—all capitalist countries developed a similar arrangement with a central bank at the top of the pyramid.

As mentioned, the problem with privately issued liabilities is that their issuer might default; furthermore, even if these are endorsed, the endorser might also default. Indeed, a *run* on liabilities (that is, widespread attempts to convert liabilities) that are lower in the pyramid can lead to a "snowball" effect that moves up through the pyramid as each agent that is lower calls on its endorser that is higher. These, in turn, call on *their* endorsers. Ultimately, the central bank is called upon to provide its liabilities on demand to its correspondents that are lower in the pyramid so that their liabilities can be converted into central bank liabilities. If the central bank provides its liabilities through loans, it is engaging in the *lender of last resort* function; this is ultimately the only way to stop a run that has snowballed upward through the debt pyramid as all who hold private liabilities attempt to convert them into debts higher in the pyramid. In a panic, only central bank liabilities (or gold) will do.

After the creation of central banks, it took several centuries to understand that they *should* act as lenders of last resort.[24] This is because it is not obvious that the central bank should behave in this manner because it appears that this would be against the interest of the central bank. Narrow self-interest would appear to dictate that the central bank should actually refuse to lend whenever there is a run on private banks lower in the pyramid precisely because these are facing financial difficulty. (No private agent relishes lending to those who are on the verge of bankruptcy.) And, in fact, the Bank of England would cut off lending whenever a run developed during its first two centuries of existence; this would virtually ensure that private banks would not be able to convert their liabilities into central bank liabilities. They would then be forced to close their doors—which would often fuel the panic. However, by the late nineteenth century it was recognized that central banks *must* provide their reserves without limit during such panics in order to stop runs.

This conflicted with the gold standard itself; if the central bank's liabilities were convertible into gold, then it would be unable to issue liabilities without fear that a run might develop to convert *its* liabilities into gold. Since gold reserves would be limited, the central bank might be forced to suspend convertibility once its reserves were depleted. Indeed, countries invariably went off the gold standard during financial crises to protect gold reserves. The discovery of the lender of last resort function greatly enhanced the stability of domestic financial systems because a run could be stopped if the central bank provided reserves without limit. Similarly, abandoning the gold standard removed the last obstacle to stopping domestic financial panics as it made it possible to provide central bank liabilities without limit. However, as we shall see, this does not prevent the possibility of an *international* run on a country's liabilities.

The Post-Keynesian View of Monetary Production

Unlike the orthodox story that begins with markets based on barter, post-Keynesians emphasize that money exists once private property develops, *before* production for market. Indeed, markets are not viewed as the place where one barters for needed items; rather, the market is the place where one obtains the means of retiring debts—that is, money-denominated means of payment. Production for market is undertaken not to barter, but to obtain money, and not to satisfy "needs" but to satisfy the desire to accumulate wealth in money form. Production is not undertaken by a Robinson Crusoe–type agent who is both a producer and consumer; instead there are those who own private property, and those who do not—and so must work for wages. The existence of propertyless workers extends market demand, and extends the use of money as a *medium of exchange*. The capitalist employer must hire workers to produce the goods that will be sold on markets; since production takes time, wages must be paid *now* before sales receipts can be realized *later*. These sales receipts are uncertain; this means that capitalist production will be undertaken only on the expectation that profits will be realized to compensate the capitalist for the possibility that sales receipts will not be sufficient to cover costs. Thus, capitalist production always involves "money now for more money later" propositions.

Typically, capitalist production begins with the issue of money denominated liabilities that allow the capitalist to obtain media of exchange used to pay wages. The primary medium of exchange used for wage payments during the nineteenth century took the form of bank notes; today, it is in the form of bank deposits. Banks issue these liabilities as they purchase the short-term IOUs of firms (making "loans" to them of bank liabilities, which are used to pay wages). Workers use these media of exchange primarily to buy the commodities that are the result of capitalist production; thus, capitalists receive the bank liabilities as sales receipts, allowing them to use these as means of payment to discharge their own IOUs. At this point, the banks receive their own liabilities; they "destroy" them much as you would destroy your IOU when you repay a debt.

Because of uncertainty, all privately issued money-denominated liabilities must pay interest; as mentioned previously, the amount of interest depends on the existential uncertainty faced by the holder of the liability. Due to this uncertainty, individuals have a preference for liquidity—liquidity preference determines the interest rates that must be paid on liabilities. It is beyond the scope of this chapter to go into this in detail, except to note that the liquidity of any particular money-denominated liability depends on a number of factors. The two most important concern the existence of good secondary markets (so that liabilities can be sold—"liquidated"—easily) and the "orderliness" of these markets (defined as stability of the price of the liabilities). If a money-denominated liability has good secondary markets that permit sale at any time at a price that does not fluctuate much, it is said to be liquid. For example, a short-term Treasury bill in the United States is highly liquid because it can be sold almost immediately at a price that does not change much from day to day. In an uncertain world, holding liquid assets is always desirable as a hedge against unfavorable events because they can be sold to allow one to meet debt obligations or to obtain media of exchange that allow one to purchase commodities. The more liquid a liability, the lower the interest rate it must pay to induce someone to hold it.

Since all private money-denominated forward contracts must include interest, and because contracts are always of the nature of "money now for more money later," all such contracts will grow over time in nominal value at a rate determined in part by the rate of interest.[25] This was summarized in an alternative manner in Marx's famous formulation, $M–C–M'$. The capitalist begins with a bank loan (M) to produce commodities (C) that will be sold in markets; because of uncertainty and promised interest, this will be undertaken only on the expectation of realizing "more money" (M') in the form of sales receipts; this means that M must exceed M' by enough to pay interest and to leave a net profit for the capitalist. This then generates a *logic of accumulation*: all monetary economies must grow because the M' *later* must be greater than the M today.[26]

According to this view, money can never be neutral; indeed, it is not too far from the truth to say that money is the objective of economic activity and that nominal values matter while real values do not. This is not due to money illusion. Because of uncertainty, all forward contracts are written in money terms. The money of account becomes the *social* measure of wealth; it is the universal measure of success and the representation of social value. Now, of course, it is true that consumers care about their *real* standard of living (as measured by the quantity of widgets consumed); however, the object of production from the perspective of those who make the decisions to undertake production (the capitalists) is *never* to produce widgets but instead to realize sales receipts in the form of money-denominated assets. Production is always "money now on the expectation of more money later."

However, production of real goods (e.g., widgets) is not the only path to "more money later." One might purchase financial assets rather than purchasing widget-producing machines and hiring labor. If financial assets are expected to generate greater money-denominated returns than are expected to be realized from widget production, then capitalist "money" will be directed toward financial assets rather than toward real capital assets. This, according to post-Keynesians, is primarily a function of the degree of liquidity preference. When uncertainty is high, resulting in high liquidity preference, the estimated returns to highly liquid financial assets will exceed the expected returns to real capital assets. In this case, production of physical capital falls, lowering employment and aggregate wages. This can then cause falling aggregate effective demand, through the process known as the Keynesian multiplier.

Financial assets generate returns in three ways.[27] First, they explicitly promise to pay an interest rate; second, they may be expected to rise in price, generating capital gains for their holder; and third, they generate a *subjective* return, liquidity, to their holder that is valuable in an uncertain world. In contrast, real, physical capital rarely is expected to generate capital gains and is normally exceedingly illiquid. This is because capital assets cannot be sold readily in secondary markets because of their firm-specific nature; furthermore, the value of such assets depends almost solely on the expected sales receipts to be realized from the sale of the commodities produced by the capital (e.g., from sales of widgets). It was Keynes's proposition that the expected return to capital must exceed that to financial assets before it can be produced. As he said, the return to liquidity ("the interest rate") sets the minimum standard that must be achieved by *all* assets. When liquidity preference is high, the return to liquidity is high so that it becomes unlikely that new capital assets will be produced because their expected receipts cannot compete with the notional return to liquid assets. This is why Keynes argued that a high interest rate inhibits investment, lowering aggregate demand and creating unemployment.

The Post-Keynesian View of the International Financial System

As discussed above, each domestic economy develops a money of account in which each debt within the pyramid of liabilities is denominated. Some of these debts then function as the means of payment, used to discharge liabilities. Normally, one uses the debt issued by someone *higher* in the debt pyramid to discharge one's own debt (the rules of the game prohibit use of one's own liabilities to discharge one's debts; this is why one must use third party liabilities to do so).[28] Some liabilities also circulate as media of exchange, used to hire labor and to purchase commodities and assets. Somewhat surprisingly, over time there has been substantial *narrowing* of the range of liabilities that would circulate as means of payment and media of exchange to those issued by agents high in the pyramid.[29] Thus, while bills of exchange served as the primary medium of exchange and means of payment until the late nineteenth century (with bank notes playing a smaller role, and bank deposits playing almost no role), by the twentieth century, bank deposits became predominant.

This narrowing can be explained by recognizing that although each liability in the pyramid is denominated in the unit of account, each varies in its perceived liquidity. This means that each may pay a different interest rate to compensate its holder for giving up some liquidity; only the asset at the apex of the pyramid is fully liquid and need not pay interest. In a central bank mono-reserve system, only central bank liabilities are fully liquid so that they may necessarily avoid paying interest. A liability that promises to pay, say, $100 a year hence is thus worth only, say, $90 today—the purchaser would pay $90 now and would expect to receive $100 in a year; the expected yield over the year would be $10, so the interest rate would be approximately 11 percent on this liability. The *spot price* of this liability on secondary markets would be $90, while the *forward price* would be $100—the difference between spot and forward price is, again, a function of liquidity preference and the liquidity of this particular liability. If the economic position of the issuer of this liability worsened, there would be fear that the issuer might default before delivering the $100 at the end of the year. This would cause the spot price to fall, say, to $75, so that any secondary-market purchaser would receive interest of $25 (rather than $10) to compensate for the greater likelihood that the issuer might default.

If the spot price of a money-denominated liability can fall before payment comes due, it obviously will not make a good means of payment or medium of exchange. If you are a worker, you do not want to be paid in the form of liabilities that might fall in value *relative to the money of account* before you can use these as media of exchange to buy widgets. This is why money-denominated liabilities that have *fixed spot prices* measured in terms of the unit of account are preferred as means of payment and media of exchange. Again, we are now so accustomed to using bank demand deposits as our medium of exchange that we find it difficult to imagine a society that uses media of exchange that fluctuate in value relative to the unit of account. A *dollar* bank demand deposit is *always* worth a dollar in the United States today; its spot price is always one; it always exchanges *at par* against the dollar unit of account. But this has not always been the case. During the nineteenth century, the bank notes issued by U.S. banks fluctuated in value relative to the dollar of account and relative to one another; a "dollar" bank note issued by Bank X might be worth a two "dollar" note issued by Bank Z and only worth half a dollar unit of account. When spot prices of bank liabilities fluctuated, they were no different from other privately issued liabilities; on this score, thus, they were *not* the preferred medium of exchange. However, all modern capitalist countries eventually adopted a system in which at least some bank liabilities are *guaranteed* to exchange at par against the unit of account; these then become the dominant medium of exchange.

How can this guarantee be made? The primary method by which spot prices of bank liabilities are fixed is through the willingness of the central bank to act as lender of last resort for the banking system. Because central bank liabilities are *perfectly liquid*, their spot price is always one; so long as the central bank promises to substitute its liabilities on demand for those of banks, bank liabilities can also maintain spot parity with the unit of account. This is why guaranteed bank liabilities need not pay interest—others will hold them because their spot price is one.

Such a system greatly enhances the use of forward contracts that are required for capitalist production. Workers are always willing to accept bank deposits as the form in which wages are paid because they know these will maintain parity; retailers are also willing to accept these in payment for widgets for similar reasons. Agents are willing to write long term contracts that deliver "money" today on the promise of "more money" at some distant date in the future, knowing that the "money" to be delivered on that date (almost always in the form of a bank liability) will exchange at par against the social unit of account. The importance of this fact can be driven home if one realizes how difficult it would be to write such contracts if one could not know the value of the "money" against the dollar on that future date.

And this is precisely the problem faced in international trade under flexible exchange rates. If the value of the dollar fluctuates against the pound sterling, it becomes very difficult for the American importer to write a forward contract with an British exporter in terms of a unit of account that is stable—indeed, it generally will not be possible to write a contract that is stable in terms of *both* the dollar unit and the pound unit. We need not go into the various "derivative" instruments that are designed to hedge such contracts in order to protect the importer and exporter from unfavorable exchange rate movements. However, it is now well-recognized by post-Keynesian observers that these attempts actually *increase* the volatility of exchange rates, making it even more difficult to protect parties to forward contracts from the negative effects of flexible exchange rates![30]

As a joke, economists often say "if it moves, differentiate it"—a reference to the neoclassical marginal analysis. The real world counterpart aphorism is: if its price moves, profit seekers will speculate against it. Fluctuating exchange rates open profit opportunities for those who can predict better than the "average opinion" which way an exchange rate will move. Post-Keynesian theory, and real-world experience, show that speculation itself is *destabilizing*—causing exchange rates to fluctuate wildly. This makes it difficult to write forward contracts by greatly increasing uncertainty involved in international trade. As a result, by the early 1990s, many observers believed that fully 90 percent of international financial flows had nothing to do with circulation of *goods*; that is, these flows represent speculative and hedging behavior as agents attempt to take advantage of, or protect themselves from, exchange rate movements.[31]

Furthermore, fluctuating exchange rates have consequences for national monetary policy. No country can tolerate rapid depreciation of its currency, which can be brought about through speculative and hedging activity. First, rapid depreciation raises the price of foreign goods, causing domestic inflation. Second, rapid depreciation of a currency will cause a run out of that nation's liabilities—causing a "debt deflation"—a rapid fall in the spot prices of its liabilities. This is because foreign holders must calculate the value of these liabilities in terms of their own unit of account; if the domestic currency is falling in value relative to the money of account of the foreigner, then the value of that liability must also fall. This can then lead to a run out of the liabilities of the country facing currency depreciation, causing the currency to depreciate even faster—fueling the run. An international run out of a nation's liabilities is very similar to a domestic run out of bank liabilities in terms of causes and consequences. Third, the possibility of currency appreciation/depreciation and resulting capital gains/losses must be incorporated in the expected returns of foreign assets that go to determine asset prices. A liability denominated in a unit of account that is expected to depreciate must carry a yield high enough to compensate for the depreciation. In other words, the interest rates of countries whose currencies might depreciate must be higher, which can have the depressionary effects discussed earlier regarding high interest rates on aggregate effective demand and employment.

International runs and debt deflations can be solved in the same manner that countries have eliminated *domestic* runs and deflations: through lender of last resort operations. For example, assume that a run develops on Italian liabilities that are held by foreigners due to expected depreciation of the lira against the dollar. The foreigners want to exchange lira-denominated liabilities for dollar-denominated liabilities. The Italian central bank can try to stop this run by agreeing to substitute dollars for lira; however, because its dollar reserves are limited, it may soon find that it cannot meet the demand for dollars. At this point, if the Fed will step in and lend dollars *without limit* to the Italian central bank, it can stop the run. It will also be able to stop depreciation of the lira, which eliminates the speculation against the lira.

The problem with the current international financial system is that it does not have an *international* lender of last resort willing to stabilize exchange rates. Thus, while a mono-reserve system with a central bank at the apex has evolved for domestic economies, we have not been able to develop a similar system for the international economy. As we shall see in the final section, Keynes called for something like an international central bank. However, his plan was not adopted. Instead, the roles that should be played by a central bank were shared, ineffectually, by the Fed, the International Monetary Fund (IMF), the World Bank, and other strong central banks. This system has not served us well, particularly since 1973 when the Bretton Woods system fell apart.

Before we turn to policy proposals, we should note that the international system, like the domestic system, requires three essential features:

1. A fixed exchange-rate system: In the domestic economy, all liabilities are denominated in a universal unit of account; certain liabilities are then guaranteed spot parity. In the international economy, while each country will use its own unit of account and will decide which liabilities will have parity, it is necessary that each central bank's liabilities maintain parity against all others.
2. An accommodative mono-reserve system: In the domestic economy, the central bank stands at the apex, providing reserves through loans to banks so they may clear accounts. In the international financial system, an international and elastic reserve is required for clearing among central banks.
3. A lender of last resort: In the domestic financial system, the central bank stands ready to provide reserves without limit as necessary to stop debt deflation. The international economy needs a lender of last resort for similar reasons.

Conclusions: Monetary Policy for the Twenty-first Century

The orthodox approach, as discussed earlier, emphasizes the medium of exchange function of money, central bank control over the money supply, and the role of money in determining inflation. Thus, domestic monetary policy should be directed toward minimization of inflation, and international monetary policy should be based on laissez-faire and free-market determination of exchange rates. Orthodox monetary policy has been closely followed in the domestic sphere since 1979 (although orthodox policy experiments began in the mid-1960s), and in the international sphere since 1973.[32] In both spheres, it has been disastrous. This is because orthodox policy is based on a theory that has no room for money—thus, that is inapplicable to our world.

Periodic attempts to "control money" in order to "fight inflation" have led to a series of credit crunches in the U.S. economy, to rising trend unemployment (unemployment never falls to the levels achieved before monetarist experiments, even at business cycle peaks), to rising trend interest rates (known as the "ratchet effect"), and to falling rates of productivity growth. The monetarist policy experiment that began in 1979 is the best example; its results included the worst recession since the Great Depression, record interest rates, the saving and loan industry crisis, and loss of U.S. international competitiveness. In the international sphere, flexible exchange rates have led to speculative booms and busts of exchange rates; laissez-faire has generated trade imbalances that compound the problems associated with flexible exchange rates. The only orthodox proposal to deal with trade deficits has been to impose austerity on domestic economies to impoverish the population sufficiently that it cannot afford imports. However, because of world aggregate demand effects, these policies are generally ineffective because depressed international aggregate demand lowers the *exports* of the deficit countries even as it lowers their imports.[33] Instead, orthodox policy prescriptions have led to a stagnant international economy even as some countries (such as the United States) continually run trade deficits.

Our alternative view has stressed the unit of account function of money, the nature of monetary production, and the role of the central bank at the apex of the debt pyramid. In this view, money has no direct relation to inflation of the prices of *current* output, and the central bank has no direct control over the "money supply" or over inflation.

Rather, money is the unit of account in which liabilities are denominated and the only "price" the central bank can influence is the *floor* price of liabilities. By standing ready to substitute its liabilities for any other, it can always set the minimum spot price of a liability at par with the unit of account. Thus, the lender of last resort sets price floors to assets, which can eliminate debt deflation. This then can indirectly influence investment by helping to keep interest rates low (a price floor on liabilities helps to maintain something of a ceiling on interest rates), which maintains a low standard return to be achieved by capital assets. The only way the central bank can impact "inflation" of the prices of current output is by pushing interest rates higher, lowering investment (the production of capital assets), raising unemployment, and causing aggregate demand to falter. But even this may not halt inflation unless it causes a recession so severe that firms decide that further price increases would negatively affect demand more than they would increase profits.[34]

The primary purpose of domestic policy, then, should be to set asset price floors and prevent debt deflation. Low interest rates are encouraged if the central bank's provision of reserves takes place at a low discount rate; this, in turn, can stimulate aggregate demand. The primary problem with accommodation and lender of last resort activity, however, is that it might remove "market discipline" in some cases. If depositors of a bank know that the central bank will not allow the bank to default on its liabilities, they needn't worry about the assets purchased by the bank; in some situations, bank management might then make excessively risky loans. If the central bank always intervenes to prevent failure, profit-seeking agents will take this into account and may behave in a risky manner, knowing the central bank will bail them out. This "absence of market discipline" argument is frequently carried much too far, but it does incorporate an element of truth. This is why a central bank that sets a floor to asset prices must also try to encourage practices that set price *ceilings* on assets. If you believe an asset's price can only go up, and particularly if you believe "the sky is the limit" to its price, you (and everyone else) will be encouraged to speculate that its price will indeed rise. Perhaps the most important way a central bank can limit such behavior is by prohibiting those institutions it protects from failure (e.g., banks) from buying assets that are likely to experience speculative booms in price (e.g., equities traded on the stock market).

Similarly, the central bank must actively intervene in an attempt to limit speculation in real estate, "junk bonds," and complex financial instruments. In other words, the central bank should focus on *qualitative* controls rather than on *quantitative* credit controls. In this way, it not only can reduce the riskiness of bank "lending" (by prohibiting purchase of certain types of assets), but can also help to direct credit to activities deemed socially desirable. This is not a radical suggestion—every country in the world attempts to direct credit in this manner. For example, it is common to encourage provision of home mortgage loans in order to increase home ownership (thought to be socially desirable) through provision of government guarantees (reducing risk to the financial institution), through development of secondary markets for the mortgages (increasing their liquidity), and through favorable rediscount treatment (providing reserves at lower interest rates to institutions that make mortgage loans). In addition, those types of assets that are favored by regulators can be treated differently for supervisory purposes. For example, required capital-to-asset and reserve-to-liability ratios might be reduced for institutions that pursue the kind of lending that is deemed socially worthy. Institutions that finance speculative booms, on the other hand, would be subject to increased supervision and tighter regulation. When the central bank sees a speculative boom developing (say, in the real estate market in a particular region), it should be able to move quickly to make it more difficult for financial institutions to finance the boom (for example, it could require that regulated institutions increase collateral requirements, it could raise equity-to-asset ratios, it could increase supervisory rules of thumb regarding the amount of lending made to any individual borrower, and it could increase pressure for diversification).

Achieving such socially desired objectives is not easy because private profit seekers cleverly subvert central bank intentions whenever these constrain the ability to make profits. This underscores the fact that clever central bankers are needed—ideally they would be even sharper that those they intend to regulate, but in practice this is almost never the case. The subversion of central bank intentions also suggests that the most clever private agents must be punished on occasion by allowing them to fail (and it is a safe bet that they will, indeed, push things so far that failure is inevitable in the absence of central bank intervention). This no doubt serves to reward those of limited intellectual capacity who work at the central bank.

Achieving socially desired objectives is also complicated by the fact that failure by a large institution could snowball and bring down others. This has led to the doctrine of "too big to fail," which may encourage large institutions to take on risk even as it puts smaller institutions at a competitive disadvantage because holders of their uninsured liabilities realize failure is possible. While some observers have advocated breaking up large institutions so that none is too big to fail, this is politically infeasible and probably not desirable because any country that did so would likely have institutions too small to compete in international financial markets. Instead, any institution deemed too big to fail should be subject to increasingly close supervision as it engages in activities thought to be risky.

Observers note that new financial instruments tend to be "underpriced"—that is, for example, financial institutions do not charge a sufficiently high interest rate on innovative types of lending to compensate for risk. In the junk bond fiasco of the late 1980s, it was discovered that default rates were much higher than projected; thus, yields were not nearly sufficient to cover losses. Many have advocated the creation of "fire walls" in which positions in risky assets and in new, unproven types of assets would be financed by issuing liabilities whose return would depend on yields earned on those specific assets. In other words, a bank would have a specific subdivision that would purchase riskier and innovative assets and issue liabilities whose value would not be guaranteed (and not subject to deposit insurance). In this case, holders of these liabilities would recognize that although the government would not allow the financial institution to fail, there would be no guarantee of the value of the liabilities issued by the riskier subdivision. If, say, junk bonds purchased by the subdivision collapsed in value, holders of liabilities issued by the subdivision would absorb these losses. Thus, those holders of such liabilities have an incentive to closely monitor the activities of this subdivision.

The aforementioned approach cannot work, however, unless government supervisors ensure that firewalls are not broached. Thus, there will continue to be a fine line between the appropriate amount of oversight (allowing innovation while discouraging excessive risk) and imposing excessive regulatory and supervisory burden on institutions (inhibiting innovation and raising costs). In short, flexible and intelligent regulators and supervisors are indispensable if domestic monetary policy is to improve as we enter the next century.

Turning finally to the international sphere, we find that the current flexible exchange rate system discourages forward contracts, encourages speculation, and exerts a stagnationist influence upon the world economy.[35] An alternative that is consistent with the "rules of the game," but that can provide a way out when necessary, is required. In this spirit, Keynes called for the creation of an International Clearing Union (ICU) based on a bancor unit of account; the bancor, in turn, would be fixed in value relative to gold and then all the currencies of all countries participating in the ICU would be fixed in value relative to the bancor.[36] The bancor would be used only for clearing purposes among countries; countries could buy bancor balances from the ICU using gold, but bancors could not be redeemed for gold. In this way, bancor reserves could never leave the system—eliminating any possibility of a run on bancors.

The initial quantity of bancor reserves would be allocated among countries based on their previous levels of imports and exports. Countries that then ran trade surpluses would accumulate further bancor reserves, while deficit countries would lose reserves. The ICU would provide overdraft facilities to those countries that exhausted their reserves. Since reserves could not leave the system, the ICU could always expand the supply of bancor reserves merely by making advances to deficit countries. In addition, surplus countries could use bancor reserves to make loans to, investments in, or unilateral grants to deficit countries. The ICU would adopt rules regarding sanctions to be placed on such debtors *and* on countries that ran persistent surpluses (thus, accumulated bancor reserves). Keynes called for a charge on excessive overdrafts *and* on excessive reserve balances of one or two percentage points in order to encourage balanced trade. Other possible actions to be taken in the case of chronically *deficit* countries would include: currency devaluation, capital controls, seizure of gold reserves, and domestic policy "which may appear to be appropriate to restore the equilibrium of its international balance."[37] Actions to be taken in the case of chronically *surplus* countries include: measures to expand domestic demand, appreciation of the currency, reduction of tariffs and other trade barriers, and encouragement of international development loans.[38] Finally, the ICU could use its power to encourage economic development through the use of overdrafts for relief work, for development of buffer stocks of commodities to provide "ever-normal granaries," for the establishment of an International Investment Corporation, and to help stabilize prices.[39]

As Keynes explained, his scheme allows creditor nations to share the burden of adjustment with deficit nations. This has three justifications: (i) creditor nations can "afford" to bear the costs of adjustment; (ii) creditor nations may share the "blame" for deficits of others; (iii) placing the full burden of adjustment on deficit countries contributes to worldwide stagnation if it forces them to use austerity.[40] Under the Keynes scheme, the creditor nations will lose their bancor reserves if they don't use them; these nations would then have an incentive to stimulate their economies so that the bancors would be used to support greater imports or greater foreign investment; alternatively, excess bancors could be given as grants. The international central bank would act as lender of last resort for the deficit countries once they have lost their bancor reserves. This intervention, however, would come with strings attached, comprising a combination of rules and discretionary actions taken by the ICU. Because the creditor nations would be similarly forced to rectify their balance sheet flows, adjustment by the deficit nations would not be so difficult—they would be trying to increase exports precisely when the creditors are trying to increase imports.

Since the bancor reserves could always be expanded without limit by the ICU, it could always maintain fixed exchange rates among international units of account by purchasing the liabilities of the central bank of any nation facing pressure to depreciate. Essentially, the ICU would operate as the international central banker, with its bancor at the very top of the debt pyramid. It would guarantee that the liabilities of all central banks were fully liquid *internationally*; each central bank would then choose which liabilities would be fully liquid *nationally*. However, the threat of sanctions to be imposed by the international central banker on those countries that continually experienced a clearing drain would force the national central banker to behave in an appropriate manner domestically. It must be remembered that it is very easy to set a floor to asset prices (whether domestically or internationally); it is much harder to set price *ceilings*. If depreciation is eliminated and full liquidity is guaranteed, this fact is taken into account when asset prices are determined. Thus, lender of last resort guarantees cannot be adopted without a system of sanctions to be applied when intervention does occur.[41]

In summary, establishing fixed exchange rates, a bancor, and an ICU or international central bank has the following benefits:

1.   Expected appreciation/depreciation of a currency no longer plays a role in determining asset prices.
2.   Use of forward contracts is encouraged because uncertainty over exchange rates is removed.
3.   Speculation in currencies is eliminated.
4.   The volume of reserves (of gold and foreign currencies) held (for speculative and precautionary purposes) by national central banks and private agents is reduced.
5.   A method of dealing with trade imbalances is created that does not rely on austerity. This carries over to the international sphere practices that are frequently adopted domestically. (A nation normally doesn't force austerity onto a region that runs a trade deficit with the rest of the nation. Of course, the United States could deal with such imbalances more rationally than it has in the past.)
6.   It reduces the need for international coordination. In spite of the claim of free marketers, the flexible exchange rate system actually increased intervention into foreign currency markets by governments as they attempted to deal with problems brought on, for the most part, by flexible exchange rates.

Notes

1. I would like to thank Jan Kregel and Charles Whalen for helpful comments.

2. According to Paul Samuelson, *Economics*, 9th ed. (Boston: Beacon Press, 1973), pp. 274–76:

Inconvenient as barter obviously is, it represents a great step forward from a state of self-sufficiency in which every man had to be a jack-of-all-trades and master of none. . . . If we were to construct history along hypothetical, logical lines, we should naturally follow the age of barter by the age of commodity money. Historically, a great variety of commodities has served at one time or another as a medium of exchange: . . . tobacco, furs, slaves or wives . . . huge rocks and landmarks, and cigarette butts. The age of commodity money gives way to the age of paper money. . . . Finally, along with the age of paper money, there is the age of bank money, or bank checking deposits.

This view is very similar to the exposition in every money and banking book with which I am familiar. It is also historically incorrect and logically flawed.

3. As Bruna Ingrao and Giorgio Israel demonstrate (in *The Invisible Hand: Economic Equilibrium in the History of Science* [Cambridge, MA: MIT Press, 1990]), the invariant paradigm of general equilibrium theory (GET) has been to demonstrate the existence, uniqueness, and global stability of equilibrium. While it has been shown that equilibrium does exist for the hypothesized barter economy under quite general assumptions, uniqueness of this equilibrium can be shown only under unacceptably restrictive assumptions; proof of stability is even more difficult to obtain. Furthermore, as Frank Hahn acknowledges, GET has no room for money: "The most serious challenge that existence of money poses to the theorist is this: the best developed model of the economy cannot find room for it. The best developed model is, of course, the Arrow-Debreau version of a Walrasian equilibrium. A world [which operates like this model] neither needs nor wants intrinsically worthless money" (*Money and Inflation* [Cambridge, MA: MIT Press, 1983]).

4. Paul Davidson, *International Money and the Real World*, 2d ed. (New York: St. Martin's Press, 1992).

5. More technically, orthodox economists assume the money supply is perfectly inelastic with respect to money demand; in textbooks, the money supply curve is normally drawn as a vertical line in money–interest-rate space while the money demand curve is downward-sloping.

6. Again, in textbooks, the money-supply curve is vertical in money–interest-rate space at the quantity of money determined by the central bank.

7. Daniel L. Thornton, "The Borrowed-Reserves Operating Procedure: Theory and Evidence," *Federal Reserve Bank of St. Louis Review, 70,* 1 (1988), 30.

8. Paul Davidson, *International Money and the Real World.*

9. Frank Hahn, *Money and Inflation.*

10. Ibid.

11. For a detailed discussion of the origins and development of the modern financial system, see L. Randall Wray, "The Origins of Money and the Development of the Modern Financial System," The Jerome Levy Economics Institute, Working Paper no. 86, 1993.

12. George Dalton, "Barter," *Journal of Economic Issues, 16,* 1 (March 1982), 181–90; Gunnar Heinsohn and Otto Steiger, "Private Property, Debts and Interest, Or: The Origin of Money and the Rise and Fall of Monetary Economics," *Studi Economici, 21* (1983), 3–56; Bronislaw Malinowski, *Argonauts of the Western Pacific: An Account of Native Enterprise and Adventure in the Archipelagoes of Melanesian New Guinea* (London: George Routledge and Sons, 1932); Karl Polanyi, "Aristotle Discovers the Economy," in Karl Polanyi, Conrad M. Arensberg, and Harry W. Pearson (eds.), *Trade and Market in the Early Empires* (Chicago: Regnery Company, 1971), p. 64.

13. John Maynard Keynes, *The Collected Writings of John Maynard Keynes*, vol. 28, ed. by Donald Moggridge (London: Macmillan, 1982).

14. Ibid. Also, Gunnar Heinsohn and Otto Steiger, "Private Property, Debts and Interest."

15. John Maynard Keynes, *The Collected Writings*, vol. 28.

16. Duncan Foley, "Money in Economic Activity," in John Eatwell, Murray Milgate, and Peter Newman (eds.), *The New Palgrave: Money* (New York: W.W. Norton, 1989); L. Randall Wray, *Money and Credit in Capitalist Economies: The Endogenous Money Approach* (Aldershot, UK: Edward Elgar, 1990); also L. Randall Wray, "The Origins of Money."

17. L. Randall Wray, *Money and Credit in Capitalist Economies*; and L. Randall Wray, "The Origins of Money."

18. John Maynard Keynes, *The Collected Writings*, vol. 28; Gunnar Heinsohn and Otto Steiger, "Private Property, Debts and Interest."

19. Richard Ehrenberg, *Capital and Finance in the Age of the Renaissance: A Study of the Fuggers and Their Connections* (New York: Harcourt, Brace, 1985).

20. Georg Friedrich Knapp, *The State Theory of Money* (London: Macmillan, 1924); John Day, *The Medieval Market Economy* (New York: Basil Blackwell, 1987); and Luigi Einaudi, "The Theory of Imaginary Money from Charlemagne to the French Revolution," in Frederic C. Lane and Jelle C. Riermersma (eds.), *Enterprise and Secular Change: Readings in Economic History* (Homewood, IL: Richard D. Irwin, 1953), p. 494.

21. Georg Friedrich Knapp, *The State Theory of Money*; Charles Goodhart, "Central Banking," in John Eatwell, Murray Milgate, and Peter Newman (eds.), *The New Palgrave: Money* (New York: W.W. Norton, 1989), p. 88.

22. R.S. Sayers, *Lloyds Bank in the History of English Banking* (Oxford: The Clarendon Press, 1957).

23. Walter Bagehot, *Lombard Street: A Description of the Money Market* (London: John Murray, 1927).

24. Ibid.

25. L. Randall Wray, "Money, Interest Rates, and Monetarist Policy: Some More Unpleasant Monetarist Arithmetic?" *Journal of Post Keynesian Economics*, *14*, 4 (1993), 543.

26. John Maynard Keynes, *The Collected Writings of John Maynard Keynes*, vol. 29, ed. by Donald Moggridge (London: Macmillan, 1979), p. 89; Robert Heilbroner, *The Nature and Logic of Capitalism* (New York: W.W. Norton, 1985).

27. L. Randall Wray, "Alternative Theories of the Rate of Interest," *Cambridge Journal of Economics*, *16*, 1 (March 1992), 69; John Maynard Keynes, *The General Theory of Employment, Interest and Money* (New York: Harcourt Brace Jovanovich, 1964).

28. In earlier times, one might be forced through "debt bondage" to actually work off debt commitments by placing one's person (or even one's family) in involuntary servitude to the creditor. However, this practice has been discontinued in developed capitalist economies with the outlaw of slavery such that debt contracts are now enforceable in money terms only.

29. Rondo Cameron (ed.), *Banking in the Early Stages of Industrialization: A Study in Comparative Economic History* (New York: Oxford University Press, 1967).

30. J.A. Kregel, "International Financial Markets and the September Collapse of the EMS, or 'What George Soros Knew That You Didn't' " (mimeo, 1993).

31. Ibid.; also, William Greider, *The Trouble with Money: A Prescription for America's Financial Fever* (Knoxville, TN: Whittle Direct Books, 1989).

32. L. Randall Wray, "Money, Interest Rates, and Monetarist Policy"; Hyman P. Minsky, *Stabilizing an Unstable Economy* (New Haven, CT: Yale University Press, 1986).

33. Amit Bhaduri and Josef Steindl, "The Rise of Monetarism as a Social Doctrine,"

Thames Papers in Political Economy (Autumn 1983); Paul Davidson, *International Money and the Real World*. See the former for a discussion of austerity as a policy proposal and the latter for an evaluation of its effects.

34. Post-Keynesians also emphasize that innovations by banks subvert central bank attempts to control the quantity of money: when the central bank tries to control a particular type of money-denominated liability, others are created to allow the "money supply" to react to "money demand."

35. Paul Davidson, *International Money and the Real World*.

36. When Keynes developed this proposal, it made sense to design the ICU with a bancor-gold reserve because most countries (and most economists) attached a special significance to the gold standard. Today, since the gold standard has been all but abandoned and because gold reserves are distributed unequally and without regard to the distribution of world trade, the ICU could be established without including gold as a reserve and without making bancors convertible into gold (John Maynard Keynes, *The Collected Writings of John Maynard Keynes*, vol. 25, ed. by Donald Moggridge [London: Macmillan, 1980]; Paul Davidson, *International Money and the Real World*).

37. John Maynard Keynes, *The Collected Writings of John Maynard Keynes*, vol. 25, p. 462.

38. Ibid., p. 463.

39. Ibid., p. 190.

40. Paul Davidson, *International Money and the Real World*.

41. We should not underestimate the political barriers to creation of something like an international central bank. As Keynes explained, this would lead to, if not require, much greater international economic integration. Perhaps the use of a bancor as the international unit of account would work only with world integration—that is, with a truly international financial system and a single central bank—because of the *social* nature of the unit of account. Perhaps the right to determine which liabilities always have spot parity against the unit of the account is the last refuge of national economic autonomy. Keynes seemed to recognize this when he argued that an ICU "might become the pivot of the future economic government of the world" (Keynes, *The Collected Writings of John Maynard Keynes*, vol. 25, p. 189).

Part IV

Macroeconomics, Structural Change, and Distribution

8

Macroeconomics and the Theory of a Monetary Economy

Wallace C. Peterson

The purpose of this chapter is to analyze and reflect upon the future shape of macroeconomics and macroeconomic policy within the context of a theory of a monetary economy. The idea of a monetary economy—or a monetary theory of production—is the fundamental essence of Keynes's *The General Theory.*

In a prescient 1933 article, Keynes described a *monetary economy* as one in which money plays a role of its own. In such an economy, money is not neutral, as in neoclassical economics. Rather, money "affects motives and decisions and is, in short, one of the operative factors in the situation, so that the course of events cannot be predicted, either in the long period or in the short, without a knowledge of the behavior of money between the first state and the last. And this is what we ought to mean when we speak of a *Monetary Economy*."[1]

Keynes's ideas about a monetary economy are different in a fundamental way from contemporary *monetarism*, as invented and developed by Milton Friedman and his followers. Money in monetarism is still neutral in the classical sense of being an external or exogenous factor. It is not, as Keynes saw it, an essential, internal, or endogenous part of modern systems of market capitalism. Through the manipulation of money as an external variable, Friedmanite monetarists believe that the short-term course of the economy can be affected, but they do not see money as either a key institution of market capitalism or a crucial part of the system. Money is not "one of the operative factors in the situation."

What is involved in analyzing macroeconomics and macroeconomic policy within the context of the theory of a monetary economy? This requires, first, a separate examination of some key ideas in both institutionalism and Keynesian economics, and, second, an analysis of how these ideas come together through the institution of money to create the essentials of a monetary theory of production. Such a theory is not static, but evolutionary, involving the contributions of economists as diverse as Karl Marx, Thorstein Veblen, Wesley Mitchell, John Maynard Keynes, Dudley Dillard, and Hyman Minsky. In a broad sense, the development and perfection of a monetary theory of production have been the common goal of both Keynes and the institutionalists.

Why Is This Important?

One might well ask: Why does this matter? Why is there a need for such a theory? Doesn't the standard textbook version of Keynes offer insights sufficient for policy purposes in today's world? Not really. With the collapse of the Soviet Union, market-style capitalism is now the dominant economic system, destined to shape the world and the global economy in the twenty-first century. Thus, it is crucial to understand how market capitalism works, its key characteristics, its problems, what it does well, and what it does not do well. The sterile, excessively abstract general equilibrium model that is the centerpiece for mainstream, neoclassical economics is of little practical value in yielding answers to these crucial questions. The theory of a monetary economy—a theory directly descended from American institutionalists and Keynes—offers the best theoretical paradigm for making sense out of the messy real-world economic system that will shape our lives into the next century.

This leads directly to the ultimate objective of this chapter—namely, to sketch out the principles of macroeconomic policymaking appropriate to our turbulent, changing market economy, one that increasingly is part of a global economic system. What policies will work in such a setting? What won't work? In what ways must we change our perspectives on macroeconomic policy as the nation moves toward the twenty-first century?

Some Essentials of Institutionalism

The appropriate place to begin is with a discussion of some general characteristics of institutionalism, followed by a similar analysis of the ideas of Keynes. Unlike neoclassical, general equilibrium economics, there is no precise, unified body of ideas that can be readily and clearly identified as institutionalism. As John Gambs has said, there is "no one authoritative school of institutional theory."[2] But institutionalism is not without boundaries, though there is a certain vagueness to its boundaries. Some see this vagueness in combination with the diversity of the content of institutionalism as a weakness. A more appropriate view is that the vagueness of boundaries and diversity of content reflect the wide-ranging interests, insatiable curiosity, and probing spirit of those who have made enduring contributions to this branch of economics. Persons like Thorstein Veblen, Wesley Mitchell, John R. Commons, Clarence Ayres, Gardner Means, Gunnar Myrdal, Allan Gruchy, Dudley Dillard, John Kenneth Galbraith, and others have refused to let their minds be shackled, or be forbidden to transcend a narrow, mechanistic view of the economic universe.

There is one viewpoint common to institutionalists of practically every persuasion. They reject the key theme in neoclassical, general equilibrium economics—namely, the belief that the economic system can be organized *adequately* through markets and the free and unrestrained play of individual self-interest. In the neoclassical view, competition restrains self-interest, forcing it to work in ways that are socially beneficial. Their economic world is a self-contained and self-regulating system, requiring only the barest minimum of governmental action to keep it going. At best, institutionalists argue, this view fails as an adequate description of the real economic world, and, at worst, it is simply an apology for contemporary capitalism.

Beyond this, institutional economics is best described not in terms of a mechanistic "model," but as a "vision," a view of how things fit together and what forces are strategic in making the economy function. The institutionalist vision embraces a series of critical ideas that have much in common with those found in Keynes's *General Theory*.

First, there is the basic view that *all* economic activity is part of an ongoing process, not part of a mechanistic system that tends toward a state of balance or equilibrium. If one needs an analogy to clarify the nature of economics, the analogy should be biology, not mechanics or physics.

There are several characteristics of the economic process worth noting. It is both cultural and evolutionary. Allan Gruchy defined the institutional approach to economics as the "study of the changing patterns of cultural relations which deal with the creation of scarce material goods and services by individuals and groups in the light of their private and public aims."[3] Economics cannot be divorced from its cultural and historical setting, which means in practical terms that there are limits to the extent that economic principles can be developed that are independent of time, culture, and place. Thus, effective policy actions must consider the economic, political, and social milieu within which they will operate.

The evolutionary character of the economic process is also of prime importance. Veblen believed that the evolutionary aspect of economics was the most distinctive feature of his writing. Evolutionary implies a system that is constantly changing, always different today from what it was yesterday. The economy is part of a complex historical process, moving from a known past to a mostly unknown future. The past always conditions the future, yet never wholly determines it. So uncertainty is a fundamental aspect of the human condition. Uncertainty provides a crucial link between institutionalism and Keynes. The view that the economy moves continuously from a known past to a largely unknown future negates the belief that the economic process involves movement toward a balance of forces—toward equilibrium, which is the heart of the neoclassical view.

Seeing the economy as part of an ongoing, historical process leads to a different view of human behavior from the individualistic, rational, maximizing postulate that undergirds the neoclassical perspective. Since the latter involves a balancing of gains against cost, it requires accurate information about the future, precisely something humans do not possess. This opens the door to a different view of human behavior, a view that sees behavior shaped by uncertainty and institutions, not exclusively by rational calculations based upon self-interest. Keynes's belief that investment decisions are often the result of "animal spirits— of a spontaneous urge to action rather than inaction, and not as the outcome of a weighted average of quantitative benefits multiplied by quantitative probabilities" is far closer to the institutionalist than to neoclassical ideas on human behavior.[4]

Institutionalist thinking about human behavior involves more than uncertainty. It also stresses conflict, aggression, and a struggle for power as part of the economic process. These forces often overshadow the neoclassical notion that market processes lead to a harmonious outcome with respect to resource allocation and the distribution of income. Some regard coercion, not harmony, as the central fact of economic life.[5] From an institutionalist perspective, the crucial economic problem is not resource allocation, but how, by whom, and for whose benefit the economic system is organized and controlled. This is why power is a central theme in institutionalism. Prices, markets, and competition play important roles, but their roles in the economic process are often subordinate to the use and distribution of power. In the neoclassical world, for example, prices primarily represent signals for the allocation of resources, whereas in the institutionalist world, *control* over prices is a major means to gain, retain, and enhance economic power.

What flows from an altered conception of human behavior based upon coercion and power is a radically different view of the modern state and its role. Rooted in eighteenth-century fears of the absolute state, and the nineteenth-century experiments with laissez-faire, neoclassical economics accords only a small role for the state. Twentieth-century liberalism takes a more benign view of state power, seeing it as a means to control and redress the worst abuses and excesses of market capitalism. This view had its greatest validity in the 1930s and immediately after World War II, but reality today is far more complex. As John Kenneth Galbraith has pointed out, the character of the modern state has become contradictory.[6] Because the economic actions of the modern state affect one-quarter to one-third of economic activity, controlling the power of the state leads to enormous control over the economy itself. Yet, the fact remains that it is only through the state power that the excessive concentration and abuse of power exercised privately can be controlled. The enormous sums spent by political action committees—the so-called PACs—to influence and control elections attest to the crucial but ambivalent role now played by the modern state in the control and exercise of power in the modern economy. Neoclassical economics, based upon assumptions that deny the existence of economic power, serves to dull public awareness of the degree to which the power of the state has fallen under the sway of private interest groups.

Another important consequence of a shift away from the neoclassical stress on self-interest and competition to the institutionalist's concern with coercion and power is to bring the distribution of income and wealth to the forefront of economic concern. This is so because the distribution of income and wealth is an economic mirror that reflects the power struggles of society. Income and wealth distribution is a "natural" subject for institutionalism, both because neoclassical analysis has practically nothing useful to say on the subject, and because power relationships are manifest in and work through the key institutions of society, such as the corporation or trade unions. The matter is broader than this. Beneath the surface of power struggles and conflicts over the distribution of income and wealth lie fundamental issues of equity and justice that must be resolved. Until they are resolved, the use of Keynesian techniques for the effective macromanagement of the economy will remain elusive and difficult.

The Essentials of Keynesian Economics

This brings us to the ideas of Keynes, clearly the dominant economist of the twentieth century. Not since Karl Marx has one person had greater influence upon how we think about the economy, and how we perceive the economic process. To perceive and understand the linkages that exist between Keynes and institutional economics—and how the two must be melded together to develop a monetary theory of production—we should start with the proposition that post–World War II Keynesianism (like institutionalism) is not a unified body of theory. This chapter identifies only two main streams of Keynesian thought, although some economists argue that there are at least three, and maybe as many as five variants of Keynesianism.[7]

The dominant stream in Keynesian economics is the standard postwar textbook interpretation of Keynes, an interpretation that Paul Samuelson once described as the "neoclassical synthesis." The essential feature of this version of Keynesian economics is the income-expenditure model, the roots of which are in Keynes's principle of aggregate demand as developed in *The General Theory*. This widely accepted version of Keynes (the IS-LM model) first appeared in J.R. Hicks's article, "Mr. Keynes and the Classics," in which he sought to show that the economics of *The General Theory* were not very different in their essentials from Marshallian or neoclassical economics.[8] Money and financial variables enter into the model as exogenous variables that affect key functional relationships, a development that pushes Keynes's analysis back toward the neoclassical belief that the endogenous processes of the system automatically lead to full employment. By adding neoclassical demand and supply curves for labor to the system, and by retaining the assumption of the neutrality of money, Keynes's theory is forced back into the general equilibrium mold. The "New Keynesian Macroeconomics" introduced wage and price rigidities and credit rationing into the model during the 1980s as factors that may cause periods of involuntary unemployment, but left its general equilibrium character unchanged.

Several consequences flow from the mainstream interpretation. On the plane of pure theory, Keynes becomes a figure of no great importance, because widespread and prolonged unemployment can only result from special circumstances, such as wage rigidity or a liquidity trap. Unemployment is not endemic to the system. On a philosophical level, the effect has been to defuse the "Keynesian revolution," drawing the attention of economists and the public away from the fact that *The General Theory* contains a devastating critique of an inherently flawed economic system. What is lost from sight in the textbook version of Keynes is the inherent instability of market capitalism, the existence of money as a significant institutional barrier to full employment, an inequitable distribution of income and wealth, the pervasive fact of uncertainty, and that the economy exists in real, historical time. According to Joan Robinson, ignoring the last point is essential to keep Keynesian economics within the "straitjacket of equilibrium." She said, "once we admit that an economy exists in time, that history goes one way, from the irrevocable past into the unknown future, the conception of an equilibrium . . . becomes untenable."[9]

The second, alternative stream in Keynesian economics—today called post-Keynesianism—is not readily reduced to the kinds of abstract models found in standard textbook versions of macroeconomics. Like institutionalism, this version of Keynesian thought is more readily described as a series of insights and attitudes that pertain to the functioning of the economy, not in terms of a formal, mathematical model. So, this side of *The General Theory* is largely neglected in conventional analysis. Yet in many ways these neglected insights and attitudes—which have ties to institutionalism—are closer to the true spirit of the Keynesian revolution than the formal textbook model. If institutionalists see coercion and power as the central fact of economic life, uncertainty occupies this role in Keynesian theory. G.L.S. Shackle says that "uncertainty is the very bedrock of Keynes's theory of employment."[10] Uncertainty pervades economic life because the economy exists in real time, and because it cannot be separated from history. This means that the system is indeterminate because the future is indeterminate. Keynes was emphatic about uncertainty. In his famous 1937 *Quarterly Journal of Economics* article in which he replied to his critics, he said with respect to the future, "We simply do not know."[11]

What emerges from Keynes's preoccupation with uncertainty is a view of the economic process foreign to neoclassical general equilibrium theory, but a view similar to institutionalism. The economy does not have an inherent tendency toward equilibrium, even an equilibrium of underemployment. Because of uncertainty and the institutions that reflect this fact (money and money-related financial practices), systems of market capitalism are inherently flawed, subject to continuous cyclical instability. Instead of equilibrium, *disequilibrium* is the normal state of affairs. The economy is always in motion, but most of the time it moves erratically, not tending toward a state of rest or balance. Nothing stands still, the system moves on, and the future is always different from the past. In a brief article that Keynes wrote for *The New Republic* before completing *The General Theory*, he said plainly that the economic system is not self-adjusting.[12] Like Veblen, Keynes saw the economy as a process involving movement through time.

Uncertainty also leads to a view of human nature very much at odds with neoclassical ideas. Joan Robinson says simply that since the future is uncertain, rational behavior in the neoclassical sense is impossible.[13] This means that economic activity must be conducted through accepted conventions—that is to say, institutions. As Keynes also pointed out in his *Quarterly Journal of Economics* article, the roots for such behavior are often flimsy, subject to "sudden and violent changes."[14] Shackle goes much further; he argues that Keynes's ideas about behavior strike at the most fundamental tenet of neoclassical economics— namely, that "men apply reason to their circumstances."[15] We are not, he goes on to say, the "assured master of known circumstances via reason, but the prisoners of time."[16] If, as these comments suggest, the behavior of human beings is frequently irrational and erratic, then the best way to understand that behavior is to understand the institutions that shape and direct that behavior. Thus, human behavior offers yet another bridge between Keynesian economics and institutionalism.

The Institution of Money

In institutionalism and in Keynesian economics, money is of the utmost strategic importance. In both approaches, money emerges as a dominant—if not the single most important—institution in systems of market capitalism. Dudley Dillard puts the matter clearly and succinctly, saying, "What is special about money under capitalism is that the private owners of capital assets may be deterred from making them available to wage earners because of uncertainty concerning the terms on which real output can be converted into money in the future at time of sale."[17] When such deterrence happens, unemployment is the result.

There are, of course, no formal intellectual ties between Keynesian economics and institutionalism, but their respective attitudes toward money are not only the most important link between the two schools, but the basis for a theory of a monetary economy.[18]

Since the time of Veblen, institutionalists have viewed capitalism as a pecuniary order in which people are torn continuously between making money and making goods. It is a curious fact that neoclassical economics continues to gloss over this distinction, considering money to be little more than a convenience, a means of exchange. Why neoclassical economists do this is hard to fathom, especially in contemporary American society where money penetrates into every nook and cranny of our economic life. Money is the ultimate consumer good, the thing that people want above all else! Money opens the door to power, attention, status, prestige, even love and affection. In a money-loving society like modern America, money flows to those who control whatever commands a price, what has value in the marketplace. Marketplace value originates, of course, in productive activity, but it also can result from the activities of persons skilled in the arts of financial manipulation or those who have attained the power needed to control the terms upon which market exchanges take place. The marketplace is indifferent, since money is the common denominator for all activity, inherently unable to distinguish between productive and nonproductive activity.

Veblen in all his writings always hammered away at this theme, stressing continually that making money is the aim and motivation for all businessmen, whereas the actual production of goods is incidental to this fact. Fortunately for the well-being of society, most people in business have to produce something to make money, although the temptation is always present to create scarcities—not goods—as a road to riches. Among institutionalists, Wesley Mitchell is well known for his life-long study of the business cycle, but like his teacher Thorstein Veblen, Mitchell believed that making money was the dominant force driving the economy. According to Dudley Dillard, Mitchell hoped his major contribution to economics would be a study of "the money economy," but he never returned to this task after becoming immersed in analysis of the business cycle. Nonetheless, he regarded the business cycle as a special aspect of a money economy.[19]

Keynes approaches the institution of money from a different perspective, although the institution of money is no less important in his analysis than it is in institutionalism. He rejects outright the neoclassical notion that money is neutral, asserting that we cannot understand the economy without a knowledge of the behavior of money. His liquidity preference theory of interest tries to provide this understanding, and also to open the way to abandon neoclassical notions about the neutrality of money.

Keynes's preoccupation with money goes much further than his formal theory of liquidity preference. Money is crucial because it provides a critical and necessary link between the present and the future. The possession of money, Keynes said, "lulls our disquietude" when we are confronted with an uncertain future.[20] By according this role to money, Keynes points to a basic dichotomy in the economic process, a split similar in its consequences to the institutionalist division of activity into pecuniary and nonpecuniary forms. In the textbooks, this dichotomy shows up as the distinction between the demand for output (the *real* sphere) and the demand for liquidity (the *monetary* sphere). Keynes used this distinction to show that, periodically, fear and uncertainty about the future created so great a demand for the safety and liquidity found in money that collapse was inevitable in the goods-producing sphere of the economy. The mechanism that brings about such a collapse is the impact of rising interest rates (the price paid for liquidity) upon real investment spending.

It is the institutional peculiarities of money that are the real source of the problem. Money, in Keynes's view, is not like other commodities. It fails to obey the normal laws of the market; it does not increase in supply when liquidity demand increases, and other things do not substitute for it when its price (the rate of interest) goes up. These unique characteristics of money, combined with its capacity to lull our worries about the future, are keys for understanding what Keynes saw as the fundamental flaw of market capitalism—namely, the inherent and inescapable tendency of the system toward instability and excessive unemployment.

Essentials of a Monetary Theory of Production

In the same essay in which he described a monetary economy as one in which money is not neutral, Keynes said the next task for economics was to establish the details of a monetary theory of production, something he was doing, confident that he was not wasting his time.[21] This task was writing *The General Theory*, which in the earliest surviving draft (1932) of the table of contents for the planned work carried the title *The Monetary Theory of Production*.[22] In *The General Theory*, he noted in the Preface that he had thought after finishing his *Treatise on Money* he had made some progress "towards pushing monetary theory back to becoming a theory of output as whole."[23] Subsequently, he realized the *Treatise* did not deal thoroughly with the effects of *changes* in the level of output, a deficiency he believed he had corrected in *The General Theory*. A monetary economy, Keynes goes on to say in the Preface, is "essentially one in which changing views about the future are capable of influencing the quantity of employment and not merely its direction."[24] Much later, in chapter 21 on "The Theory of Prices," he says a great fault of classical economics is that while the "homely but intelligible concepts" of supply and demand explain individual prices, when it comes to explaining all prices, economists move into another world entirely. It is a world in which the quantity of money, its velocity, and related variables explain prices in general. It is a false division to explain individual prices by one set of forces (supply and demand) and all prices by another set (money and velocity).[25]

The right dichotomy, Keynes declares, is between "the Theory of the Individual Industry or Firm . . . and the Theory of Output and Employment *as a whole*."[26] At the level of the individual firm or industry, economists need not be concerned about the significant characteristics of money, but once they move to the problem of what determines output and employment *as a whole*, what is required is "the complete theory of a Monetary Economy."[27] In *The General Theory* itself, these observations are the closest Keynes came to a precise definition of a monetary economy, although in an earlier but discarded draft for chapter 3 of *The General Theory*, he wrote that, "An entrepreneur is interested, not in the amount of product, but in the amount of money which will fall to his share," and that the business firm "has no object in the world except to end up with more money than it started with. That is the essential characteristic of an entrepreneur economy."[28]

Dudley Dillard was the first economist in the post–World War II era to understand and grasp the significance that Keynes in *The General Theory* believed he was establishing a body of theoretical ideas appropriate to the behavior of a monetary economy, which in a fundamental sense is one in which money is not neutral. The subtitle of Dillard's highly regarded 1948 book (*The Economics of John Maynard Keynes*) explaining Keynes's masterwork is *The Theory of a Monetary Economy*.[29] Later, in a seminal 1954 article, "The Theory of a Monetary Economy" that appeared in *Post Keynesian Economics*, edited by Kenneth K. Kurihara, Dillard analyzed in detail why *The General Theory* contains the essentials of a monetary theory of production, but did not develop such a theory in its entirety.[30] Throughout his long and productive intellectual life, Dillard returned continuously to this theme, making it the centerpiece of his remarks upon receipt of the Veblen–Commons award in 1986 from the Association for Evolutionary Economics. Besides filling in some gaps in Keynes's theoretical treatment of a monetary theory of production, Dillard stressed in his writings the roots of this theory in the works of Marx, Veblen, and Commons.

Dillard succinctly describes a monetary theory of production as "a model of production in which business firms (owners of non-personal means of production) produce output and try to convert it into money."[31] This brief statement captures the essence of Marx's view that production in capitalist societies involves a continuous movement from money to goods to money ($M\text{–}C\text{–}M'$) in a relentless drive for profits, Veblen's pervasive theme that the pursuit of pecuniary gains dominates the industrial process (producing goods), and Keynes's view that the force that drives the business firm is the need to end with more money than it started with.

Behind Dillard's clear but simple statement lies a view of the economic world that is profoundly different from what one finds in current mainstream economics. A part of this difference lies in the meaning of the term "real," as used in economics and in the world of business. To the economist, what is real are the actual goods (and services) currently produced (output) or goods produced in the past and not used up (capital). For business firms—and probably for most people as they view matters in their everyday lives—money is what is real. As Dillard says, goods for the individual producer are an artificial form of wealth until converted into money—*real* wealth for the producer.[32]

The most important theoretical idea coming from *The General Theory* is that output in systems of market capitalism depends upon aggregate demand, which equals expected spending by all domestic and foreign end-users of output—consumers, business firms, and governments. This principle is common to all contemporary macroeconomic schools. What has been grossly neglected in the mechanistic models of Keynes that dominate mainstream macroeconomic theory is that aggregate demand—an *expected* variable—governs the terms upon which business firms can convert the goods they produce into what to them is real wealth—money.

Since, overwhelmingly, both consumer and capital goods are produced for future sale, uncertainty always exists with respect to the terms on which business firms can convert their output into money. Uncertainty in combination with the peculiar characteristics of the institution of money is the Achilles heel that accounts for the periodic breakdowns of production and increased unemployment in market economies. When uncertainty mounts, holding money (money "lulls our disquietude") becomes preferable to producing goods for future sale, resulting in less output and more unemployment. The situation is not self-correcting, because, as noted earlier, market forces do not increase the money supply when the demand for liquidity rises, and its price (the rate of interest) "rules the roost." By this Keynes means that interest sets the standard that the rate of return on all assets—but especially on investment goods—must attain or exceed if they are to be produced. As uncertainty increases, the demand for liquidity also increases, setting a floor below which the rate of interest will not fall. As Keynes said, "Unemployment develops . . . because people want the moon—men cannot be employed when the object of desire (i.e., money) is something that cannot be produced and the demand for which cannot be readily choked off."[33] Because money has a low elasticity of production and substitution, the rate of interest is sticky. The practical meaning of this is that, left to themselves, market forces cannot bring interest rates low enough to generate enough investment spending and a level of aggregate demand that leads to full employment.

The foregoing represents in bare outline the core ideas of a monetary theory of production as developed in *The General Theory* and amplified by Dudley Dillard. Its major deficiency is that it treats the institution of money too narrowly, both in its conception, and in terms of the mechanism through which output is affected. To put the latter point differently, Keynes's notion of liquidity preference carries too great a burden. In *The General Theory*, as well as most textbook interpretations of Keynes, money is treated as an exogenous variable whose quantity is determined by the central bank. A modern, realistic view is that money is as an endogenous variable whose supply—at least in the form of credit—is *not* independent of the demand for money.[34] The liquidity preference approach limits the impact of money on economic activity to the effect of changes in the rate of interest on investment spending. Today's reality is far more complex, not only because "money" includes a vast and complex array of financial instruments, but also because the influence of financial institutions permeates the entire production process, not just the production of investment goods. The economist who has captured this best and, thereby, taken a giant step toward completing Keynes's theory of a monetary economy is Hyman Minsky, Professor Emeritus from Washington University and Distinguished Scholar at the Jerome Levy Economics Institute of Bard College.

Minsky, like Keynes, places volatile investment spending at center stage. But he goes beyond Keynes and shows how, in an economy with a highly developed and sophisticated financial system, the volatility of investment spending has roots in the periodic and *systemic* inability of business firms to meet the cash payment commitments that grow out of obligations undertaken in the past.[35] This is the "financial-instability hypothesis"—Minsky's investment theory of business cycles. In the "paper world" of Wall Street that dominates the real economy, real investment in capital assets is typically financed by borrowing from banks and other financial institutions. Indeed, one of the major characteristics of the modern market economy is the ingenuity and skill displayed in the continued invention of new means to finance investment spending—means often invented in a deliberate attempt to circumvent central bank constraints. Borrowing to finance the acquisition of real capital by business firms sets up dual money flows stretching into the future. First, there is a cash inflow from the earnings produced by the real capital assets acquired, a flow that is both uncertain and volatile. Second, there is a cash outflow in the form of payments to the firm's creditors, a flow that is fixed and contractual. In this real economic world, the flow is always from money and debt, to capital spending and the production of goods for sale, and then back to money and profit. When the flow of expected earnings falters (and this occurs due to endogenous forces, not just unexpected changes in the state of business confidence), investment falters, the economy falters, and unemployment results. The severity of the crises that erupt when the expected earnings flow falters is often magnified because during good times business firms leverage their debts as they overestimate the expected profitability of additional capital.

In Minsky's view there are two major reasons why up to now—and in spite of the seriously flawed character of modern market capitalism—the U.S. economy has not experienced another economic debacle on the scale of the Great Depression of the 1930s. The first is the stabilizing effect of big government. When the economy slows, federal government spending and the federal deficit increase, thus tending to underwrite income and business profits. This acts as a floor under any downturn, so none of the recessions since World War II have had the depth and severity of the decade-long slump of the 1930s. The second is the willingness of the Federal Reserve to act as the lender of last resort, a role that has prevented the collapse in asset values and the kind of debt-deflation crisis that used to be characteristic of economic downturns.[36] This process is flawed, because while preventing the economy from falling into another 1930s-style deep depression, it leaves a legacy of highly liquid assets that not only may feed inflation, but may support another investment boom built upon highly leveraged debt. Preventing a recurrence of the 1930s is not, as Minsky says, "a trivial gain," but something better is still needed.[37]

Implications for Macroeconomic Policy

The dominant thrust of the foregoing comments is that we live in a complex, basically unstable economic system, dominated by the institutions of money and finance, an economy in which the foremost goal of the business enterprise is to use money to make goods in order to make more money. Together, Keynes and the institutionalists give us an accurate picture of the economy's real nature. The question now becomes: What policies are appropriate to tame and stabilize this economy?

Three propositions undergird the macroeconomic policies appropriate to the modern monetary economy. The first is the clear necessity for managing the economy. Instability is the norm of the economy. There is not a shred of credible evidence that a system of market capitalism will adjust to an equilibrium of full employment if left on its own with a minimum of government interference. As Walter Heller pointed out in 1986 at a symposium on the fortieth anniversary of the Employment Act, the record of activist governments in promoting output, high employment, growth, and economic stability is far better than the record of the antigovernment era that began with the Nixon administration.[38]

Second, and as Minsky has made clear, big government is necessary as a stabilizing element in the modern economy. The crucial question is how big should government be to play this stabilizing role? Minsky suggests that total federal spending in the range of 16 to 20 percent of gross domestic product (GDP) will generate deficits during an economic downturn large enough to offset profit losses for business firms following a sharp decline in investment spending.[39] The irony is that under the Republican administrations of Reagan and Bush, federal spending climbed to more than 24 percent of GDP, while tax revenues lagged behind at 19.3 percent of GDP (in 1992).[40] Deficits of an unprecedented magnitude resulted, negating almost totally the possibility of using fiscal action for stabilization purposes. Ronald Reagan did not succeed in his cherished goal of shrinking government's size, but through the deficits his administration created he succeeded in crippling the federal government's role in managing the economy. Consequently, reducing the size of the federal government and getting the deficit under control are essential if fiscal policy is to be used effectively once again. This is true even though the operational federal deficit would be smaller if the U.S. government had a capital budget, as do the governments of most other modern states.

Finally, the Keynesian principle of aggregate demand is the key strategic instrument for carrying out macroeconomic policy in a monetary economy. In an economy in which business firms produce goods and services primarily in order to make money, nothing will be produced if there are not buyers or the expectation that buyers will appear when the goods and services reach the market. Keynes's concept of aggregate demand reflects this. Thus, management of the economy must take place through actions that focus on aggregate demand.

Macroeconomic policy as it has evolved since Keynes should not be discarded or radically transformed. But policy must be modified and updated before it can be used successfully in management of the complex kind of monetary economy that has evolved since Keynes published his classic work more than half a century ago.

A major failure of post–World War II mainstream Keynesian economics was not recognizing that a serious inflationary problem would arise out of the combination of sustained full employment and the concentration of economic power that exists in strategic areas of the economy. This came about in part because orthodox economic theory simply refuses to admit the existence of economic power, let alone acknowledge that in many areas of the economy market power is stronger than competition. As Galbraith has noted, one outstanding feature of our society is the rise of organizations—trade unions and corporations are prime examples—whose primary purpose is to shield people from the market or to control the terms on which transactions in the market take place.[41] Negotiation based upon organization and power frequently is more important than impersonal market forces in determining prices, incomes, and what gets produced.

One consequence is that a strong inflationary bias is built into the economy, even though economic stagnation since 1972 has dampened inflationary pressures.[42] During the forty-three years from 1950 through 1992, consumer prices rose by nearly 500 percent, or at an annual average rate of 4.2 percent, a pace that cuts the value of the dollar in half in just under seventeen years. During this same period, unemployment averaged 5.8 percent of the civilian labor force, a figure well in excess of the full employment target of a 4.0 percent unemployment rate set by the Kennedy–Johnson administrations, or the 3.0 percent goal written into law in the Full Employment and Balanced Growth Act of 1978.[43] It does not take any great theoretical wisdom to understand that if the economy had performed during these years close to a genuine full employment level, inflation would have been far more severe than it was.

The logical consequence of this, given the existing institutional structure of the U.S. economy, is an incomes policy. Such a policy has never found favor with mainstream economists, but it is difficult to see how another explosive round of inflation can be avoided if the economy *ever* gets back to a path of full employment growth. Orthodox economists avoid the issue altogether, being content to define unemployment rates in the 5 to 6 percent range as "natural," thereby implying that there is little that public policy can do to change the situation. This is not acceptable.

As far as macroeconomic theory is concerned, the "Guideposts" that the Kennedy administration set forth in the 1962 *Economic Report of the President*[44] are sound, reflecting Keynes's insights in chapter 21 of *The General Theory* on the close relationship between wage increases, productivity gains, and the price level.[45] Between 1964 and 1992, labor productivity grew at an annual average rate of 1.6 percent, worker compensation per hour at 6.2 percent, and, not unexpectedly, unit labor costs rose at a 4.7 percent rate. Since markup pricing is widespread throughout the economy, increases in unit labor costs are a major factor in price increases. During the 1964–92 period, consumer prices rose at an annual average rate of 5.5 percent.[46] The fault of the Kennedy Guideposts was not in design, but in the absence of effective machinery for enforcement. The latter has yet to be devised.[47]

A majority of economists remain hostile to an incomes policy, enamored as they are with the market and market solutions to most economic problems. This will change only when greater realism penetrates the profession, leading to recognition that most prices and wages in the economy are more administered than competitive. Under current circumstances, administered processes for prices and wages reflect private interests. An incomes policy is an appropriate way to inject the public interest into the process of wage and price determination. It is also the only way to spring the social trap of a wage–price spiral.[48]

Once an incomes policy is accepted and in place, full employment must become the major macroeconomic goal for the U.S. economy. The nation has not had a full employment policy since the Kennedy–Johnson years, a worthy effort that collapsed because of the disastrous war in Vietnam. A modern full employment policy must be conceived and constructed differently than it was thirty years ago. Then it was simply sufficient to stimulate aggregate demand, as the Kennedy–Johnson administrations sought to do with such devices as the investment tax credit and the tax cuts of 1964. In part because of technology and automation, the link between jobs and production is much looser than it used to be. Over the last two decades, large numbers of well-paying jobs have been lost in the goods-producing sectors, jobs that are not being replaced by expanding employment in services. Furthermore, the United States' growing involvement in an increasingly integrated and highly competitive global economy has pushed many firms to relocate to low-wage, low-cost Third World countries.

Economics traditionally has viewed labor as a "factor of production," a means to the larger end of more output. Work, though, is much more than simply a means to an end. It is an end in itself, because it is through work that people achieve self-expression and self-realization. An anthropologist, Elliott Liebow, expressed this idea eloquently, saying, "Work is not only the fundamental condition of human existence, but it is through work . . . that the individual is able to define himself as a full and valued member of society. It is almost impossible to think of what it means to be human without thinking of work."[49]

If we look at jobs and work from this perspective, it means that the opportunity for productive and useful work is something the economic system ought to produce just as much as it produces goods and services. It can be argued, of course, that this idea is implicit in a full employment policy. This may have been true in the past but it is less true now. The reason is not just because of the weakened links between production and jobs, but also because so little is really known about how to create "good jobs"—that is, jobs that enable workers with less than a college education to earn incomes on which they can support a family. Thus, a contemporary full employment policy involves more than stimulating aggregate demand. Policy must also embrace explicitly the goal of quality job creation, one of the toughest challenges confronting policy makers.

Any full employment policy is made operational through measures that raise aggregate demand—this is fundamental to macroeconomic policy—but how this is done is vital. In the brief experience the nation has had with a full employment policy under Presidents Kennedy and Johnson, the focus was on stimulating demand in the private sector, primarily by tax credits to spur investment and tax cuts to increase personal consumption. This is not what is currently needed, especially after the go-go years of the 1980s when the consumption as a share of GDP rose to the highest level of the entire post–World War II period.[50] A part of the price for the nation's consumption binge of the 1980s—a binge enjoyed primarily by the upper quintile of the population—was the continued and accelerated neglect of public investment. In current dollars, the nation's shortage of public capital—the infrastructure of roads, bridges, sewer and water systems, airports, rail networks, mass transit systems, and the like—is at least $1 trillion![51]

The route to a full employment economy under current conditions is a massive program of public investment to rebuild and modernize the nation's infrastructure. With the Cold War over, resources for such a program can be provided through major reductions in military spending. A carefully designed program for infrastructure investment is probably the best way to make a start on providing jobs with adequate pay for many persons seeking full-time work. Further, and contrary to conventional economic wisdom, infrastructure investment does not "crowd out" private investment. Rather, as David Alan Aschauer has found, over a period of four to five years, every dollar increase in public investment leads to an increase of approximately forty-five cents in private investment.[52] By its very nature, such an investment program will be highly decentralized. This is because the overwhelming bulk of infrastructure investment spending is done at the local level. This should continue, even though most of the financing will have to come from the federal government.

In his agenda for reform, Minsky argues for a shift in full employment policy away from subsidizing private investment to a revival of some of the employment-based programs of the 1930s, like the Civilian Conservation Corps (CCC), the National Youth Administration (NYA), and the Works Progress Administration (WPA).[53] These are worthy objectives, easily attained within the framework of a massive program for infrastructure investment. Programs like the CCC, NYA, and WPA from the 1930s not only provide jobs, but also result in visible outputs, something that does not result from transfer spending for welfare purposes.

The idea of linking a full employment policy to investment in the nation's sadly neglected infrastructure is neither unrealistic nor radical. The resources are there, currently locked up in our oversized military establishment, while financing state and local government activities through the federal government is an old story. An infrastructure investment program is good economics. All economists understand that investment in capital and investment in people is the true road to full employment and economic growth. Economists must enlarge their horizons to include public as well as private investment in this formula.

In conclusion, a few observations are in order about monetary policy, the rate of interest, and the global economy. As for monetary policy, which has had to carry most of the stabilization burden because of Reagan–Bush deficits, its proper role should be to supply the economy with the necessary purchasing power required by a full employment fiscal policy buttressed by an incomes policy. With respect to the rate of interest, it is time to take seriously Keynes's admonition that interest rates must remain low for capitalism to function effectively. It is true that interest rates have recently been at their lowest level since the mid-1960s, but given the strong propensity of the Federal Reserve to fight inflation by raising interest rates, any upsurge in prices will bring a return of interest rates to the levels of the 1980s.[54] In *The General Theory*, Keynes expressed hope, too, that someday we might see the "euthanasia of the rentier," but our society has moved steadily away from that objective. In 1992, interest income accounted for 9.1 percent of the national income, far above the 1.3 percent share in 1950.[55] Keynes also argued that "interest today rewards no general sacrifice, anymore than does the rent of land," a philosophical position that economists ought to examine, particularly in view of the fact that interest on the nation's debt is the third largest item in the federal budget, following military spending and social security payments.[56] The more than $200 billion spent on interest by the federal government in fiscal year 1994 did not lead *directly* to the production of anything or the employment of any person.[57]

As for the global economy, two comments are in order. First, we now live and produce in the context of a global economic system in which national economic sovereignty is increasingly limited, transnational flows of money and finance are calling the tune, and the international economic order is one of almost unrestricted laissez-faire. On a global scale, as was the case on the domestic scale in the 1930s, few institutions and instruments exist through which a reasonable degree of social control can be exercised over global markets. This latter condition leads to a second observation. The single, basic lesson we learned from the economic debacle of the 1930s is that a regime of unrestrained laissez-faire did not work for the domestic economy. It will not work on a global scale either. Economists should be in the forefront of forging the ideas, the theory, and the institutional arrangements whereby the market forces at loose in the global economy can be harnessed to the social interest. In the meanwhile, it is vital that the leading industrial nations—especially the G–7 countries—coordinate their macroeconomic policies to a far greater extent than they have to date.[58]

One final comment: Keynesian economics bolstered by a sound knowledge of the institutions through which the real-world economy of money making operates still offers the best intellectual tool available to shape our economic lives at the macroeconomic level. Market capitalism is a turbulent, unstable system, not self-adjusting if left to its own devices, but one that is enormously productive and, when tamed and managed, will provide full employment, reasonable growth, and a decent standard of life for most people.

Notes

1. John Maynard Keynes, *The Collected Writings of John Maynard Keynes*, vol. 13, ed. by Donald Moggridge, *The General Theory and After*, Part I (London: Macmillan, St. Martin's Press, 1973), pp. 408–11.

2. John S. Gambs, *Beyond Supply and Demand: A Reappraisal of Institutional Economics* (New York: Columbia University Press, 1946), p. 8.

3. Allan Gruchy, *Modern Economic Thought: The American Contribution* (New York: Prentice-Hall, 1947), p. 552.

4. John Maynard Keynes, *The General Theory of Employment, Interest and Money* (London: Macmillan, 1936), p. 161.

5. John S. Gambs, *Beyond Supply and Demand*, p. 13.

6. John Kenneth Galbraith, "Power and the Useful Economist," *American Economic Review*, *63* (March, 1973), 10.

7. Paul Davidson, *Money and the Real World* (New York: John Wiley and Son, 1972), p. 4.

8. J.R. Hicks, "Mr. Keynes and the Classics: A Suggested Interpretation," *Econometrica*, *5* (April 1937): 147–59.

9. Joan Robinson, "What Has Become of the Keynesian Revolution?," *Challenge*, *16* (January–February 1974), 446.

10. G.L.S. Shackle, *The Years of High Theory* (Cambridge: The University Press, 1967), p. 112.

11. John Maynard Keynes, "The General Theory of Employment," *Quarterly Journal of Economics*, *51* (February 1937), 214.

12. John Maynard Keynes, "A Self-Adjusting Economic System," *The New Republic*, *20* (February 1935), 35–37. Reprinted in the *Nebraska Journal of Economics and Business*, *2* (Autumn 1963).

13. Joan Robinson, "What Has Become of the Keynesian Revolution?"

14. John Maynard Keynes, "The General Theory of Employment," p. 214.

15. G.L.S. Shackle, "Keynes and Today's Establishment in Economic Theory: A View," *Journal of Economic Literature*, *11* (June 1973), 518.

16. Ibid.

17. Dudley Dillard, "Money as an Institution of Capitalism," *Journal of Economic Issues*, *21* (December 1987), 1623.

18. While it is doubtful that Keynes knew much about American institutionalism as a body of thought, he did receive a reprint of an essay on monetary theory and policy from John R. Commons in 1927, and responded with a letter that included the following:

> Many thanks for sending me your article in the "An[n]alist." I am entirely in sympathy with it. Indeed, a good deal of your analysis runs on very closely similar lines to some material which I already have in my manuscript for a forthcoming book [i.e., the *Treatise on Money*] . . . [Moreover,] I quite agree with your practical proposals. . . . I should very much like to have some conversations with you on this and other matters. Judging from limited evidence and at great distance, there seems to be no other economist with whose general way of thinking I feel myself in such genuine accord.

This letter, dated April 26, 1927, is reproduced in *John R. Commons Papers* (microfilm edition 1982), State Historical Society of Wisconsin. For more on the monetary economics of John R. Commons, see Charles J. Whalen, "Saving Capitalism by Making It Good," *Journal of Economic Issues*, *27* (December 1993).

19. Dudley Dillard, "Money as an Institution of Capitalism," p. 1629.

20. John Maynard Keynes, "The General Theory of Employment," p. 216.

21. John Maynard Keynes, *The Collected Writings of John Maynard Keynes*, vol. 13, p. 411.

22. John Maynard Keynes, *The Collected Writings of John Maynard Keynes*, vol. 29, ed. by Donald Moggridge, *The General Theory and After* (London: Macmillan 1979), p. 49.

23. John Maynard Keynes, *The General Theory of Employment, Interest and Money*, p. vi.

24. Ibid., p. vii.

25. Ibid., pp. 292, 293.

26. Ibid., p. 293 (emphasis in original).

27. Ibid.

28. John Maynard Keynes, *The Collected Writings of John Maynard Keynes*, vol. 29, p. 89. In his early drafts of *The General Theory*, Keynes used the term "an entrepreneur economy" to mean a monetary economy.

29. Dudley Dillard, *The Economics of John Maynard Keynes: The Theory of a Monetary Economy* (Englewood Cliffs, NJ, Prentice-Hall, 1948).

30. Dudley Dillard, "The Theory of a Monetary Economy," in Kenneth K. Kurihara (ed.), *Post Keynesian Economics* (New Brunswick, NJ: Rutgers University Press 1954), pp. 3–30.

31. Dudley Dillard, "The Evolutionary Economics of a Monetary Economy: Remarks upon Receipt of the Veblen-Commons Award," *Journal of Economic Issues, 21* (June 1987), 580.

32. Dudley Dillard, "The Theory of a Monetary Economy," p. 28.

33. John Maynard Keynes, *The General Theory of Employment, Interest and Money*, p. 235.

34. L. Randall Wray, "Minsky's Financial Instability Hypothesis and the Endogeneity of Money," in Steven Fazzari and Dimitri B. Papadimitriou (eds.), *Financial Conditions and Macroeconomic Performance: Essays in Honor of Hyman Minsky* (Armonk, NY: M.E. Sharpe, 1992), p. 169.

35. Hyman P. Minsky, *Stabilizing an Unstable Economy* (New Haven, CT: Yale University Press, 1986). This is the most comprehensive statement of Minsky's views.

36. Ibid., part II, pp. 13–99.

37. Ibid., p. 95.

38. Walter Heller, "Activist Government: Key to Growth," *Challenge, 29* (March–April 1986), 7.

39. Hyman P. Minsky, *Stabilizing and Unstable Economy*, p. 299.

40. *Economic Indicators* (Washington, DC: U.S. Government Printing Office, October 1993), pp. 1, 34.

41. John Kenneth Galbraith, "Reaganomics: A Midterm View," in *Reaganomics: Meaning, Means, and Ends* (New York: The Free Press, 1983), p. 28.

42. Wallace C. Peterson, "What Is to Be Done? Remarks upon Receipt of the Veblen-Commons Award," *Journal of Economic Issues, 27* (June 1992), 337–48.

43. *Economic Report of the President* (1993), pp. 390, 411.

44. The 1962 *Economic Report of the President* stated that "The general guide for noninflationary wage behavior is that the rate of increase in wage rates (including fringe benefits) in each industry be equal to the trend rate of over-all productivity increase." This is the essence of the "Guideposts" worked out by President Kennedy's Economic Council, whose members were Walter Heller, Kermit Gordon, and James Tobin. For full details, see the 1962 *Economic Report*, pp. 185–90.

45. John Maynard Keynes, *The General Theory of Employment, Interest and Money*, p. 309.

46. *Economic Report of the President* (1993), pp. 398, 411. Inflation that results when money-wage gains run ahead of productivity increases is usually described as a "wage-push" inflation. Such an inflation originates on the cost side of the price equation. There also can be "profits inflation," resulting from increasing markups during periods of slack demand, or "interest inflation," brought about by rising interest rates.

47. The most effective machinery for enforcement of an incomes policy is likely to be devised, as Ray Marshall has suggested, through a cooperative process involving representatives of all major economic interests. See Marshall, *Unheard Voices: Labor and Economic Policy in a Competitive World* (New York: Basic Books, 1987), pp. 290–93.

48. See Charles K. Wilber, chap. 3 in this volume, for a further discussion of the important role of collective action in resolving a wage–price spiral and other social traps.

49. Elliot Liebow, *The New York Times Magazine, 5* (April 5 1970), 28.

50. *Economic Report of the President* (1991), p. 286; (1993), p. 348.

51. Calculated by the author in his book, *Silent Depression: The Fate of the American Dream* (New York: W.W. Norton, 1994), p. 183.

52. David Alan Aschauer, *Public Investment and Private Sector Growth* (Washington, DC: Economic Policy Institute, 1990), p. 19.

53. Hyman P. Minsky, *Stabilizing and Unstable Economy*, p. 310.

54. This monetary policy—monetarism—is flawed for three reasons: (1) it contributes to unemployment by causing a slowdown in economic activity; (2) it contributes to inflation by raising price markups in sectors with market power; and (3) it adds to the federal deficit by raising the government's interest costs in the face of reduced tax receipts.

55. *Economic Report of the President* (1991), p. 312; *Economic Indicators* (October 1993), p. 4.

56. John Maynard Keynes, *The General Theory of Employment, Interest and Money*, p. 376; *Economic Indicators* (October 1993), p. 33.

57. See L. Randall Wray, chap. 7 in this volume, for more on monetary policy.

58. France, Japan, the United States, the United Kingdom, Germany, Italy, and Canada.

9

Economic Inequality and the Macrostructuralist Debate

Barry Bluestone

During the 1992 U.S. presidential campaign, candidate Bill Clinton criss-crossed the nation championing a proactive partnership between the federal government and the private sector. After three terms of Republican-style "laissez-faire," Clinton's economic manifesto *Putting People First* advocated a more aggressive public sector—one not banished to the economic sidelines or limited to the sphere of macroeconomic policy. A Clinton government, promised the campaign, would be committed to structural reforms purposely aimed at creating "good jobs at good wages" and reversing the country's stubborn trend toward economic and social inequality.[1]

Although, for political purposes, it eschewed the standard vocabulary, the Clinton program resurrected what many economists malign as "industrial policy" and "managed trade." The specific structural remedies in the program ranged from infrastructure investment and incentives for defense industry conversion to worker training and education, aggressive trade negotiations to open foreign markets, and direct assistance to private-sector research and development efforts. In advocating such initiatives, *Putting People First* gingerly entered the fray of the economic profession's most timeless controversy: where, when, and to what extent the public sector should be allowed to trespass on the private market. The objective in this chapter is to explore the current state of the controversy in the context of the advancing globalization of the U.S. economy.

The "Killingsworth–Heller" Debates

It is helpful to begin with a bit of history. With the national unemployment rate topping 6 percent in 1961—high by postwar standards—economic advisers to the newly elected President Kennedy urged an explicitly Keynesian tax cut to stimulate the economy. Disputing traditional conservative dogma about the dangers of deficit finance, those within the administration most concerned with the social distress caused by anemic economic growth became enthusiastic supporters of an expansionary fiscal policy.

A vocal minority outside the administration argued that a pro-growth macro policy was necessary, but not sufficient, to handle the structural unemployment facing a substantial and growing segment of the jobless—those with limited skills and education and, most particularly within this group, disadvantaged African-Americans. They argued that rapid technological change, combined with persistent discrimination in the allocation of educational opportunities, was responsible for a widening mismatch between the skills required on the job and the skills that workers brought to the labor market.[2] As a result, no matter how much the federal government stimulated aggregate demand, there would be a core of workers who would remain structurally unemployed. Dealing with this problem would require a greatly expanded set of job-training programs to shore up the supply side of the labor market as well as a public-sector jobs program to generate employment opportunity on the demand side.

Kennedy's Council of Economic Advisers, led by Professor Walter Heller, was firmly in the tax cut camp.[3] "A rising tide lifts all boats" was the council's refrain. Heller went so far in his support of the tax cut as to predict before a U.S. Senate subcommittee in late 1963 that "the sharpest declines [in unemployment] will occur where the incidence of unemployment is the highest: among teenagers, the Negroes, the less-skilled."[4]

The council's most persistent critic was a professor of labor and industrial relations at Michigan State University, Charles C. Killingsworth. In a series of policy papers first written in 1963, Killingsworth argued that Heller and his colleagues had seriously underestimated the impact of automation on the labor market and thereby had overestimated the ameliorative powers of standard macroeconomic policy.[5] New technology and changing consumption patterns, he warned, "had caused a long-run decline in the demand for low skilled, poorly educated workers and a long-run rise in the demand for high skilled, well-educated workers." He called this phenomenon a labor market "twist" and argued that it had "proceeded farther and faster than adjustments in the supply of labor, resulting in a growing imbalance in the labor market."[6] A tax cut would stimulate demand, but it would do nothing to adjust supply to meet it.

The test of the structuralist claim presumably turned on whether the tax cut would produce a growing gap in unemployment rates between skilled and unskilled workers and specifically between whites and blacks. If this was indeed the appropriate measure, readily available data seemed to furnish conclusive support to the macroeconomic position of the tax cut advocates. In percentage terms, between 1962 and 1967, unemployment rates declined among those with eight years or less of schooling about as much as those with a high school or college degree. The ratio of unemployment rates remained roughly constant—

double for blacks as for whites—testifying to the apparent evenhandedness of the Kennedy tax cut and the utility of standard fiscal policy. That the national aggregate unemployment rate fell below 4 percent for the last four years of the 1960s added weight to the argument that boosting aggregate demand—initially through the 1963 tax cut and then through Vietnam War spending—had satisfactorily dealt with the jobless problem facing all but a handful of workers.

The claim of structural unemployment now seemed a tempest in a teapot. As Gardner Ackley, chairman of President Johnson's Council of Economic Advisers, summed it up in a 1966 address at Southern Illinois University, "It is as clear today as it can possibly be that . . . the inadequate demand camp was right and the structuralists were wrong."[7]

Despite what appeared to be an overwhelming case against the structuralist position, Killingsworth stuck to his guns. In a meticulously researched series of papers, he demonstrated that the nearly uniform decline in unemployment rates could not be used as conclusive proof of the tax cut's efficacy. He began by showing that the declining unemployment rates experienced during the mid-1960s masked significant countertrends in labor-force participation.[8] Instead of adding to the official unemployment count, many of automation's long-term jobless had actually exited the labor force. Between 1962 and 1967, participation declined for men with less than twelve years of schooling, while it increased for those with more education.[9] This "twist" in labor-force participation, according to Killingsworth, reflected the twist in demand toward highly educated workers and against those with less than a high school diploma.

Even more compelling was Killingsworth's argument that the Kennedy–Johnson era could not be used as a germane test of pure aggregate demand policy. What confounded any assessment was that along with fiscal stimulus, the government had implemented powerful structural policies during the 1960s which helped to lower the unemployment rates of less skilled workers, and particularly those of young black men. One of these—the wartime equivalent of a massive public jobs program—was the expansion of the armed forces by nearly 600,000 between early 1964 and late 1966. Those drafted into the military were young and a disproportionate number were black. This alone was responsible for lowering the official civilian unemployment rate in the latter year to 3.8 percent from what would have been an estimated 4.5 percent.

Also contributing to the decline in labor-force participation as a direct consequence of the Vietnam War were the nearly 185,000 young men who avoided the draft by maintaining their full-time student status rather than attempting to enter the labor market. A third factor was the expansion in federally funded job training programs—an explicit structural policy. More than 400,000 workers participated in the newly created Neighborhood Youth Corps, the Job Corps, New Careers, and other so-called "manpower programs" during this period. Enrollment in these programs automatically lowered the official unemployment rate since the Bureau of Labor Statistics counted participants as either "employed" or "out of the labor force" even though most would have been unemployed in the absence of these programs. Where successful, they also did what structural programs are supposed to do: they improved the match between labor supply and labor demand.[10]

During the 1960s, Killingsworth never received the full credit he deserved for his careful research on structural imbalances in the U.S. labor market. But history would soon bear out his structuralist revelation. The rise in *both* unemployment and inflation after 1969—leading to the imposition of wage and price controls in 1971—suggested a level of structural unemployment well above anything the pure fiscal stimulus enthusiasts predicted. A surplus supply of low-skilled workers contributed to unemployment while an insufficient supply of high-skilled workers led to a wage-led escalation in prices.

Structural Problems since the 1960s

In retrospect, Charles Killingsworth—and a small band of structuralist contemporaries—were a generation ahead of their time. The labor-market twist identified during the 1960s was, in retrospect, no more than a mild precursor to what we would witness in the 1990s as a serious structural imbalance in the labor market. Thirty years after Killingsworth's seminal work, a rapidly growing body of economic analysis suggests that the twist can be observed not only in official unemployment rates, but in labor market outcomes more generally.

One of the most conspicuous aspects of the new structural imbalance in the U.S. economy is the sharp deterioration in labor market outcomes among young workers who have no more than a high school education.[11] Recent research by Barry Bluestone, Mary Huff Stevenson, and Chris Tilly[12] compares the "jobless" rates and annual earnings of white and black twenty-year-olds in the mid-1980s (1983–87) to those of a generation earlier in the mid-1960s (1963–67). Using *Current Population Survey* (CPS) data, this new research demonstrates that the jobless rate—defined in this case as the proportion of a cohort reporting no hours worked, no weeks worked, and no wages earned during the entire year previous to the annual March survey—rose modestly among white male twenty-year-olds. It went from 1.1 percent in the 1960s to 4.8 percent in the 1980s. However, among comparably educated twenty-year-old black men, the rate soared from 3.8 to 21.6 percent. For black high school dropouts, there was a sixfold increase between the two periods in this measure of employment distress—from 6.0 to 36.1 percent.

As a consequence of the increase in joblessness and a related decline in weekly earnings among those who held jobs, real annual earnings stagnated over the twenty-year period for white male high school graduates (–3.3 percent), it declined for white male high school dropouts (–17.1 percent) and black high school graduates (–22.4 percent), and it plummeted for black high school dropouts (–47.4 percent). The term "underclass," referring to a group totally divorced from the U.S. economic mainstream, has been applied to at least the last of these cohorts.[13]

What is happening at the very bottom of the United States' social class structure represents a particularly severe case of a more general change occurring throughout the U.S. labor market. A new labor market twist is affecting white workers as well as black, prime age as well as young. It is reflected in estimates of overall wage inequality and particularly in the growing earnings gap between groups of workers with different levels of schooling. There has been a nearly monotonic increase since the early 1970s, for example, in a standard measure of inequality, the variance in the log of annual wages among year-round full-time workers. This measure of wage dispersion has increased from 0.461 in 1973 to 0.505 in 1979 to 0.627 in 1987.[14]

Further analysis of the same CPS data demonstrates the growing significance of schooling as a source of the widening gap in the earnings distribution. In 1963, the mean annual earnings of those with four years of college or more stood at just over twice (2.11) the mean annual earnings of those who had not completed high school. By 1979, this ratio had increased to 2.39, a harbinger of things to come. The earnings gap was nearly three to one (2.91) by 1987.[15]

In fact, the entire pattern of wage growth during the 1980s reflects an unmistakable labor market twist as shown in Table 9.1. During this decade, the real wages of male high school graduates fell by nearly 13 percent. Even those with some college saw an erosion in earning power. Men who completed college found their higher education had been purely defensive in nature—the undergraduate degree did no more than prevent a decline in inflation-adjusted hourly wages. Only those who had at least the equivalent of a master's degree saw their earnings increase. Women fared better than men in terms of wage growth, but the imprint of a labor market twist is clearly discernible here as well. That approximately 70 percent of U.S. workers have not completed college provides some indication of how large a proportion of the entire labor force has been adversely affected.

Not surprisingly, this pattern of wage inequality is recapitulated in the distribution of family income. During the 1980s, the top fifth of all families by income class enjoyed a robust 22.9 percent increase in their pretax average income. In contrast, as Table 9.2 indicates, the bottom three-fifths of all families sustained a real income loss while even the second highest fifth of all families experienced little improvement in their living standards.[16] This reverses a trend toward less income inequality during the entire postwar period up through the 1970s.

With real income falling the most for those in the bottom of the income distribution, it is not accidental that poverty increased during the 1980s despite an expanding economy and declining unemployment. In 1973, the official poverty rate was 11.1 percent; by 1991 it was 14.2 percent. Nearly 13 million more Americans were in poverty in the early 1990s than in the early 1970s. Like

Table 9.1

Percent Change in Real Average Hourly Wages by Education 1979–89

	Men	Women
High school graduates	−12.7%	−2.9%
1–3 years college	−8.3	4.3
4 years college	0.3	12.7
6 years college	9.8	12.5

Source: Lawrence Mishel and Jared Bernstein, *The State of Working America* (Washington, DC: Economic Policy Institute, 1993).

Table 9.2

Income Growth of Families
(1992 dollars)

	Average family income		Percent change
	1980	1989	1980–89
Top fifth	$89,031	$109,424	22.9%
Second fifth	45,827	47,913	4.6
Middle fifth	32,948	32,681	−0.8
Fourth fifth	21,009	20,140	−4.1
Lowest fifth	8,791	8,391	−4.8

Source: Lawrence Mishel and Jared Bernstein, *The State of Working America* (Washington, DC: Economic Policy Institute, 1993).

family income inequality, poverty had taken a "Great U-Turn," declining from the 1950s through the 1970s and rising more or less ever since.[17]

The Shrinking Power of Macroeconomic Growth

The labor market twist reflected in employment and wage data is a prime indicator of structural imbalance. But there is also a cyclical component suggesting just how dominant structural factors have become relative to macroeconomic growth.

Historically, inequality has been countercyclical, growing during recessions and declining during expansions. During economy-wide contractions, lower-skilled workers usually bear the brunt of rising unemployment and stagnating wages—leading to a wider gap in outcomes between themselves and more skilled workers. During past economic recoveries, these lower-skilled workers have benefited the most in terms of reemployment and rising wages. Family incomes have followed suit.

Beginning in the late 1970s, however, earnings inequality has defied the cycle. It has increased during recessions as in times past, but then has continued to increase right through recovery. In 1979, the ratio of real average hourly wages of workers in the eightieth percentile of earnings to those in the twentieth was 2.42. Throughout the 1980s, despite overall economic growth following the 1980 and 1981–82 recessions, the advantage of well-paid workers continued to accelerate. By 1989, the 80/20 percentile wage ratio had risen to 2.77. Family income inequality did exactly the same. In the recession year 1980, the top one-fifth of all families enjoyed an average income ten times that of the bottom fifth. After seven straight years of economic expansion, the richest fifth earned thirteen times their poorer counterparts.[18]

If macroeconomic growth could not reliably counter the labor-market twist of the 1960s, it has been wholly inadequate to the task ever since. In entering a new economic regime, "rising tide" policies are leaving more and more boats on the bottom.

The Sources of Labor-Market Twist in the 1980s and 1990s

What Killingsworth and his colleagues could not have easily foreseen from their vantage point in the middle of the 1960s was a phalanx of structural forces beyond machine automation that would magnify the mismatch between labor supply and labor demand and generate the inequality just described. These include: (1) the accelerated shift in employment from manufacturing to services or "deindustrialization"; (2) an accompanying "deunionization" of the work force; (3) an explosion in global trade and transnational capital mobility; (4) a chronic U.S. trade deficit; and (5) increased immigration particularly from newly industrialized and developing countries. All of these, when added to the early structuralists' concern about technical progress, help to explain the explosion in economic inequality in the United States since the late 1970s.

Note, for example, the distributional impact of the shift of employment from goods-producing industries (construction, mining, and manufacturing) to services. In 1963, nearly one-third (32.7 percent) of all wage and salary workers in the United States were employed in this sector. Thirty years later, the proportion is little more than one-fifth (20.8 percent). This exodus from goods-producing sectors into services might simply have led to a decline in overall wages since mean annual earnings in services remain about 20 percent lower than in manufacturing, mining, and construction. But this same shift in industry composition has had a profound secondary effect: an accelerating earnings gap between skilled and unskilled workers. Between 1963 and 1987, the earnings ratio between college graduates and high school dropouts working in the goods-producing sector widened from 2.11 to 2.42—an increase of 15 percent. In services, however, the school-related earnings ratio moved from 2.20 to 3.52—a 60 percent increase.[19] That virtually all of the employment growth in the economy during the 1980s came in the sector polarizing most rapidly explains part of the dramatic increase in earnings inequality.

Reinforcing the inequality-inducing shift in industry composition has been the decline in unionization. At one point during the 1950s, more than a third of the U.S. labor force belonged to unions. By the early 1990s, the proportion was under 16 percent and falling. The combination of a shrinking manufacturing sector where organized labor has traditionally been strong and rapidly expanding services where unions have traditionally been weak explains in large measure the decline in union strength. That unions have generally negotiated wage packages that narrow earnings differentials is one of the reasons for the lower wage dispersion in manufacturing.[20] That unions have made only modest inroads into the service economy explains in part why earnings inequality in this sector outstrips that elsewhere.

What can be described as skill-biased technological change is also an element in the earnings dispersion story. New computerized technologies generally boost the demand for skilled workers while displacing the need for workers of more common skill and education. This turns out to be particularly true in such industries as communications; business services; and finance, insurance, and real estate.[21]

Still, even more fundamental to the recent restructuring of the labor market—and a proximate cause of deindustrialization and deunionization—has been the accelerating "globalization" of the economy. Globalization entails more than increased foreign trade. It covers such interrelated phenomena as the withering of trade barriers, transnational capital flows, chronic trade deficits, and increased immigration. As we shall presently see, the combination of these four is largely responsible for recent changes in the American earnings distribution. Figure 9.1 provides a elementary schematic of these interrelationships.

Figure 9.1. **The Impact of International Economic Forces on the Domestic Earnings Distribution**

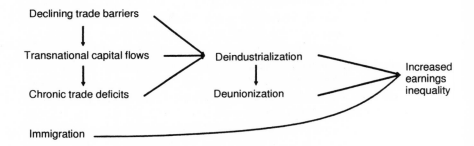

The impact of trade itself can best be understood by considering a rather abstract piece of economic theory—the "factor price equalization" theorem first postulated during the 1920s and early 1930s by Eli Heckscher and Bertil Ohlin.[22] According to the theory, under a particular set of conditions, unfettered international trade is sufficient by itself—*without* any accompanying capital mobility or immigration—to induce the price of each input factor (for example, the wages of unskilled workers) to equalize across trading countries. There are stringent conditions for this to occur: (1) there must be as many or more commodities produced as there are factors; (2) "tastes" must be broadly similar across countries; (3) countries must use identical production functions with some factor substitution; (4) transport costs must be negligible; (5) there must be no barriers to trade; (6) perfect competition must characterize all markets; and (7) something of every commodity must be produced and consumed in every country after trade.

Thirty years ago, these Heckscher–Ohlin conditions were far from being met. As such, elegant as it might be, the theory had no practical use. People from different countries and cultures appeared to favor different goods and services; different production technologies were used to produce similar goods in different countries; transportation costs, tariffs, and nontariff barriers were formidable; monopoly characterized the markets in key industries; and countries were highly specialized in the commodities they produced and consumed. Under these conditions, there would have been little trade-induced equalization and, indeed, wages for similar kinds of labor as well as profit rates varied substantially across countries.

Since the 1970s, reality is coming more and more to imitate theory. The real world seems more like the Heckscher–Ohlin world. In part this is due to technology, in part to the ascendancy of laissez-faire economic policy. Transportation and communications revolutions have reduced the cost of trade and multinational production. The worldwide proliferation of "best practice" manufacturing techniques in industries that range from textiles to high-tech semiconductors has contributed to the use of virtually the same production processes worldwide. Deregulation of key industries plus liberalized trade under GATT have moved virtually all nations toward more competitive product markets and freer trade. Hence, a theory that held only academic interest in the 1920s, or for that matter as late as the 1960s, provides a reasonable starting point for understanding wage trends in the 1980s and 1990s.

One might still ask, how does Heckscher–Ohlin theory, which predicts factor price *equalization*, contribute to an understanding of income *inequality*? The answer is that while individual factor prices will tend to equalize, the worldwide gap in prices between different factors will tend to expand with the disparity depending on the relative abundance of each factor and the nature of derived demand. With low-skilled workers in the United States competing with a practically unlimited supply of similarly skilled workers elsewhere, low-skilled wages here will tend to fall toward world standards. Wages in less-developed countries will rise slightly while wages of less-skilled workers in advanced nations will fall dramatically. On the other hand, with high-skilled labor generally scarce in less-developed countries, skilled workers will suffer only moderate downward pressure on their wages. The result in advanced countries should be an evolving pattern of wages indistinguishable from the actual U.S. experience previously described in Table 9.1.

Empirically, there is some dispute over whether factor price equalization is responsible for the sharp increase in U.S. earnings inequality. Ironically, a number of neoclassical trade theorists tend to discount its impact. Arguing that the Heckscher–Ohlin conditions are still far from being fulfilled, they tend to attribute increased earnings polarization exclusively to changes in domestic technology that favor skilled workers whether trade takes place or not.[23] In contrast, a much larger cohort of labor economists have all demonstrated a significant trade-induced impact on the American wage structure.[24]

As noted above, commodity trade is only one of the global factors possibly responsible for changes in the U.S. wage structure. Modern transportation and communications technologies, combined with fewer government restrictions on foreign capital investment, have led to increased multinational capital flows between countries. As just one example, the number of "maquiladoras"—manufacturing plants along the Mexican border established with U.S. government approval—has expanded from 65 employing 22,000 workers in 1970 to more than 1,700 employing between 400,000 and 500,000 in 1991.[25] While companies move for many reasons, the search for unskilled labor at wages only a fraction of U.S. levels is one of them. Such transnational investment adds to the effective supply of lesser-skilled labor available to American firms, reinforcing factor price equalization and accelerating the entire disequalizing process.

Increased immigration has a similar effect. Growing immigration from Latin America, the Caribbean, and Southeast Asia has augmented the supply of lesser-skilled labor in the United States, putting downward pressure on existing wages at the low end of the skill spectrum. It is estimated that in the first half of the 1980s, immigration (including illegal aliens) was responsible for at least a quarter of all population growth.[26] The top ten sources of immigration into the United States in the mid-1980s were Mexico, the Philippines, Korea, Cuba, Vietnam, India, Dominican Republic, China, Jamaica, and Iran.[27] Merely the threat of moving operations from the United States to other countries or employing immigrant labor at home provides an advantage to companies in wage and benefit negotiations with their employees.

In the very long run, capital mobility to less-developed countries will raise productivity and wages alike. In the very long run, rising wages in less-developed countries will reduce emigration (on economic grounds) to advanced countries. In the very long run, wage differentials tied to skill will induce rational individuals to pursue greater education and training in all countries. But for the foreseeable future, existing labor supply conditions in less-developed and

Table 9.3

Factors Responsible for the Increase in the Male College/High School Wage Differential during the 1980s

Deindustrialization	25–33%
Deunionization	20%
Trade and immigration	15–25%
Trade deficit	15%
Technological change	7–25%

Source: Richard B. Freeman and Lawrence F. Katz, "Rising Wage Inequality: The United States vs. Other Advanced Countries," *National Bureau of Economic Research*, May 1993.

advanced nations will lead to greater wage inequality in both.

For the United States, at least, still another factor is at work—chronic trade deficits of $70 to $160 billion a year since 1983. The surplus of manufactured imports over manufactured exports has contributed to the decline in precisely those sectors of the economy that have in the past helped to keep earnings inequality in check.

Richard Freeman and Lawrence Katz have attempted to parse out how much of the overall increase in wage dispersion can be attributed to each of these factors.[28] While it is difficult to do this with any great precision, the relative magnitudes are of interest. Drawing on their research and that of others,[29] we summarize their findings in Table 9.3.

What is interesting is that the factors described in Figure 9.1—from trade, immigration, and trade deficits to deindustrialization and declining union strength—are responsible for at least three-quarters of the total increase in school-related wage differentials among men. Automation—the phenomenon that presumably drove structural unemployment in Killingsworth's day—explains at most 25 percent of the contemporary labor market twist. The consequence of this much more powerful set of structural factors is the sharply rising earnings and income inequality we have seen since the early 1970s—an inequality increasingly correlated with the distribution of education and training.

None of these factors appears to be weakening. If anything, they are strengthening. The passage of the North American Free Trade Agreement (NAFTA), the formation of the European Economic Union (EU), and the successful completion of the Uruguay Round of the General Agreement on Tariffs and Trade (GATT) all contribute to freer international trade and increased transnational capital investment. Corporations are becoming more global, less bound by national borders and national loyalties.[30] Immigration, both legal and illegal, has not slowed. Mass layoffs and plant closings in the manufacturing sector—now fashionable even among profitable firms—continues the trend toward services and away from goods production. The ranks of organized labor continue to shrink. Under these conditions, the structural imbalances and the inequality of the 1980s will almost assuredly accelerate during the 1990s and into the twenty-first century.

Poor Productivity and Stagnating Income

There is an additional problem. At the same time that the forces behind the labor-market twist are stronger than ever, the overall economy is much weaker. This is manifest in falling real wages and stagnating family incomes. Average real gross weekly wages, which grew by 15.3 percent during the 1960s, have actually declined by 14.9 percent since then. Median family income rose by 71 percent between 1953 and 1973. In the following sixteen-year period through 1989, despite rising female labor-force participation rates and the more common occurrence of two-earner families, the median rose by less than 2 percent.[31]

The proximate cause is sluggish productivity growth. In the era when Killingsworth was writing about structural unemployment (1959–69), productivity growth averaged 2.5 percent per year. Since 1969, it has averaged no better than half that rate.[32]

What is responsible for the slowdown in productivity growth is not well understood. Macroeconomic factors such as aggregate savings and investment rates turn out to explain only a small fraction of the overall decline in the nation's efficiency growth rate. The Brookings Institution's Edward Denison, the economist most often credited with inventing "growth accounting," has investigated dozens of factors that might explain the slowdown in national output ranging from declines in capital spending to changing weather conditions for farming. Only about 40 percent of the productivity slowdown after 1973 can be explained by these factors.[33]

What is left out of the Denison calculations and more likely explains the United States' weak productivity performance are such culprits as "outdated competitive strategies," "short time horizons," "technological weaknesses," "neglect of human resources [beyond formal schooling]," "failures of cooperation," and "government and industry working at cross purposes."[34] The important point is that like the underlying causes of the labor market twist, all of these factors are structural in nature. They are not particularly susceptible to improvement through even the most interventionist of macroeconomic policies.

Structural Problems and Traditional Liberal Public Policy

Motivated by the preponderance of these trends, a growing number of economists have come to recognize the limits of a macroeconomic rising tide. Still, the longstanding reticence toward any intervention on the demand side of the labor market has restricted the search for solutions to three types of policies: education and training, immigration reform, and direct tax and transfer policy.

Education and Training Strategy

In theory, equalizing education can counteract the disequalizing effect of skill-biased technological change and factor price equalization. By upgrading less-skilled workers, the surplus of low-skilled workers is reduced and the shortage of skilled workers is relieved. If, by doing this, the overall level of education is increased, this strategy has the added advantage of improving overall labor productivity.

A number of education and training programs have widespread appeal. Expanding the Head Start program for disadvantaged preschool children, charging a corporate tax levy to finance on-the-job training, instituting a national apprenticeship program, and converting current grant and loan programs into income-contingent loans for college and university students are among them. Setting national standards for school performance, introducing merit systems to reward successful teaching, and providing for teacher/parent centered control of schools have all been put forward as possibilities for education reform. Those on the conservative end of the spectrum generally favor an alternative education/training approach, one based on voucher systems that provide public subsidies for private schools or academies.

Although the exact means of augmenting education is contested, there is virtually no disagreement within the economics profession and even less in political circles that schooling and training are the keys to both improving economic growth and ameliorating maldistribution. Indeed, "more training, more schooling" has become something of a mantra in the 1990s—presumably good for whatever ails the economy.

Controlling Immigration

Another direct method for affecting labor supply entails regulating immigrant flows. Canada has a higher rate of immigration than the United States. But immigration laws in the two countries have produced very different effects on their respective labor markets.[35] Since the 1960s, U.S. policy has stressed family reunification. Canada, in contrast, employs a "point system" designed to produce a more skilled immigrant labor pool. According to Borjas, this approach has produced legal immigrants in Canada who average 1.3 more years of education than native Canadians.[36] In the United States just the reverse is true: the typical immigrant has nearly a year less schooling than the native-born.

If we ignore the thorny ethical issues surrounding the rights of political refugees and judgments about the worthiness of individuals seeking to emigrate, one could imagine tilting immigration policy toward greater use of skill-based criteria. This would eventually reduce the supply of legally documented, but poorly educated and trained, workers in the domestic low-skill labor force. Moreover, adding resources to border patrols and strengthening sanctions on employers who hire undocumented workers would presumably cut down on the number of "illegal" immigrants. Political pressure to do just this took the form of the Immigration Reform and Control Act (IRCA) which was approved by the Congress and passed into law in 1986.

Tax and Transfer Redistribution

Finally, if education and immigration control cannot do the job satisfactorily, one can turn to progressive tax and transfer policy to redress inequality directly. Instead of directly altering labor inputs so as to affect the distribution of earnings, this approach redistributes income after it is generated in the private market. Traditional liberal economists favor this method for it theoretically entails the least interference with market forces.

The 1993 Clinton budget package, which narrowly won approval in the Congress, was strongly endorsed by the so-called "deficit hawks" who urged tough measures against mounting national debt. But it also won support from those who worried about growing inequality. The package included higher marginal tax rates on the very wealthy and expansion of the earned income tax credit (EITC) for the working poor. Universal programs such as national health insurance also reduce "postmarket" inequality if they provide similar benefits to all citizens while being underwritten by progressive taxes or fees. Economists may debate the merits of how the Social Security system is financed, but only a hard core of conservatives still advocate its elimination.

Assessing Traditional Liberal Policy

The case for improved education and training programs, rethinking immigration policy, and more actively pursuing redistributive tax and transfer policies is increasingly easy to make on equity grounds. Yet, given the national and global forces we have outlined here, it is necessary to ask whether any of these, even if pursued more vigorously, could effectively reverse present trends toward earnings polarization and income inequality.

Take education and training. The distribution of formal education in the United States has actually become significantly more equal during the past two decades. Based on CPS data for year-round, full-time workers, the coefficient of variation in years of schooling for all Americans age 16 and over has declined from 0.274 in 1963 to 0.204 in 1987.[37] On the surface, this should have generated a more equal earnings distribution. Nonetheless, the income-equalizing effect of this trend has been more than offset by the growing returns to education primarily driven by skill-biased technological change and factor price equalization. In effect, schooling gaps are shrinking but increasingly smaller educational differentials have greater earnings clout.

Typically, job training programs have had even less success. While the fed-

eral government has experimented with a bevy of programs from the original
Manpower Development and Training Act (MDTA) of the Great Society days to
the Job Partnership and Training Act (JTPA) program in the 1980s, repeated
evaluations suggest mixed results at best. Some programs like the Job Corps,
which provide long-term training opportunities to disadvantaged youth, have
been found cost-effective. The vast majority have dubious cost–benefit ratios. In
any case, even when these programs are "successful," the earnings advantage
they give participants makes only a dent in the trend we saw in Table 9.1. James
Heckman has actually estimated how small this dent really is. Assuming a generous 10 percent rate of return on investment, he notes that a staggering $284
billion would need to be spent on the U.S. work force simply to restore male
high school dropouts to their 1979 real incomes. Even more staggering, to restore skill differentials to their real 1979 levels without reducing anyone's real
income would take more than $2 trillion dollars![38]

To be sure, further investments in human capital programs may have a somewhat better track record than past attempts, particularly if they are well targeted.
But one cannot ignore the enormous increases in inequality that have already
taken place, nor can one overlook the *Alice in Wonderland* nature of the problem. To counter the accelerating trend of disequalizing global competition and
technological change, these programs must be expanded faster and faster simply
to keep inequality from growing worse. Immigration reform may have a marginal impact as well, but any improvement will be largely limited to regions of
the country where immigration flows have been disproportionately large.

A similar conclusion is warranted for tax and transfer programs. On paper, a
suitably progressive set of tax rates combined with sufficiently generous transfer
assistance can be constructed that radically redistributes postmarket income. But,
in practice, even with such measures as the Clinton 1993 tax initiatives, the
degree of redistribution is sufficiently small that it can hardly offset the inequality trends set in motion under Heckscher–Ohlin conditions, multinational capital
flows, migration, and skill-biased technical change. In 1977, when the federal tax
system was significantly more progressive than it is today, the pretax ratio of
shares of total income between the richest fifth and the lowest fifth of family
income groups was 9.5 to 1. Federal taxes reduced the gap in relative shares by
less than 20 percent; state and local taxes, if anything, increased the gap. Given
the current trend toward greater reliance on regressive payroll taxes and an
aversion to any further increase in progressive income taxation, it is unlikely that
much more redistribution is possible through the tax system.

The same is true of public transfer programs. Over the past twenty years, the
New Deal "social safety net" of unemployment insurance and welfare assistance
has come under attack. Unemployment insurance (UI) covered over 60 percent
of the jobless during the 1961 and 1975 recessions. Despite the greater severity
of the 1982 recession, only 43 percent of the unemployed collected jobless
benefits. During the 1991 recession, coverage was down to 40 percent. While

there may be important reforms of the federal UI system under the Clinton administration, it is unlikely that the states or the federal government will greatly expand coverage to the unemployed.

The traditional welfare system, including Aid to Families with Dependent Children (AFDC), has also been eroded during the past decade. Real benefit levels have been cut in many states and the system has imposed greater eligibility restrictions. Again, there may be major reforms in the structure of programs, but it is unlikely that coverage or benefits will be greatly expanded.

In sum, education and immigration reform as well as redistributive tax and transfer policy can contribute to turning the tide of inequality, but by themselves—and under the best of political scenarios—they are no match for the forces now driving the labor market.

Labor-Market Regulation, Industrial Policy, and Managed Trade

In the late 1970s, as import competition surged and the economy was experiencing a painful round of stagflation with both rising unemployment and inflation, the macrostructuralist debate briefly considered whether industrial and managed trade policies, like those allegedly used in Japan and Europe, could assist U.S. manufacturing industries and accelerate aggregate growth. Not much came of the debate over demand side structural policy before the whole issue was made moot by the election of Ronald Reagan and the political triumph of conservative "supply-side" nostrums. The election of Bill Clinton and the campaign promises in *Putting People First* made it possible once again to consider a more aggressive structural approach to economic problems—particularly the labor-market twist and income inequality.

Demand-side structural policies fall into three primary areas: labor-market regulation, industrial policy, and managed trade.

Regulating the Labor Market

As the empirical evidence suggests, the growth in earnings inequality has come about in part because of a serious erosion in wages at the bottom of the skill distribution and a sharp decline in unionization. Rectifying these two trends is seen as one element in reversing inequality. Imposing higher minimum wage standards and mandating employer benefits such as health insurance are therefore advocated as a direct way for government to affect the distribution of employee compensation.

While raising the mandatory wage minimum theoretically entails some tradeoff in the form of job loss, recent evidence suggests that the positive earnings impact of at least modest increases in the statutory minimum far outweighs the employment effect—that is, total wage payments to less-skilled workers increase.[39] Given that the benefits are concentrated in the bottom of the earnings distribution, raising wage floors should militate against earnings inequality.

Labor law reform, making it easier for unions to organize unorganized work-ers, provides an indirect method to accomplish a similar objective. While there are many reasons why union membership is dwindling, there is strong evidence that unions do not face a level playing field when it comes to organizing drives.[40] That employers can permanently replace striking employees reduces the ability of unions to organize and to freely negotiate collective-bargaining agreements. That unions do not have free access to employees during membership drives and that the penalties for employer "unfair labor practices" are so trivial tilt the playing field toward management.

Legislation that would ban permanent striker replacements, permit union or-ganizers access to in-plant bulletin boards and public forums, and impose more costly penalties on employers who violate the legal rights of union organizers would all presumably increase union strength. The empirical evidence regarding the impact of deunionization suggests that these measures have their place in the redistribution arsenal.

Industrial Policy

Beyond labor market regulation are various industrial policies aimed at retaining or expanding employment, particularly in the nation's manufacturing sector. Ironically, one of the most comprehensive plans for a national industrial strategy was spawned by a federal commission established by the Reagan administration. The Commission on Industrial Competitiveness, comprised of corporate execu-tives, union leaders, and academics, and chaired by John Young, the president of the Hewlett-Packard Company, urged the White House to create an Economic Security Council to plot U.S. global economic strategy.[41]

In its report, the commission called for the creation of a Federal Department of Science and Technology to promote national policies for research and innova-tion, enhanced R&D tax credits to "maximize innovation," the elimination of antitrust barriers to joint R&D efforts, the streamlining of patent laws to promote product development, the expansion of Export–Import Bank services to assist U.S. industries in foreign markets, the initiation of a federally funded Export Promotion campaign, and the encouragement of state and local government ini-tiatives in the area of joint management/labor/government programs to enhance competitiveness and promote exports.

The commission avoided any mention of a National Development Bank and was silent on the government's role in picking "winners" and "losers" among manufacturing sectors. Still, the commission advocated the replication in the United States of some of the public policies used successfully in other countries, particularly Japan, to maintain more of the United States' manufacturing base.[42] The commission said nothing about the impact of such policies on the earnings distribution, but as noted above, empirical evidence compiled since the commission's report at least indirectly suggests that policies that help to retain manufacturing jobs are likely to reduce overall earnings inequality.

Advocates of industrial policy point to the success of the U.S. aircraft industry and agriculture as examples where government R&D subsidies and government purchases help to create and maintain industries that dominate world markets. The Carter administration's Chrysler Loan Guarantee, which provided an eleventh-hour reprieve from certain bankruptcy for the hapless automaker, played a critical role in turning around an old "smokestack" company and saving tens of thousands of well-paying jobs—not only at Chrysler but at hundreds of its suppliers. With a new lease on life supplied by the federal government, Chrysler has surged back as a world leader in automotive technology. While there are many instances of failed industrial policy—the government's ill-fated Synfuels Corporation, for example—there are an ample number of cases on the other side of the ledger.

Managed Trade

Finally, there are structural policies to influence global trade. Under "fair trade" provisions, global trading relationships are negotiated between nations so as to smooth economic transitions within and between countries.[43] One way of doing this is to use tariffs and trade barriers designed to give *temporary* protection to key industries so as to promote industrial revitalization and economic transition. Another type of managed trade ties the offer of reduced protection to a trading partner's compliance with certain environmental and labor standards. Critics of NAFTA argued for side agreements that would have linked the pace of tariff reduction to the rate at which Mexican wages caught up with Mexico's rapidly rising productivity.

By linking tariff reduction to the fulfillment of specific conditions, fair trade can potentially fulfill three objectives. First, it can slow down the transition to wide open markets, giving workers and firms a respite to allow an adjustment to unlimited competition. Second, it can temporarily reduce the disparity in effective production costs between countries, thus diminishing the downward pressure on wages in the higher wage country and somewhat reducing the short-term incentive for capital mobility. Finally, where managed trade involves negotiating the opening of markets in other countries (e.g., Japan), such policies can help trim the size of trade deficits in countries like the United States.

There is virtually no doubt that government-imposed limits on trade can have detrimental effects on prices and therefore reduce average real incomes from what they might be under a free trade regime. Nevertheless, a carefully crafted set of trade policies that condones temporary protection of selected domestic markets can soften the distributional impact of factor price equalization. The trick is to keep such protection from becoming permanent or prompting a trade war.

The Case for More Aggressive Structural Policies

To be sure, standard neoclassical theory condemns such structural policies. Traditional economists including most liberals are quite hesitant, if not openly hostile, when it comes to more aggressive "demand side" efforts. In general, they doubt the ability of government agencies to carry out industrial or trade policies effectively and fear that even the most carefully formulated government attempts will be undermined by political machinations. As such, inefficient and outmoded, but politically powerful, industries will be aided; agile small startups will be ignored.[44] Such concerns are not without foundation.

Yet, given the limited efficacy of macro policy and rejiggered labor supply to reverse growing inequality, such policies need to be carefully considered. Economic growth per se cannot be counted upon to reverse the impact of freer trade, deindustrialization, and the imperatives of technological change. Education, training, immigration reform, and progressive tax and transfer policies all can contribute to solving the inequality problem. But by themselves they are no match for the inexorable forces of global free markets.

Still, one might ask, is there any evidence that more aggressive structural policies can help? An affirmative reply comes from comparing recent trends in an international context. We know that all nations now face nearly identical pressures from technological change and global competition. Yet not all are experiencing the same degree of growing inequality.[45] Comparative income distribution data present a strong case that "corporatist" economies—those with strong unions, national wage solidarity agreements, generous social welfare programs, and more vigorously pursued industrial and trade policies—have much less inequality than countries that have pursued laissez-faire policies, notably the United States and the United Kingdom.[46]

Reviewing a range of comparative studies based on the Luxembourg Income Study, Freeman and Katz conclude that while educational and occupational skill wage differentials were growing rapidly in the United States and the United Kingdom during the 1980s, the experience elsewhere was acutely different. The Netherlands saw an actual decline in inequality; France, Germany, and Italy experienced no noticeable change at all in wage differentials; and Australia, Canada, Japan, and Sweden suffered at most modest increases in wage dispersion.[47]

In all of these countries, intensified global competition and technological innovation were pushing the distribution of earnings and income in the same direction of greater inequality as in the United States and the United Kingdom. Structural protection against this onslaught was simply greater in countries that did not follow the Reagan–Thatcher road to full-scale deregulation and laissez-faire trade policies.

The "flexibility" of the U.S. market may be partly responsible for lower overall unemployment rates compared with these countries, but the price of this flexibility seems to be much higher levels of economic polarization and social inequality. Interestingly, recent comparative research by Rebecca Blank suggests that there is little empirical evidence that labor market flexibility is substantially affected by the presence of social protection programs nor does limiting social protection automatically enhance the speed of labor market adjustment. Instead, she finds that by enhancing worker well-being, enhanced social protection may actually permit flexibility that would not otherwise be possible.[48]

Conclusion

Where does this leave economics and economic policy on the eve of the twenty-first century? Despite all the apparent victories of standard neoclassical economic theory during the past decade and half—the rise to power of such political leaders as Ronald Reagan and Margaret Thatcher, the movement toward free trade in North America and Europe, and the demise of the so-called socialist republics of Eastern Europe—it is my contention that the continued trend toward inequality as a consequence of rapid advances in technology and freer trade will keep the debate over structuralist policies wide open in the years to come.

Modern advances in technology and increased global economic integration—for all the benefits they provide—have the unfortunate consequence of leading to greater inequality and social polarization in totally unfettered markets. As such, the political pressure to impose market imperfections in the form of greater labor-market regulation, industrial policy, and managed trade will be almost irresistible as we approach the twenty-first century. In the absence of a much greater redistribution effort tied to human-capital investment and tax and transfer policy, an industrial policy/managed-trade strategy may end up as a sine qua non for the maintenance of civil society. Indeed, in the *Alice in Wonderland* world we have described, a frontal assault on inequality will require major efforts on *all* sides of the market. Strong macroeconomic stimulus will be necessary periodically to maintain employment growth. Education and training efforts targeted to the disadvantaged will be needed to keep skill-based earnings differentials from further widening, and demand-side policies will be needed to keep manufacturing employment opportunities from disappearing. The hard work—both practically and politically—is to devise policies that generate more equality without unduly sacrificing economic efficiency. Quite clearly, the issues raised by Charles Killingsworth and his colleagues in the 1960s are more relevant than ever.

Notes

1. Bill Clinton, "Putting People First: A National Economic Strategy for America" (Clinton for President Campaign Program, 1992).
2. National Commission on Technology, Automation, and Economic Progress, *Tech-*

nology and the American Economy (Washington, DC: U.S. Government Printing Office, 1966).

3. Council of Economic Advisers, "The American Economy in 1961: Problems and Policies," *Economic Report of the President, 1961* (Washington, DC: U.S. Government Printing Office, January 1961); also *Economic Report of the President, 1964* (Washington, DC: U.S. Government Printing Office, January 1964).

4. U.S. Senate Subcommittee on Employment and Manpower, *Hearings*, 88th Congress, 1st Session, pt. 5, October 28, 1963.

5. Charles C. Killingsworth, "Automation, Jobs and Manpower," Statement before the U.S. Subcommittee on Employment and Manpower, *Hearings*, 88th Congress, 1st Session, pt. 5, October 28, 1963.

6. Charles C. Killingsworth, "The Continuing Labor Market Twist," *Monthly Labor Review* (September 1968).

7. Quoted in Charles C. Killingsworth, *Jobs and Income for Negroes* (Ann Arbor: Institute of Labor and Industrial Relations, University of Michigan/Wayne State University, Policy Papers in Human Resources and Industrial Relations, no. 6, May 1968).

8. Eleanor G. Gilpatrick, *Structural Unemployment and Aggregate Demand* (Baltimore: Johns Hopkins Press, 1966).

9. Charles C. Killingsworth, "The Continuing Labor Market Twist."

10. Charles C. Killingsworth, *Jobs and Income for Negroes.*

11. Bennett Harrison and Barry Bluestone, *The Great U-Turn: Corporate Restructuring and the Polarizing of America* (New York: Basic Books, 1988); McKinley L. Blackburn, David E. Bloom, and Richard B. Freeman, "The Declining Economic Position of Less Skilled Men" (as well as other contributions) in Gary Burtless (ed.), *A Future of Lousy Jobs?* (Washington, DC: The Brookings Institution, 1990); John Bound and Richard B. Freeman, "What Went Wrong? The Erosion of the Relative Earnings and Employment among Young Black Men in the 1980s," *Quarterly Journal of Economics 107*, 1 (February 1992), 201–32; and Frank Levy and Richard Murnane, "U.S. Earnings Levels and Earnings Inequality: A Review of Recent Trends and Proposed Explanations," *Journal of Economic Literature 30*, 3 (September 1992), 1333–82.

12. "An Assessment of the Impact of 'Deindustrialization' and Spatial Mismatch on the Labor Market Outcomes of Young White, Black, and Latino Men and Women Who Have Limited Schooling," *John W. McCormack Institute of Public Affairs* (August 1992).

13. William Julius Wilson, *The Truly Disadvantaged* (Chicago: University of Chicago Press, 1987).

14. Barry Bluestone, "The Impact of Schooling and Industrial Restructuring on Recent Trends in Wage Inequality in the United States," *American Economies Review 80*, 2 (May 1990), 303–7.

15. Barry Bluestone, "The Great U-Turn Revisited: Economic Restructuring, Jobs, and the Redistribution of Earnings," in John D. Kasarda (ed.), *Jobs, Earnings, and Employment Growth Policies in the United States* (Boston: Kluwer Academic Publishers, 1990).

16. Lawrence Mishel and Jared Bernstein, *The State of Working America* (Washington, DC: Economic Policy Institute, 1993).

17. Bennett Harrison and Barry Bluestone, *The Great U-Turn.*

18. Computed from Lawrence Mishel and Jared Bernstein, *The State of Working America.*

19. Barry Bluestone, "The Great U-Turn Revisited."

20. George E. Johnson and Kenwood C. Youmans, "Union Relative Wage Effects by Age and Education," *Industrial and Labor Relations Review 24*, 2 (January 1971), 171–79; Richard B. Freeman and James Medoff, *What Do Unions Do?* (New York: Basic Books, 1984).

21. McKinley L. Blackburn, David E. Bloom, and Richard B. Freeman, "The Declining Economic Position of Less Skilled Men"; John Bound and George Johnson, "Changes in the Structure of Wages in the 1980s: An Evaluation of Alternative Explanations," *American Economic Review 82,* 3 (June 1992), 371–92; Larry Katz and Kevin Murphy, "Changes in Relative Wages, 1963–87: Supply and Demand Factors," *Quarterly Journal of Economics 107,* 1 (February 1992), 35–78; Kevin Murphy and Finis Welch, "The Structure of Wages," *Quarterly Journal of Economics 107,* 1 (February 1992), 285–326; and Richard B. Freeman, "How Much Has De-Unionization Contributed to the Rise in Male Earnings Inequality," in Sheldon Danziger and Peter Gottschalk (eds.), *Uneven Tides: Rising Inequality in America* (New York: Russell Sage Foundation, 1993).

22. Charles P. Kindleberger, *International Economics* (Homewood, IL: Richard D. Irwin, 1963).

23. Gene M. Grossman, "The Employment and Wage Effects of Import Competition in the United States," *Journal of International Economic Integration 2* (1987); Robert Z. Lawrence and Matthew J. Slaughter, "Trade and U.S. Wages: Great Sucking Sound or Small Hiccup?," paper presented at MICRO-BPEA Meeting, The Brookings Institution, June 1993.

24. Including Kevin Murphy and Finis Welch, "The Role of International Trade in Wage Differentials," in Marvin H. Kosters (ed.), *Workers and Their Wages: Changing Trade Patterns in the United States* (Washington, DC: American Enterprise Institute Press, 1991); Steven J. Davis, "Cross-Country Patterns of Change in Relative Wages," in Olivier J. Blanchard and Stanley Fischer (eds.), *1992 Macroeconomic Annual* (Cambridge, MA: MIT Press, 1992); Larry Katz and Kevin Murphy, "Changes in Relative Wages, 1963–87"; Edward E. Leamer, "Wage Effects of a U.S.–Mexico Free Trade Agreement," National Bureau of Economic Research, Working Paper no. 3991, 1992; Ana L. Revenga, "Exporting Jobs: The Impact of Import Competition on Employment Wages in U.S. Manufacturing," *Quarterly Journal of Economies 107* (1992), 255–84; and Richard B. Freeman and Lawrence F. Katz, "Rising Wage Inequality: The United States vs. Other Advanced Countries," *Working under Different Rules Conference*, National Bureau of Economic Research, 1993.

25. United Automobile Workers, *Research Bulletin* (February 1991); Philip Mirowski and Susan Helper, "Maquiladoras: Mexico's Tiger by the Tail?" *Challenge 32,* 3 (May–June 1989), 24–30.

26. Leon F. Bouvier and Robert W. Gardner, "Immigration to the U.S.: The Unfinished Story," *Population Bulletin* (Population Reference Bureau) *41,* 4 (November 1988).

27. Martin K. Starr, *Global Competitiveness: Getting the U.S. Back on Track* (New York: W.W. Norton, 1988).

28. "Rising Wage Inequality."

29. For example, George J. Borjas, Richard B. Freeman, and Lawrence F. Katz, "On the Labor Market Effects of Immigration and Trade," National Bureau of Economic Research Working Paper no. 3761, 1991.

30. Robert B. Reich, *The Work of Nations* (New York: Knopf, 1991).

31. Council of Economic Advisers, *Economic Report of the President, 1993* (Washington, DC: U.S. Government Printing Office, 1993).

32. Paul Krugman, *The Age of Diminished Expectations* (Cambridge, MA: MIT Press, 1990).

33. Edward F. Denison, *Accounting for Slower Economic Growth: The United States in the 1970s* (Washington, DC: The Brookings Institution, 1979); Martin Neil Baily and Alok K. Chakrabarti, *Innovation and the Productivity Crisis* (Washington, DC: The Brookings Institution, 1988).

34. Michael L. Dertouzos, Richard K. Lester, and Robert M. Solow, *Made in Amer-*

ica: The Report of the MIT Commission on Industrial Productivity (Cambridge, MA: MIT Press, 1989).

35. David Card, "Small Differences that Matter: Labor Market Institutions, Policies, and Outcomes in Canada and the United States," *Working under Different Rules Conference*, National Bureau of Economic Research, May 7, 1993.

36. George J. Borjas, "Immigration Policy, National Origin, and Immigrant Skills: A Comparison of Canada and the United States," as summarized in David Card, "Small Differences that Matter."

37. Barry Bluestone, "The Impact of Schooling and Industrial Restructuring on Recent Trends in Wage Inequality in the United States."

38. James Heckman, "Assessing Clinton's Program on Job Training, Workfare, and Education in the Workplace," National Bureau of Economic Research, Working Paper no. 4428, August 1993.

39. Larry Katz and Alan B. Krueger, "The Effect of the Minimum Wage on the Fast-Food Industry," *Industrial and Labor Relations Review 46*, 1 (October 1992), 6–21; David Card, "Do Minimum Wages Reduce Employment? A Case Study of California, 1987–89," *Industrial and Labor Relations Review 46*, 1 (October 1992), 38–54. Editor's note: see also David Card and Alan B. Krueger, "Minimum Wages and Employment: A Case Study of the Fast-Food Industry in New Jersey and Pennsylvania," *American Economic Review 84*, 4 (September 1994), 772–93; and David Card and Alan B. Krueger, *Myth and Measurement: The New Economics of the Minimum Wage* (Princeton, NJ: Princeton University Press, 1995).

40. Paul Weiler, "Who Will Represent Labor Now?," *American Prospect 1*, 2 (Summer 1990), 78–87.

41. Commission on Industrial Competitiveness, *Global Competition: The New Reality* (Washington, DC: U.S. Government Printing Office, January 1985).

42. Lester Thurow, *The Zero-Sum Solution* (New York: Simon and Schuster, 1985).

43. Robert Kuttner, *The Economic Illusion: False Choices between Prosperity and Social Justice* (Boston: Houghton-Mifflin, 1984).

44. Charles L. Schultze, "Industrial Policy: A Dissent," *The Brookings Review* (Fall 1983), 3–12.

45. Bennett Harrison and Barry Bluestone, "Wage Polarization in the U.S. and the 'Flexibility' Debate," *Cambridge Journal of Economics 14*, 3 (1990), 351–73; Peter Gottschalk and Mary Joyce, "Changes in Earnings Inequality—An International Perspective," *The Luxembourg Income Study*, Working Paper no. 66, June 1991.

46. Francis Green, Andrew Henly, and Euclid Tsakalotos, "Income Inequality in Corporatist and Liberal Economies: A Comparison of Trends within OECD Countries," *Studies in Economics* (University of Kent at Canterbury, U.K.), *92/13* (November 1992); David Card, "Small Differences that Matter."

47. Richard B. Freeman and Lawrence F. Katz, "Rising Wage Inequality."

48. Rebecca Blank, "Social Protection vs. Economic Flexibility: Is There a Tradeoff?" *Working under Different Rules Conference*, National Bureau of Economic Research, May 7, 1993.

10

Not Markets Alone: Enriching the Discussion of Income Distribution

Chris Tilly and Randy Albelda

Income distribution matters to us because we care about equity. Distribution also matters because it shapes and constrains patterns of consumption, savings, and investment. Finally, distribution matters because it affects the long-term viability of capitalism—as well as of alternative economic systems, including socialism. For all of these reasons, economists working in all of the great theoretical traditions—classical, Marxian, neoclassical, Keynesian—have felt compelled to address the distribution of income.

Yet, an underdeveloped and distorted conception of income distribution dominates Anglo-American economics today. At the macroeconomic level, economists have primarily theorized about and proposed policies to aid growth rather than distribution. At the microeconomic level, neoclassical economics posits a theory of income determination denuded of institutions. The key factor market—labor—is itself institutionally impoverished, while class, family, and state are assumed away to allow for a single-minded focus on factor markets, and are only then reintroduced as modifiers of factor market outcomes.

Fortunately, many economists as well as researchers in other disciplines have worked to build alternatives to this dominant conception. In this chapter we draw on their work to critique conventional economic analysis and to outline some of the elements of a richer theory of distribution.

The current economic situation in the United States and the world lends this task particular urgency. Harrison and Bluestone's felicitous title, *The Great U-Turn*, captures the reversal of the last two decades—with growing inequality accompanied by increasingly vociferous defenses of inequality.[1]

This does indeed mark a reversal. Since the 1930s we have seen a proliferation of political movements setting equality as their goal: parties in power ranging from the New Deal Democrats in the United States to social democrats elsewhere; popular movements such as the civil rights and women's movements; movements in the Third World for independence and for parity with the industrialized nations. These movements had their share of success: inequality decreased along many dimensions during the early postwar decades.

But in the last two decades, inequality has grown anew. In the United States, income dispersions have widened among families and individuals.[2] Categorical disparities grew by race, educational level, occupation, industry—virtually every criterion except gender.[3] Inequality also rose *within* groups defined by these criteria.[4] Meanwhile, inequality among countries worsened as well.[5] Strapped by debt and dependency, many developing countries saw a declining standard of living for the majority.

In parallel arose a resurgence of movements and ideologies declaring the sovereignty of the market and the inefficiency of efforts to redistribute. These were neither a direct cause nor an effect of the trends described above, but served to ratify and reinforce them. In the United States, Reaganism ushered in a decade of inequality in the name of free markets, while conservative governments in Britain, Germany, and elsewhere joined the chorus. Multilateral lenders—the International Monetary Fund and World Bank—imposed austerity in the name of free markets on much of Latin America and Africa.[6]

Hence the title of this chapter. We maintain that there is no such thing as a "free market"; markets invariably are influenced mightily by their institutional contexts. Income inequality is shaped by many factors other than markets alone, and remedying inequality will require action in spheres other than the market. We focus on issues and findings from the industrialized countries (chiefly the United States), but we believe that with some modifications our argument can be generalized to the rest of the capitalist world.

Growth and Distribution

Two Big Ideas

Conventional economic views of income distribution have been greatly shaped by two big ideas: Simon Kuznets's notion that inequality first increases, then decreases as economies develop; and Arthur Okun's formulation of the equity/efficiency trade-off.

In 1955, Simon Kuznets set the stage for post–World War II discussions of income distribution in his American Economic Association presidential address, "Economic Growth and Income Inequality," in which he proposed the "inverted U" time pattern of inequality. His main argument was compositional.[7] With development, populations move from a low-income agricultural sector to a higher-income industrial sector. Incomes are relatively equal in the early stage, when almost everybody is concentrated in agriculture, and in the late stage, when virtually all work in industry. Inequality peaks in between, when the work force is equally divided between the two sectors.

For mature industrial economies, Kuznets's proposition counsels focusing on growth, since equity follows directly from it. In developing countries, it calls for enduring current inequality for the sake of future equity and prosperity. In both cases, income distribution is a corollary to growth.

Twenty years later, in 1975, Arthur Okun took the discussion in a different direction, suggesting that, as far as government redistribution policies were concerned, equity is not a corollary to growth, but an alternative to it.[8] Okun posited a "big trade-off": redistributive equity comes at the expense of efficiency, largely because income redistribution reduces incentives for work and investment.

Good liberal that he was, Okun argued for the "humane" side of the trade-off. But others used Okun's idea to justify a U.S. transfer system that was (and remains) meager compared with the country's industrial counterparts, and to rationalize a growing wealth concentration in the United States. As Okun wrote, the almost continuous growth that had characterized the United States in the postwar period was coming to an end. In short order the supply-siders and the New Classicals (as well as scholars in other disciplines, notably Charles Murray) claimed that negative incentive effects overwhelm the positive impacts of income redistribution.[9] Further, revitalizing eighty-year-old neoclassical theory, they argued that having a larger economic pie to share depends on more rapid growth, which calls for increased investment, which requires more savings, which requires greater wealth. Even liberals concluded in the mid-1980s that the key problem in the U.S. economy was stagnant growth, not rising inequality.[10]

Three Challenges

We challenge the subordination of distributive concerns to growth on three grounds: moral, theoretical, and empirical.

At a moral level, we contend that income distribution deserves attention in its own right both simply because we *should* care who gets what, and because economic inequality breeds social instability. This is hardly a novel idea. David Ricardo declared in 1821 that "To determine the laws which regulate distribution, is the principal problem in political economy."[11] Similarly, Marx and Malthus focused on economic inequality because they saw in it a threat to capitalism—whether through revolution or starvation. More recent research confirms that people care deeply about their level of income *relative* to other people, not simply their absolute standard of living.[12] At the close of the 1980s, as evidence of widening inequality in the United States mounted, a growing number of researchers—including both liberal economists and at least one conservative political analyst—acknowledged anew the autonomous importance of distribution.[13]

On a theoretical plane, we note that the apparent consensus subordinating distribution to growth conceals a wide variety of conflicting long-run models. For every economic theory dismissing income distribution as secondary to growth or even damning redistribution as an obstacle to growth, there is another established theory taking the opposite stance. The three most durable theoretical traditions within economics—neoclassical, Marxian, and Keynesian—accommodate a wide range of views on the relationship between equity and growth. For the most part, growth theorists have limited distributive considerations to the functional division of income between capital and labor—that is, the *average* profit rate and wage.

In a standard neoclassical model (the "golden rule" model), the growth rate of the economy is simply determined by the rate of growth of the employed work force, which is exogenous (since labor markets are assumed to clear). This growth rate, in combination with the savings function, determines the profit rate; the real wage level is determined as a residual.[14] In this framework, distribution is a straightforward consequence of growth. Given the usual neoclassical microfoundations for this model, attempts to raise wages above labor's productivity level or redistribute via welfare benefits are likely to prevent labor market clearing and interfere with growth.

The standard Marxian theory adopts the classical convention that the wage is set exogenously by a combination of tradition and class struggle; the profit rate is then determined as a residual. Since growth depends solely on reinvestment by capitalists (the size of the work force is endogenous, given the existence of a labor reserve of variable size), the level of wages sets the pace of growth in an inverse relationship.[15] Far from being a corollary of growth, distribution *determines* growth, but a version of Okun's trade-off still obtains. However, many economists working within a Marxian tradition have gravitated instead toward a stagnationist version of Keynesian growth theory (see below).[16]

Keynesian theory with regard to growth and distribution has split into a variety of competing camps. Keynes himself commented, "I believe that there is social and psychological justification for significant inequalities of incomes and wealth, but not for such large disparities as exist today."[17] However, some self-described Keynesians essentially adopt the neoclassical long-run growth model, with its bias against redistribution. Others—the post-Keynesians—hold that equilibrium growth occurs where intended savings from profits equal intended investment as a function of the profit rate; wages are then determined as a residual.[18] Finally, a stagnationist school posits that in modern economies dominated by large corporations, the profit rate is a (more or less) fixed markup, and that growth is driven by wage levels via consumption.[19] According to this last theory, redistribution from capitalists to workers via unions, minimum-wage laws, or transfers actually *stimulates* growth.

What have we learned from this theoretical roundup? First of all, current theories speak with many voices regarding the relationship between distribution and growth. All of these models describe possible—and, in many cases, actual—economic regimes, but none of them can serve to characterize all capitalist economies in all historical periods. Second, macroeconomic theorists rarely disaggregate the work force to examine the effects of inequality *among* workers—in part because this poses problems of mathematical complexity.

Finally, we turn to the empirical relationship between growth and distribution—focusing this time on short-run, business-cycle patterns. Until recently, U.S. economists generally agreed that "a rising tide lifts all boats": growth lessens inequality.[20] They appealed to the Phillips curve: whereas the unemployment that results from slow growth disproportionately hurts the poor, the inflation that results from rapid growth has little redistributive effect, and may even hurt the rich to the extent that they hold fixed-interest-rate assets and are net creditors. They also argued that labor shortages due to speedy growth push up wages fastest at the low end, since low-wage jobs tend to have more flexible wages.

This hypothesis fit the data relatively well from roughly 1950 to 1980. But during the 1980s, economic expansion was accompanied by *growing* inequality, and by far smaller than expected reductions in poverty.[21] Economists might have been less surprised by this turn of events had they examined pre-1950 data. Over U.S. history, the relationship between growth and distribution has shifted a number of times: for example, the Great Depression, despite high unemployment rates, compressed U.S. incomes.[22] The lesson is simple: The relationship of growth to distribution depends on the institutional environment.

In short, the theoretical subordination of income distribution to growth is morally inappropriate, theoretically indeterminate, and empirically unwarranted. Rather than supposing any fixed relationship between distribution and growth, we must analyze inequality directly, in a way that is historically specific and institutionally grounded. To do so we now turn to microeconomic theories of personal income distribution.

Putting the Labor Market in Context

About two-thirds of U.S. income is earned in labor markets, but labor markets surely receive more than two-thirds of economists' attention in discussions of income distribution. The dominant, neoclassical theory of labor markets is institutionally naked. Largely lost are the rich contributions of institutionalist labor economists from the 1940s through the 1960s.[23] Instead, we are left with a short-run model that derives labor supply from individual preferences and prices, and demand from marginal revenue product and prices, with prices (wages, in this case) clearing the market. The long-run model incorporates investment (human capital) that affects individual productivity.[24]

What does this omit? Among other things: the family, race, ethnicity, gender, community, employer strategy, non-Walrasian power, unions, culture, customary wage patterns, and level of worker effort.[25]

Economists have employed a variety of approaches to attempt to remedy these shortcomings. Within the neoclassical tradition, the "New Institutional Economists" such as Edward Lazear and Joseph Stiglitz have attempted to derive labor-market institutions from a model peopled with individual maximizers.[26] Their key innovation has been the efficiency wage model, which posits that employers may pay a wage above the market clearing level in order to elicit effort from workers.[27] But their insistence that institutions must flow from individual optimization precludes them from incorporating culture or power into their analyses.

More promising is the labor market segmentation theory pursued by a number of institutionalists and neo-Marxists.[28] Segmentation theories hold that historically, jobs cluster in segments that differ systematically by the skill and training involved, job security and attachment, opportunities for advancement, breadth of job definition, level of worker participation in decisions, and compensation. "It is not possible," writes Paul Osterman, "to pick a rule from each category and establish a stable set of employment relationships. Rather, only certain configurations of rules fit together."[29] However, segmentation theory to date has focused excessively on the work situations and transformation of job clusters as they affect white males; generalization requires more attention to women and people of color.[30]

To advance their understanding of labor markets, economists must grit their teeth and prepare to learn from sociologists and historians. Insights from sociology could illuminate numerous aspects of labor markets: labor productivity, norms about a fair wage and a fair day's work, and labor–management relations are inherently collective, social phenomena. Historical analysis throws into sharp relief the rise and decline of particular labor market institutions.

For example, economic discussions of earnings inequality could benefit greatly from the sociological literature on the importance of networks for finding and succeeding in jobs.[31] Search/recruitment and matching, usually conceptualized by neoclassical economists as activities of individual job seekers and firms, typically involve the overlap between recruitment networks through which employers seek workers, and supply networks through which workers find jobs. Economists concerned with the contingent work force can learn from extensive sociological work on the informal economy, as well as research on the history of subcontracting in other eras of capitalism.[32] Indeed, historians of work would be quick to point out that fundamental concepts such as "worker," "job," "occupation," and "unemployment," far from being timeless, originated at particular points in time and have evolved ever since, reflecting a changing social reality.[33]

Putting Income in Context

Along with an expansion of our understanding of wage income, economists need to enrich their understanding of other forms of income. A first step toward contextualizing income distribution is to note the historical uniqueness of capitalism. Neoclassical economists tend toward ahistorical, even naturalistic conceptions of the economy. As an antidote to this approach, it is refreshing to read Karl Polanyi's impertinent remarks about the artificiality of the three main markets that yield income under capitalism:

[Under capitalism,] labor, land, and money are essential elements of industry; they also must be organized in markets; in fact these markets form an absolutely vital part of the economic system. But labor, land, and money are obviously *not* commodities; the postulate that anything that is bought and sold must have been produced for sale is emphatically untrue with regard to them. . . . Labor is only another name for a human activity which goes with life itself, which in its turn is not produced for sale but for entirely other reasons, nor can that activity be detached from the rest of life, be stored or mobilized; land is only another name for nature, which is not produced by man; actual money, finally, is merely a token of purchasing power which, as a rule, is not produced at all, but comes into being through the mechanism of banking or state finance.[34]

What is fundamental to understanding income distribution is not the particular factor markets that have become so familiar over the last few hundred years but rather that humans must find ways to satisfy their physical, emotional, and social needs. There are three chief ways to meet such needs: make, share, or buy. Under capitalism, a growing share of needs are commoditized: fulfilling them requires buying. Thus, income becomes essential—a prerequisite for consumption, and by extension, a measure of status. Indeed, in countless analyses (including, we confess, some of our own) economists have used income as a readily measurable proxy for consumption of goods and services, and even for well-being. But even in a capitalist mode of production, needs are also met via sharing and making—most notably in the household and via government transfers. Adequately analyzing these locations of income distribution requires looking beyond market relations.

By freeing the exchange of goods and services from many of the bonds of custom, capitalism has brought to the fore what could be called Walrasian power—the power to buy from and sell to whomever one chooses. Many neoclassical models assume Walrasian power is the only significant type of power affecting income distribution. But in fact, this is only one dimension of economic power. For example, a firm's degree of monopoly power has important income consequences for the firm's owners—and its employees. In addition, what Bowles and Gintis call "short-side" power—the power of a seller faced by excess demand or a buyer faced by excess supply (notably an employer in a labor market that has unemployment)—upsets the power symmetry of Walrasian exchange, with dramatic effects on income determination.[35]

In more detail, the key non-labor-market institutions shaping income distribution are class, family, and the state.

Class

Discussion of economic power asymmetries leads naturally to a consideration of class in income determination. The classical economists, including Marx, devoted intense attention to the shares of income accruing to the various ownership classes. However, outside of the rarefied world of macroeconomic growth models (see above), most economists' attention has shifted from the class distribution to the size distribution of income. Researchers define rich and poor in terms of income quintiles rather than relationship to the means of production.[36]

This shift in attention can be attributed in part to the empirical finding that stock ownership is widely dispersed in the United States, but more importantly to neoclassical economists' conceptual replacement of class with endowments (which may in principle be distributed in any pattern among the population). In the neoclassical theory of income distribution, economic agents are rewarded according to the marginal productivity of the factor(s) of production they bring to the market—a rule that applies symmetrically to owners of labor power and owners of capital alike, and initial endowments are taken as given. Of course, the jettisoning of class also has a strong ideological motivation. J. B. Clark, the American economist who pioneered marginal productivity theory at the turn of the century, explicitly sought a theory that would justify unequal allocation.[37]

Rather than abandon class, it seems to us more fruitful to enrich class-based models. Two overlapping directions seem particularly promising. First, it seems essential to recognize that modern capitalism, rather than simply polarizing people into proletariat and bourgeoisie as Marx forecast, has in fact led to a proliferation of classes and subclasses.[38] In particular, capitalist labor markets have segmented the work force into distinct groups with differing compensation, privileges, and systems of control—contradicting Marx's prediction of an increasingly homogeneous and deskilled working class.[39] Second, within any given class, distinctions by race, ethnicity, and gender remain decisive.[40]

Family

The family has always proven a conceptual trouble spot for research on income distribution. On the surface, the problem appears at first as a measurement issue. Any income distribution study must first decide on the relevant unit to study (households, families, or individuals) and how to adjust for the different needs based on the number and ages of family members. Any choice of units and adjustments has both advantages and drawbacks, and in practice, investigators have made a wide variety of choices, rendering comparison of studies quite difficult.[41]

But in fact the problem goes far beyond measurement. It has four main aspects. First, in industrialized capitalist economies, the family is the main site where people make or share goods rather than buying and selling them. Thus, the distinctions among income, consumption, and well-being yawn widest in this context. As is well known, neither macroeconomic national income accounts nor most microeconomic data series measure unpaid household labor at all.[42]

Second, family structure greatly affects the income to which family members have access. This is true in an epochal sense: the shift from extended family to nuclear family, the reduction of child labor, and increases in life expectancy have all profoundly affected income distribution. It is also true in cross-section among families in any given time period. In recent work, we explore empirically the income consequences of the number of working-age adults in the family, the gender of those adults, and the presence of children requiring care.[43] These factors conspire most dramatically against single-mother families, which (by definition) consist of one female adult with one or more dependent children. It is not surprising, therefore, to discover that poverty rates for single mothers are nearly four times as high as for the average family.

Third, income opportunities affect family structure. Once again, this is true in both an epochal and a short-term sense. The centuries-long process of separation of home and workplace undermined the extended family, pulling workers centrifugally toward their own jobs and nuclear family units. The growing incorporation of women into the paid work force in the United States and other industrialized countries shifts power relations within the family, alters the type of care children receive, and makes single motherhood more thinkable.[44] Debt-linked structural adjustment in Africa and Latin America has in many cases thrust women into the labor market while pushing men out, turning family structures topsy-turvy.[45] In combination with the second point, this causal link between income and family structure means that the family is not simply a stable sphere of reproduction: it is a moving target.

Finally, existing economic theory offers no satisfactory analysis of the distribution of work and rewards within the family. For neoclassical economics, the family—like production—can be seen as a black box. How work gets done and who does it are largely technical questions (comparative advantage) or questions of preferences—not subject to analysis by economists. Neoclassical models generally compress a family into a single utility function, skipping over the process by which family members jointly make economic decisions in a situation of unequal power and authority. Standard Marxian models offer little more.

However, research driven by a feminist critique of economics has begun to crack open these issues.[46] Folbre extends the standard Marx/Sraffa model of exploitation to allow exploitation of one family member (say, a wife) by another (say, a husband). Recent empirical research confirms that intrafamily resource allocation is shaped by age and gender.[47] Notably, studies of Asia and Africa have pointed to the higher mortality rates of women due to the systematic denial of resources to women.[48] In one of the few studies of intrahousehold distributions in the United States, Lazear and Michael found that division of consumption between parents and children changes dramatically with the number of adults in a household: as the number of adults increases, children's share decreases more than proportionally.[49]

The State

The state is the chief agent of redistribution in most industrialized economies. In the neoclassical framework the state is the locus of the equity–efficiency trade-off, while treatments of transfers, subsidies, and taxes focus primarily on incentives. Since most neoclassical economists subsume income distribution to growth, they would advocate that the state structure incentives to encourage saving (and hence a future stream of property income) rather than consumption, and work rather than leisure—although most would also support provision of some minimal degree of state-sponsored safety net, despite the fact that this is held to cut against these two incentives. The U.S. federal government adopted an extreme version of these policies over the last fifteen years, resulting in redistribution from poor to rich.

Even among mainstream economists who opposed the supply-side experiment, many hold a strong set of priors about the incentive effects of transfers, particularly on the nonelderly poor: higher transfers will depress labor-force participation and encourage births. However, time series and cross section data analyses suggest otherwise. Within the United States, states with higher Aid to Families with Dependent Children (AFDC) benefits do *not* have a larger welfare population.[50] Sweden, which has a relatively generous social support system, boasts a 93 percent labor force participation rate among single mothers—in large part because much of the cash grant is kept intact as a mother works more—though most work only part-time.[51] Further, the negative income tax experiments in the United States showed that higher transfers do not encourage single mothers to have more children—but they *do* result in more women living on their own.[52] Conversely, recent U.S. tax breaks and subsidies for the wealthy have done little—if anything—to revive savings and investment, which remain low by historical standards, despite substantial increases in property income. Indeed, one recent study finds that the level of *public* investment—which has fallen as the tax base has eroded—is one of the major predictors of private investment.[53]

Bad policies based on bad economics have taken their toll on the U.S. income distribution. The United States is distinguished among industrialized nations for having the greatest income disparity between top and bottom quintiles. Further, it has the highest levels of child poverty—attributable primarily to the threadbare transfer system.[54]

Progressive economists must offer better theories of the state's role, as well as better policies. As a starting point, we question the neoclassical conceit that state policies are impositions on a logically prior market economy. In fact, the state has historically always been the guarantor, builder, and shaper of that economy. Redistribution is no more of an imposition than the right to private property itself.

What, then, determines the possibilities for income redistribution? The state under capitalism serves purposes of legitimation as well as capital accumulation, offering a leverage point for redistribution.[55] Historically, a growing array of constituencies have exerted that leverage, expanding the sphere of democracy under capitalism.[56] In light of the problems just highlighted concerning economists' understanding of income distribution, we would identify three policy priorities: policies must be effective in ending poverty, democratically designed and administered, and capable of garnering broad political support.

First, then, in the interest of effectiveness, transfer policies must be linked to family policies that compensate for women's low wages and child-care responsibilities—since being female brings structural earnings disadvantages. Such family policies could include family allowances to all parents of young children; government-guaranteed health benefits, child care, and other supports for low-wage workers; and requirements that employers provide added flexibility to meet family-care needs, building on U.S. family-leave legislation enacted in 1992.

Second, redistributive policies must connect redistribution of income to an expansion of democracy and poor people's power over their lives and communities. Measures pegged solely to a model of individual mobility will not suffice to end poverty; in addition, we need policies that help to build *collective* institutions: laws facilitating union organizing in low-wage jobs, broader opportunities for voter registration, and tax and subsidy advantages for community-based organizations.

Finally, transfer policies should include universal policies to build widespread political support, while preserving targeted benefits for those worst off. For example, child allowances could garner some of the support enjoyed by Social Security, but there will continue to be a need for a means-tested welfare safety net to provide for those with no other option.

Conclusion

We have done our best to argue for a richer, more complex theory of income distribution. We claim that:

- Distribution does not follow a fixed, determinate relationship to growth; that relationship is contingent.
- The labor market itself is institutionally dense, so that the tools of sociology and history as well as the conventional tools of economic market analysis are required to understand it.
- Income is only meaningful within a given mode of production. Capitalism expands the need for income.
- Further, the mode of production generates a class structure—and power relationships—that shape income inequality.
- Family structure mediates the distribution of income, affects that distribution, and is affected by it. Indeed, distribution of consumption *within* the family can be a matter of life and death.
- The state is not simply a redistributive overlay on top of a presumptively efficient private market, but rather—for good or ill—the fundamental arbiter of the ground rules that allow an economy to function.

We have cast a broad net—but it could be still broader. Shanahan and Tuma point out that the concept of distribution—"the allocation of scarce values . . . associated with social exchange," in their words—can apply to far more than income.[57] It can apply to inputs (such as human capital) as well as outputs, and it can apply to outputs as disparate as health, status, and power, and even happiness. Economist Amartya Sen, in conjunction with several philosophers, is working to develop concepts and measures of quality of life that include not only income resources, but also the degree of security in one's home, job opportunities, and exposure to the threat of disease.[58] In this context, poverty is not understood as lack of income, but rather as the inability to use one's potential resource capacity to provide an adequate quality of life. Our final word, then, is that not only must we look beyond markets, but we must go farther to look beyond income in order to develop a satisfactory theory of the distribution of human well-being.

Notes

1. Bennett Harrison and Barry Bluestone, *The Great U-Turn: Corporate Restructuring and the Polarizing of America* (New York: Basic Books, 1988).
2. For recent accounts see Lynn A. Karoly, *The Trend in Inequality among Families, Individuals, and Workers in the United States: A Twenty-Five Year Perspective* (Santa Monica, CA: Rand, 1992); Frank Levy and Richard Murnane, "U.S. Earnings Levels and Earnings Inequality: A Review of Recent Trends and Proposed Explanations," *Journal of Economic Literature*, 30, 3 (September 1991), 1333–81; and Chris Tilly, "Understanding Income Inequality," *Sociological Forum*, 6, 4 (December 1991), 739–56.
3. Richard Freeman, *Factor Prices, Employment, and Inequality in a Decentralized Labor Market* (Cambridge, MA: National Bureau of Economic Research and Corporation for Enterprise Development, 1986).
4. Lawrence F. Katz and Kevin M. Murphy. *Changes in Relative Wages, 1963–1987: Supply and Demand Factors*, National Bureau of Economic Research, mimeo, April 1990.
5. Denny Braun, *The Rich Get Richer: The Rise of Income Inequality in the United States and the World* (Chicago: Nelson-Hall, 1991).
6. Susan George, "Debt as Warfare: An Overview of the Debt Crisis," *Third World Resurgence*, 28 (December 1992), 14–19.
7. Simon Kuznets, "Economic Growth and Income Inequality," *American Economic Review*, 45 (1955), 1–28.
8. Arthur Okun, *Equality and Efficiency: The Big Trade-off* (Washington DC: The Brookings Institution, 1975).
9. Charles Murray, *Losing Ground: American Social Policy, 1950–1980* (New York: Basic Books, 1984). For a supply-side account, see Jude Wanniski, *The Way the World Works: How Economies Fail—And Succeed* (New York: Basic Books, 1978); and for the New Classical position, see Robert J. Barro (ed.), *Modern Business Cycle Theory* (Cambridge, MA: Harvard University Press, 1989).
10. A good example of the liberal view is Frank Levy's *Dollars and Dreams: The Changing American Income Distribution* (New York: Russell Sage Foundation, 1987).
11. Quoted in Massimo Pivetti, "Distribution Theories: Classical" in John Eatwell, Murray Milgate, and Peter Newman (eds.), *The New Palgrave: A Dictionary of Economics* (New York: Stockton Press, 1987), p. 872.

12. Richard Easterlin, "Does Money Buy Happiness?," *The Public Interest, 30* (1973), 3–10.

13. Liberal analyses are provided by Paul Krugman, *The Age of Diminished Expectations: U.S. Economic Policy in the 1990s* (Washington, DC: Washington Post, 1990); Frank Levy and Richard Murnane, "U.S. Earnings Levels and Earnings Inequality"; and Sheldon Danziger and Peter Gottschalk, *Uneven Tides: Rising Inequality in America* (New York: Russell Sage, 1992). For a conservative approach, see Kevin Phillips, *The Politics of Rich and Poor: Wealth and the American Electorate in the Reagan Aftermath* (New York: Random House, 1990).

14. See Robert M. Solow, *Growth Theory* (New York: Oxford University Press, 1970) and Stephen Marglin, *Growth, Distribution, and Prices* (Cambridge, MA: Harvard University Press, 1984).

15. For Marxian treatments of growth theory see Stephen Marglin, *Growth, Distribution, and Prices*, and David Gordon, "Distribution Theories: Marxian" in John Eatwell, Murray Milgate, and Peter Newman (eds.), *The New Palgrave: A Dictionary of Economics* (New York: Stockton Press, 1987), pp. 878–83.

16. Stagnationist growth theories can be found in Paul Baran and Paul Sweezy's *Monopoly Capital: An Essay on the American Economic and Social Order* (New York: Monthly Review Press, 1966), as well as Samuel Bowles, David Gordon, and Thomas Weisskopf's *After the Wasteland: A Democratic Economy for the Year 2000* (Armonk, NY: M.E. Sharpe, 1990).

17. John Maynard Keynes, *The General Theory of Employment, Interest, and Money* (New York: Harcourt Brace Jovanovich, 1964 [1935]), p. 374.

18. Examples of post-Keynesian treatments can be found in Nicholas Kaldor, *Essays on Value and Distribution* (London: Duckworth, 1960); Luigi I. Pasinetti, *Growth and Income Distribution: Essays in Economic Theory* (Cambridge: Cambridge University Press, 1974); and Stephen Marglin, *Growth, Distribution, and Prices*.

19. See Michal Kalecki, *Collected Works, Volume II. Capitalism: Economic Dynamics* edited by Jerzy Osiatinsky (Oxford: Oxford University Press, 1991), and John B. Foster and Henry Szlajfer (eds.), *The Faltering Economy: The Problem of Accumulation under Monopoly Capitalism* (New York: Monthly Review Press, 1984).

20. See, for example, Rebecca Blank and Alan Blinder, "Macroeconomics, Income Distribution, and Poverty" in Sheldon Danziger and Daniel Weinberg (eds.), *Fighting Poverty: What Works and What Doesn't* (Cambridge, MA: Harvard University Press, 1986), pp. 180–208.

21. Two recent papers document this trend: Rebecca Blank, *Why Were Poverty Rates So High in the 1980s?*, Paper prepared for the Levy Institute Conference on Income Inequality, Bard College, June 18–20, 1991, and Patricia Ruggles and Charles F. Stone, "Income Distribution over the Business Cycle: The 1980s Were Different," *Journal of Policy Analysis and Management, 11*:4 (Fall 1992), 709–15.

22. Jeffrey Williamson and Peter Lindert, *American Inequality: A Macroeconomic History* (New York: Academic Press, 1980), and Eugene Smolensky and Robert Plotnick, *Inequality and Poverty in the United States: 1900 to 1990*, Discussion Paper no. 998–93, Institute for Research on Poverty, University of Wisconsin-Madison, March 1992.

23. Sanford M. Jacoby, "The New Institutionalism: What Can It Learn from the Old?," *Industrial Relations, 29* (1990), 316–40.

24. Gary S. Becker, *Human Capital: A Theoretical Analysis with Special Reference to Education* (New York: Columbia University Press for National Bureau of Economic Research, 1964).

25. For an extended discussion, see Chris Tilly and Charles Tilly, "Capitalist Work and Labor Markets," in Neil Smelser and Richard Swedberg (eds.), *Handbook of Eco-*

nomic Sociology, (Princeton, NJ: Princeton University Press, 1994).

26. Edward P. Lazear, "Labor Economics and the Psychology of Organizations," *Journal of Economic Perspectives*, 5 (1991), 89–110, and Joseph Stiglitz, "Symposium on Organizations and Economics," *Journal of Economic Perspectives*, 5(1991), 15–24.

27. See Carl Shapiro and Joseph Stiglitz, "Equilibrium Unemployment as a Worker Discipline Device," *American Economic Review*, 74 (1984), 433–44, and George A. Akerlof and Janet L. Yellen (eds.), *Efficiency Wage Models of the Labor Market* (Cambridge: Cambridge University Press, 1986).

28. Paul Osterman, "Choice of Employment Systems in Internal Labor Markets," *Industrial Relations 26* (1987), 46–67; and David M. Gordon, Richard Edwards, and Michael Reich, *Segmented Work, Divided Workers: The Historical Transformations of Labor in the United States* (New York: Cambridge University Press, 1982).

29. Paul Osterman, "Technology and White-Collar Employment: A Research Strategy," *Proceedings of the 38th Annual Meeting of the Industrial Relations Research Association* (1985), 58.

30. Randy Albelda and Chris Tilly, "Toward a Broader Vision: Race, Gender, and Labor Market Segmentation in the Social Structure of Accumulation Framework," in David Kotz, Terence McDonough, and Michael Reich (eds.), *Social Structures of Accumulation: The Political Economy of Growth and Crisis* (Cambridge: Cambridge University Press, 1994).

31. Reviewed by Walter W. Powell and Laurel Smith-Doerr, "The Role of Networks in Economic Life," in Neil Smelser and Richard Swedberg (eds.), *Handbook of Economic Sociology* (Princeton: Princeton University Press, 1994.

32. For treatments on the informal economy, see Alejandro Portes, Manuel Castells, and Lauren Benton (eds.), *The Informal Economy: Studies in Advanced and Less Developed Countries* (Baltimore: Johns Hopkins Press, 1989); and for subcontracting, see David Nelson, *Managers and Workers: Origins of the New Factory System in the United States* (Madison: University of Wisconsin Press, 1975).

33. See, for example, Alex Keyssar, *Out of Work: The First Century of Unemployment in Massachusetts* (Cambridge: Cambridge University Press, 1986), and Chris Tilly and Charles Tilly, "Capitalist Work and Labor Markets."

34. Karl Polanyi, *The Great Transformation: The Political and Economic Origins of Our Time* (Boston: Beacon Press, 1957), p. 72.

35. Samuel Bowles and Herbert Gintis, "The Revenge of Homo Economicus: Contested Exchange and the Revival of Political Economy," *Journal of Economic Perspectives*, 7,1 (Winter 1993), 83–102.

36. See, for example, Lynn A. Karoly, *The Trend in Inequality among Families, Individuals, and Workers in the United States*.

37. Historian Mary O. Furner makes this argument in *Advocacy and Objectivity: A Crisis in the Professionalization of American Social Science, 1865–1905* (Lexington: The University Press of Kentucky, 1975).

38. Pat Walker (ed.), *Between Labor and Capital* (Boston: South End Press, 1979), and Erik Olin Wright, *Class Structure and Income Determination* (New York: Academic Press, 1979).

39. Peter B. Doeringer and Michael J. Piore, *Internal Labor Markets and Manpower Analysis* (Lexington, MA: D.C. Heath, 1971); Richard C. Edwards, *Contested Terrain: The Transformation of the Workplace in the 20th Century* (New York: Basic Books, 1979); and David M. Gordon, Richard Edwards, and Michael Reich, *Segmented Work, Divided Workers*.

40. Authors who make this argument include Gerald Jaynes and Robin Williams (eds.), *A Common Destiny: Blacks and American Society* (Washington, DC: National

Academy Press, 1989); Teresa L. Amott and Julie A. Matthaei, *Race, Gender, and Work: A Multicultural Economic History of Women in the United States* (Boston: South End Press, 1991); and Randy Albelda and Chris Tilly, "Toward a Broader Vision."

41. Compare, for example, Frank Levy, *Dollars and Dreams*; Bennett Harrison and Barry Bluestone, *The Great U-Turn*; and Lynn A. Karoly, *The Trend in Inequality among Families, Individuals, and Workers in the United States.*

42. For a review, see Lourdes Beneria, "Accounting for Women's Work: Assessing the Progress of Two Decades," paper delivered at ASSA meeting, New Orleans, January 1991.

43. Randy Albelda and Chris Tilly, "All in the Family: Family Types, Access to Income, and Family Income Policies," *Policy Studies Journal*, 20, 3 (1992), 388–404, and Chris Tilly and Randy Albelda, "Family Structure and Family Earnings: The Determinants of Earnings Differences among Family Types," *Industrial Relations*, 33, 2 (April 1994), 151–67.

44. Barbara R. Bergmann, *The Economic Emergence of Women* (New York: Basic Books, 1986), and Heidi Hartmann, "Changes in Women's Economic and Family Roles in Post–World War II United States," in Lourdes Beneria and Catherine Stimpson (eds.), *Women, Households, and the Economy* (New Brunswick: Rutgers University Press, 1987), pp. 33–64.

45. Lourdes Beneria and Shelley Feldman (eds.), *Unequal Burden: Economic Crises, Persistent Poverty, and Women's Work* (Boulder, CO: Westview, 1992).

46. See, for example, Heidi Hartmann, "The Family as the Locus of Gender, Class, and Political Struggle," in Sandra Harding (ed.), *Feminism and Methodology* (Bloomington, IN: Indiana University Press, 1981), pp. 109–34.

47. Nancy Folbre, "Exploitation Comes Home: A Critique of the Marxian Theory of Family Labor," *Cambridge Journal of Economics*, 6 (1982), 317–29.

48. Amartya Sen, "Women's Survival as a Development Problem," *Bulletin of the American Academy of Arts and Sciences*, 43 (November 1989).

49. Edward P. Lazear and Robert T. Michael, *Allocation of Income within the Household* (Chicago: University of Chicago Press, 1988).

50. David Ellwood and Lawrence Summers, "Poverty in America: Is Welfare the Answer or the Problem?" in Sheldon Danziger and Daniel Weinberg (eds.), *Fighting Poverty: What Works and What Doesn't* (Cambridge, MA: Harvard University Press, 1986), pp. 78–105.

51. Richard Hauser and Ingo Fischer, "Economic Well-Being among One-Parent Families," in Timothy Smeeding, Michael O'Higgins, and Lee Rainwater (eds.), *Poverty, Inequality and Income Distribution in Comparative Perspective* (Washington, DC: Urban Institute Press, 1990), 126–57.

52. Gary Burtless, "The Economist's Lament: Public Assistance in America," *Journal of Economic Perspectives*, 4, 1 (Winter 1990), 57–78.

53. David A. Aschauer, *Public Investment and Private Sector Growth: The Economic Benefits of Reducing America's "Third Deficit"* (Washington, DC: Economic Policy Institute, 1990).

54. Michael O'Higgins, Gunther Schmaus, and Geoffrey Stephenson, "Income Distribution and Redistribution: A Microdata Analysis for Seven Countries," in Timothy Smeeding, Michael O'Higgins, and Lee Rainwater (eds.), *Poverty, Inequality and Income Distribution in Comparative Perspective*, (Washington, DC: Urban Institute Press, 1990), 20–56; also Timothy M. Smeeding, Lee Rainwater, Martin Rein, Richard Hauser, and Gaston Schaber, "Income Poverty in Seven Countries: Initial Estimates from the LIS Database" in the same volume, pp. 57–76.

55. See, for example, James O'Connor, *The Fiscal Crisis of the State* (New York: St. Martin's Press, 1973).

56. Samuel Bowles and Herbert Gintis, *Democracy and Capitalism: Property, Community and the Contradictions of Modern Social Thought* (New York: Basic Books, 1986).

57. Suzanne E. Shanahan and Nancy B. Tuma, "The Sociology of Distribution and Redistribution," in Neil Smelser and Richard Swedberg (eds.), *Handbook of Economic Sociology* (Princeton: Princeton University Press, 1994), p 1.

58. Martha Nussbaum and Amartya Sen (eds.), *The Quality of Life* (Oxford: Clarendon Press, 1993).

Part V

Competitiveness, Trade, and Development

11

Comparative Advantage, Factor–Price Equalization, Industrial Strategies, and Trade Tactics

Lester C. Thurow

Today's neoclassical theory of comparative advantage was developed in an era where economic location was determined by natural resource endowments and factor proportions (capital–labor ratios). This era is being replaced by an era of brainpower industries where comparative advantage is human-made rather than given by mother nature and history. At the same time, with the development of a global economy, factor–price equalization has become a reality. Together these two facts create a need for industrial strategies and trade tactics that in earlier eras could be easily dismissed from the dialogue of economists.

The Disappearance of Neoclassical Comparative Advantage

Resource Endowments and Factor Proportions

In the neoclassical theory of comparative advantage everyone benefits from free trade. Part of this conclusion flows from an underlying assumption that the location of economic activity is determined by natural resource endowments and factor proportions (capital–labor ratios). Those with good soil, climate, and rainfall specialize in agricultural production; those with oil supply oil. Industries locate next to the raw materials they need. Capital-intensive products are made in capital-rich countries; labor-intensive products are made in capital-poor countries.

In the nineteenth and for most of the twentieth century, this assumption about economic geography was essentially correct. The United States grew cotton in the South because the climate and soil were right; it made cloth in New England because that was where the water power and capital were located. New York was the biggest city in the country since it had both the best natural harbor on the East Coast and the capital to build a water connection (the Erie Canal) to the midwest; Pittsburgh was the iron and steel capital, since—given the location of the country's coal, iron ore, rivers, and lakes—there was no other place for it to be. In an age of railroads, Chicago was destined to be the United States' transportation capital and hog butcher to the world; Texas was oil, and the availability of electricity dictated that aluminum be made on the Columbia river.

Economic success depended upon natural resources. Of the twelve largest companies in the United States in 1900—American Cotton Oil Company, American Steel Company, American Sugar Refining, Continental Tobacco Company, Federal Steel, General Electric, National Lead, Pacific Mail, People's Gas, Tennessee Coal and Iron, U.S. Leather, and U.S. Rubber—ten were natural resource companies.[1] Before World War I more than one million workers toiled in the coal mines of Great Britain. Those countries with natural resources, such as Argentina and Chile, were rich; those without natural resources, such as Japan were poor.[2]

In the world described by the conventional theory of comparative advantage, governments had neither the incentive nor the means to alter the location of economic activity. Any attempt to do so would simply have burdened the economy with the inefficiency costs of having economic activities located in the wrong places. The only microeconomic role for government was to prevent private barriers to factor or product mobility (monopolies).

In the world of the twenty-first century none of the aforementioned postulates of the neoclassical theory of comparative advantage corresponds with reality.

The existence of world capital markets effectively means that an entrepreneur in Bangkok, Thailand, can build a facility that is just as capital-intensive as those that can be built in Germany, Japan, or the United States, despite the fact that the per-capita income in those countries is many times that found in Thailand. And if the Thai entrepreneur cannot access world capital markets, firms from richer countries will bring their access to capital and technology with them to Bangkok. Everyone effectively borrows in New York, London, or Tokyo. As a result, there is no such thing as a capital-rich or a labor-rich country. Labor-intensive products will not automatically be built in poor countries; capital-intensive products will not automatically be built in rich countries. Factor proportions have dropped out of the theory of comparative advantage since capital has become an international rather than a local commodity.

But natural-resource endowments have likewise become an international commodity. The green revolution and the material-science revolution have both made many more resources available and reduced the need for resources. After correcting for general inflation, natural resource prices fell 40 percent from 1970 to 1990.[3] With biotechnology speeding up the green revolution, the material-science revolution accelerating, and all of the raw materials of the old Soviet Union now becoming available to the capitalistic world, the next twenty years will witness an even bigger decline in raw-material prices.

Today Japan has the world's dominant steel industry, yet it has no coal and no iron ore. That could not have happened in the nineteenth century or for most of the twentieth century. But today ocean transportation costs are low and Japan simply buys what it needs wherever those resources are cheapest and best, brings them to coastal locations, and has every advantage that countries with natural resources have. Japan can be rich without natural resources.

Any list of the industries that are expected to grow rapidly in the next few decades is likely a list where natural resources play no role.[4] It is a list of brainpower industries—such as microelectronics, biotechnology, the new material science industries, telecommunications, civilian aircraft manufacturing, machine tools plus robotics, and computers plus software—that could be located anywhere, a list of industries that will be located wherever someone organizes the brainpower to capture them.

If natural resources are buyable, if capital is borrowable, if new product technology is easily copyable using reverse engineering, then there is only one source of long-run strategic advantage—the skills of the work force. But if human skills are the dominant factor in determining economic location, the whole distinction between capital and labor dissolves. Capital–labor ratios cease to be meaningful variables since the whole distinction between capital and labor collapses. Skills are created with capital investments, and raw labor (the willingness to sacrifice leisure) earns almost nothing when there is an entire globe of poor, underemployed workers.

Unemployment and Transition Costs

The neoclassical conclusion about the universal benefits of free trade does not always rest solely upon the view of economic geography discussed above. This conclusion is also often traceable to assumptions about unemployment and transition costs in the world in which trade occurs. These assumptions are: (1) full employment is assumed to exist; free trade does not push anyone into unemployment; and (2) transition costs are assumed to be zero; no industry- or firm-specific physical or human capital is to be destroyed when workers are forced to shift between firms or industries.

Historically, one could always quarrel with the assumptions of no unemployment and zero transition costs (and some economists have), but yesterday's perhaps unrealistic assumptions have become today's counterfactual assumptions.

In the past economists could disagree about whether economies would automatically run at full employment or whether Keynesian countercyclical economic policies would be necessary to insure the existence of full employment. In the 1990s it is clear that market economies do not run at full employment and that governments either will not or cannot use Keynesian economics to insure full employment. The industrial world suffers double-digit unemployment and has been operating at or very near those high levels of unemployment for more than a decade, and no one expects unemployment to do anything but rise in the foreseeable future. Empirically modern industrial economies do not automatically operate at or near full employment.[5]

Keynesian countercyclical full-employment policies are partially blocked by fears of inflation—an inflation that does not disappear regardless of how high unemployment goes. In Spain, unemployment stood at 23.5 percent during the first quarter of 1995; yet consumer prices rose by 6.7 percent during the same period.[6] Countercyclical full-employment policies are also partly blocked by the emergence of a global economy that has made Keynesian economics impossible to practice successfully in any one country. To cut taxes or raise government spending initially leads to faster growth, but this faster growth quickly produces balance-of-payments problems, falling currency values, higher price inflation, a sharp reversal of policies, and the imposition of austerity policies with little increase in domestic employment. New governments facing high unemployment, such as the French conservative government in the spring of 1993, adopt austerity measures (higher taxes and cuts in spending) that are just the opposite of what Lord Keynes would have prescribed.

Multicountry-coordinated Keynesian reflation is economically feasible. Growth responded rapidly to the coordinated monetary and fiscal policies put in place in the aftermath of the October 1987 stock market crash. In mid-1987, economic forecasters expected 1988 to be a mediocre year. In November 1987 it was expected to be a very bad year. But it was in fact the best year of the decade. Coordinated monetary and fiscal policies quickly accelerated the global economy.

But such policies are not politically feasible without a clear crisis. In normal times none of the big three economies (the United States, Japan, and Germany), which make up about 50 percent of the world economy, are willing to do the locally painful things that they would have to do to build a multicountry Keynesian coordinated economic locomotive for the world. Japan is not willing to reduce its trade surplus, the United States is not willing to reduce its consumption and hence increase its saving so that it becomes a lender and not a borrower on world capital markets, and Germany is not willing to reorganize its fiscal house so that it can make the necessary investments in eastern Germany without having to endure high interest rates.

Finally, in today's era of brainpower industries, transition costs are not just the costs of physically moving people and capital from one industry or geographic location to another. Human skills are often industry-, firm-, or even team-specific and, when laid off, the average worker finds his or her wages upon reemployment much lower than they were before. In effect, the worker's previous skills are of little value. This is particularly true for those over fifty years of age.

While financial capital is clearly highly mobile, if one looks at the market price of the used productive assets, it is also clear that large capital transition costs are incurred in shifting from one industry or location to another. Today's idle computer, auto, or aircraft factories could be purchased very cheaply, but there are no buyers. Typically, plants will simply be scrapped—not sold.

In short, if natural resources have ceased to dominate economic activity in a world of brainpower industries, if factor proportions have dissolved in a world of global capital markets and worldwide logistics, if high and persistent unemployment is a worldwide fact of life, and if transition costs are very large, the real world is far removed from the standard, neoclassical theory of comparative advantage.

The Appearance of Factor–Price Equalization

The theory of factor–price equalization holds that in a global economy, an American worker who does not work with more natural resources than a Korean (and none can since there is now a world market for raw material to which everyone has equal access), who does not work with more capital than a Korean (and none can since there is a global capital market where everyone borrows in New York, London, and Tokyo), and who does not work with better technology than a Korean (few will since reverse engineering has become an international art form whereby new product technologies are rapidly diffused throughout the world), must work for the wages commensurate with the pay found for that skill level in Korea. Korean wages rise and American wages fall until factor–price equalization occurs.

Falling Wages

Until the early 1970s a truly global economy did not exist and Americans got a wage premium simply because they were Americans. They would automatically work with more raw materials, employ more capital-intensive processes, and use better technology than those in Korea. But under the pressure of factor-price equalization, this premium has vanished.

From 1973 to 1992 the U.S. per-capita GNP rose 27 percent after correcting for inflation, but the U.S. Department of Labor reported that over the same time period real weekly wages for nonsupervisory workers (those who do not boss anyone else) fell 19 percent.[7] To some extent these numbers reflect the increased participation of lower-paid women, but if one looks at males' median earnings for year-round full-time workers, blacks are down $1,239 (5 percent in 1990 dollars) and white males are down $3,097 (9 percent) from their peak earnings two decades earlier.[8]

The U.S. Census reports that in 1979, 18 percent of males 18 to 24 years of age who work year-round full-time failed to earn $12,195 (in 1990 dollars).[9] This number was chosen since it fell between the poverty line for a family of three and a family of four. A fully employed young man who could not earn this amount could not expect to support a family. By 1990, that 18 percent had more than doubled to 40 percent. (The same percentages rose from 29 to 48 percent for

18- to 24-year-old fully employed women.) In the past two decades, 20 percent of American men have essentially been on an up escalator, 20 percent have been holding their own on a moving sidewalk that is working against them, and 60 percent have been on a down escalator. What President Kennedy had promised three decades ago in his inaugural address ("a rising tide lifts all boats") and what had been true in the 1960s, had, by the 1970s and 1980s, become a lie. The tide was going up but many of the boats were sinking.

What Changed in the 1970s?

High-wage jobs disappeared as U.S. firms lost market share to imports in auto, steel, and machine tools. Every 45 billion dollars in additional trade deficit means the loss of one million U.S. manufacturing jobs.[10] Those jobs were replaced not by jobs of equal wages but by service jobs with wages that were on average one-third lower than in manufacturing.

New technologies, such as just-in-time inventories or statistical quality control, requiring new skills—in this case mathematical skills—also converted what had been unskilled assembly-line jobs into jobs that require considerably more education and skill. The human welder was replaced by a robot and jobs went to those skilled enough to repair robots.

Much of the earnings decline, however, can be traced to factor–price equalization. Global trade could contribute to increasing the average U.S. per-capita GDP and at the same time lower the real earnings for most Americans.

Factor–price equalization increases the importance of industrial structure. Some industries are skill-intensive and provide a lot of opportunities for the highly skilled. Other industries generate skills endogenously through on-the-job training. If these industries do not exist, skills either cannot be used or will not exist. Effectively, the industrial structure and the skill structure can interact synergistically or negatively. Without jobs that reward skills, skill investments stop.

The existence of industry economies of scale are another factor that can produce high wages. Autos and steel were not particularly skill-intensive but they were high-wage since the economies of scale existed to make them a high value-added industry. If industries such as autos or steel are lost and new industries such as consumer electronics are not captured, average wages are going to be lower than they would be otherwise.

The composition of a nation's "industrial clusters" is also an important determinant of individual earnings. Industrial clusters are important because to some extent the economic game is a team as well as an individual game. Wages are not just dependent upon individual marginal productivities. They to a great extent reflect team marginal productivities. Economists with doctorates playing on the U.S. team make a lot more money than their counterparts on a British team. Their knowledge is not greater but their earnings are higher simply because their team's productivity is higher than that of the British team.

Industrial Strategies and Trade Tactics in the Twenty-first Century

Historically, microeconomics has been the study of how markets reach equilibrium. In a world of humanmade comparative advantage with factor–price equalization, microeconomics is going to have to become something quite different. It will have to become the study of how strategic economic advantage is created—rather than a discipline that simply seeks to understand why particular strategic advantages arise.

Creating Strategic Advantage

The ultimate objective in any economic community is high and rapidly rising productivity, where productivity growth can be used to obtain more goods and services or more leisure. To achieve this objective requires strategies and tactics for capturing those industries that can pay high and rapidly rising wages and high rates of return on capital.

To do this, an industry needs a number of characteristics. First, after correcting for the amount of physical capital used, the desired industries must be high value-added industries. Only high value-added industries can pay high wages and high rates of return. An industry may be a high value-added industry either because it is skill-intensive in the sense that it uses a lot of skills that can be acquired in formal education or training, or because it is skill-intensive in the sense that it will endogenously generate a lot skills. Computer software firms use a lot of high-skilled labor; the skills necessary for making semiconductor chips can only be acquired by making semiconductor chips.

Firms may also be high value-added if proprietary product technologies can be established. The Polaroid Corporation is a good historical example. But today the art of reverse engineering makes it very difficult for anyone to be the exclusive producer of any product. What is possible, however, is proprietary process technologies. Since they cannot be bought in the market and copied, unique production processes can still produce high value-added industries.

In some areas it is also possible to create branded products and unique marketing images that can command a premium price. Coca-Cola is the archetypical example. In addition, large economies of scale have historically been the prime source of value-added firms or industries. There are arguments that modern manufacturing technologies may be reducing the importance of economies of scale, and the willingness to pay a premium for brand names may be diminishing. Nevertheless, neither of these two characteristics is likely to disappear completely.[11] Economies of scale are important in computer software, and frequent flyer programs have been able to create brand loyalty in the airline industry.

If value-addedness is to grow, productivity must grow. A high expected growth rate of productivity means that the industry's value-added will be rising and that the wages and profits that it can pay will be increasing.

High value-added and high expected rates of productivity growth need to be combined with a third characteristic—a high income elasticity of demand. This characteristic insures that markets served by an industry will be growing rapidly and that lots of jobs and profits will be generated.

Finally, the search for strategic advantage looks at complementarities. Does success in industry A help establish a better position in industry B?

These four characteristics led to the list of the seven hot industries presented above—namely, microelectronics, biotechnology, the new-materials industries, telecommunication, civilian aircraft manufacturing, machine tools plus robots, and computers plus software.

Microelectronics is large, rapidly growing, and highly complementary with other products. The electronic controls on machine tools are almost as important as the machines themselves. Microelectronics lies at the heart of the telecommunication revolution. Electronic accident-avoidance systems may give one's auto producers an edge in conquering the world's largest market.

Biotechnology is a skill-intensive industry with the potential to displace much of today's very large conventional pharmaceutical and chemical engineering industries. Stock market price–earnings ratios indicate that the market expects these firms to earn rates of return far above average in the future.

A successful material-science industry that can build ceramic engines or the materials for making a workable battery for an electric car can lead to conquering the auto business, the world's largest industry, as well as the materials business.

Telecommunications is both large and exploding with the integration of computer and visual technologies into what had been an audio technology. Fiber optics and the computer make possible a host of uses that were once impossible.

Civilian aircraft manufacturing is seen as the technological driver that military aircraft manufacturing used to be. The most sophisticated electronics and materials of the future will be used first in this industry.

Machine tools and robots are important since no one can achieve a productive edge over the competition in the rest of the world unless they have unique proprietary process technologies. If machine tools are bought from others, it just is not possible to have an edge in process technologies.

Computers and software are increasingly being integrated into every product that is consumed, from automobiles to telecommunications.

Where these industries will be located depends upon who organizes the brainpower to capture them. Organizing brainpower means not just building an R&D system that will put a nation on the leading edge of technology, but organizing a top-to-bottom work force that has the brainpower necessary to master the new production and distribution technologies necessary to be the world's low-cost seller in each of these seven areas.

Public Policy

In a world of humanmade comparative advantage, government has an important role to play that it was spared in the world of classical comparative advantage.

Government both supplies well-educated workers and funds the R&D expenditures that makes the industries of the future possible. It must do both because capitalism has a strategic defect. Given any reasonable interest rate, the discounted net present value of a dollar ten years from now is too small to matter. As a consequence, capitalism never looks more than seven or eight years into the future.

No hard-nosed capitalistic mother or father would ever make a sixteen-year investment in the education of their children. No hard-nosed capitalistic firm would ever have spent twenty-five years pouring tens of billions of dollars into biotechnology research before there was even any prospect of building usable products. The payoffs are just too distant. Yet, long-run educational and R&D investments have to be made if the key industries of tomorrow are to be captured. There is a big collective payoff to having an educated citizenry and being a technological leader.

Only government, with its potentially much longer time horizons, is in a position to organize the necessary investments. Success will go to those human societies that can lengthen capitalistic time horizons. As a result, government activities are going to be much more central in the microeconomics of the future than they have been in the microeconomics of the past.

To generate high-wage job opportunities tomorrow, a civilian R&D technology policy is necessary today. But that technology policy cannot be developed without a national industrial strategy. Countries have to decide where they want to play the game.

In the last fifty years the United States let its military strategy drive its technological investments. The great thing about the military was that it knew what it wanted—a missile that landed within fifteen feet, a submarine that stayed underwater forever, a fighter aircraft that flew at 3,000 miles per hour. Technologies were developed to meet these goals. With the end of the Cold War, military R&D is fading away and the United States' military R&D system will have to be replaced with a civilian R&D system. But to be effective, that system must know what it wants—and it cannot know what it wants unless the nation has an industrial strategy.

Those directing government R&D spending need to know where to bet. Experience teaches us that just giving money to researchers and telling them to do good things does not work. One has to know what one wants and to be able to set goals so that failure can be distinguished from success. Walking around an institution like MIT, for example, one will see many fabulous technologies, but only some of them will lead to big important industries. Where are the development dollars that will make these technologies into usable products going to be bet?

In today's global economic game, technology strategies have become central. Even if they do not want to play the civilian technology policy game, Americans will face others with strategies for conquering the key strategic industries of tomorrow. Europe's Airbus Industries is the best current example of this reality. What is the American answer to Airbus Industries? Whatever arguments Americans advance to prove that Europe has "wasted" too much of its money in developing the Airbus, it exists, and it is not going away. The United States will have to develop defensive industrial policies to deal with situations where the rest of the world targets one of its key industries—even if Americans decide not to have offensive industrial policies. But if one plays defense all of the time and never offense, what is true in sports is equally true in economics: One never wins.

How does one reorganize a market-incentive system to lengthen time horizons? This is not a question that can be asked in traditional microeconomics. Rates of time preferences are what they are and governments should not intervene to lengthen them. But it *is* a question that has to be asked and answered in an era of humanmade comparative advantage.

A technology strategy does not mean that government has to pick winners and losers. The European Common Market, for example, merely announces that it has identified some hot technologies and that it has matching funds available for industries (in programs such as JESSI, ESPRIT, and EUREKA)—if at least three companies from two different countries come through the door with both a good project and half the money, these private·funds will be matched with government money.[12] Government is not picking winners and losers but it is expanding time horizons and the scale of operations.

Today's global economic game requires a trade policy in addition to a technology policy. But trade tactics, like technology initiatives, cannot be formulated without an industrial strategy. Again it becomes necessary to ask, where does one want to play the game? What is strategic and what is not?

The United States, for example, places restrictions on New Zealand lamb imports, while Japan places restrictions on imports of amorphous metals (American inventions that have some very desirable electrical properties). Both are restrictive but only one is strategic. The Japanese believe that amorphous metals are a high value-added industry, with an upside potential for large productivity gains and rapidly growing use. These metals may also have an important complementary impact upon electrical equipment manufacturing. No one believes that lamb production meets any strategic criterion. As the Japanese say, the United States has an industrial strategy and a trade policy. It is just "loser"-rather than "winner"-driven.[13]

The world is moving into an era of quasi-trading blocks with freer trade within regions but more managed trade between regions. The semiconductor agreement with Japan is an illustration of managed trade. The United States is guaranteed a 20 percent market share in Japan. But when and where should such agreements be negotiated? There is no theoretical answer to this question. It depends upon the development of an integrated technology-trade strategy.

A winning industrial strategy requires a technology policy along with trade tactics. These flow partly from hard analysis and partly from widespread consultations with those in the private sector who must cooperate in the execution of the policies and tactics that are adopted. American skill and technological strengths and weaknesses have to be analyzed as well as those of its principal competitors.

One has to understand where the keys to achieving economic success are located. For example, is leadership in the telecommunications industry of tomorrow to be obtained by strengthening the United States' laboratory leadership in key technologies, or in building a fiber-optics test bed such as the one Germany is now building in eastern Germany?

A winning industrial strategy also requires a theory of strategic retreats. How does a country get out of an industry with the least pain and damage to human capital when it is clear that it cannot compete? The Japanese retreated from aluminum production after the OPEC oil shocks, when it became clear that they would not successfully compete in energy-intensive industries. Successful exit means that you do not let weak airlines drive healthy airlines into bankruptcy, as is currently happening in the United States.

Conclusion

In an era of brainpower industries and humanmade comparative advantage with factor-price equalization, industrial strategies and trade tactics become central variables in determining the difference between success and failure. The real issue is how government and industry can work together to generate the strategies and tactics that will be necessary for success. We know that neither socialism nor laissez-faire works. Governments cannot successfully give orders to industrial firms; markets cannot successfully make the necessary long-run investments. The Japanese have a working third way where the phrase "administrative guidance" is the operable term, but their third way is probably peculiar to their culture and not transferable to the Americas or Europe. A workable American third way has yet to be discovered.

Notes

1. *The Wall Street Journal* (January 1, 1900), 1.
2. Lester Thurow, *Head to Head* (New York: Morrow, 1992), p. 204.
3. International Monetary Fund, *Primary Commodities: Market Development and Outlook* (July 1990), 26.
4. Lester Thurow, *Head to Head*, p. 45.
5. Editor's note: See "World Employment Crisis Worst Since 1930s Depression," *ILO Washington Focus* (Washington, DC: International Labor Office, Winter 1995).
6. *The Economist*, Economic and Financial Indicators (July 1, 1995), p. 96.
7. Council of Economic Advisers, *Economic Report of the President, 1993*, pp. 350, 381, and 396.
8. Ibid., p. 380.

224 COMPETITIVENESS, TRADE, AND DEVELOPMENT

9. U.S. Bureau of the Census, *Workers with Low Earnings 1964 to 1990*, Current Population Reports, Consumer Income, Series P-60, no. 178, p. 2.

10. U.S. Department of Commerce, *Survey of Current Business* (July 1992), pp. 82, 84.

11. *The Economist*, "Shoot Out at the Check-out" (June 5, 1993), 81.

12. JESSI is a project to advance the European semiconductor industry; ESPRIT is the European Strategic Programme for Research and Development in Information Technologies; EUREKA is the European Research Co-ordination Agency. Yet another project is Prometius, designed to develop a computer-driven auto accident-avoidance system.

13. *Journal of Japanese Trade & Industry, 4* (1988), 15.

12

International Trade and the Governance of Global Markets

Brent McClintock

The free traders, as has been said, win the debates but the protectionists win the elections.[1]

Frank H. Knight

International trade is the spice of economic life. It allows us both to enjoy the goods and services that we are unable to provide at reasonable cost from within our own community and to earn a livelihood by the sale of exports in a wider market than our own. But trade also has the ability to disrupt community life. The rapid penetration of imports into the domestic market or a decline in the competitiveness of our exports in world markets may lead to lost employment, declines in real income, plant shutdowns, and the deterioration of affected communities. The challenge for society is to savor the taste of trade without allowing trade to become an all-consuming force that threatens the development of social and economic life within a community.

Mainstream economics has yet to provide a workable theory of trade management to explain why society steps in to govern the activities of markets when those markets create significant disruption of the life process. It has not been able to interpret fully Frank Knight's observation that the free traders win the arguments but lose the elections. Is the preference of so many societies for managed trade rather than free trade simply the outcome of the power and persuasion of a few vested interests, or is there something more to be explained?

A fuller explanation is offered by institutional economics. Its method is to investigate how the economic process interacts with the wider cultural process. The task of the economy, in the institutionalist view, is to ensure social provisioning or the maintenance of society as a going concern. Whenever economic changes threaten this social provisioning, intervention in the economic process may be expected in an effort to restore continuity and to allow the pursuit of values beyond simply achieving economic efficiency. It is from this perspective that institutional economics approaches the explanation of intervention in international trade.

Since institutional economics treats the economy as part of an ongoing historical process, investigation of international trade at the end of the twentieth century requires a consideration of the trends in the global economy that have led to present trade arrangements and practices. While much international trade has been organized through markets, those markets have been altered substantially by the interventions of corporations and national governments. Increasingly, nations and corporations have realized that social provisioning can only be assured if intervention occurs at the supranational level. A key challenge for the twenty-first century is to reduce the social dislocation created by international markets through the extension of supranational governance.

The Trend of Trade and Production

National economies have become more interdependent since World War II. Over the past twenty-five years, world trade has grown annually in real terms by 5.5 percent while world real gross domestic product (GDP) has grown at a slower 3.4 percent annual rate.[2] Improvements in production systems, communications, and transportation have all contributed to this greater integration of national markets into a global system. The structure of trade has also changed: in the 1950s and 1960s much of world trade was between developed nations; from the beginning of the 1970s the less developed countries began to provide a rapidly rising share of developed countries' imports.[3]

While the various negotiating rounds of the General Agreement on Tariffs and Trade (GATT) produced multilateral tariff reductions after World War II, the loss of these protective measures led to the increasing use of nontariff barriers (NTBs) and domestic subsidies to counter the effects of freer trade. The recently concluded Uruguay Round of the GATT became protracted as negotiations shifted to the reduction of NTBs in agriculture, trade in services, and intellectual property rights.

The governance of global markets is not limited, of course, to nation-states. Multinational corporations have responded to the vagaries of markets by engaging in the management of international trade and production. The extent of multinational dominance in trade may be seen in U.S. trade data: in 1990 nearly three-quarters of all U.S. exports involved transactions by American and foreign multinationals.[4] On the import side, two-thirds of all imports were associated with the activities of multinationals.

A form of corporate-driven trade management of increasing importance is intrafirm trade. This replaces arms-length market transactions with hierarchical, redistributive transactions between elements of the same firm. Some 30 percent of U.S. exports and 35 to 40 percent of U.S. imports in 1990 are estimated to have involved intrafirm transactions between the parent groups of multinationals and their affiliates.[5] Studies of Japan, Germany, and the United Kingdom also underscore the rising significance of intrafirm transactions.[6]

International production has become increasingly integrated too, and must be understood in terms of the evolution of production systems under capitalism. Over the course of the twentieth century, the organization of production has evolved from craft to mass production to lean production. Mass production, exemplified by Henry Ford's application of the system in the automobile industry, combined the interchangeability of parts, ease of assembly, equipment dedicated to single tasks, and a fine division of labor with low skill requirements with a continuous-flow assembly line.[7] It led to substantial economies of scale, which contributed to higher real incomes for workers and stockholders and lower prices for consumers. On the downside, product selection was limited (because of the high cost of introducing new products) and the de-skilling of workers led to worker alienation.

Corporate organization under mass production involved vertical integration, dictated both by the technological exigencies of standardized parts and by efforts to build and exert market power. In large measure an American invention, the mass production system spread to Europe and beyond to form the basis of international production and trade strategies for many industries.

In the final decades of the twentieth century, lean or flexible production has emerged as a strong competitor to mass production in organizing international production. Developed by Toyota and other Japanese auto companies, this system allows producers to improve final product quality, change production levels and products relatively quickly in response to shifts in market demand, and develop new products in less time. The result is a wider assortment of higher-quality, more customized products or models produced in lower volume *and* at lower cost than under mass production.

Corporate organization under lean production has tended to rely less on vertical integration and more on horizontal linkages between firms, often of different national origin. Rather than compete among themselves for market share, many national monopolistic or oligopolistic firms in a range of industries are establishing cooperative oligopolies in the form of joint ventures, strategic alliances, international subcontracting, and production sharing arrangements that focus on supranational market strategies. Such experiments in corporate organization are best referred to as instances of oligopolistic cooperation instead of oligopolistic competition.[8]

Cases of oligopolistic cooperation from several industries may be illustrative. In the automobile industry, international production has moved beyond the horizontal and vertical integration of manufacturing within one firm to such joint ventures as those formed by General Motors and Toyota, Ford and Mazda, and Chrysler and Mitsubishi, as well as production sharing arrangements in which ostensible competitors produce components and even complete vehicles for one another. The airline industry has begun to circumvent the strictures of the international airline cartel by forming strategic alliances through cross-shareholdings, shared marketing arrangements, and joint ownership of reservation systems. Examples include the British Airways minority stockholding in U.S. Air, KLM's ties to Northwest Airlines, and the Galileo International reservation system owned by eleven international airlines including United Airlines, British Airways, U.S. Air, KLM, and Swiss Air. Finally, in the telecommunications industry, the foundations of a global information highway are being laid by various strategic alliances across national borders. Thus far, four such alliances have been formed. In May 1993, AT&T launched World Source, a joint venture with five foreign phone companies including Kokusai Denshin Denwa of Japan and Singapore Telecom to provide voice and data transmission for multinational corporations. British Telecom (BT) and MCI set up a $1 billion joint venture to operate in the same global market, with BT also taking a 20 percent stake in MCI. A third alliance between Deutsche Telekom and France Telecom expanded their joint-venture Eunetcom network for multinationals around the globe, while Unisource, the fourth alliance, formed around the national phone companies of the Netherlands, Sweden, and Switzerland.

The Challenge of Structural Dislocation

The trade and production changes described above have often led to significant economic and social dislocation. Managing adjustment to this structural dislocation has presented substantial challenges to corporations, labor unions, local communities, and governments.

The winds of international competition and other structural changes in the economy have imposed an especially steep adjustment burden on labor. When mass production replaced craft production early in this century, many displaced, skilled craft workers found new employment opportunities in the new mass-production industries. The opposite holds for the transition from mass to lean production at the close of the century. Since workers under mass production have relatively low skill levels, they are not well prepared for the multiskill work requirements of lean production. Consequently, as the recent history of the auto, steel, and textile industries has made clear, mass-production workers have found (and will continue to find) it difficult to shift from one production system to another. While much of the burden of this transition has fallen on low-skill, low-wage blue-collar workers, increasing numbers of pink- and white-collar workers have also begun to feel the burden.

The alternatives faced by society are either to resist the transition by trying to insulate itself from the changing structure of global markets or to adapt to the evolving set of circumstances. The insular strategy of protectionist trade barriers and unilateral foreign investment controls is likely simply to delay the day of reckoning, postponing adjustment that over the long run is likely to be more

costly. Slower rates of productivity growth and declining international competitiveness, resulting in slower income growth and higher unemployment, are the
costs of an inability or unwillingness to adapt.

The adaptive strategy requires the diffusion of lean production and the search
for new adjustment policies. Such adaptation may occur through markets alone
or through a mixed-market approach. Leaving adjustment to free trade alone is
likely to precipitate extensive short-run dislocation in terms of lost jobs, income,
and community stability, which has and will generate a protectionist backlash.
More beneficial over the long haul is an adaptive strategy that combines open
but managed trade with adjustment programs to retrain and support displaced
workers. Adjustment programs at the national level, however, are insufficient to
meet the challenges of a more integrated global economy. Nation states may be
able to moderate the dislocation caused by international markets through retraining and relocation assistance, but they may increase the fiscal pressures on
already overburdened states without directly creating an environment for sustain-
able growth. Increasingly, it is becoming apparent that greater supranational
governance is required to bolster national economic policies.

The Conventional Wisdom on Trade Intervention

Although Adam Smith was the first to formulate a theory of free trade, David
Ricardo's theory of comparative advantage laid the foundation for modern neoclassical trade theory. The theory of comparative advantage holds that nations
should specialize in the production and exchange of products in which they are
relatively efficient even if they do not have an absolute cost advantage.
Ricardo's theory set the precedent for the theoretical development of trade models based on a harmonious, frictionless world where all would experience greater
welfare upon the adoption of free trade. Short-run adjustment costs to trade
disturbances and the resulting effects on income distribution were largely assumed away.

Later, neoclassical trade theory, exemplified by the Heckscher–Ohlin model
and the Stolper–Samuelson theorem, explicitly introduced the distributional effects of trade into economic analysis by exploring the changes in marginal productivity of resources resulting from a change in trading conditions.[9] Under free
trade, countries would specialize in trading goods that used intensively their
most abundant resource. At a national and global level, welfare would be enhanced by higher production and consumption levels. In terms of income distribution, the owners of the abundant resource would tend to gain from trade, while
other resource owners would tend to lose.

Neoclassical trade theory is set within a larger vision of the economy as a
self-regulating market system in which resources are allocated according to the
directions of the supply-demand-price mechanism. This vision of the market
economy is reflected in the assumptions of free trade theory. In the Heckscher–

Ohlin model, for example, the beneficial outcomes of free trade are underpinned by key assumptions of perfect competition, full employment, perfect mobility of resources in the domestic economy, the dominance of self-interested gain as a guide to human behavior, no transaction or adjustment costs, and the association of welfare maximization with efficiency in production and consumption. Implicitly, government intervention in the trade sector is assumed to be limited to establishing the rules under which the market exchange of free trade may take place. Set up in this way, free trade models may point to the undesirability of government intervention; they do not, however, explain why intervention occurs.

Whenever any of these assumptions breaks down, the analysis changes and the desirability of free trade may weaken. In an economy operating at less than full employment and facing substantial adjustment costs to changing trade patterns, free trade may not be the "first best" or even "second best" solution.

"The New International Economics" developed by Paul Krugman, James Brander, and Barbara Spencer, among others, emerged in the early 1980s as an investigation of the implications of imperfect competition for trade theory and policy.[10] In contrast to neoclassical trade theory's assumption of perfect competition, the new international economics holds there are sectors in which supernormal profits exist and under particular circumstances—the presence of increasing returns to scale and gains from "learning by doing" external economies—these industries may be designated as strategic to the national interest. The strategic trade policy to capture the beneficial effects of imperfect competition in trade may be classified as taking the form of either "profit-shifting subsidies," which lower production costs for domestic firms and allow them to capture a larger share of rents, or "protection from home market effects," through the use of export subsidies or import tariffs to allow domestic firms to capture the external economies of learning by doing.[11]

Rather than a rationale for an activist trade policy to pick winners and losers, Krugman has argued that the new international economics provides "a sadder but wiser argument for free trade as a rule of thumb in a world whose politics are as imperfect as its markets" because of the rent-seeking activities of vested interests.[12] If this statement comes to reflect the end point of the new international economics' deliberations, then its position will be little different from that of public-choice theorists.

The task of explaining the motives for protectionism has largely fallen to public choice theory. Its interpretation focuses on how utility-maximizing individuals or "rent seekers" form special interest groups to extract rents by lobbying politicians to impose tariffs or quotas.[13] Politicians, who are assumed to be self-interested and thus wish to improve their chances of re-election, allocate protection according to how their electoral benefits may be maximized.

According to James Buchanan, this rent seeking does nothing to add to social product since it merely alters the way the economic pie is sliced—that is, it redistributes current income between interest groups, rather than making the economic pie any larger.[14] How adequate an explanation of intervention in trade is the public-choice approach? The available evidence suggests that rent seeking is not simply motivated by short-run, self-interested gain. Robert Baldwin, himself a public-choice theorist, concludes from an extensive econometric study of trade protection that in addition to self-interest, "interpersonal effects and broad social concerns are also needed to explain trade policies."[15]

It is to these broader social concerns that institutionalist critics of public choice turn when they seek to explain intervention in the market system. Major objections advanced by these critics center on public choice's narrow conception of the individual as a maximizer of consumer satisfaction to the exclusion of her or his role as a creator of productive capacities; its rejection of the existence of a public interest above and beyond individual interest; and its neglect of values other than market efficiency, such as security, democracy, and equity.[16] In these alternative conceptions of society and economy, the center of attention shifts away from economic and political exchange to the working rules of society that give expression to collective action. The policy issues become issues not so much of determining the institutions necessary for market efficiency but of establishing the working rules for the administration of international trade, finance, and the environment that will foster the mix of values society deems vital to social provisioning.

An Institutionalist Theory of the State and the International Economy

The institutionalist theory of the state is captured in James Ronald Stanfield's concept of "the dichotomized state."[17] The state may perform both repressive and socially integrative functions. The coercive powers of the state may be used to further or suppress the conflicts between individuals, classes, and societies in such a way as to redistribute income and wealth to further the ends of vested interests. Yet the state may also be used to further the provisioning or reproduction of society as a going concern. The integrative state may act as a counterbalance to private interests that jeopardize social reproduction. Thus, under market capitalism, the state may act as a check to the excesses of the market system illustrated by fluctuations in macroeconomic activity, the degradation and alienation of labor, instability in the financial system, and environmental damage.

This integrative function of the state is encapsulated in Karl Polanyi's concept of "the double movement" generated by market capitalism. As the market system encroached upon greater areas of social life, it was met by a socially protective response aimed at limiting the social disruption caused by market shocks.[18] The source of this disruption, in Polanyi's view, was the market's treatment of labor, natural resources, and productive organization as fictitious commodities. The significance of these elements to society is their ability to promote the life process, not the fiction that their ultimate role is to be produced for sale in markets.

Social protection or the integrative function of the state also occurs in response to dislocation generated by international markets. Although acknowledging the efforts of rent-seeking interests to gain protection from international competition, Polanyi identifies the greater motivation for protection as the desire to stabilize social provisioning:

> No purely monetary definition of interests can leave room for that vital need for social protection, the representation of which commonly falls to . . . the governments of the day.[19]

This social protection goes beyond mere self-interested rent seeking to encompass the promotion of the social and economic stability of society. Evaluating the protectionist repercussions of the excesses of laissez-faire capitalism, Polanyi notes:

> Customs tariffs which implied profits for capitalists and wages for workers meant, ultimately, security against unemployment, stabilization of regional conditions, assurance against liquidation of industries, and perhaps most of all, the avoidance of that painful loss of status which inevitably accompanies transference to a job at which a man is less skilled and experienced than at his own.[20]

What this suggests is that there is some greater social or public interest to be met by intervention in markets—namely, assuring at a minimum that social provisioning will not be disrupted. In addition, the reference to both monetary and nonmonetary costs and benefits indicates these must all be incorporated in any comprehensive analysis of proposals for protection and adjustment policies.

Drawing upon his model of the "double movement," Polanyi sees the two-edged nature of change which he characterizes as a struggle over "habitation versus improvement."[21] The need to protect the social fabric very often conflicts with the need to bring about economic improvement. While neoclassical economics assumes the two objectives coincide, there is no guarantee that this will happen, except by chance. In the event of conflict, social intervention may be expected to occur in an attempt to preserve the social fabric. The guiding principle for this interventionist policy, Polanyi holds, ought to be whether or not:

> the dispossessed could adjust themselves to changed conditions without fatally damaging their substance, human and economic, physical and moral; [and] whether they would find new employment in the fields of opportunity indirectly connected with the change.[22]

To Polanyi then, as to many other institutionalists, the smooth, rapid adjustment of society and its citizens to significant changes in markets, whether domestic or international, is not a given. Rather, in the absence of managed adjustment, dislocation generated by markets is likely to initiate resistance that may impede economic improvement. The solution is to realize that although society may not always be able to determine the direction of economic change, it very often has the ability to alter the pace at which change takes place. This integrative task need not be reactive but may be by conscious design, that is, intervention to correct the excesses of the economic system may be planned and implemented *before* social reproduction is being threatened.

The welfare state emerged in the twentieth century as one institutional form of the socially protective response. It is something of a social and economic hybrid, often summed up under the heading "mixed economy," which reflects the mix of private and public involvement in the economic process. Because it evolved from the spontaneous, nonideological protective response of the double movement, the welfare state has lacked a clear theoretical purpose for responding to market excesses and has exhibited only weak policy coordination. Yet, it has intervened under a wide variety of circumstances to counter social costs associated with unemployment, safety and health risks, environmental degradation, instability of the banking system, and international competition.

An institutionalist theory of the welfare state should clarify both the repressive and the integrative functions of the state. It must, in essence, make the case for the social benefits of collective action when the state performs the integrative task. On this point there are strong differences between institutionalist and public choice theorists.[23] Public choice contends that rent seeking is deleterious to society because the high social costs of protective measures on third parties outweigh the private benefits to producers and workers. The institutionalist perspective is less emphatic. Most certainly it concedes the presence of the motive of self-interested gain in protective action, but it also introduces the social benefits of collective action to the analysis. The social desirability of a protective measure depends upon the weighing of the expected private and social benefits against the expected private and social costs. Furthermore there must be an assessment of the ability of those gaining from the measure actually to compensate the losers. Since social costs and benefits may not always be expressed appropriately in terms of market values or, more importantly, related to market efficiency because they are extramarket phenomena, it is necessary to assess protective measures not in terms of market efficiency but in terms of a wider set of social values.

Identification of social costs and benefits calls for scientific determination of "social minima" or "basic needs," which might include minimum environmental, health, education, nutrition, housing, transportation, and employment standards.[24] These social minima would reflect certain value minima, or value floors, of society. This suggests supplementing market valuations in cost–benefit analyses of trade policies with social indicator analyses and environmental impact statements. Where social minima are not met, society might be expected to intervene either to reduce social costs or to increase social benefits.

The willingness of society to intervene where the market fails indicates that market valuations are not the only values of importance to society. A number of investigators of the welfare state have identified a well-defined, representative set of welfare values: equality, security, freedom, democracy, efficiency, and solidarity or community.[25] These values reflect the attempt of the welfare state to move beyond the market mentality's overemphasis on the motive of self-interested gain and the value of market efficiency to a broader interpretation of the ends of human endeavor. A further value, a land ethic, may be added to this set of values to underscore the importance to human life of conserving the ecological system.[26]

The importance of the state in institutional analysis derives from society's need for an institution that can represent and help form social values, resulting in a sum of valuations that is greater than the parts. This contrasts sharply with the role of the state in the public-choice approach, where it is a broker state of vested interests giving expression to individualistic values, a mere summing of the parts.

The Case of Labor

The integrative functions of the state may be seen in the ways in which social protection is accorded labor in the economic process. In the United States a range of labor market policies are used to assist workers displaced by the effects of international competition; regrettably, they generate rather ineffective adjustment because of poor targeting and funding. Compared with most other industrialized nations, U.S. federal labor-market programs are heavily focused on providing short-term income maintenance and at lower levels of expenditure as a percentage of national income. The United States spends only half as much as OECD countries as a percent of GDP on labor-market adjustment assistance and only two-thirds the level of the OECD country average on income maintenance.[27] Since relatively little is expended on adjustment-enhancing assistance in the form of retraining, job search, and relocation, this expenditure mix engenders longer periods of unemployment for the average worker and larger numbers of discouraged workers.

Adjustment programs are organized primarily through the Job Training Partnership Act (JTP), the Economic Dislocation and Workers Adjustment Assistance Act (EDWAA), a subprogram of the JTP, and the Trade Adjustment Assistance Act (TAA). Advance notice to workers and communities of mass layoffs and plant closures is required under the Worker Adjustment and Retraining Notification Act (WARN). The JTP and EDWAA programs provide retraining and job search assistance to all dislocated workers, while the TAA focuses on workers displaced by international competition.

The performance of these adjustment assistance programs has been poor. Advance warning of impending mass layoffs and plant closings under the

WARN act is ineffective in many cases because of poor enforcement.[28] The level of assistance is often low, assistance fails to reach many of those eligible, and retraining is slow to materialize. In 1990, the JTP and EDWAA programs paid benefits averaging only $1,354 to 288,000 participants.[29]

Little comfort can be taken from the experience with the Trade Adjustment Assistance program either. While substantially more is expended on average assistance, at $7,000 per worker, total expenditures are small and the placement rate in new employment is low, at just 35 percent.[30] Moreover, Robert W. Bednarzik found only some 6 percent of the long-term unemployed between 1982 and 1987 were certified as eligible for trade adjustment assistance.[31] This underscores the evidence that groups at high risk from freer trade—women, minorities, older workers, and less skilled workers—are left to carry the burden of adjustment largely on their own.

In sum, if the policy objective is to enhance adjustment to international competition, the current mix of federal labor-market programs is greatly ineffective. Existing programs emphasize short-term income support and do little to promote retraining, job search, counseling, and relocation. The track record for current adjustment programs indicates that the few displaced workers fortunate enough to qualify for retraining receive relatively small amounts of assistance. If the social costs of trade adjustment are to be minimized, then existing labor programs will require substantial restructuring to promote more rapid and extensive adjustment assistance.

The burden of adjustment is not only borne by the unemployed and those working in sunset or declining industries. Even those employed in comparatively advantaged, sunrise industries such as telecommunications are affected by rapid changes in trade patterns. Greater productivity and higher incomes have not meant increased leisure for Americans. Over the past two decades, annual hours worked by the average American have risen by an amount equivalent to an extra month's work per year.[32] The length of the average work week has changed little from forty hours since the 1930s, even increasing slightly since the late 1960s.

Not surprisingly, the homefront was squeezed by expanding work effort in the marketplace. Working women found themselves working a double shift in the market and the home. The conservative economic message of the 1980s, exemplified by Reaganomics, reversed the logic of the linkages between the economy and society. More market work and of greater intensity and a conservative moral code of individual self-interest will not in and of themselves improve the realization of family values. Indeed, this strategy simply made things worse in the 1980s. It is the unhindered disruption of social life by markets that undermines family values.

These social outcomes are not created by some natural order but by our present institutional arrangements. It is quite within human capabilities to re-shape our institutions to meet our requirements should we resolve to rebalance our effort between the market economy and social life. Fundamentally, society has failed to ask clearly, loudly, and often enough: progress for what? Affluent societies need to undertake a re-envisioning of the role of work in individual and social life. Such a new vision will necessitate a reassessment of what institutions are needed both to smooth adjustment to trade and other dislocations generated by the economic system and to build a world in which there is greater time for leisure.

Supranational Governance of Global Markets

Attempts by nation-states to manage adjustment to market-induced change initiated in the international economy may simply generate the further export of jobs and capital, thus worsening a country's position. A national government may be unable or unwilling to persuade firms to behave in a socially responsible manner when its sovereignty ends at national borders. Increasingly, the management of adjustment to trade and financial flows between countries requires coordinated effort at the supranational level.

Two important reasons for the development of supranational governance are the technological and integrative imperatives of modern life. In the first case, the employment of technologies on a global scale calls forth the need for their standardization and regulation. International transport, communications, and meteorological services all fall within this category. Their efficient operation depends on supranational organization. The second major reason, which might be called the integrative imperative, is the perceived need to embed the international economy more firmly within social relations.

At the close of the World War II there was much interest in experimentation in supranational government in order to cement the peace and diminish the new threat of a nuclear holocaust raised by the onset of the Cold War. Just as important, societies wanted to avoid a repetition of the Great Depression and the ensuing tariff wars that broke out in world markets. The United Nations and its special agencies, such as the International Monetary Fund (IMF) and the World Bank, emerged out of these efforts. But some visionaries went beyond the limited scope envisioned for the United Nations' operations to explore more extensive versions of supranational governance.

Rexford Guy Tugwell, Henry Wallace, Clarence Ayres, Gunnar Myrdal, and others suggested that economic development could not be adequately achieved on a national level but required international coordination.[33] In this view, what was required to rebuild the world's economies after the devastation of the war and to improve the lot of the world's poor was a World New Deal. The world's wealthier nations would not only help one another rebuild via the Marshall Plan but also provide the demand and market access for products from poorer nations. All this was to be achieved within the context of a more progressive, democratic world order that would allow for a high degree of decentralized decision making.

A concrete instance of this thinking on supranational governance emerged from the work of Tugwell and others on a World Constitution.[34] Offering their proposal for a World Government as a starting point for discussion rather than a blueprint, the authors outlined a global federal system of governance. This system would be governed by a president, a World Council, and three special bodies: a House of Nationalities and States, a Syndical or functional Senate (a type of occupational parliament), and an Institute of Science, Education, and Culture. A Grand Tribunal of justices would supply the members of the World Supreme Court to decide judicial cases of world law. At the macroeconomic level, the World Government would be responsible for the conduct of fiscal and monetary policy, while a division of powers would occur on the more microeconomic issues of regulation and provision of public goods.

To Tugwell, the move to World Government would allow for a shift away from trade protectionism to equality of opportunity.[35] Tariff wars between nations would become a thing of the past as national borders became obsolete. World citizens would have a social safety net to cushion them from the disruptions of the trade and financial systems irrespective of their geographic location, ethnicity, or social status. Administratively, World Government, according to Tugwell, could foster diversity within unity. A federal system might at one and the same time generate a sense of oneness at the world level while encouraging diversity and autonomy at the regional and local levels.

But the vision of World Government was not to be realized in the mid twentieth century. The Cold War precipitated a heightening of international tensions between capitalist and communist nations, resulting in a tightening of trade flows. Furthermore, the slowing of New Deal reformism at home put an end to any consideration of launching a World New Deal. The United Nations became just one of many possible international forums for national governments and for limited experiments in supranational governance.

At the founding of the U.N. system in the mid-1940s, it was envisioned that there would be three specialized agencies charged with the supranational governance of the world economy. The International Trade Organization (ITO) would be responsible for the supervision of the international trading system; the IMF would attend to the international monetary system; and the International Bank for Reconstruction and Development, or World Bank, would be a conduit for financial capital flows between developed and less developed nations. As originally planned, the ITO was to have a far-reaching brief to oversee the trading system. Its main objectives were to be to foster economic growth and full employment; to assist in the transfer of resources from developed to less-developed countries; to oversee developments in national trade policies; and to establish price stabilization programs for primary products. But instead, the GATT was founded as what was meant to be an interim measure.

That interim measure has thus far lasted almost half a century. The GATT is less ambitious in its objectives than the ITO, limiting its efforts to the long-run reduction of trade barriers rather than pursuing management of trade through better integration of economic and social values.[36] Increasingly, as the experience with the latest Uruguay Round of negotiations has shown, the process has become drawn out and is subject to steeply diminishing returns. The larger concern with the administration of the trading system has been lost from view. While the IMF played a coordinating role in the Bretton Woods exchange-rate system, it has played a relatively minor part in the managed exchange-rate arrangements of the end of the twentieth century; most decision making has rested in the hands of the G–7 major industrial countries. In addition, the IMF failed to establish the Special Drawing Right as a key international reserve currency, primarily because of the reluctance of nation-states to surrender sovereignty over money creation. The World Bank has actually created further social disruption in the Third World by imposing structural adjustment programs that magnify the effects of market disturbances on social life. Hence, the United Nations system may have created a range of institutions to help govern the international economy but it has largely failed to fulfill the integrative function of a supranational state.

Regional Experiments in Integration

Regional experiments in supranational state governance may provide better working models than the U.N. system. The best known and most developed of these is the European Union (EU). Undoubtedly, the EU's extension of representative democracy and a system of justice to the supranational level takes the EU further along the path to the realization of social values of democracy, freedom, security, and equity than does the current U.N. system. In this system, social considerations firmly dominate the market economy. To interpret the union as some experiment in laissez-faire market economics at a regional level would be wrong. The EU economy has at all times been subject to significant social and political oversight.

Evidence of this governance may be seen in the process of instituting the Single Market for the EU in 1992. A raft of preexisting and new measures have been used to encourage the technological imperative within the EU and to provide social protection at the international level. The development and diffusion of technology within the union are assisted by programs such as ESPRIT (European Strategic Programme for Research and Development in Information Technologies) and EUREKA (European Research Co-ordination Agency).[37] The social imperative at the EU level is instituted through a range of interventions that modify the market outcomes of corporate activity in the Single Market. Anthony Scaperlanda finds three major areas in which the social control of industry has been exerted at the union level.[38] First, the EU Commission is empowered to enforce antitrust or competition policy. Second, the competitiveness of small to medium-size businesses is encouraged as an offset to potential market dominance by large corporations. Third, there are a range of social policies that are meant to limit the impact of big business on the environment, labor, consumers, and regions.

A key component of the introduction of the EU Single Market was the ratification of the Social Charter by all members except the United Kingdom. This nonbinding document affords, on paper at least, social protection of labor through a set of worker rights to a minimum wage, health coverage, the right to strike, and worker participation in management. Social legislation at the EU level of governance is likely to be based on the provisions of the Charter.

Despite the substantial measures by the EU to institute supranational governance in response to the technological and integrative imperatives, the task is incomplete. Many significant conflicts between national and supranational sovereignty lie ahead, as do conflicts between the economic and social spheres. Supranational democracy and justice are also underdeveloped; citizen participation in the political process at the union level is low and there is friction between the national and international political and legal systems. Despite fits and starts in the supranational governance experiment, as exemplified by recent difficulties along the path to European monetary union, the trend within the EU continues to be toward a re-embedding of the supranational economy in the evolving EU society.

North American nations have embarked upon their own regional experiment in supranational governance in the form of the North American Free Trade Agreement (NAFTA) among Canada, Mexico, and the United States.[39] The NAFTA involves far less social oversight of the integration process than has occurred in the EU. There is no supranational legislature or supranational court of justice to monitor the effects of the NAFTA. Instead, a North American Trade Commission has been established to implement and manage the treaty, as well as to settle disputes arising from the agreement.[40] Dispute-resolution panels of experts will decide cases. Failure of a country to abide by panel recommendations would allow the complainant country to introduce trade restrictions or other punitive measures equivalent to the degree of damage incurred. Although the Trade Commission's panels entail a lower degree of supranational governance than do EU institutions, these measures do involve some surrender of national sovereignty.

Labor and environmental side agreements to the NAFTA have also been negotiated. These agreements are to be administered by NAFTA labor and environmental commissions charged with establishing whether or not governments have been enforcing their own national labor and environmental laws.[41] Countries found not to be enforcing their laws may be fined up to $20 million and, should they continue to infringe commission findings, may ultimately be subject to the imposition of trade sanctions by the other NAFTA partners. These side agreements are modest steps toward supranational governance in North America. Nonetheless, the Trade Commission's establishment involves a further surrender of national sovereignty to a supranational body. Much, of course, remains to be done. Checking the enforcement of disparate laws of the partner countries is a fragmented approach to adequate labor and environmental protection in North America. NAFTA social and environmental charters are essential components of a fully functioning experiment in regional integration.

Conclusion: An International Economic Policy for the Twenty-first Century

Conventional economics is an inappropriate guide for developing an international economic policy for the twenty-first century. Neoclassical economic theory—in its focus on perfectly competitive markets, free trade, and a static conception of economic efficiency—assumes away too many of the realities of the world in which we live. While public choice provides an explanation of trade intervention, it takes too narrow a perspective of the motives for protection. Institutionalists readily agree with public choice theorists that much protectionism is motivated by self-interest. They differ from public choice theory in their consideration of a larger, social interest in protective measures aimed at fostering values, such as economic security, democracy, and equity, that allow a smoothing of the adjustment process. Unlike much of neoclassical and public choice theory, institutional analysis recognizes that adjustment to economic progress can be a painful and socially costly process.

In the institutional view, international trade is a dichotomous process in which technology tends to outpace the ability of institutions to adapt to the new exigencies. Both national societies and common humanity need better institutions to serve them in the twenty-first century. This necessarily involves improvements in national and supranational governance to promote the development and diffusion of technological advances. The early twenty-first century will require societies to come to terms with all the ramifications of the information age in which digital technologies such as virtual reality bring about changes in production, consumption, and the way we pass our leisure time.

In the short term, much can be done to improve the national governance of international trade and production. The burden shouldered by labor could be greatly eased by more socially protective adjustment assistance programs. As discussed above, current programs deliver assistance at low levels for relatively short periods, are poorly administered, and do not reach many of those in most need of assistance. A universal program of assistance to displaced workers, available irrespective of the cause of displacement and emphasizing longer-term retraining and relocation, would not only improve conditions for affected workers but raise overall productivity. These labor-market programs need to be coordinated with an industrial policy that encourages basic research and development and its diffusion across sectors of the economy. Such an industry policy would be charged with the conduct of adjustment-enhancing policy and not adjustment-retarding policies. One task would be to assist in the transition of both the private and public sectors from mass to lean production.

More fundamentally, society must re-envision the roles of work and leisure in the twenty-first century. What does "full employment" mean in the twenty-first century? Is now the time to "cash in" those long annual hours of work for more leisure time? If so, adjustment-assistance programs might be needed not only for work but also for leisure. New institutional arrangements would need to be developed to give effect to the new realities of work. Flexible scheduling, job sharing, a thirty hour work week or a three-day weekend, even a guaranteed annual income might become routine institutions.

Social protections mean nothing if they are not widely accepted and honored. One of the great social problems of the twentieth century has been the ease with which social protections have been overturned because of political expediency or alleged economic crisis. A cascading set of bills of rights, backed up by appropriate monitoring and enforcement, might improve the integration of the economic process in overall social provisioning. These bills of rights would run the gamut from local communities to the national and supranational levels. Robert Schlack has proposed a Community Bill of Rights that would oblige corporations to honor the rights of local communities to quality job opportunities, long-term job protection, fair treatment and compensation in the event of plant shutdowns, and environmental protection.[42] In addition, a number of economists are now developing and discussing proposals for supranational oversight of multinational enterprises and direct foreign investment.[43] At the national level, an Economic Bill of Rights was proposed in the mid-1940s and again in the 1980s.[44] Commitments to economic security and fairness, economic democracy in the workplace and in the community, a national health policy, and environmental sustainability might be some of the elements of an Economic Bill of Rights at the national level.

A Supranational Bill of Rights is not unthinkable. Already, the EU has a Social Charter with many of the same individual rights as the proposed Economic Bill of Rights, though they are not yet regarded as inalienable rights. The NAFTA would be much more effective and garner greater social support if it were tied to a North American Social Charter. As the experience with the UN Declaration of Human Rights demonstrates, it is very unlikely, however, that any bill of rights at the supranational level would mean anything until judicial and enforcement institutions exist to give it effect.

In the interim, experiments in social protection at the supranational level are likely to continue. While these experiments are currently at their most advanced stage in the EU, others are increasingly trying them. The labor and environmental side agreements to the NAFTA are small but useful steps to greater social oversight of international trade and production. Even the GATT, for all its weaknesses as an institutional mechanism to ensure social protection, might be modified by inserting social clauses on labor and environmental protection. On the environmental front, the United Nations has brokered global agreements on the reduction of greenhouse emissions and efforts to limit the damage of the ozone layer.

Much further into the twenty-first century, nations and supranational regional groupings will likely consider seriously the establishment of truly global forms of social oversight of the world economy. Perhaps this will ultimately take the form of a world constitution and government. This will probably be a gradual, evolutionary process in which there will be much resistance from vested corporate and national interests reluctant to relinquish yet more of their sovereignty.

The role of a twenty-first century economics is to explore the place of the economy in the cultural context. It must assist in working out institutional arrangements that will allow societies to continue to engage in international trade and production without substantial damage to the social fabric. This will involve extending social oversight of the economy to the supranational level within a democratic, participatory process. To do otherwise is to risk continuing market dislocation of society, increasing isolationism, or a shift to antagonistic regional trade blocs. The task of building an international economics fit for the twenty-first century awaits us.

Notes

1. Frank H. Knight, "The Role of Principles in Economics and Politics," in *On the History and Method of Economics: Selected Essays* (Chicago: University of Chicago Press, 1956), p. 253.

2. Author's calculation over the period 1965–90 based on International Monetary Fund, *International Financial Statistics Yearbook, 1993* (Washington, DC: International Monetary Fund, 1993).

3. While this section traces the trend of trade and production, one must recognize that trends in international finance are inextricably intertwined with trade and production. These issues are, however, beyond the scope of this chapter. For more on international finance in the present volume, see chap. 7 by L. Randall Wray. For more on international finance and supranational governance, see my "International Economic Policy and the Welfare State," unpublished Ph.D. dissertation, Colorado State University, 1990, and "International Financial Instability and the Financial Derivatives Market," *Journal of Economic Issues* (forthcoming [March 1996]).

4. The data on MNC shares of U.S. trade are the author's estimates based on Raymond J. Mataloni, Jr., "U.S. Multinational Companies: Operations in 1990," *Survey of Current Business* (August 1992), 60–74; Steve D. Bezirganian, "U.S. Affiliates of Foreign Companies: Operations in 1991," *Survey of Current Business* (May 1993), 89–99. The author's estimates of double counting are based on Betty L. Barker, "U.S. Merchandise Trade Associated with U.S. Multinational Companies," *Survey of Current Business* (May 1986), 55–72.

5. Author's estimates based on sources in note 4.

6. For British data, see Stuart Holland, *The Global Economy* (New York: St. Martin's Press, 1987), table 4.2, p. 143, and for German data, see Werner Olle, "Company Data–Preliminary Results of a 1983 Survey," *CTC Reporter, 20* (Autumn 1985), 55–59.

7. For an excellent investigation of this evolution of production strategies, with a

focus on lean production, see James P. Womack, Daniel T. Jones, and Daniel Roos, *The Machine that Changed the World* (New York: Rawson, 1990).

8. For more on oligopolistic cooperation, with specific reference to the automobile industry see John R. Munkirs, "The Automobile Industry, Political Economy, and a New World Order." *Journal of Economic Issues*, *27* (June 1993), 627–38.

9. Bertil Ohlin, *Interregional and International Trade* (Cambridge, MA: Harvard University Press, 1933), and W.F. Stolper and P.A. Samuelson, "Protection and Real Wages," *Review of Economic Studies*, *9* (November 1941).

10. For examples of such work, see Paul Krugman, "Import Protection as Export Promotion: International Competition in the Presence of Oligopoly and Economies of Scale," and James Brander and Barbara Spencer, "Tariff Protection and Imperfect Competition," both in Henryk Kierzkowski (ed.), *Monopolistic Competition and International Trade* (Oxford: Clarendon Press, 1984); and the contributions in Paul Krugman (ed.), *Strategic Trade Policy and the New International Economics* (Cambridge, MA: MIT Press, 1986).

11. James Brander, "Rationale for Strategic Trade and Industrial Policy," in Paul Krugman (ed.), *Strategic Trade Policy and the New International Economics*, p. 43.

12. Paul Krugman, "Is Free Trade Passé?," *Economic Perspectives*, *1*, 2 (Fall 1987), 131–44 (quote on p. 143).

13. For a pathfinding example of public-choice analysis of trade protection, see Anne O. Krueger, "The Political Economy of the Rent-Seeking Society," *American Economic Review*, *64* (June 1974), 291–303.

14. James M. Buchanan, "Reform in the Rent-Seeking Society," in J.M. Buchanan, R.D. Tollison, and G. Tullock (eds.), *Toward a Theory of the Rent-Seeking Society* (College Station: Texas A&M University Press, 1980), pp. 359–67; see p. 359.

15. Robert E. Baldwin, *The Political Economy of U.S. Import Policy* (Cambridge, MA: MIT Press, 1985), p. 165.

16. For critical views of public-choice theory, see Allan G. Gruchy, *The Reconstruction of Economics* (Westport, CT: Greenwood Press, 1987), p. 156, and Glen W. Atkinson, "Political Economy: Public Choice or Collective Action?," *Journal of Economic Issues*, *27* (December 1983), 1057–65.

17. James Ronald Stanfield, "The Dichotomized State," *Journal of Economic Issues*, *25* (September 1991), 765–80.

18. See Karl Polanyi, *The Great Transformation* (Boston: Beacon Press, 1957), p. 76, for Polanyi's statement of the double movement. Part three of the book contains his elaboration of the protective response.

19. Ibid., p. 154.

20. Ibid., p. 154.

21. Ibid.; "Habitation versus Improvement" is the title of chapter 3.

22. Ibid., p. 37.

23. For an institutionalist approach to social costs and benefits, see K. William Kapp, *Social Costs of Business Enterprise 1963* (Nottingham, UK: Spokesman Press, 1978), and "Social Costs and Benefits—Their Relevance for Public Policy and Economic Planning," in *Hindu Culture, Economic Development, and Economic Planning* (New York: Asia Publishing House, 1963), pp. 171–201.

24. Kapp, "Social Costs and Benefits," p. 183.

25. Norman Furniss and Timothy Tilton, *The Case for the Welfare State* (Bloomington: Indiana University Press, 1977) pp. 28–39; and Samuel Bowles, David M. Gordon, and Thomas E. Weisskopf, *Beyond the Wasteland* (Garden City, NY: Doubleday, 1983).

26. Aldo Leopold, "The Land Ethic," in *A Sand County Almanac* (New York: Oxford University Press, 1968 [1949]), pp. 201–26.

27. Organization for Economic Cooperation and Development, *Labour Market Policies for the 1990s* (Paris: OECD, 1990), table 14, and OECD, *Economic Outlook* (December 1991), table 13.

28. In a survey of eleven states, the General Accounting Office found more than half of all employers failed to provide advance notice to state agencies, and about 30 percent gave workers less than the sixty days notice required by law. See General Accounting Office, *Dislocated Workers: Worker Adjustment and Retraining Notification Act Not Meeting Its Goals* (Washington, DC: GAO, February 1993).

29. Author's calculation based on General Accounting Office, *Dislocated Workers: Comparison of Assistance Programs* (Washington, DC: September 1992), p. 1.

30. Reported in Hufbauer and Schott, *North American Free Trade* (Washington, DC: Institute for International Economics, 1992), p. 116. The higher average spending and lower placement rate relative to EDWAA tend to reflect the fact that recipients of TAA assistance require greater retraining effort compared with the wider population of displaced workers.

31. Robert W. Bednarzik, "An Analysis of U.S. Industries Sensitive to Foreign Trade, 1982–87," *Monthly Labor Review, 116*, 2 (February 1993) 15–31; see table 5, p. 28.

32. See Juliet B. Schor, *The Overworked American* (New York: Basic Books, 1991), table 2.3, p. 35.

33. For a sampling of these proposals for supranational governance see Clarence Ayres, *The Theory of Economic Progress* (Kalamazoo, MI: New Issues Press, 1978), pp. 278–82; Gunnar Myrdal, *Beyond the Welfare State* (New Haven, CT: Yale University Press, 1960); and Rexford Tugwell, "Notes on Some Implications of Oneness in the World," *Common Cause, 1* (November 1947), 165–72.

34. Rexford Guy Tugwell, et al., "Preliminary Draft of a World Constitution," *Common Cause, 1* (March 1948), 325–46.

35. Rexford Guy Tugwell, "Notes on Some Implications of Oneness in the World."

36. Evan Luard, *The Management of the World Economy* (New York: St. Martin's Press, 1983), pp. 77–78.

37. Anthony Scaperlanda, "The European Community and Multinational Enterprises: Lessons in the Social Control of Industry," *Journal of Economic Issues 26* (June 1992), 421–32.

38. Ibid., pp. 427–29.

39. For a summary of treaty details, see The Governments of Canada, Mexico, and the United States, *Description of the Proposed North American Free Trade Agreement*, August 12, 1992.

40. Ibid., pp. 39–41.

41. "NAFTA Is Facing Tough Journey in the Congress," *The Wall Street Journal* (August 16, 1993), A3, A16.

42. Robert F. Schlack, "Plant Closings: A Community's Bill of Rights," *Journal of Economic Issues, 25* (June 1991), 511–18; see p. 516.

43. See C. Fred Bergsten and Edward M. Graham, "Needed New International Rules for Foreign Direct Investment," *International Trade Journal, 7* (Fall 1992), 15–44; and Anthony Scaperlanda, "Multinational Enterprises and the Global Market," *Journal of Economic Issues, 27*, (June 1993): 605–16.

44. Norman Markowitz, *The Rise and Fall of the People's Century* (New York: Free Press, 1973), pp. 85, and 144–46; and Samuel Bowles, David M. Gordon, and Thomas E. Weisskopf, *Beyond the Wasteland*, part III.

13

Late Industrialization: Can More Countries Make It?

Alice H. Amsden

Furthering the Frontiers of Institutionalism

Many of the best and brightest Anglo-American economists in the 1950s turned their attention to solving the underdevelopment problems of the postcolonial world. This fad was short-lived, however. The subject matter of economic development did not lend itself easily to mathematical abstraction, and after the war abstraction overwhelmed the economics profession. Economic development involves a transformation, often violent or turbulent, of virtually all of a country's major private and public institutions, whereas in the last half of the twentieth century abstract modeling coalesced around the concept of equilibrium. The great classical economists—Smith, Ricardo, Malthus, and Marx—of course, were absorbed in the analysis of growth and distribution. They were fortunate enough to live before the marginalist revolution.

Traditional neoclassical theory predicts that poor countries will converge in income levels with rich countries because in poor economies where capital is scarce, returns to investment are highest and, therefore, investment is expected to be relatively great, thereby narrowing income differences over time. If anything, however, after the 1950s the per capita income differential between most rich and poor countries widened.[1] This created a *credibility* gap between neoclassical theory and practice, which led in the 1980s to innovative attempts by leaders of the profession to save the basic model. For instance, the "New Growth" theorists, as they came to be called, borrowed the old heterodox idea of "increasing returns" and, through the mathematical construct of a "knowledge production function," succeeded in introducing increasing returns into the old neoclassical framework without sacrificing its assumption of perfect competition.[2]

Yet, despite "New Growth" theories, "New Trade" theories, and other creative attempts at model saving, the gap between traditional market theory and the realities of economic development widened. Perhaps the most serious and important challenge came from the rise of the East Asian economies—first Japan, next Hong Kong, Singapore, South Korea, and Taiwan, then Thailand, Indonesia, and Malaysia, and finally China and Vietnam. Here for the first time in the postwar period were ex-colonies of the great powers that actually managed to develop. Here were the first of a large generation of poor economies after the war to experience rapid growth in per-capita income at relatively full employment levels and balance-of-payments equilibria. What is more, the general approach of government in most of these economies was one of pervasive intervention on both the supply and demand sides, in direct contradiction to the principles that define the traditional laissez-faire model of markets.

The East Asian "miracle" created a challenge to development economists—even heterodox ones—as never before. Instead of abstract models, whether neoclassical or Marxist, the discourse shifted to demonstrably successful "country models." These models were proven and real, and, therefore, exerted more claim to legitimacy than theoretical abstractions. The question became whether or not poor countries could emulate Eastern Asia's experiences—not in whole, of course, but in terms of selected *systems and subsystems*, possibly even shorn of the repressive political structures that were typical of Eastern Asia's growth.

The analytical challenge to development economists was immense because the transfer of intragenerational country models, rather than the mathematical manipulation of abstract models or the far-fetched comparisons between late twentieth-century and late nineteenth-century development experiences, required a distinct set of skills and empirical knowledge. Indeed, it required a whole set of new theories to understand how the various systems and subsystems of successful country models fit together. It required a more systematic way of thinking about institutions, not least of all those that had to be changed in countries wishing to import the economic systems of successful cases—how the emulators' existing institutions could be transformed (if at all!), under what conditions they were likely to adapt, and the degree to which they had to be modified to suit new soil.

Countries have always borrowed ideas, policies, technologies, organizations, and economic systems from one another—the factory system of eighteenth-century England and the mass production system of nineteenth-century North America are two cases in point. History is also replete with examples of dramatic changes in the major institutions of emulators—one need only think of Meiji Japan. But anything approximating a systematic understanding of which specific (possibly deep-seated) institutions could be expected to change and under what circumstances was still at a very primitive stage at the time of Eastern Asia's success.

It is the analytical issue of country-model transfer, and the new long-run research agenda it creates for development economists, that are this chapter's concern. If more countries are to follow in Eastern Asia's footsteps (Eastern Asia in this chapter refers to South Korea, Taiwan, and Hong Kong to a lesser extent), then the complexities of country-model transfer must be better understood.

Country-model transfer may be divided into three conceptual parts: the interpretation of the successful model to be transferred (the "input"), or analysis of what made a country succeed; the agents involved in the importation and transformation of the model; and the institutions of the emulating country that have to be changed in order to arrive at a workable retrofit (the "output"). This chapter is concerned mainly with the first and highly contentious process of how to analyze what made a country succeed. In the 1990s there was a fierce debate among development economists concerning whether Eastern Asia's success confirmed orthodox or heterodox economic principles.[3] The second issue (the agents responsible for emulation) and the third (institutional uprooting) are left for a more ambitious day.

Ideology and Interpretation

Both sociologists and historians have much to teach development economists about the country model transfer problem. Emulation, with institutional change at its core, is their bread and butter.[4] Nevertheless, in three critical respects (at least) the analytical difficulties currently confronting development economists differ from those confronting sociologists and historians.

First, historians studying how the United States caught up with Britain, or how European countries caught up with the United States, were dealing with a catch-up process among countries with income differentials on the order of at most 2:1. By contrast, the per capita income gap among countries that all started poor after World War II—say, Taiwan and Laos—grew cavernous by the end of the century, on the order of at least 10:1.[5] Consequently, system transfer even among countries of the same generation became more problematic.

Second, the nature of "inputs" differ for the sociologist and the development economist. The organizations the sociologist Westney was concerned with in her investigation of Japan's import of Western models included the post office, army, navy, and primary school system.[6] Even the "economic" organization Westney studied—banks—was discrete, with fairly easily determined empirical and conceptual boundaries. By contrast, development economists looking at a country model for purposes of accelerating growth in another country are interested in much more diffuse and less neatly bound phenomena—say, a whole financial system rather than just a central bank or even network of commercial banks; or an entire trade system, or an export promotion subsystem, and so forth. These systems and subsystems are harder to transfer than simply discrete organizations owing to a "conflation" problem. They have more "path dependence"— the success of their transfer depends more on their historical context, and "codependence"—their success depends more on related and interconnected systems. For example, the efficiency of both a post office and a financial system depends on a country's budgetary institutions, but in different degrees. Unless a country's fiscal system is sound, its financial system will almost certainly fail, although its post office (and even commercial banks) may still operate tolerably well. Contingent, interconnected economic systems are a major complication in country transfer.

Third, the development economist, unlike the sociologist or historian, operates in an academic discipline that is dominated by a single theoretical paradigm, that of the free market, with a small but vocal number of dissenters (many of whom happen to be development economists). This paradigm has become highly ideological in its interpretation of how economies work, if only because at its heart lies the question of the proper economic role for the state. The appropriate degree of state intervention in the economy generates emotional feelings because it touches on the relationship between the individual and political power. It also differentiates the platforms of political parties. Therefore, shades of opinion among "worldly economists" about the proper role for the state tend to depend on political affiliations, which political party is in power at any given moment, and what the public mood is at the time, rather than simply on new theoretical wisdom or empirical insight about the success or failure of state intervention. Public sentiment, moreover, can change capriciously. In 1943, for example, Joseph Schumpeter wrote about the United States: "The public mind has renounced allegiance to the capitalist scheme of values . . . Political forces strong enough to liquidate the organs of the war economy as they were liquidated in 1919 are not in sight."[7] By 1953, with the United States in the throes of McCarthyism, the public mind had already been manipulated in an about-face, and the mood of economists seemed to shift accordingly.[8]

A belief in the virtues of free markets at an ideological level of intensity, with a hegemonic paradigm polarizing opinion, makes it extremely difficult for development economists even to begin the process of analyzing country model transfer. So much is at stake in defending (or attacking) the paradigm that debate stops at the stage of interpretation: there is no consensus on what *caused* a successful country to prosper (or an unsuccessful one to fail) because there is no agreement on the importance of the state's role in that country's transformation. If economists cannot first agree on the nature of a model, they certainly cannot proceed to consider how to transfer it.

A case in point is provided by the stupendous economic success of South Korea and Taiwan. Contention over the role of the state in their development was crystalized in a study of Eastern Asia prepared by the World Bank, and a series of responses to the Bank's report.[9] It is worth reviewing this debate in order to try to advance the art of "model interpretation." In what follows, therefore, the conflict over what caused the postwar "East Asian miracle" is analyzed briefly,[10] with a view toward trying to establish certain methodological principles that all development economists might agree upon in order to improve country-model interpretation, a starting point for furthering the cause of country model transfer.

Country-model Interpretation: Example of the World Bank's "East Asian Miracle" Study

The World Bank's "East Asian Miracle" study was commissioned by the Japan Delegation to the Bank in order to determine the state's role in Eastern Asia's economic development. Consequently, the *Report* was written from the outset with the question of state intervention in mind. Unambiguously, the *Report* concluded that state intervention in Eastern Asia's economic transformation was enormous:

> Policy interventions took many forms—targeted and subsidized credit to selected industries, low deposit rates and ceilings on borrowing rates to increase profits and retained earnings, protection of domestic import substitutes, subsidies to declining industries, the establishment and financial support of government banks, public investments in applied research, firm- and industry-specific export targets, development of export marketing institutions, and wide sharing of information between public and private sectors. Some industries were promoted while others were not.[11]

Despite the absence of any ambiguity about the scope of state intervention, the Bank claimed that the responsibility of the state for Eastern Asia's success could not be determined:

> It is very difficult to establish statistical links between growth and a specific intervention, and even more difficult to establish causality. Because *we cannot know what would have happened in the absence of a specific policy*, it is difficult to test whether interventions increased growth rates.[12]

Of course, if "it is difficult to test whether interventions increased growth rates" (and it clearly is), then it is also difficult to test whether *non*interventions increased growth rates. Yet the Bank goes on to argue (in the form of an "essay in persuasion") that, in fact, Eastern Asia prospered not because of interventionist policies but because the economies of Eastern Asia "got the basics [a twist on prices] right":

> What caused Eastern Asia's success? In large measure the high performing Asian economies [HPAE's] achieved high growth by getting the basics right. Private domestic investment and rapidly growing human capital, were the principal engines of growth [along with an export orientation]. In this sense there is little that is "miraculous" about the HPAE's superior record of growth; it is largely due to superior accumulation of physical and human capital.[13]

In addition to this general conclusion downplaying the role of the state, a particularly controversial part of the *Report* concluded that industrial policy was ineffective: "We find very little evidence that industrial policies have affected either the sectoral structure of industry or rates of productivity change. *Industrial policies were largely ineffective.*"[14] Here is how the *Report* arrives at this conclusion.

The Bank's own tests of the effect of industrial policy on industrial structure (of South Korea primarily) elicited the conclusion that industrial policy has "no effect" on sectoral configuration based on the following analytical reasoning: "The manufacturing sector seems to have evolved roughly in accord with neoclassical expectations; industrial growth was largely 'market conforming.' "[15] Since industrial policy created an industrial structure that was market-conforming (in the neoclassical sense of comparative advantage), the *Report* reaches the astonishing conclusion that industrial policy was "ineffective." Thus, the *Report* declares Korea's industrial policy ineffective because it created the same market structure that neoclassical theory predicts would have evolved if South Korea had no industrial policy at all (just a neutral neoclassical policy).

As this test result is formulated, industrial policy can't win: if it fulfills neoclassical expectations, it is "ineffective"; if it violates them, it is inefficient! More to the point, the underlying (and *unverifiable*) presumption is that, in the absence of an industrial policy, South Korea's industrial structure would have been as "market-conforming" as neoclassical theory predicts—instead of simply underdeveloped, or under the control of foreign capital, or in serious balance-of-payments straits, or advancing at a slower rate than it actually achieved.

Of course, it is quite possible that if the Bank had determined Eastern Asia's overall growth strategy, the outcome might have been a lot worse—rather than as good as or better—than what did happen. Without capital controls and other financial market "imperfections," for instance, an undisciplined private sector might have sent its money to Switzerland, speculated more intensely in real estate, or consumed rather than invested. Without an investment policy, expenditures on primary and secondary schooling might simply have led to unemployment, and tertiary school leavers might merely have added to "brain drain." The presumption of the Bank's "market-friendly" approach is that investments in education obey a kind of "Say's Law," with the supply of educated people creating the demand necessary to employ them. Instead, investments in education may behave in accordance with Keynesian "ineffective demand." (Sub-Saharan African governments, for example, have invested more than Eastern Asian governments in education—4.1 percent versus 3.7 percent of GDP[16]—but unemployment of primary and secondary school leavers in Africa is rampant.) With respect to industrial structure, in varying degrees the high-performing Eastern Asian economies protected their strategic industries from foreign competition and offered them tax and other financial incentives. In contrast, Bank neoliberal policy rigidly opposed *any* form of subsidies to industry, whether for exports or import substitutes, and enforced its will by means of the conditionality it attached to its structural adjustment loans. Why, however, should one presume that such minimalism is superior to any of the varieties of industrial policy found in the high-performing Eastern Asian economies?

The above references may not do justice to the richness of the World Bank's Eastern Asian study, but they are enough to make two general points about "country-model interpretation." To appreciate these points, it is useful to apply them not just to Eastern Asia, where growth has been superlative, but to a set of countries whose growth performance has been abysmal—say, a fictitious amalgam of poor-performing countries called "Zaimalia."

"Nassau Senior"–Type Error

The first point that emerges from examining the World Bank's Eastern Asian *Report* is that if country models are to be interpreted fruitfully, interpretation must be free from what may be called the "Nassau Senior"–type fallacy. Confusing stocks and flows, economist Nassau Senior argued in the 1830s against reducing the ten-hour work day on the ground that all profits were made in the tenth hour. In effect, the Bank also fallaciously argues that government intervention in Eastern Asia accounted for only a small fraction of total growth and, therefore, was of minor consequence ("getting the basics right" was allegedly what mattered)! In countries where state intervention has been pervasive, as the Bank demonstrated was the case in Eastern Asia, one cannot divorce the "basics" from the state's role. If, for example, Eastern Asia has had high rates of saving and investment (most East Asian countries began the postwar period with very low rates), then these arose only in conjunction with, say, a particular structure of business enterprise and financial system (all banks in Korea and Taiwan, for instance, were publicly owned). If the high-performing Eastern Asian countries have exported a lot and have been aided in doing so by reasonable exchange rates, then their exchange-rate regimes have operated only in conjunction with extensive import-substitution policies (tariffs or quotas on competing imports) and elaborate export-incentive systems.

Thus, one cannot separate Eastern Asia's high investment rates from its financial repression, or its high export growth from its import substitution or deliberate export-promotion policies. *By the same token*, since the government in Zaimalia was also ubiquitous, one cannot divorce its poor performance from the government's role. Any sensible "essay in persuasion" would have to conclude from these two cases that the role of the state in Eastern Asia was highly positive, while in Zaimalia it was highly negative.

Errors of Doctrinalism

Second, if one is to make sensible country-model interpretations, one cannot conclude, as the Bank does in its assessment of industrial policy in Eastern Asia, that growth in a country would have been as fast or possibly even faster if laissez-faire policies had been adopted instead of the set of policies that actually were introduced. To argue along these lines is simply doctrinaire since no proof can be offered as evidence. The boasts that laissez-faire policies can do better are theoretical rather than real.

By the same token, one cannot argue that because the state was so pervasive in Zaimalia, and performance was so poor, the best policy to fix Zaimalia's problems is laissez-faire. There is no evidence to support this policy, if one uses as a guide the country models of Eastern Asia. What can be said is that state intervention in Zaimalia has to change; it must be *different*, which, applying the East Asian model, may mean less interventionist government policies in some areas and altered (and possibly greater) interference in other areas.

No doubt systems or subsystems of the East Asian model may be difficult to apply in Zaimalia, given cultural, historical, and institutional differences in the two cases. But it may be equally difficult to apply laissez-faire policies; after all, markets are little more than sets of institutions. Moreover, the political repression that accompanied East Asian growth in its early phases may be an integral aspect of the East Asian model, making it unattractive to transfer. On the other hand, the political system associated with laissez-faire in any given country may be equally undesirable. All these issues deserve further study. But the point is to study them using evidence derived from country models. With concrete cases of successful development in existence, a new mirror, rather than neoclassical theory, is worth a try.

What Is Admissible Evidence?

Orthodox and heterodox economists both claimed that Eastern Asia's economic success confirmed their own models.[17] How could this be so? The reason for the conflict was the absence of any clear, agreed-upon conventions of what constituted admissible evidence for support of a particular theory. The heterodox pointed to Eastern Asia's highly interventionist policies as confirmation for their approach. They argued that Eastern Asia grew by "getting the prices wrong," or rigging prices to favor capital accumulation.[18] The orthodox claimed that despite intervention, governments in Eastern Asia still "got the prices right." What, precisely, did they mean by this? One meaning they emphasized was creating "level playing fields." According to Jagdish Bhagwati, Eastern Asia succeeded because its effective exchange rates were "neutral," favoring neither import-substitution nor export activity.[19] Another meaning they emphasized related to productivity. They took zero total factor productivity growth as confirmation of orthodoxy because it allegedly implied that economic development was due to high rates of investing and saving, rather than with any institutional factors that might have contributed to increasing returns (despite the "New Growth" theories) and rising productivity.

This debate suggests that some simple rules of thumb are necessary for determining what right and wrong prices signify. One of the most simple and operational is to define the "right" prices as those determined by supply and demand. If fundamental prices in Eastern Asia's development—say, interest rates or foreign-exchange rates—are found to reflect not the government's hand but the forces of supply and demand, then one might conclude that orthodoxy lay behind Eastern Asia's success.

In my own work I demonstrate that key prices in South Korea were "wrong."[20] In the case of real interest rates, for instance, due to government intervention three real interest rates applicable to the same group of borrowers, with the same term structure of borrowing, existed side by side—the curb market interest rate, which was competitively determined; the commercial bank interest rate, determined by government-owned (or controlled) commercial banks; and the foreign loan interest rate, influenced by domestic inflation and exchange-rate policy. These real interest rates varied widely, so all three could not have been "right" simultaneously.[21] Moreover, while South Korea let market forces determine the exchange rate (more or less), neither exporters nor most firms competing against imports faced market-determined exchange rates. Exporters received subsidies and targeted import-substitution industries received trade protection (as well as many other incentives). The ultimate exchange rate that influenced the decisions of private economic actors, therefore, was "wrong"—that is, it deviated from what market forces determined.

All this implies that the Bhagwati criterion for attributing Eastern Asia's success to orthodoxy is inadmissible evidence.[22] Even if South Korea's effective exchange rate regime was "neutral" (in fact, it appears to have been slightly *anti-export*-biased), this does not mean that South Korea's key prices were determined by the forces of supply and demand. Manufacturers may have found it equally profitable to export or sell in the domestic market. But if their profit rates were determined by subsidies or tariff protection, and their decision to invest at all and sell in the domestic market or export was influenced by incentive regimes that included subsidies and protection against imports, it cannot be concluded that market forces were driving economic development. What can be concluded is that industrial policy succeeded in creating a neutral trade regime.

As for using zero total factor productivity growth as confirmation of orthodoxy, it also does not conform to the rule of thumb outlined above, of determining whether market forces or government intervention set key relative prices. If it turns out (the debate is ongoing) that total factor productivity growth was zero in economies like those of Eastern Asia, where output growth was rapid and government influence over the price of capital and foreign exchange was key, then one might conclude that government policies succeeded in stimulating investment, or that they failed to raise productivity. But one cannot conclude that orthodox policies of laissez-faire contributed to anything, because they did not exist.

Methodology of Country-model Mirrors

The shift from using an abstract, theoretical model to using a country model as a guide to policy change in poorly performing developing countries necessitates additional methodological shifts in analysis. Two necessary methodological changes are discussed below (one in this section and one in the final section), while the substantive focus continues to be on the role of the state.

Market Failures versus Historical Trade-offs

When abstract theoretical models are used as a mirror or reference point for improving the performance of low- or no-growth countries, typically the analysis of the role of the state in that process is considered from the perspective of *market failure*. When, instead, country models are used, the analysis of the role of the state should be considered from the perspective of *history*, and a historical examination of the real reasons why governments initially intervened in fast-growing countries. Typically the reasons for intervention (or nonintervention) involved (a) the inadequacy (or adequacy) of any country's competitive asset bundle (to compete in world markets), and (b) a *trade-off*, with significant economic, political, and social implications. Approaching the issue of why governments have intervened from the perspective of competitive asset bundles and historical trade-offs, rather than market failure, forces potential emulators to examine the choices their own governments face, rather than simply the issue of static or dynamic efficiency.

The virtues of the historical method may be appreciated by using the Eastern Asian example. Presumably all poor Eastern Asian countries started their postwar industrialization with highly imperfect markets; that is, there were abundant market failures. Yet, the degree of government intervention varied considerably *within* the Eastern Asian region, with the state in Taiwan and especially South Korea (we ignore Japan) playing a maximalist role, and that in Hong Kong playing a minimalist one. As Perkins pointed out, there are several Eastern Asian models, not just one (although for expositional purposes, the "East Asian model" in this chapter refers to Taiwan and South Korea).[23] If market failure was pervasive in Hong Kong as well as in Taiwan and South Korea, but the degree of government intervention was dramatically different, a market failure approach cannot explain such differences.

Explaining Intervention Differences

Historically, the government in Hong Kong intervened little because, given Hong Kong's existing asset bundle in the 1950s, it did not have to in order for enough industries to attain international competitiveness. Because Hong Kong was a "first mover" in garment manufacture, it gained protected foreign-market share in this commodity, which was more labor intensive and, therefore, more competitive on the basis of low wages than cotton textiles, the "leading sector"

of Taiwan and South Korea. There was little need for the government to intervene in order to facilitate capital accumulation since the amount of capital that
any single productive entity required was small (or foreign-owned) and wage
rates were a decisive competitive advantage. Certainly capital requirements in
garment making were smaller than they were for integrated spinning. To keep
wages low, the Hong Kong government sometimes encouraged immigration
flows from China (whereas social pressure in South Korea and Taiwan kept
low-wage labor immigration to a minimum). Moreover, government intervention
in Hong Kong was unnecessary insofar as Hong Kong's financial sector (services now account for as much as 70 percent of GNP) could build global competitiveness on the basis of political stability and excellent geographical location.

Ironically, Hong Kong's garment industry became strongly protected by the
very type of market interference its economic philosophy deplored: "Because of
its comparatively longer history of development, Hong Kong possesses *larger
export quotas* than Taiwan and South Korea, and especially other LDCs."[24]
These quotas allowed Hong Kong to delay a painful process of industrial restructuring, although in anticipation of the need to create higher value-added manufacturing activity, the government, in fact, became more interventionist.[25]

By contrast, government intervention in Taiwan and South Korea was greater
because initially textile manufacturers could not compete on the basis of market
determined production costs. In the mid-1960s, after Korea and Taiwan dutifully
devalued their real exchange rates and liberalized the imported inputs they
needed to manufacture their exports, they still could not compete against Japan,
even in their labor-intensive leading sector, cotton textiles, on the basis of "getting the prices right." They were uncompetitive in spite of the fact that they had
benefited from American aid–financed investments in physical and human infrastructure, and access to the American market, which was far more open than it is
today. Japan had higher wages but proportionately higher productivity (and
product quality) than either Korea or Taiwan. Therefore, Korea and Taiwan
faced an immediate choice, as depicted in figure 13.1. They could either *cut real
wages further* to become internationally competitive (a movement from B to C),
or they could *subsidize business*, in this case the textile industry, offering it
preferential credit and protecting it from Japanese exporters and Japanese foreign
investors, until it learned enough to raise productivity (and quality) to reach
Japan's level (at A) of unit labor costs (a movement from B to D, with subsidies
financed through either foreign borrowing or taxation).

Thus, looking at competitiveness historically reveals another advantage of the
"trade-off" approach over the "market-failure approach" to assessing the need
for government intervention: poorly performing countries can get a better idea of
which of several country models is more appropriate for their immediate needs.
The Hong Kong model is closest to laissez-faire, but probably furthest from the
competitive realities of most remaining poorly performing countries. In the
1980s real wages fell sharply throughout the Third World, thereby improving

Figure 13.1 **Cutting Real Wages or Subsidizing Learning**

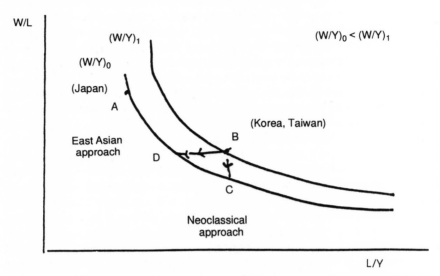

L = labor; Y = output; W/L = real wage per worker (expressed in a common currency); W/Y = unit labor cost. Unit labor cost loci are rectangular hyperbolas, the product of the real wage and labor-output ratio. They, therefore, are constants.

Source: Alice H. Amsden, "Why Isn't the Whole World Experimenting with the East Asian Model to Develop? Review of the World Bank's *The East Asian Miracle: Economic Growth and Public Policy*," *World Development, 23*, 4 (April 1994).

their chances of competing in advanced country markets on the basis of low costs. Nevertheless, because cuts in real wages were so broad based, and covered such a wide array of poor countries, the poorest among them, with the lowest productivity and worst infrastructure, probably did not improve their own chances against other low-cost competitors. Most labor-intensive industries in such countries today appear to face competitive conditions more akin to those of Taiwan and Korea in the 1960s than to those of Hong Kong in the 1950s. Therefore, the very immediate trade-off they face is one of cutting real wages (which follows from neoclassical theory) or subsidizing learning (which follows from Eastern Asia's experience).

Conclusion

Toward Country-model Theory

In this chapter I have tried to suggest analytical principles that development economists might fruitfully follow in order to facilitate the transfer of country

LATE INDUSTRIALIZATION   257

models to poor countries—that is, models based on the experiences of countries that have already successfully managed to transform themselves rather than on abstract market theory. This is a preliminary effort in many respects, not least of all because this chapter considers only the first stage of the transfer problem: the rules to apply and methods to follow in order to arrive at the most accurate conception or interpretation of country models themselves. This is necessary because there is typically no consensus among development economists about the causes of a successful country's transformation. In the case of the East Asian model, which I use to illustrate the general arguments of this chapter, some economists have attributed the East Asian "miracle" to "getting the basics right,"[26] while others, myself included,[27] have attributed it to a set of institutional arrangements in which the government played a disciplined and central role. How can a poor country wishing to learn from the East Asian experience discriminate between two such different interpretations? Further, should they follow the "East Asian model" based on the experience of South Korea and Taiwan, or the experience of Hong Kong?

By way of approaching these questions, several operational principles have been introduced. First, in developing countries where an inventory of trade, investment, and financial policies reveals extensive government intervention, an interpretation of that intervention must avoid a *"Nassau Senior"–type error*: the government's role cannot be reduced to a small percentage of growth. Whether in fast-growth or no-growth countries where government intervention has been extensive, the government must take the credit *or the blame* for overall economic performance.

Second, in fast-growth cases with extensive government intervention, one cannot conclude that growth *would have been* as fast or even faster if overall policy had been one of laissez-faire. Such a conclusion commits an *error of doctrinalism*, since there is no evidence from the fast-growth model to substantiate it. By the same logic, one cannot conclude that the optimal policy for the no-growth country to follow is laissez-faire since, again, the fast growth model does not provide any evidence for a laissez-faire approach. Rather, the fast-growth country model suggests that the nature of government intervention should be different.

Third, in choosing which country model to follow, from the angle of overall degree of government economic intervention (the substantive focus of this chapter), it is best for emulators to employ a *historical trade-off approach* rather than a "market-failure" approach. That is, in order for borrowing countries to evaluate the specific country model to adopt, the actual history rather than market failures of successful countries should be examined. If a market failure approach is adopted to understand different degrees of government intervention in different country models, it is impossible to discriminate among country models since all underdeveloped countries initially suffered from pervasive market imperfections and hence market failures. By the market failure reckoning, all developing countries should exhibit roughly the same amount of government intervention. Yet, from the East Asian experience, Hong Kong, South Korea, and Taiwan had vastly different experiences.

The actual choice of whether an existing poor country should follow the extreme of either Hong Kong or Korea and Taiwan (assuming these are the only two choices) should be determined according to whether an existing poor country has competitive assets to enter world markets comparable to those Hong Kong possessed in the 1950s, or Korea and Taiwan possessed in the 1960s (the decades when these economies began to grow). Government intervention in Hong Kong was minimalist because existing wage levels, in conjunction with world export quotas for Hong Kong's garment manufactures and an excellent geographical location for financial services, were sufficient assets to enable entrepreneurs (many of them foreign) to compete internationally without subsidies (although roughly 50 percent of Hong Kong's housing for workers was, in fact, public). Government intervention in Korea and Taiwan was maximalist because low wages, in conjunction with U.S. aid–supported education and infrastructure, were insufficient for Korean and Taiwanese entrepreneurs to compete in cotton textiles against the higher productivity of Japanese cotton spinners and weavers—despite repeated exchange-rate devaluations. Therefore, the governments in Korea and Taiwan faced a trade-off: they could either cut real wages further, which market efficiency models recommend, or they could subsidize learning, which is what the East Asian model is all about.

A historical trade-off approach rather than a market failure approach thus gives emulating countries (1) a way of selecting the most appropriate country model to follow, based on a comparison at the outset of growth of their own existing endowments of competitive assets and those of different successful countries, and (2) a way of estimating the alternatives to government subsidization of learning if the existing competitive assets of emulating countries are insufficient to compete in world markets in labor-intensive (or raw-material-intensive) industries.

Finally, it has been argued that transparent rules are necessary to arrive at a consensus about whether a country model confirms the operation of orthodox or heterodox policies. A simple rule of thumb is that orthodox policies are at play when key prices are determined by the forces of supply and demand, and heterodox policies are at play when governments set the "wrong" prices to stimulate growth. By this criterion, tests such as Jagdish Bhagwati's "neutral" trade regime or the contribution of total factor productivity growth to total growth tell us nothing about how key prices are determined. As pieces of evidence of either orthodox or heterodox policies at work, they are beside the point or inadmissible.

Reducing the Problem of "Conflation"

Nevertheless, the operating principles and methodological approaches just summarized are not in themselves sufficient to ensure analytically sharp interpretations of country models with a view toward cross-national transfer. New modes of theorizing are necessary in order to reduce a general problem of "conflation," or interdependence of different economic systems or subsystems within a country model. If, for example, Korea's and Taiwan's (repressed) financial systems in the 1970s were dependent on their (egalitarian) systems of income distribution to generate, say, high savings rates, then we need some theory to persuade potential borrowers that the institutional relationship between saving and income distribution was either integral (codependent) or incidental (independent). Without an understanding of how one set of systems interacts with another set of systems in the same country, transferring that country model will be difficult. By the same token, effective country model transfer necessitates greater understanding of the historical path dependence of given systems (for instance, whether the export success of Korea and Taiwan depended on international market growth in the 1960s or simply on the displacement of entrenched competitors from stagnant markets).

The laissez-faire model has to its great credit the fact that it is, after all, a theory, however empirically irrelevant. Laissez-faire (or "neoclassical" theory) contains a set of predictions about how abstract markets work. Therefore, what is needed if country models, rather than market abstractions, are to guide policy making in poor countries are theories about how *institutionally specific markets* work in particular countries. Such theorizing need not start from scratch because there is already a literature of "structuralist" theories about how developing countries behave.[28] Structuralist theorists model developing economies from an empirical vantage point (say, a certain type of financial market, or a certain trade constraint). Nevertheless, structuralist theories have largely been macroeconomic in nature and have not typically been constructed with a view toward transferring the financial, trade, industrial, or bureaucratic systems or subsystems of one country to another country (although not discussed in this chapter, bureaucratic systems in both firms and governments are critical for implementation, or transforming one country's model into a workable form in another country). The transfer problem necessitates more *sensitivity analysis* of the path and codependence of a country's systems and subsystems than is typical of past structuralist theorizing.

In addition to orienting new structuralist theories deliberately toward this end, two opposite approaches to advancing country-model sensitivity analysis generally may be mentioned. First, the analysis of technology—its generation, adaption, and transfer—has benefited from what Richard Nelson calls "appreciative theorizing,"[29] and such theorizing may further country-model transfer analysis. According to Nelson, "Appreciative theorizing [as opposed to formal theorizing] tends to be close to empirical work and provides both guidance and interpretation. . . . It generally refers to observed empirical relationships, but goes beyond them, and lays a causal interpretation on them."[30] Country-model analysis probably requires appreciative rather than formal theorizing.

Second, whereas "appreciative theorizing" starts from the very concrete, another approach to understand cross-sectional and historical interconnections among a country's economic (sub-) systems is to start with the very abstract, as in "complexity analysis."[31] Starting, say, with a single politician, bureaucrat, and business person, it is possible to make certain assumptions about their maximizing behavior that reveal different possible outcomes for countries where such assumptions are realistic.

Such innovative theorizing may not only aid in the process of country model transfer. It may also aid in the process of creating realistic theories for economic development at the twentieth century's end. This, I would argue, is a necessary condition for more poor countries to make it.

Notes

1. Takashi Hikino and Alice H. Amsden, "Staying Behind, Stumbling Back, Sneaking Up, Soaring Ahead: Late-Industrialization in Historical Perspective," in William J. Baumol, Richard R. Nelson, and Edward N. Wolff (eds.), *Convergence of Productivity: Cross-National and Historical Evidence* (New York: Oxford University Press, 1994).

2. Robert E. Lucas, Jr., "On the Mechanics of Economic Development," *Journal of Monetary Economics, 22,* 1 (July 1988), 3–42; Nancy L. Stokey, "Learning by Doing and the Introduction of New Goods," *Journal of Political Economy, 96,* 4 (August 1988), 701–17; "Symposia: New Growth Theory," *Journal of Economic Perspectives, 8,* 1 (Winter 1994).

3. See, for example, World Bank, *The East Asian Miracle: Economic Growth and Public Policy* (Washington, DC: World Bank, 1993) [hereinafter referred to as *Report*], and "Symposium on the World Bank's *The East Asian Miracle: Economic Growth and Public Policy,*" *World Development, 23,* 4 (April 1994).

4. See, for example, D. Eleanor Westney, *Imitation and Innovation: The Transfer of Western Organizational Patterns to Meiji Japan* (Cambridge, MA: Harvard University Press, 1987) on Meiji Japan, and David S. Landes, *The Unbound Prometheus, Technological Change and Industrial Development in Western Europe from 1750 to the Present* (Cambridge: Cambridge University Press, 1969) and S. Pollard, *Peaceful Conquest: The Industrialization of Europe, 1760–1970* (Oxford: Oxford University Press, 1981) on continental Europe.

5. Takashi Hikino and Alice H. Amsden, "Staying Behind, Stumbling Back, Sneaking Up, Soaring Ahead."

6. D. Eleanor Westney, *Imitation and Innovation.*

7. Joseph Schumpter, "Capitalism in the Post-War World," in Seymour Harris (ed.), *Post-War Economic Problems* (New York: McGraw-Hill, 1943), pp. 121–22.

8. See, for example, the prominence accorded to Milton Friedman (*Essays in Positive Economics Chicago* [Chicago: University of Chicago Press, 1953]).

9. See, for example, "Symposium," *World Development* (April 1994).

10. Drawing on Alice H. Amsden, "Why Isn't the Whole World Experimenting with the East Asian Model to Develop? Review of the World Bank's *The East Asian Miracle: Economic Growth and Public Policy,*" in "Symposium," *World Development* (April 1994).

11. *Report*, pp. 5–6.

12. Ibid., p. 6, emphasis added.

13. Ibid., p. 5.

14. Ibid., pp. 21, 312, emphasis added.

15. Ibid., p. 315.

16. Ibid., p. 198.

17. See, for example, Helen Hughes (ed.), *Explaining the Industrialization Success of East Asia* (Cambridge: Cambridge University Press, 1987).

18. Alice H. Amsden, *Asia's Next Giant: South Korea and Late Industrialization* (New York: Oxford University Press, 1989).

19. Jagdish N. Bhagwati, "Export-Promoting Trade Strategy: Issues and Evidence," *Research Observer, 3*, 1 (January 1988), 27–57.

20. Alice H. Amsden, *Asia's Next Giant*.

21. Alice H. Amsden and Yoon-Dae Euh, "South Korea's 1980s Financial Reforms: Good-bye Financial Repression (Maybe), Hello New Institutional Restraints," *World Development, 21*, 3 (March 1993), 379–90.

22. Jagdish N. Bhagwati, "Export-Promoting Trade Strategy."

23. Dwight Perkins, "The East Asian Miracle: Not One Model but at Least Three: Review of the World Bank's *The East Asian Miracle: Economic Growth and Public Policy*," "Symposium," *World Development* (April 1994).

24. Yin-ping Ho and Tzong-biau Lin, "Structural Adjustment in a Free-Trade, Free Market Economy," in Hugh Patrick (ed.), *Pacific Basin Industries in Distress: Structural Adjustment and Trade Policy in the Nine Industrialized Economies* (New York: Columbia University Press, 1991), pp. 257–310.

25. Ibid.

26. *Report*.

27. Alice H. Amsden, *Asia's Next Giant*.

28. See, for example, Lance Taylor, *Income Distribution, Inflation, and Growth: Lectures on Structuralist Macroeconomic Theory* (Cambridge, MA: MIT Press, 1991).

29. Jan Fagerberg, "Technology and International Differences in Growth Rates," *Journal of Economic Literature, 32*, 3 (1995), 1147–75.

30. Richard R. Nelson, "What Has Been the Matter with Neoclassical Growth Theory?" in Gerald Silverberg and Luc G. Soete (eds.), *The Economies of Growth and Technical Change: Technologies, Nations, Agents* (Aldershot, U.K.: Edward Elgar, 1994).

31. Duncan K. Foley, "A Statistical Theory of Markets," *Journal of Economic Theory, 62*, 2 (Summer 1994), 321–45.

Part VI
Conclusion

14

Economics in the Twenty-first Century

Robert Heilbroner

Economics and Capitalism

How is one to write a concluding essay to a collection of such variety and yet unity—a collection that examines contemporary economics in so many areas, and finds it seriously deficient in all? I propose to do so by raising for consideration an aspect of the discipline that provides the basis for just such a sweeping critical assessment—an aspect whose recognition runs throughout the preceding essays, although not quite in the blunt terms I shall use. This vulnerable aspect of economics derives from the fact that it is concerned exclusively with the study of capitalism. I do not mean "almost exclusively," or "with some exceptions," or any other such qualifying phrase. I mean that economics has no relevance whatsoever to the study of the hunting and gathering tribes that account for over 99 percent of human history, or to the noncapitalist stratified orders—kingdoms, empires, feudalities, command societies, or self-styled socialisms—that make up most of the remaining fraction of one percent. I go even further to assert that economics will not have any place in the study of the communal, supranational, associationist, or other modes of postcapitalist social organization that may come into being in some future time. Economics is about capitalism. It has no relevance to any other form of social architecture.

In itself, this concentrated relevance is not the source of the vulnerability of the discipline to criticism. The problem is that the great majority of its practitioners are unaware of the involvement of their study with one and only one social order. This leads not only to serious mischaracterizations of how that social order works, but to misleading applications of "economics" to societies that, despite our easy use of the term, do not possess economies.

This is a conceptual starting point that flies in the face of the received wisdom, and that may seem an overstatement even to some contributors to this volume. I need hardly add that the case must appear wholly unsupportable to neoclassical economists whose conceptual orientation might well be described as the exact opposite of my own. Here I might quote the distinguished economist Jack Hirshleifer:

> [I]t is ultimately impossible to carve off a distinct territory for economics, bordering on, but separated from other social disciplines. Economics penetrates them all, and is reciprocally penetrated by them. *There is only one social science.* What gives economics its imperialist penetrative power is that our analytical categories—scarcity, cost, preferences, opportunities, etc.—are truly universal in application. Even more important is our structured organization of these concepts into the distinct, yet intertwined processes of optimization on the individual decision level and equilibrium on the social level. Thus economics does really constitute the universal grammar of social science.[1]

It is evident, then, that I have much to do to make my case plausible. I must first establish exactly what I mean by capitalism, if I am to make it the *sine qua non* for a discipline called economics. Second, I must explain why this discipline cannot be applied to any society outside such a framework. Last, I must consider the consequences, both for theory and practice, of formulating a body of knowledge called "economics" without a specific awareness of its severe conceptual constraints.

Capitalism Defined

I shall begin my task by defining capitalism, a less awesome task than might at first appear. For I believe that capitalism is clearly identifiable among the social formations of history merely by virtue of three characteristics, no one of which is sufficient, but all of which are necessary, to bring about its existence. This is a viewpoint that derives ultimately from Marx and Weber, and that is tacitly or explicitly present in many critical views of capitalism, including a number in this volume. I bring it to the fore to make as explicit as possible the analysis that will follow.

The first of the three identifying elements is the presence of an entity or process called capital. Capitalism is a social order built on capital; and capital, by its designation as a necessary, if not sufficient, condition for the existence of capitalism, is therefore unlikely to be found, save marginally, in any precapitalist, or perhaps postcapitalist, order.

At the risk of stating the obvious—a risk I am forced to assume in view of its general disregard in conventional economics—I must halt here to distinguish between two distinct meanings for the crucial term *capital*. As an enduring physical (perhaps organizational) residue of labor, capital is as ancient as social effort itself. No human society, perhaps not even some animal societies, can exist without producing or discovering artifacts by which to ease or enable social reproduction: the twig of the anteater that dislodges its food, the club of neolithic man, the machines of modern society are all exemplars of physical capital, and as such, essential to social existence. Capital, in the sense described by Marx, refers to something quite else: a process in which physical capital loses its meaning as an object of use-value to gain a new meaning as a link in a chain of transactions—a chain from money into commodities back into a larger sum of money—whose purpose is the enlargement of exchange value, itself a term that connotes a specific, although not exclusively capitalist, social setting. This circuit of M–C–M' (where $M' > M$), appears in several of the preceding essays. It is the self-reproducing genetic unit of capitalism.

As such, the unit becomes the building block of a social order whose sense of historical purpose, institutional needs, and internal dynamism are all intimately connected with, and incomprehensible without, reference to this unique social process. Many kinds of societies accumulate wealth as objects that confer virtue or power on their owners, and in some societies there are small pockets of "capital" in its self-expanding form—one thinks of mercantile enclaves within precapitalist frameworks ranging from ancient Egypt to late feudalism. But only when the capital circuit becomes central to the larger social body can we speak of a capitalist social order. And only then, by my still undemonstrated chain of reasoning, do we discover the peculiar structures of theory and analysis called economics.

The crucial role played by M–C–M' raises a question of strategic importance and elusive comprehension—namely, the source of this powerful, apparently insatiable drive. That source can, of course, be subsumed under the rubric of rational choice applied to utility maximization. The well-known difficulty with this explanation is that no behavior cannot be so described, and that explanations that apply to everything explain nothing. My own answer locates the roots of the quest for capital in the adult acting-out of infantile fantasies and frustrations. This deep-buried source is perhaps the closest we can come to ascribing the drive for capital to "human nature," although the fact that capitalism appears so late in human history makes it abundantly clear that cultural pressures can greatly restrain the reenactment out of such drives, just as rational considerations of self-defense can reinforce them in a social order of generalized predation.

I should add that it is only a short step from this level of explication to an examination of the question of power itself, with its universally recognized but ill-explained attractions. These are aspects of stratified social orders to which conventional economics pays no heed whatsoever, but they suggest a foundation for the motivations of the M–C–M' process very different from that which would follow from Hirshleifer's depiction of it as arising from "scarcity, cost, preferences, opportunities, etc.," at least to the extent that this description applies to the life force of a capitalist system.[2]

It remains, however, to complete our tripartite definition of capitalism by attending to its two other essential structures. One of these is a network of channels of exchange, established and protected by a framework of law and custom without which the process of capital accumulation could not take place. The network is, of course, the market mechanism, much celebrated as the quintessence of the social order, which it is not, although it is indeed indispensable to its operation. Like $M–C–M'$, the market network has no counterpart in any noncapitalist society, even though individual markets play highly visible and useful roles in tributary or even some hunting and gathering societies, as well as in *soi-disant* socialist ones. In the analysis of these markets as allocatory mechanisms, economics finds its most extensive and familiar application, and in its nonrecognition of a market system as a sociopolitical structure, it also demonstrates one of its most crippling handicaps, a matter also referred to more than once in the preceding essays.

The third identificatory element is "political." I put quotation marks around the word to call attention to a curious compression of its meaning in capitalist society. Like all social orders, capitalism requires an architecture of horizontal and vertical order—the former largely concerned with the maintenance of stable intraclass social relations; the latter with widely accepted interclass distinctions. As in noncapitalist societies, much horizontal orderliness in capitalism is provided by informal—that is, unwritten—customs and conventions such as familial (kinship) systems, traditional social standings of different occupations, and the like, although the relative importance of these arrangements is diminished in a setting where acquisitive behavior plays such a large role. In similar fashion, vertical order under capitalism is mainly determined by two considerations— possession or nonpossession of capital, which divides the society into its two main economic classes, and formal political power which establishes a similar, but by no means identically gradated, hierarchy of precedence and prerogatives in the various structures of government proper.

We should note, however, that the presence of a class structure, as such, or even one determined by capital, is not of unique importance for capitalism as a political order. After all, a dominant class based on capital only replaces much older hierarchical arrangements determined by genealogy, military prowess, or other such attributes. The crucial political hallmark of the order is the coexistence of two realms of power—one public, one private. In the public realm are located the institutions that have the capability to establish and enforce law and order, the quintessential function of government in all social orders—usually, but not always, used in a capitalist society to further the interests of the capital-owning class. In the private realm are found the activities of the $M–C–M'$ process whose forms, objectives, and strategies are left largely to the decisions of this class, including its managerial subordinates. The authority of capital is not absolute within the private sphere—capitalists who wield "economic" authority cannot disobey the law, or take into their hands the trial or punishment of competitors or workers—but within the general process of capital accumulation itself, their unimpeded prerogatives are very great. This bifurcation of authority is historically unique; in all other social orders the political function knows no such boundaries. It is here, obviously, that economics displays its limitations in regarding the immense social consequences that follow from the exercise of the $M-C-M'$ function as a matter that falls outside the scope of political inquiry, because it lies within the domain of private economic activity.

It is apparent that this is no more than a stylized rendition of a capitalist order. The sketch only points to the psychoanalytic and social roots of the drive for wealth, or its correlate, the pleasures of power. It does not examine the historical process by which capitalism emerged from the chrysalis of a decaying feudalism—a process that greatly influenced the specific forms assumed by the developing $M-C-M'$ core. The outline does not examine the formation of the monetary and legal institutions needed to allow capitalism to work, and is not concerned with the crucial importance of the dual realms of power with respect to political liberty. Nonetheless, I think this brief exposition is sufficient to serve our purposes in identifying the social order that also uniquely boasts the disciplinary study we call economics.

Economics and Noncapitalist Society

I now broach the crucial step in my argument by gladly conceding the conventional starting point of that discipline—to wit, the claim that all societies must undertake the activities of production and distribution, without which they could not survive. Indeed, this indisputable fact raises the disconcerting question as to whether there must not therefore be an economics of insect or avian life driven by cognitive activities similar to those that establish economics as a "universal" science. But I have a simpler question. Directing our attention solely to human societies, can we say that we need a specialized vocabulary called economics to describe, much less understand, the productive and distributive processes necessary for their continuance?

I shall put the question as concretely as possible with an illustration I have used more than once. It describes the distribution of food produced by a group of hunters in the Kalahari grasslands of Southwest Africa:

> The gemsbok had vanished ... Gai owned two hind legs and a front leg, Tsetschwe had meat from the back, Ukwane had the other front leg, his wife had one of the feet and the stomach, the young boys had lengths of intestine. Twwikwe had received the head and Dasina the udder.
> It seems very unequal when you watch Bushmen divide the kill, yet it is their system, and in the end no person eats more than the other. That day Ukwane gave Gai still another piece because Gai was his relation, Gai gave meat to Dasina because she was his wife's mother. . . . No one, of course, contested Gai's large share, because he had been the hunter and by their law

that much belonged to him. No one doubted that he would share that much with others, and they were not wrong, of course; he did.[3]

This example enables us to examine the meaning of "economic" activity with unusual clarity. For what knowledge do we require to explain this productive and allocational activity? We certainly need information regarding the mode of hunting itself—knowledge that might be generally described as technological and organizational. In addition, we must have an understanding of whatever sociological considerations apply to the distribution of the kill. Overarching the whole, we also need to be familiar with the culture of the Kalahari, for cultural usages vary considerably even among societies whose sociopolitical structures are alike, with important consequences for their provisioning and distributive activities. But economics? If we were apprised of all these particulars regarding the Kalahari, what would be left for an economist to explain?

That same question can be addressed to the activities by which other kinds of noncapitalist societies sustain themselves. Passing over ancient societies of command, such as Egypt, let us consider the ex–Soviet Union with its bevies of economists, economics journals, institutes of economics, and the like. What did these individuals or institutions study or elucidate? Techniques of production, comparative efficiencies, input–output relations, bottlenecks, externalities, bureaucratic problems, consumer demand, and elasticities of supply were certainly high on the list. But in what way are these "economics"? What knowledge do we require over and above a close familiarity with their technological, organizational, sociocultural, and political characteristics and constraints? Taking away the vital—but hardly "economic"—exercise of command, in what way was the solution to the production and distribution problems of the USSR different from that of the Kalahari? To pose again the central question, what would be the unique content of the "economic" knowledge needed to elucidate the provisioning problem for any or all of these noncapitalist societies? My answer is: none.

Understanding Capitalism.

Having devoted this much space to adumbrating what economics does not do, let us turn the inquiry around by asking whether someone reared in the Kalahari or in the former Soviet Union would be adequately prepared to understand American or Japanese or German life by studying modern technology, sociology, psychology, political institutions, and the rest, but not economics.

The answer can, I think, be put succinctly: our pupils would not be able to understand how these societies provisioned themselves. Who or what energized and directed the activity of production, given the virtual absence of tradition or central command as an animating or coordinating force? How was it that goods and services produced in such seemingly chaotic fashion appeared to match the changing "demands" of buyers? In what manner was the population provided with the wherewithal to exercise its claim on goods and services? To say the all-important word once more, our visitors would not understand the modus operandi of capitalism, which is to say, they would not understand economics.

Would they understand it if they read a conventional economics text? The answer is: yes and no. No, they would not understand the depth and complexity of the self-expanding $M–C–M'$ process—the main propulsive force of the social order they were investigating. Perhaps our Soviet visitor might see in it an analog to the idea of "power," and might then explain the accumulation of capital as the expression of some presumably universal desire to increase the form in which that social relation was denominated. Our Kalahari visitor would have a much more difficult time, coming from a social order in which power—to the minor extent that it existed—was denominated in reputation and not easily subject to indefinite expansion. Thus I fear that the core process of capital would remain as little understood by our visitors as by their instructors who, if interrogated about the basis of the dynamism of the system, would ascribe it to "human nature." Asked by the Russian student why it had not surfaced in the Soviet Union, they would perhaps answer: repression. Asked by Kalahari, I think they would be at a loss for an answer.

Things would no doubt go somewhat better when it came to explaining the market mechanism, once its driving force could be taken as a "given"; and no doubt the instructors could also shed light on the relation between the public and private realms. The public realm would be explained as a holdover from earlier times when the market had not yet appeared, now largely confined to areas in which the market was not permitted to enter, such as the application of the law; and the private realm could then be explicated as the natural realm of "economic" activity, once it had been released from its age-old captivity. Capitalism itself would then appear as a "system" where ancient political powers were constrained by the legitimation of the market which, with all its admitted shortcomings, was a benign substitute for the bloodier modes of administration characteristic of most stratified precapitalist societies. What would remain unexplained is that "the market" or the "private sector" would have no existence—not merely no place—without the subterranean foundations of a drive to amass capital, a dependency that is unrecognized by conventional economics.

Nonetheless, if we overlook this political or social innocence, there can be no doubt that economics sheds light where there would otherwise be darkness. Given a motivational structure of acquisitive behavior ("maximization of utilities") and the legal constraints of property and competition, economics bestows on the larger social process a degree of recognizable coherence and causality that would otherwise be unavailable. For all its failures of omission and commission, that is no small accomplishment. Insofar as my essay is openly driven by a critical intent, I want to register this admiration before going on to ask what might become of economics in the future. I must add, however, that in the absence of the sociopolitical roots I have tried to describe, much of the understandings of economics take on the aspect of ideology, meaning by that treacherous word not an intent to deceive others, but an unknowing deception of the self.

Economics in the Future

What now of the future possibilities for economics? If my argument has any cogency, everything depends on the evolutionary possibilities for capitalism itself. If the social order bursts its bounds, descending into a system of central planning, there will be no need for economics. Input–output studies, detailed statistical research, sociological investigations into managerial efficiency, blueprints for balanced or unbalanced expansion of various production categories will of course be indispensable. Political determinations, domestic or international, will vitally affect both production and distribution. But economics? In the absence of M–C–M' as the organizing principle and energizing belief system of the social totality—including, let us not forget, the market system itself—I must confess I cannot conceive of its existence.

There is, of course, a second possibility. Instead of a descent into authoritarianism, may there not be an ascent into some form of communitarian, participatory life, organized perhaps as casually as the Kalahari, but at a more advanced level of technology—in short, an ascent to an egalitarian, democratic, participatory socialism? I will not quarrel here with its feasibility, but only ask once again: Where is its economics? What would an economist teach its members, aside from reviewing the past as we review feudalism, and reading its texts as we read those of the Schoolmen? In such a society I see the need for many determinations with respect to who will do what, and how the level and kind of social output will be arrived at, as well as shared. But is this economics? I think not.

There remains a last possibility—this time, one that includes a role for economics. The possibility is an evolutionary movement of capitalism itself, still retaining M–C–M', markets, and its two realms of power. Here I leave the land of imaginary other-worlds and try to remain within this world, a much more precarious operation. I shall, therefore, put the answer to my third possibility in the form of questions that I must ultimately leave to my readers to resolve for themselves.

The first such question is how long capitalism can last. If my foregoing analysis carries any persuasive power, the answer must hinge on three prior questions: How long can the M–C–M' process go on? How much strain can the market network handle? How far can the public realm expand without endangering one or the other of the system's complementary elements? Let us reflect on each in turn.

The M–C–M' process faces one deadly obstacle. If, as Marx believed, it hinges on the appropriation of unpaid labor power, its death knell will sound when the working class refuses to submit to any payment less than the full exchange value of the final product. Thus, the answer to the initial question depends on one's estimate of the political power of labor, or its counterpart, that of capital. My own view is that such a class breakdown of capitalism is unlikely during the imaginable future, at least in its major Western centers, primarily because of the absence of a plausible and attractive sociopolitical alternative. That is the historic price of the débacle of the Soviet system.

In addition, there is good reason to believe that capitalism can be played for smaller stakes than those currently enjoyed in the West. Within a reduced flow of "normal" profits, unusually efficient (or lucky) firms could still enjoy technological or other rents which, however transient, would add a certain vitality to the $M–C–M'$ circuit. Thus, one might find a politically attractive argument for retaining the capitalist process on such a reduced scale, as the underpinning both for a market system that minimized bureaucratic interventions into productive and distributive activity and for the political safeguard of a two-sector society. To the extent that this is the case, an explicatory role remains that cannot be filled by any other discipline, although, as we shall see, that role will likely change to a not inconsiderable degree.

A second threat to the life-span of capitalism would be the gradual displacement of the market as the strategic means of allocation. Two current developments point in this general direction. One of these is the intensification of international competition, a process that may well encourage the growth of protective regulatory mechanisms. This is a prospect discussed in several essays in this volume. I would think the general tendency could not be described as likely to pose a serious threat to capitalism, but indeed likely to add strength to "dirigiste" tendencies within it. Far more threatening, in my view, is the advent of global warming, now regarded as a plausible threat to social reproduction by the end of the coming century. If, in fact, atmospheric warming becomes a clear and present danger, its control would require deep interventions into the quantity and kind of energy produced in both rich and poor nations. However uncertain the scenario, it raises the possibility of an unprecedented conflict between market and political determinations of output, a conflict that could pose the most profound challenge to the market mechanism, and beneath that, to the $M–C–M'$ process.

Last, there is the question of the relation between the two sectors. Within all capitalist nations, it seems clear that the balance of power has been irregularly but steadily moving toward the enhancement of the public realm, partly in response to unwanted effects of capital accumulation, and partly in response to political movements seeking greater social well-being. If, as I believe likely, this general tendency continues, it raises the possibility of national capitalisms moving in the direction of Schumpeterian bureaucracies in which capitalist firms gradually embrace a more regulated, state-directed, "socialistic" post-capitalist order.

This returns us finally to economics within the assumption that the central institutions of capitalism remain, in whatever watered-down form, always placing *M–C–M'* at the center. What could be the role of economic analysis under such conditions? I can foresee two possible, and indeed, conjoined courses. The first is the gradual erosion of the boundaries that have increasingly separated economics from sociology, anthropology, psychology, and political thought. The present isolation of economics would then become ever less tenable and the sterility of contemporary formal economic thought ever more evident. Although my mention of the medieval Schoolmen reminds us that intellectual formalism can persist despite considerable socioeconomic change, I would nonetheless think—or at least hope—that economics would then return to its sociopolitical origins, recognizing and exploring its relation to other, more universal aspects of social life, and seeking from this multidisciplinary exploration new guidance with respect to the management of the diminished, but still critical force of capital accumulation and its expression through market relationships. In many ways, the essays of this book embody just such an approach.

The second imaginable course of development for economics also reflects my assumption concerning the gradual politicization of the capitalist world. It is becoming increasingly difficult to depict economic processes as the outcomes of interactions among one-dimensionally conceived agents. In place of this depiction, I would describe the new task of economics as concerned with the formulation of policies designed to guide individual or group behavior toward the attainment of, or adjustment to, politically given ends. In the terminology of Adolph Lowe, its original formulator, this would reorient our discipline from a "predictive" to an "instrumental" purpose—that is, from a self-contained to a means–ends, policy-oriented discipline.[4] In more blunt terms, it means recognizing the inescapable subordination of economics to politics—indeed, acknowledging the inescapably political nature of economic thought as the conceptual vocabulary of a capitalist order, and making of that long-repressed secret a source of new clarity and usefulness for as long as the underlying social order permits. Here again, my own vision embodies that of many contributors to this volume, itself a welcome sign of a growing discontent with the intellectual and social status quo and of a growing determination to find remedies for that state of affairs.

Notes

1. Jack Hirshleifer, "The Expanding Domain of Economics," *American Economic Review* (December 1985), 53, emphasis in the original.

2. See my *Nature and Logic of Capitalism* (New York: W.W. Norton, 1985), pp. 46f. See also Otto Fenichel, "The Drive to Amass Wealth," *Psychoanalytic Quarterly* (January 1938), passim.

3. Elizabeth Marshall Thomas, *The Harmless People* (New York: Knopf, 1959), pp. 49–50.

4. See Adolph Lowe, *On Economic Knowledge*, 2d ed. (Armonk, NY: M.E. Sharpe, 1977), passim; and Robert Heilbroner and William Milberg, *Economic Analysis and Social Vision in Modern Capitalism*, forthcoming.

Index

Wages *(continued)*
-price controls, 54–55, 106
productivity and, 53
rate of increase, 169n.44
rigid, 128
in Third World, 255–256
See also Income; Income distribution
Wallace, Henry, 236
Want process, 38–39
Wealth distribution, 155
Wealth of Nations (Smith), xv, 25n.31
Weisskopf, Thomas, 41
Welfare state, 233, 234
Welfare system, 184, 185–186, 197, 204, 205
Westney, D. Eleanor, 247
Whalen, Charles J., 3–21
Wilber, Charles K., xv, 6, 7–8, 45–61
Williamson, Oliver, 42
Wolff, Richard D., 35, 41
Wolfson, Martin, 26n.44
Wollstonecraft, Mary, 65
Women
  economic independence of, 65
  in economics profession, 65–66, 79n.4, 83n.57
  in economic theory, 66–71
  income distribution and, 203
  labor of, 67–68, 78, 81n.28, 235
  progressive change and, 77–78
  wages of, 67–68, 111, 217, 218
  See also Feminist economics
Woolf, Virginia, 65

Work, nature of, 165
Work councils, 119
Worker Adjustment and Retraining Notification Act (WARN), 234–235
Workers
  bill of rights, 241
  displaced, 234–236, 240
  education of, 104–107
  public service, 107
  sovereignty, 51
  thinking skills of, 108–110, 113, 114–115, 116, 218, 220
  See also Labor markets; Labor relations
Workplace
  alienation in, 39
  control of, 40
  technology-intensive, 103
Works Progress Administration (WPA), 166
World Bank, 109, 140, 196, 236, 237, 238
  East Asian miracle study of, 248–253
World Constitution, 237
World Government, 237
World view (Weltanschauung), neoclassical, 47–51
Wray, Randall L., xvi, 8, 11–12, 125–145

Y

Young, John, 187

Z

Zimmerman, Erich W., 35, 37